# BLACK
# BUSINESS
# ENTERPRISE

E185.8
B145

# BLACK BUSINESS ENTERPRISE

## Historical and Contemporary Perspectives

Edited by

## RONALD W. BAILEY

Basic Books, Inc., *Publishers*

NEW YORK : LONDON

DEC 20 1972

173007

© 1971 by Basic Books, Inc.
Library of Congress Catalog Card Number 76–147008
SBN 465–00690–6
Manufactured in the United States of America
DESIGNED BY THE INKWELL STUDIO

TO

MAMA AND DADDY

How can I ever thank you?

# Foreword by Julian Bond

It is impossible to discuss what life has been like during the decade of the sixties or what we can expect in the seventies without discussing two factors that have shaped the past and are likely to be of dominating importance in years to come. These factors—war and race—combine to form the framework in which we must present and evaluate Black business and economic development and other strategies to improve the quality of our existence.

The long fingers of American might are still sticking in other people's pies. Almost 300,000 American soldiers are still engaged in perpetrating a war that has, for the last ten years, been aimed at telling the Vietnamese people what kind of government they can have and under what circumstances.

In America, although the summer of 1970 did not prove as "hot" as previous ones, over every day hangs the ominous threat of yet another explosion in protest against racial injustice in this country. This growing concern about the relations between white and Black people in the United States has been a number one item on the domestic priority list of the sixties.

These two frightening realities—the one because it threatens international annihilation, the other because it threatens genocide—greatly color our lives. There is no escaping the duality of these facts for it is within their context that we witness some very disturbing paradoxes.

America annually spends more money on pet food than on food stamps. Private citizens in this country spend more on tobacco than all government does on education. We pour vast subsidies into many industries—cotton, airlines, rail lines and others. The oil industry received government handouts upwards of 50 billions of dollars in the past ten years while supplements for the poor were laughed out of Congress.

Farmer-Senator James O. Eastland was given $140,000 in farm subsidies in a single year, in effect paying him for doing nothing. The Congress subsequently voted to place but did not pass a $20,000 limit on the amount of money a farmer could receive; but it will be sometime before it begins to think about paying $20,000 a year to poor families who cannot do for themselves. We live in a country where 5 percent of the people have 20 percent of the wealth and 20 percent of the people have 5 percent of the wealth.

These paradoxes put us on the edge of a domestic revolution that may destroy us all; we may well be a generation of people without a future. But our domestic predicament as a nation is complicated by this country's teetering on the brink of revolution on a world-wide scale.

The United States of America comprises 6 percent of the world's population; each year we consume 60 percent of the earth's consumable
resources. A careful analysis suggests that in order to continue its present
standard of living this country must maintain its present grip on the
economies of the under-developed nations of the world. It may be true
that consumption will have to be changed in this country, both in order
to redistribute what there is to be consumed and also in order to have
something to be consumed, but it is also true that preserving the U.S.
economic advantage is done at a prohibitive cost. "We cannot afford
continued imperialism, either financially or spiritually, without the nation
ceasing to function as a democratic state" (Richard J. Barnet, *The
Economy of Death*).

But the facts for Black people are more frightening and certainly more
immediate. Blacks are only closing the income gap between Blacks and
whites at an agonizingly slow pace. For example, the income of the
average white American family has increased by one hundred percent over
the past twenty years; so has the income of the typical Black family. But
twenty years ago, average family income for Blacks was about one-half
that of whites; in 1968 Black family income is still only 60 percent that of
white families. Our housing is probably more segregated than ever before.
The United States Commission on Civil Rights has said that if all Americans lived in conditions as crowded as do Black people in some sections
of Harlem, then all 200 million Americans could live in three of the five
boroughs of New York, leaving the other two and all the rest of the United
States totally unpopulated.

Four out of every five Americans are more affluent than any other
people in history. They have reached that affluence by degrading the fifth
person, the poor Black and Brown Americans and others who have neither
the power nor resources to significantly improve their lot. The American
"welfare" system taxes the poor more than our tax system taxes the rich.
A poor man on welfare must pay the government 70 cents on every dollar
he earns above $30 a month; a rich man pays the government only 25
cents on every dollar he wins on the stock market.

Half of the farmers in the United States (the half who have incomes
of less than $2,500 a year) received 5 percent of the farm subsidies pro-
vided by the government. Ten percent of the farmers in the United States
received 60 percent of the subsidies. Some Americans of thirty years
ago were afraid that this might become a welfare state. Instead, we have a
warfare state. America gives 80 percent of its wealth to the Pentagon,
and 10 percent to health, education, and welfare.

This country which has visited death on thousands of Vietnamese has
found the arrogance to ignore the centuries of pleading against American
racism from her own domestic colony—the Blacks. When these pleadings
are dismissed, then the problems of the 20th century come to the fore,
and violence is done to the notion that men can solve their problems
without using violence. In the 1970s, this is likely to be the theme of the
struggle. We have already seen ample evidence of what sort of violence has

been visited on the oppressed people of the world for centuries. We are likely in the future to see increasing answers in violence from those who have been on the receiving line all too often.

But we need to discover who is and who isn't violent in America. Violence is Black children going to school for twelve years and receiving five years of education. Violence is 30 million hungry stomachs in the most affluent nation on earth. Violence is having Black people represent a disproportionate share of inductees and casualties in Vietnam. Violence is an economy that believes in socialism for the rich and capitalism for the poor. Violence is a country where property counts more than people. Violence is spending $900 per second to stifle the Vietnamese, but only $77 a year to feed a hungry person at home. Violence is J. Edgar Hoover listening to your telephone conversation. Violence is an assistant attorney general proposing concentration camps for white and Black militants. Violence is blowing up two men and claiming that they did it themselves!

There have been several suggestions as to what should be done in the context of such violence to improve the conditions of life for Blacks in America. It has been over fifteen years since the United States Supreme Court, in *Brown v. Board of Education of Topeka*, declared that segregation in public schools was illegal. The next year, Southern schools were ordered to desegregate with "all deliberate speed." Yet, over a decade and a half later, we are only now witnessing any real attempt to integrate Black children into school systems supported by allocations of monies geared to providing quality education. During the interim we have watched a most repulsive display of racism as many people were party to attempts to deny Black school children access to equal educational opportunities.

But education alone cannot solve the problems of poverty, unemployment and other problems facing Black America. Something more far-reaching is needed. For many years Southern farmers have collected fortunes in Federal monies for not growing crops. Congress should declare that these farmers have forfeited the right to possess their land. They should then redistribute it to the landless and often unemployed people who work it for subsistence wages while its owners are made rich by Federal largesse. This type of land reform would mean important progress in property ownership for poor Black sharecroppers and would partially settle a debt outstanding since the defaulted payment on the promise of forty acres and a mule.

The Nixon administration is attempting to alter an outmoded institution that all others have been too timid to touch—the present welfare system. Its proposals, however, while providing a start, fall short of what is needed. The proposed national floor of $1,600 a year for a family of four should be raised to $5,500 to reflect the realities of what is required to meet minimum human needs. The food-stamp and commodities distribution programs should be retained, and the suggestion that recipients should be forced to work indiscriminately should be abandoned.

A national land reform program and the establishment of comprehensive welfare standards would at least be solid first steps in dealing with problems facing Black and poor people in the United States. An effective national skill training and job provision program would complement such efforts. But at the same time, the several "underprivileged," oppressed minorities must recognize the desperate need for the cultivation, singly and collectively, of the kind of power whites have monopolized since the American experiment began. Each group of us must realize that an evil system run by evil men prevents the realization of our every aspiration, and that no question of education or job training or integration of jobs and housing can be implemented without a correlated grasp of power by the powerless. A dominating reality in American society is its racism and the implementation of effective programs and cures will not willingly be done for us.

For example, instead of more measures addressed to the real needs of Blacks, President Nixon has put forth Black capitalism. Here is a man who cannot help but know that capitalism has yet to solve the problems of white poverty, yet he offers a pitifully underfinanced public-relations gimmick as an answer to our needs. What we need is not Black capitalism but something more properly called "community socialism," that we may have profit for the many instead of the few; so that neighborhoods and communities shall have the major say in who gets what from whom. Black people need to find ways to control what we can. This includes our politics, our economy, and other aspects that give us a greater measure of control over our own destiny.

We have had some small victories. All are important, but some are more surface than others. We now have free access to restaurants only to find that we can barely afford to eat at those five-and-dime store lunch counters of the kind where Black students in Greensboro made the first stand; the same is true with similar types of "integration." The system grudgingly conceded to Black people the right to sit in the front of the bus—a hollow victory when one considers that the longest journey is likely to be from the overtly racist South to the not so overt racism in the North. And Blacks now have relative freedom to vote in a system which in 1968 still selected a President who was obviously not our choice.

A significant number of Black folk have decided that the right to sit at lunch counters or to vote or to peacefully petition the government for a redress of grievances means nothing to a people who are living in a colony. We live in a social, educational, and economic colony that is as effectively administered and controlled from the outside as was the American colony in 1776, or the Vietnamese colony before the Vietnamese decided that they could rule themselves better than could any Frenchmen, Japanese or Americans.

The question for us as Blacks in America, then, is how to escape from this colonial status. Ought we to follow the example set by the Minutemen at Concord, or the hardy band of revolutionaries who looted ships in the Boston Harbor? Or ought we instead wait for the Mother Country—in this case White America—to grant us freedom only when we have demonstrated that we are ready for it?

Within the Black community at this very moment are dozens of proposals, scores of ideas, all focusing on the basic question of what are the most promising techniques for bringing about substantial improvement in the position of Blacks in this country. Whites have a variety of ideas, and Black folk have even more. Reputations and careers are being built on this very topic. Presumably, some of them have merit. All of them cannot, because many of them are mutually exclusive or proceed from mutually contradicting premises. But in the absence of any remarkable wisdom as to which proposals are the more promising and which the less, one is constrained to sample them all.

For this reason, Ronald Bailey has rendered a great service to everyone concerned with this problem. By bringing together into one volume a rich compendium of the thoughts of those who are in the forefront of action and analysis in the area of Black economic development, he has made it possible for us all to submerge ourselves deeply into the discussion and its many ramifications. He has also made these thinkers available to students, from whom the solutions to our problems are ultimately very likely to come. By including the broad spectrum of contemporary thought on paths to Black economic development—from capitalism to socialism, from integration to separation—Ronald Bailey has insured that the reader will lay *Black Business Enterprise* down considerably broadened by his reading experience.

Which path to follow? The oppressed people of this nation have several options available to them; we quite properly ought to exercise them all. That is to suggest that an oppressed people cannot choose a single means of freeing themselves from oppression, but that any and every method must be explored and attempted. The power of our oppressor and our powerlessness dictate that we do no less. The old saying of Black abolitionist Frederick Douglass is as applicable now as ever:

*Power concedes nothing without a demand; it never has and never will. Find out just what people will quietly submit to, and you have discovered the exact measure of injustice and wrong which will be imposed upon them and these will continue until they are resisted with either words, or blows, or both. The limits of tyrants are prescribed by the endurance of those whom they oppress.*

# The Authors

LOUIS L. ALLEN is president of Chase Manhattan Capital Corporation, which has invested heavily in ghetto businesses. His writings include *Starting and Succeeding in Your Own Small Business* (1968).

RICHARD F. AMERICA, JR., a Black economist, is director of the Urban Programs Division of the Graduate School of Business, University of California at Berkeley. He was formerly associated with the Stanford Research Institute as a development economist in the Urban and Regional Economics groups specializing in urban systems studies.

TALMADGE ANDERSON is director of Black Studies at Washington State University, Pullman, Washington. He holds a Master's of Business Administration degree from Atlanta University with further course study in finance at the University of Missouri.

JAMES BOGGS is a veteran Black activist in the labor movement and an internationally known social theoretician. The article appearing in this volume appears in his book, *Racism and the Class Struggle* (Monthly Review Press).

ANDREW F. BRIMMER is the first Black member of the Board of Governors of the Federal Reserve System.

ROBERT S. BROWNE teaches economics at Fairleigh Dickinson University and is director of the Black Economic Research Center. He is also interim editor of *The Review of Black Political Economy.*

HORACE CAYTON, who died in 1969, was a Black sociologist who made many scholarly contributions to the study of social problems.

THEODORE L. CROSS is currently with the Office of Economic Opportunity, Washington, D.C. He is formerly editor-in-chief and publisher of *The Bankers Magazine.*

HAROLD CRUSE has recently served as visiting instructor at the University of Michigan. He is a leading Black intellectual whose *Crisis of the Negro Intellectual* and *Rebellion or Revolution?* have sparked considerable debate.

ST. CLAIR DRAKE, an outstanding Black scholar, is currently Professor of Sociology and Anthropology and head of the Afro–American Studies Program at Stanford University. He has written books and articles on the Black experience, race relations, and social change.

GEOFFREY FAUX is a former chief of the Economic Development Branch of the Policy and Evaluation Division of the Community Action Program in the Office of Economic Opportunity.

JAMES FORMAN, long active in the struggle for Black liberation, is director of international affairs for the Student National Coordinating Committee and head of the Black Economic Development Conference United Black Appeal.

E. FRANKLIN FRAZIER, who died in 1962, was Professor and Chairman of the Department of Sociology at Howard University. He also served as president of the American Sociological Association. Among his many published works are *The Negro Family in the United States* and *The Negro in the United States*.

GERSON GREEN is director of the Research and Demonstration Division of the Community Action Program of the Office of Economic Opportunity.

ALAN HABER is a writer and economist engaged in research on strategies of ghetto economic development. He was the first president of Students for a Democratic Society. He is co-editor of *Poverty in America*.

BENNETT HARRISON is a doctoral candidate in economics at the University of Pennsylvania. When his article appearing in this volume was written, he was serving as Teaching Associate, Graduate Faculty of Political and Social Science, The New School for Social Research, New York City.

PATRICIA HETTER is a political science writer, and director of the Institute for the Study of Economic Systems in San Francisco.

JOHN F. KAIN is Professor of Economics at Harvard University. He is co-author of *Urban Transportation Problem* and has written numerous professional articles on urban problems.

LOUIS O. KELSO is the senior partner of a financial and corporate law firm in San Francisco. Among his writings are *The Capitalist Manifesto*, *The New Capitalists*, and articles in many scholarly journals.

ROBERT KINZER is a Black graduate of West Virginia State College. When the piece appearing in this volume was written, he was a student at the Graduate School of Business Administration of New York University.

ROBERT MCKERSIE is Professor of Industrial Relations at the University of Chicago's Graduate School of Business.

DUNBAR S. MCLAURIN is the founder and president of a ghetto-oriented consultant firm, Ghettonomics, Inc. He is a Black economist who has spent over twenty-five years in the field of underdeveloped nations and ghetto economics.

JOSEPH J. PERSKY is a visiting professor at Fisk University and a parttime staff member of the National Bureau of Economic Research.

JOSEPH A. PIERCE was formerly dean of the graduate school and acting president of Atlanta University.

EDWARD SAGARIN once a chemist, is the author of *The Science and Art of Perfumery*. He is now a member of the Department of Sociology at City College in New York.

ARNOLD SCHUCHTER is currently associated with the Arthur D. Little Company in Cambridge, Massachusetts. He has had extensive experience with urban renewal planning in Baltimore, Boston, and Chicago.

FREDERICK D. STURDIVANT is Associate Professor of Marketing Administration in the Graduate School of Business at the University of Texas. He is the editor of a recent volume, *The Ghetto Marketplace* (New York: The Free Press, 1969).

CHARLES TATE is a community organizer and former chairman of the Dayton, Ohio, chapter of CORE, the Dayton Alliance for Racial Equality, and the Afro–American Cultural Center. He is presently an urban fellow at The Urban Institute in Washington, D.C., and is engaged in the area of Black community development.

AL ULMER has been closely associated with the cooperative movement, as a director of Community Organization for the Southern Regional Council and as a consultant to various coops. He authored a previous Southern Research Council report, *Cooperatives, Credit Unions, and Poor People* (March, 1966).

ROBERT E. WRIGHT is a recent Black graduate of the Law School of the University of Pennsylvania.

# Acknowledgments

It is surprising to realize that I am indebted to so many people so soon. The customary apology for being unable to thank them all here is even more in order. I mention only a few of those whose help led to the completion of this reader.

Dr. T. Harry McKinney provided an initial opportunity to systematically explore topics related to urban economics when I was a teaching assistant in Justin Morrill College. A summer internship with the Joint Economic Committee of the U.S. Congress, sponsored by Congresswoman Martha Griffiths of Michigan, was a rewarding experience. John Stark, executive director of the committee, and his staff contributed much to my interest in the economics of poverty and urban areas.

I want to acknowledge the generous support of the Sam Wyly Foundation in Dallas, Texas, while I was a White House Intern in 1969. The summer experience on the staff of Robert Brown, special assistant to the president, gave me an ample opportunity to study, discuss, and observe many aspects of Black business enterprise and economic development. To express my appreciation to the many people who patiently shared their views and insights is impossible; to them I am most grateful.

In the preparation of this volume, Clarissa Stevenson, as a friend and critical conversationalist, provided encouragement at times when the project was almost abandoned. I wish also to thank the several people who read and critiqued the introductory essay. Lois Gray, Linda Foster, Janet Saxe, Wilma Fuller, and Henry Organ were of immeasurable assistance in the preparation of the manuscript for publication.

The bulk of any proceeds from this volume will be contributed to an effort to strengthen research aimed at alleviating the socioeconomic plight of Black people in America. Many of the authors have given their usual permission fees for the same purpose. To them, and to Basic Books, Inc., I express my appreciation.

Finally, to the spirit of Black folk—living, dead, and even yet unborn—I owe the deepest measure of gratitude for the constant inspiration to right the many wrongs inflicted on oppressed people the world over.

R.W.B.

# Contents

Foreword      vii
JULIAN BOND

Introduction/Black Business Enterprise: Reflections on
its History and Future Development     3
RONALD BAILEY

## PART I

### *Recurring Themes: An Historical Overview*

Introduction     23

1]] The Evolution of Negro Business     25
JOSEPH A. PIERCE

2]] Roots of the Integrationist–Separatist Dilemma     47
ROBERT KINZER AND EDWARD SAGARIN

3]] Negro Business: Myth and Fact     61
ST. CLAIR DRAKE AND HORACE CAYTON

4]] Negro Business: A Social Myth     73
E. FRANKLIN FRAZIER

5]] The Black Economy     86
HAROLD CRUSE

## PART II

### *Black Capitalism: Will (or Should) It Work?*

Introduction     99

6]] Vitalize Black Enterprise     IOI
ROBERT MCKERSIE

7]] The Limits of Black Capitalism     II4
FREDERICK D. STURDIVANT

8]] "What Do You People Want?"     124
RICHARD F. AMERICA, JR.

9]] Making Capitalism Work in the Ghettos     138
LOUIS L. ALLEN

10]]  The Myth and Irrationality of Black Capitalism            150
      JAMES BOGGS

11]]  Toward Controlled Development of Black America           159
      ROBERT E. WRIGHT

12]]  Small Business and Economic Development in the
      Negro Community                                         164
      ANDREW F. BRIMMER

13]]  Brimmer and Black Capitalism: An Analysis               173
      CHARLES TATE

# PART III

## Alternatives to Black Capitalism

      Introduction                                            183

14]]  Ghetto Economic Development and Industrialization
      Plan (Ghediplan)                                        184
      DUNBAR S. MCLAURIN

15]]  Economic Development Planning for American
      Urban Slums                                             193
      BENNETT HARRISON

16]]  Conjoining Black Revolution and Private Enterprise      205
      ARNOLD SCHUCHTER

17]]  Equality of Economic Opportunity through
      Capital Ownership                                       233
      LOUIS O. KELSO AND PATRICIA HETTER

18]]  Cooperatives and Poor People in the South              243
      AL ULMER

19]]  Magnets of Profit: A Program for
      Categorical Corrective Incentives                       251
      THEODORE L. CROSS

20]]  Community Development Corporations:
      A New Approach to the Poverty Problem                   269
      HARVARD LAW REVIEW

# PART IV

## Black Economic and Business Development: The Future

      Introduction                                            293

21]]  The Social Utility of Black Enterprise                  294
      GERSON GREEN AND GEOFFREY FAUX

Contents                                                                      xxi

22]]  Alternatives to the Gilded Ghetto                                        309
      JOHN F. KAIN AND JOSEPH J. PERSKY

23]]  Economic Development: Liberation or Liberalism                           316
      ALAN HABER

24]]  The Black Manifesto: Total Control as the Only
      Solution to the Economic Problems of Black People                        320
      JAMES FORMAN

25]]  Toward an Overall Assessment of Our Alternatives                         330
      ROBERT S. BROWNE

26]]  Black Economic Liberation under Capitalism                               339
      TALMADGE ANDERSON


      Bibliographical Notes                                                    345
      Index                                                                    349

# BLACK BUSINESS ENTERPRISE

# Introduction / Black Business Enterprise:

# Reflections on Its History and

# Future Development

*Ronald W. Bailey*

The struggle of African people to liberate themselves has been characterized by the recurrence of certain themes—regardless of where their struggle has taken place. This has certainly been the case in the United States. It is as if the laws of oppression dictate a periodic swing back to philosophies and methods of some past era, in an attempt to make some sense of the current scheme of things. The recent rhetoric surrounding "Black power," for example, is quite similar to concepts espoused much earlier by W. E. B. DuBois, Booker T. Washington, Marcus Garvey, and others. Both the 1900 period and the recent 1960 movement recall the 1850s when the ideologies of racial solidarity, self-help, and Black nationalism were espoused as viable means to Black freedom.[1]

But there has been another closely related and very significant consistency throughout the history of Black people in this country. I am speaking of fluctuations in emphasis with respect to the most beneficial relationship between Black folk and whites in America. Integration or separation? This philosophical tension between integrationists and separatists lies at the root of ideological differences in all spheres in which Black people have been and are engaged—cultural, economic, and political.[2] As Harold Cruse has noted, "the present-day conflict within the Negro ethnic group, between integrationist and separatist tendencies, has its origins in the historical arguments between personalities such as Frederick Douglass and Martin R. Delany."[3]

The economic and business sphere, the topic of this volume, offers an illuminating example of this ideological conflict. Ever since Africans were first enslaved here, the question whether Blacks would become a part of the national economy or be relegated to a separate Black economy has been posed repeatedly. The answer, to my mind, is no more obvious today than it might have been a century or more ago. But the persistence of the question strongly suggests that a knowledge and appreciation of the past is a necessary though not a sufficient key to understanding the complexities of the present. Only when both past and present are fully utilized can we expect to plan effectively for our future.

## The Historical Setting

Indeed, it is impossible to discuss economic and business development in Black America without some brief mention of the general socioeconomic condition of Black people. Following Myrdal's *The American Dilemma*, we shall divide the economic history of Blacks in America into three periods, roughly approximating a pre-emancipation period, a period between emancipation and the start of World War II, and a third from World II to the present.[4]

The full extent of slavery's damaging impact on the social and economic conditions of Africans in the United States may never be completely revealed. Historians will be uncovering new twists in this cause–effect analysis for years to come. However, some obvious effects can be identified. Perhaps the most significant of these might be labeled social rather than economic, for they revolve around the very conscious effort to replace the African personality with a slave mentality—a belief in one's own inferiority and in the superiority of those who enslaved him. This was at the crux of the impact of slavery. The racist sentiments which emerged from this institution were embedded in the constitutional documents underlying this country's existence and were quite naturally implanted as deeply in the minds of men.

Many writers tend to ignore these "social" consequences of slavery and are thus unable to place its economic consequences into a sensible perspective. For example, "there has been a great deal of controversy about the profitability of slavery in the antebellum South and about whether slavery was an efficient and viable form of economic organization."[5] That so much effort is still spent on such academic debates is surprising. No amount of scholarly diatribe can ever convince Black folk of any viability in such a racist institution.

Another major effect of slavery was containment. Black people, until the outbreak of the Civil War, were largely confined to the South. This geographical concentration and over-representation in a soon-to-decline southern agricultural economy was to have rather dire economic consequences. The primary effect of emancipation was perhaps the disruption of the "plantation regime," the system that had so well ordered the day-to-day routine among the enslaved. Upon emancipation, many slaves immediately applied the true test of their newly acquired status–mobility. They had to "leave the plantation for at least a few days or weeks in order that they might really feel sure that they were free."[6]

But assuring a lasting and meaningful freedom to the exslaves would have required much more than either the North or the South was willing to undertake. It is a simple fact that "Emancipation was not related to any change of mind on the part of white people."[7] Consequently, attempts to educate the freedmen, abolish discrimination, and institute land reforms, when not brazenly resisted, were unenthusiastically undertaken.

In the face of northern complacency, the South found an ample opportunity to avenge its defeat in war by dismantling the few policies aimed at protecting the freedmen. Slowly, but surely, the failure to provide the groundwork for the economic independence of freedmen led to the reestablishment of the old plantation regime. Soon the development of the sharecropping system and the passing of certain laws were to create conditions as oppressive as had existed during slavery.

The great migration to the "Promised Land"—the mass movement of southern Blacks to the urban North—affected the economic position of Black people as much as slavery had. Before 1940, almost four out of every five Blacks lived in the rural and economically depressed South. The South's per capita income was only three-fifths of the nation's, and at that it was the misfortune of Black folk to be concentrated in those southern states with the lowest per capita incomes. Blacks moreover were concentrated in a declining agricultural section, a situation that greatly worsened their economic position.

So the North seemed to offer Blacks some things not available in the South—more job opportunities, a covert and more subtle form of discrimination, and a seeming sense of being a part of the scheme of things. The continuing downward spiral of the southern agricultural economy after the Civil War and the concurrent industrial expansion in the North (except during the depression) contributed to a significant regional shift of Black people in the United States. Around 1940, only 20 percent resided outside the South. Just twenty years later, in 1960, that percentage had almost doubled to 37 percent. Although the claim that this migration has led to some real improvement in the economic position of Black folk can be substantiated, its validity is debatable.[8]

But despite substantial improvements, the fact remains that the economic position of Blacks in America is still grossly inferior to the position of whites.[9] In 1968 the median annual income of Black families ($5,590) was only 60 percent of that for white families ($8,936). The incidence of families below the poverty level is almost three and one half times greater among Blacks than among whites. The unemployment rate among Blacks was twice the rate for whites in 1969, and that ratio had remained relatively unchanged over a ten-year period. The median income for a Black male high school graduate between the ages of twenty-five and fifty-four was less than that of a white male with only an eighth grade education. The litany of inequities continues. It has been in the context of such economic disparity—in the face of such racist absurdities—that we, as Blacks in America, have had to maintain our sanity *and* struggle to gain the economic, political, and social opportunities that are supposedly ours by virtue of being born here.

Having briefly looked at the general socioeconomic condition of Black people in America from slavery to the present, let us turn specifically to the development of business-related activity during this same period. Business activity among Blacks did not begin with their appearance on the American scene. African people had developed extensive experience in trade at home and in other societies where they could move freely. But the impact of a forced separation from our natural environment and the peculiar differences in the economic arrangements in America left Africans at a great disadvantage.

Before the Civil War, the institution of slavery in the South, and in the North, a small, scattered population and more developed economy tended to confine Blacks to small business ventures. In the South, these ventures were usually based on skills acquired in performing tasks that whites did not wish to engage in. Barbering, catering, and similar services comprised the bulk of Black business activity under the well-established patterns of racial segregation. In the North, population scarcity and keener competition joined racial oppression as the major barriers to the development of large-scale Black business enterprise. And yet there were individual success stories in several lines of business endeavor. For example, Paul Cuffe of Boston financed several "Back to Africa" expeditions with money made in sail-making and shipping.

The history of Black business ownership shows how tightly economics was woven with political and social development. The years following Reconstruction witnessed a stress on economic activity as a means of solving the "race problem." It was thought that through materialistic aggrandizement Black folk would then be accorded their rights as citizens and the respect due them as human beings. Economic activity, along with self-help and racial solidarity, became dominant values in Black communities. The economic theme became the center of the Black movement, even to the exclusion of concern for the suppression of political and civil rights.[10] Some espoused a philosophy of thrift and hard work as a means of elevating Black people to economic independence, while others stressed economic solidarity among the working class as a more practical means.

Although emancipation radically altered the legal framework in which Black businesses could develop, for many years there was no appreciable increase in the number of Blacks engaged in business. Much more than a proclamation was needed to overcome the handicaps stemming from racist oppression. But from 1885 on there was a noticeable increase in the number of Black businesses—banks, insurance companies, undertakers, and retail establishments. Contributing to this development was the increasing urbanization of Black people and the simultaneous decline in white support for Black business.

As time passed, racial prejudice and discrimination became a greater barrier to those Black businesses that had previously catered to whites, and these businesses now became increasingly dependent on the Black community. Increasing technology and the consequent need for greater capitalization in order to compete with whites forced many Black people out of business. In the face of such obstacles, the appeal to self-help and racial solidarity intensified.

The narrative of Black business activity after 1890 is filled with very rugged, very inspiring, but also very sparsely scattered individual success stories—with many more "unsuccess" stories. There were some related events worth noting. In 1900, Booker T. Washington took the initiative in founding the National Negro Business League, designed to foster business development through publicizing individual success stories and instilling faith in business as a means to racial equality. Several conferences on business development and economic cooperation were held and the organization is still in existence.

But the trend of Black business activity over the last sixty years followed a general pattern: there were brief periods of "expanding opportunities" and then sustained periods of depression. The most significant factor affecting these cycles of expansion and depression was the shifting tendencies toward segregation and integration in American society. In closely related debate over the integrated versus the separate economy, this ambivalence is still with us today.[11] It is this conflict that must be thoroughly treated if we are serious in our efforts to unravel the intricacies of economic and business development among Blacks in America.

One general comment should be made regarding the historical sketch just presented. There has been a tendency to attribute only selfish motives to those Blacks who advocated business development as a means to racial equality. Abram Harris has been a prime perpetrator of this mistaken conclusion.

Although ostensibly sponsored as the means of self-help or racial cooperation, as it was sometimes called, through which the masses were to be economically emancipated, Negro business enterprise was motivated primarily by the desire for private profit and looked toward the establishment of a Negro capitalist employer class.[12]

Such a conclusion ignores that these advocates had a very clear, though naïve, faith in the impact of business on race relations and the economic conditions of the Black masses. Such men as John Hope were quite explicit on the role of business enterprise:

Industrial education and labor unions for Negroes will not change this condition. They may modify it, but the condition will not be very materially changed. . . . We must take in some, if not all, of the wages, turn it into capital, hold it, increase it . . . as a means of employment for the thousands who cannot get work from old sources. Employment must be had, and this employment will have to come to Negroes from Negro sources. . . . Negro capital will have to give an opportunity to Negro workmen crowded out by white competition. . . . Employment for colored men and women, colored boys and girls must be supplied by colored people.[13]

Such optimism coupled with the emphasis placed by society on business as a means to many social ends, effectively masked certain trends that might have dulled this faith in business as the means whereby Black people would "generally advance to all the rights and privileges which any class of citizens enjoy."[14] But this faith stemmed not from a desire to exploit their brothers but rather from the economic tenor of the times and the unfounded optimism in a future for Black folk in this country.

## The Current Emphasis on Black Economic Development

Today, Black business enterprise and economic development have again regained prominence as *the* solution to the long-standing plight of Black people. The impetus to this resurgence is not entirely clear. Some claim that the recent "official" thrust was sparked, in part, by the Report of the National Advisory Commission on Civil Disorders which suggested, as part of its recommendations for national action that "we . . . give special encouragement to Negro ownership of business in ghetto areas."[15] Their suggestion may have, in part, stemmed from their analysis of the minimal effectiveness of previous governmental efforts aimed at fostering Black business ownership.[16]

Yet when one considers the state of Black business enterprise at the time of this resurgence, particularly in the context of the rebellions which had occurred in urban areas, it is surprising that the swing back to "Black economic development" did not occur much sooner. A national survey of U.S. business conducted by the Small Businesses Administration in 1969 estimated that there were some 112,500 Black-owned businesses, or roughly 2.25 percent of the over 5 million businesses in the U.S. (See Table 1.) If Blacks owned businesses roughly proportional to their reported 11 percent total of the population, they would be owning about 550,000 businesses. The SBA figure for Black ownership thus falls 437,500 businesses short of proportional representation.

### TABLE 1
*Minority Share of Business Ownership — By Industry*

| Industry | Share of Black Ownership |
|---|---|
| Personal Services | 8.4% |
| Other Services | 1.4 |
| Construction | 2.6 |
| Manufacturing | 1.2 |
| Retail Trade | 1.9 |
| Other Industries | 1.4 |
| All Industries | 2.25% |

*Source:* Small Business Administration, 1969.

This quantitative difference, however, is made even worse when we consider the qualitative distribution of Black-owned businesses. Almost 60 percent of minority-owned businesses* are found in personal services

* Although the category is "minority" (or "nonwhite"), Blacks constitute over 90 percent of this group.

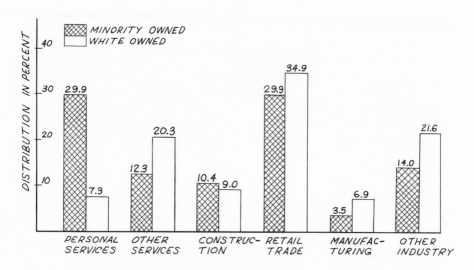

FIGURE. 1. *Industry Distribution of Minority\* and White Owned Businesses.*

SOURCE: National Survey of U.S. Business by Small Business Administration—1969.

\* Blacks Comprise over 90% of the Census Category "Minority".

and retail trade, compared with 42 percent of white businesses. (Figure 1). This leads to all sorts of related inequities.

The average business equity of nonwhites is approximately $14,000; white-owned business equity averages $25,000 in value. Since, moreover, as Levitan and Taggert have pointed out, "the median value of business equity owned by nonwhites is only $3,700, the large majority own small enterprises."[17] Only 5.1 percent of minority-owned business employed ten or more people, compared with almost 20 percent for other businesses. Finally, while almost 50 percent of white-owned business activity enjoys gross receipts of $50,000 or more, this is true of only 33 percent of minority-owned businesses (Table 2).

These figures, while they represent gains over past years, also reflect the almost negligible impact of Black business activity on the nation's economy. Federal and private programs to foster Black ownership of productive enterprise were bound to meet with some success; there was no way to go except up!

Federal efforts to increase Black business ownership were also related to other factors:

1) Minority citizens have significantly improved their position in skilled, professional, and technical occupations. Between 1960 and 1967, nonwhite

employment in professional and technical occupations increased at an annual average rate of 37,000 persons, craftsmen and foremen occupations increased 30,000 per year, while clerical occupations increased 56,000 annually.

2)There is an expanding economic base for business opportunity within the minority population itself. Between 1960 and 1967, the increase in disposable income of nonwhite persons is estimated at $16 billion, reaching a total of $37 billion in 1967, about half of which was concentrated in urban areas.

3) Average family incomes among nonwhite families are rising faster than the national average. This growing minority purchasing power can support both a growing number of businesses and a greater range of products.

**TABLE 2**

*Size Distribution, Minority-Owned Business*

| Number of Paid Employees | Minority-Owned (Percent) | Other (Percent) |
|:---:|:---:|:---:|
| 0 | 31 | 26 |
| 1-9 | 64 | 55 |
| 10-49 | 4 | 13 |
| 50-99 | 1 | 3 |
| 100+ | * | 3 |

| Gross Receipts (in Thousands of $) | Minority-Owned (Percent) | Other (Percent) |
|:---:|:---:|:---:|
| 0.9.9 | 33 | 19 |
| 10-19.9 | 15 | 12 |
| 20-49.9 | 19 | 19 |
| 50-99.9 | 14 | 15 |
| 100-999.9 | 17 | 26 |
| 1,000-4,999.9 | 2 | 9 |
| 5,000 and over | | |

*Source:* Small Business Administration, 1969.

*Less than 0.1 percent.

So the stage was set for the reemergence of economic development as the panacea of the problems of Black America and many people were self-cast for leading roles. "Black capitalism" became the order of the day.[18] President Nixon's interest in Black business ownership led to the formation of a new division within the Commerce Department, the Office of Minority Business Enterprise (backed by a sixty-three-man National Advisory Committee), several interagency task forces, as well as increased attention to the subject by many other federal agencies.[19] Many businessmen, academicians, and foundations began to discuss the problem, and in Congress there was bipartisan sponsorship of bills aimed at facilitating

Black ownership. These moves were even joined by "militant" Blacks who saw the program as being consistent with their drive for Black control over Black communities. But the flurry of activity under the rubric of "Black capitalism" (and Black economic development) was confusing in the number of things meant by different people.

Yet perhaps this will prove to be the most fruitful contribution of "Black capitalism"—the phrase has evoked widespread discussion that is more meaningful than the concept it attempts to describe. It is fortunate that the alternatives are being thoroughly aired and even tested. There remains much to be resolved. To many advocates, the current emphasis is no more than the transfer of traditional economic practices from the white to the Black community. The critique of this notion has been that it implies the creation of a Black capitalist class "where Blacks merely exploit other Blacks or where Blacks merely become cogs in the traditional western monopoly capitalist system."[20] But others have a completely different definition. Roy Innis of CORE, for example, views the thrust as

the acquisition of the instruments of black capitalism, the community-owned means of operation of shops, factories, stores, and industry. We're not just interested in creating ten or fifteen more black capitalists. . . . What we want is broad black industrialism, based on community action, ownership and management, in the hands of blacks, all the blacks in the community.[21]

Here the emphasis is on *community-based economic development*—the broad-based ownership and control of productive resources as a basis for effective community development. Between these two definitions fall a host of others which tend to suggest that the only limits to the generation of new definitions are those imposed by a creative imagination.

A recent discussion of Black economic development suggests three broad categories of activity.[22] One stresses skills training, job placement, or employment opportunities; a second emphasizes Black capitalism, or Black ownership and operation of businesses; and the third is described as the elimination or dispersal of ghettos. Considerable controversy has developed within and around each of the categories. For example, the "individual Black capitalist" and the community-based models represent opposite poles within the Black ownership category. The limitations of the employment thrust are now accepted by most Blacks; after all there was "full employment" under slavery. And advocates of ghetto eradication must counter the argument that even if white America were prepared to accept a much greater Black presence in its midst, this alternative would still provide little meaningful and lasting benefits to large numbers of Black people.[23]

It is a simple fact that there is no consensus on the nature of Black economic development. As always, and of necessity, our decisions in the economic sphere must be closely linked to Black social and political ends. It is essential, therefore, that some attempts be made to establish a basis for evaluating the many efforts occurring in the area of Black economic development.

## *Toward an Analytical Framework*

Black folk often react quite strongly against those who call for more analysis of our situation and further clarification of our goals and strategies. And rightly so! We have discussed, defined, and delineated (and have heard others discuss, define, and delineate for us) the various aspects of our predicament to the point of exhaustion. Nevertheless, it is still necessary to remind ourselves that *goals* and an understanding of what action–orientations they imply are essential to the success of our struggle.

There are two related questions which can be asked in helping us to structure a framework for the analysis of Black economic and business activity.

1) What are our goals in undertaking Black economic and business developmental efforts?
2) What are the obstacles to building viable Black business and economic enterprise?

These questions should clearly be asked in the order above. Yet in many instances this has not been the case. Some activities have been undertaken with well-defined goals but with little careful assessment of existing obstacles. Even more serious have been programs designed to alleviate certain perceived obstacles to Black economic development, but with no further goals beyond the removal of such barriers.[24]

From all the comments and activity we can isolate at least three levels of goals advocated by different groups concerned with Black economic development:

Level 1: to give a few more Blacks "a share of wealth and a piece of the action." (This is the thrust of President Nixon's Black capitalism program.)
Level 2: to give Black Americans collective income parity with whites. (This is the position of, among others, Andrew Brimmer, the Black member of the Board of Governors of the Federal Reserve Board.)
Level 3: to overcome Black dependence and powerlessness and to institute maximum broad-based control over the economic activity of Black communities. (This is the essential position of Roy Innis of CORE.)

Similarly we can identify these levels of obstacles to, or causes of, the economic and business underdevelopment of Black communities:

Level 1: lack of managerial skills and attitudes. Thus, in the words of Robert McKersie, a well-known labor economist, "Negroes as a race have been little exposed to business operations and lack the technical experience and entrepreneurial values that are necessary for succeeding in business.[25]
Level 2: the accumulation and institutionalization of prerogatives in

existing economic institutions that are exercised to the detriment of Blacks —for example, hiring practices, seniority, union membership rules, "testing," etc.[26]

Level 3: The basic structure of U.S. capitalism. This position was well put by James Boggs, when he recently wrote: "Black underdevelopment is a product of capitalist development. Black America is underdeveloped today because of capitalist semi-colonialism, just as Africa, Asia, and Latin America are underdeveloped today because of capitalist colonialism."[27]

I suggest that it is possible, indeed helpful, to view these three levels of goals and obstacles as reflecting either the increasing importance of a goal to larger numbers of Black people, or the increasing complexity in the nature of a particular obstacle. The gist of my argument is that, at worst, actions dictated by a low level analysis of goals or obstacles may defeat the achievement of higher level (and more important) goals. At best, lower level programs may contribute little, if anything, to the removal of the real obstacles to Black economic development.

An excellent example of a Level 1 goal involves those programs which are essentially geared to the production of *individual* entrepreneurs—and these embrace most programs under the "Black capitalism" rubric. But "Black capitalism" is intended to benefit Black *communities* only indirectly, for it does not address itself to the massive needs of large numbers of Black people. I have already cited the widening gap in both income and employment opportunities between Blacks and whites. Moreover, disadvantages in housing, health, educational opportunities, and almost any other standard measure of social well-being reflect the oppression Blacks face as a people. Thus, considering the seriousness of our plight, the emphasis on individualist Black capitalism is diversionary.

The Black capitalist orientation perpetuates the myth of economic individualism and the illusion of competition as a viable tool in the quest for Black liberation.[28] It is sheer folly for a Black person to suggest that we can all be individually secure in white man's America. Black people in America have not been oppressed primarily as individuals, but as a group. The history of this country suggests that it is only on this group basis that any people, once excluded, have struggled successfully to enjoy whatever America has to offer. Black economic, political, and social freedom must also be sought on this basis.

The fact of the matter is that advocates of Black capitalism tend to ignore the whole problem of securing maximum broad-based control of economic activity as a means for effective *community* development. The relationship between control of economic activity and political power is an important one. Exclusionary policies have contributed to widespread alienation and frustration among substantial segments of American population, especially among Blacks who are now rightly demanding more say in those decisions shaping their lives. In fact, Black people are, individually or collectively, only recent participants in these arrangements. Regardless of the outcome of this move toward greater Black participation, the present state of affairs is a sad commentary on the effectiveness of past practices.

The Level 2 goal—to give some Black Americans collective income parity with whites—is perhaps best articulated by Andrew Brimmer. Brimmer does not advocate major efforts to encourage Black-owned businesses because he believes that higher earnings are possible through salaried employment in white firms. His chosen emphasis, therefore, is jobs "in an integrated national economy." But as Charles Tate, in his critical assessment of Brimmer's position appearing in this volume, points out, such a strategy "writes off the masses of Black people who are excluded from competition for white collar jobs, and condemns them to a marginal, sub-human existence" and the same is true of the myriad of job development and skills training programs that have emerged in recent years. The "victims" of many of these programs were trained with skills or for jobs either already or soon to be outmoded by technological advances (or man-induced manipulations). In addition to almost wholly ignoring the significance of business ownership and control, the program approaches under the income equality goal (Level 2) were never geared to providing full income parity for Black folk in the American economy.

A similar analysis can be applied to the obstacles which are alleged to explain Black economic and business underdevelopment and the programs aimed at alleviating them. For many years the tendency has been to blame Black folk for their economic plight. We were admonished to "pull yourselves up by your own bootstraps like . . ." when, in view of economic realities, Blacks had been amputated from the knees, if not the waist, down. Programs which perceived this type of obstacle as a major one were designed to strengthen the "entrepreneurial heritage" of Blacks by exposing them to the white heritage through business school fellowships, counseling programs, seminars with retired white executives, and the like. But as the National Advisory Commission on Civil Disorders pointed out, a more complex obstacle to Black development in general, and to economic development, specifically, has been the racism that pervades the major institutional arrangements in American society.[29] Many programs and much legislation of the "civil rights" era were intended to challenge and alter the practices of racial discrimination in employment, education, housing, public accommodation, and other areas.

On another, even more complex level, a convincing argument is made that "racism in the U.S. is so pervasive in the mentality of whites that only an armed, well-disciplined, Black-controlled government can insure the stamping out of racism in this country." Such an analysis leads James Forman, for example, to suggest "total control as the only solution to the economic problems of Black people." This seizing of state power, according to Forman, will enable Blacks to create a society where productive economic resources are owned collectively for the benefit of all people.

Another example of the three levels of obstacles involves the rather innovative "Ghediplan" proposed by Dr. Dunbar McLaurin, which seeks to revitalize the depressed Harlem economy through such mechanisms as guaranteed financing, guaranteed markets, and local ownership and control. The objectives of the "Ghediplan" place them as Level 3 goals—the attainment of local control over economic activity to enable meaningful improvement in the quality of Harlem life.

It would be extremely naive to claim that the Level 1 obstacle—lack of an entrepreneurial heritage—is all that prevents maximum community development through control of local economic activity. A Level 2 obstacle like institutional racism is certainly more reflective of the plight of Black folk in this country. But there is perhaps a stronger argument for choosing a Level 3 obstacle—the nature of American capitalism. The argument based on the analogy that Black communities, particularly of the Harlem variety, exist as colonies to be used by America for the same purposes that overseas colonies and other "territories" were (and are) used cannot be so easily dismissed. The failure to undertake programs with a reasonable chance of rehabilitating ghetto economies across the country is seen by many as stemming not only from institutional racism (Level 2), but from a desire (sometimes unconscious) to maintain the exploited, dependent, powerless, in short, the colonized state of Black communities (Level 3). The upshot from this multilevel analysis of obstacles illustrated by the above examples is simply that some factors are more responsible for the economic plight of Black folk than others.

There is a natural tendency to select those obstacles which are relatively simple to deal with (Level 1), but are not the real causes of our predicament. If the three levels of goals are seen as related to the levels of obstacles, then it is obvious that any actions that stem from a Level 1 analysis of goals and obstacles do not contribute as much to the attainment of higher goals as programs which result from a Level 2 or Level 3 analysis. For example, a very real obstacle to the participation of Blacks in the construction trades is the kind of discretionary racism practiced by many of the vested interests that have built up around that industry (Level 2). For many years the problem was being diagnosed as a lack of "trained" construction workers and Black construction firms with "good track records" (Level 1). But, in spite of advances in both of these areas, racism was rampant and Blacks showed no significant advances in the industry. The analysis that led away from Level 1 and up to Level 2 viewed the problem as one of institutionalized discrimination and suggested a series of steps—similar to the Philadelphia Plan—to systematically hold unions and contractors responsible for the hiring of a meaningful number of minority personnel—on a contractural basis. The results have been significantly different from the counseling and "good faith" tactics that had for too long impeded progress. To state the matter differently, if Black economic equality and maximum community economic control are our goals, then dealing with obstacles (like racism and massive concentrations of wealth) which grow out of the existing socioeconomic system is much more meaningful than dealing with factors (like the lack of an entrepreneurial heritage) which are mere symptoms of what really ails Black folk in this country.

Much of the debate today stems from a disagreement over the selection of goals, on the one hand, and a disagreement on the obstacles preventing the attainment of any goal, on the other. It would seem that Blacks could agree on the Level 3 goal above—maximum broad-based control of community economic activity. This goal does not preclude the Level 1 or Level 2 goals, but is rather, as I see it, a necessary condition for their attainment. But it is this goal which perhaps causes greatest difficulty. The current debate reflects again the integrationist–separatist dilemma in the Black community. Economic nationalism (control of one's economy) has nothing necessarily to do with race. It is universal among nations—and among states, countries, cities, and even local neighborhoods. The strength and control of one's economic base determine the well-being of the people. History has amply demonstrated the outcome of outside control for the well-being of African people the world over.

The question becomes, then, not whether Blacks should control and develop our economy, but how we are to do so. And to rule out any mechanism on a priori anticipations of even miniscule contributions toward the ends of control and development is inconsistent with the strategy dictated by the nature of our situation.

So the two questions that Black people must constantly ask and discuss are (1) what are our goals? and (2) what are the obstacles to their attainment, in what order should we deal with them, and how? Of course, this does not mean we should declare a moratorium on our economic and business development efforts until such questions are conclusively answered. Until a new consensus is reached, we must forge a provisional operational unity that will enable us to work on different goals with a variety of strategies.

The situation Black people must avoid, however, is fixation with regard to ends or means, or both. Blacks cannot allow themselves to be lulled into agreement on any goal less than the total liberation of all Black people. Similarly, we must constantly attempt to spur our perspectives about what barriers Black economic development faces to higher levels of analysis and adopt programs that are geared to deal directly with the real causes of our problems.

It is in this context of ends and means—total liberation of Black folk everywhere by any and all means dictated by our situation—that the seemingly endless debate over separation or integration becomes, as succinctly stated by Lerone Bennett, "abstract, false, and diversionary."[30] Participants in the debate have tended to view separation or integration as ends in themselves. But they are more properly viewed as alternate tactics to be used at various times, in various places, and perhaps even in combination, to deal with the realities of racist America. It is the recognition and acceptance of this fact which will free Blacks in America of an ideological halter that has for years been consciously perpetrated to impede our struggle for total liberation.

The readings selected in this book elaborate on themes treated in this introductory essay, and on many other issues related to economic and business development in Black America. The selections are organized in four major sections. Part I provides the historical background needed to place contemporary Black economic and business activity in proper perspective. The second part presents the current debate over Black capitalism as a strategy for Black economic development. The readings in this section are extensive; no other debate has generated as much attention or as many alternative models. Part III contains many of the models and suggestions for action proposed as alternatives (or complements) to the "Black capitalism" model. Part IV is concerned with the future. The selections treat, more than anything else, the implications of the various strategies and philosophical questions that have emerged during the brief period in which economic and business development have seemingly reemerged as the prime instrumentality for Black liberation.

The selections are certainly not exhaustive. There are limitations. One is that the emphasis is more on business and business-related development than on other facets linked to the Black economic development thrust—job development, broadening employment opportunities, guaranteed income plans, and the like. To these important topics ample space has been devoted in other sources. Although the focus is primarily on Black folk, the Black experience is certainly relevant to other oppressed people, and the strategies that evolve will surely be applicable to our common struggle. But the major limitation of this volume of readings is that it treats only one activity that has rapidly risen to a status similar to previous schemes offered as panaceas in the quest of Blacks for human rights. Others include integration, education, political participation. Hopefully, the lesson to be learned from this rapid rise of economic and business development as *the* solution to the problems of Blacks—a lesson not sufficiently reiterated in the selections herein—will be remembered. There exists no "the solution." Viewed in perspective, it has become patently obvious that the solutions must be numerous and as multifaceted as the kinds of oppression facing African people in America and wherever we find ourselves.

## Notes

1. Harold Cruse, *Crisis of the Negro Intellectual* (New York: Morrow, 1967).

2. An excellent review of this ideological debate appeared in a special issue of *Ebony* (August 1970) under the subtitle "Which Way Black America—Separation? Integration? Liberation?"

3. Cruse, *op. cit.*, p. 6.

4. Gunnar Myrdal et al., *An American Dilemma: The Negro Problem and Modern Democracy* (New York: Harper, 1944) contains a discussion of the economic history of Africans in America between the Civil War and World War II. For an excellent economic study of the role of slavery, see Eric Williams, *Capitalism and Slavery* (New York: Capricon, 1966); for a treatment of more recent times, see Andrew Brimmer, "The Negro in the National Economy," in *The American Negro Reference Book* ed. John P. Davis, (Englewood Cliffs, N.J.: Prentice–Hall, 1966), pp. 255–336.

5. John F. Kain, *Race and Poverty: The Economics of Discrimination* (Englewood Cliffs, N.J.: Prentice–Hall, 1969), p. 6.

6. Booker T. Washington, *Up From Slavery* (New York: A. L. Burt Co., 1901), p. 23.

7. Myrdal, *op. cit.*, p. 223.

8. Kain, *op. cit.*, p. 8 ff. See also Paul A. Baran and Paul M. Sweezy. *Monopoly Capital* (New York: Monthly Review Press, 1966). p. 258. The authors argue that "the bottom of the urban industrial ladder is higher than the bottom of the southern agricultural ladder." But the fact that Blacks made no real progress after reaching urban areas raises serious questions about any urban gains from migration.

9. U. S. Department of Labor and U. S. Department of Commerce, "The Social and Economic Status of Negroes in the United States" (Washington, D.C., 1969).

10. The philosophy of Booker T. Washington can be cited as generally illustrative of this trend, although the Negro Convention movement of the 1870s provides much earlier examples.

11. The work of Harold Cruse referred to above is an admirable effort to provide the historical background of the contemporary Black movement, and the separatist–integrationist tension is discussed quite thoroughly.

12. Abram Harris, *The Negro As Capitalist* (Philadelphia: The American Academy of Political and Social Science, 1936), p. 49.

13. John Hope, Proceedings of the Fourth Atlanta University Conference (1898), *The Negro in Business*, ed. W. E. B. DuBois (Atlanta University Press), pp. 56–57.

14. Washington, *op. cit.*, p. 19 ff.

15. National Rdvisory Commission on Civil Disorders, *Report* (Washington, D.C.: Government Printing Office, 1968), p. 236.

16. Federal programs in aid of Black business enterprise have never been of the magnitude that the public has been led to believe. Even since the initiation of the highly touted "Project Own," an analysis of Small Business Administration statistics suggests that while there may have been increases in the number of loans to Blacks, there has been little if any increase in the share of the total dollar value of these loans. In other words, the loans to Blacks, while increasing in number, are much smaller than the average loans to white businessmen. Further, the bulk of loans to Blacks are concentrated in the secondary industries (services, retail trade, etc.) instead of in the more important primary industries (manufacturing, wholesaling, construction) where whites "happen" to be concentrated. This pattern is a familiar one and argues strongly for a much closer scrutiny of federal and private efforts in support of Black business ownership. See the tables of Small Business Administration statistics appearing in Anthony Mason, "Black Capitalism: Rhetoric and Reality," (New York: Equity Research Associates, 1969).

17. Sar A. Levitan and Robert Taggert III, "Entrepreneurship—Another Option Toward Equal Opportunity," *Poverty and Human Resources Abstracts*, March 1969, p. 15.

18. Not only are the ideas expressed in today's use of the phrase "Black capitalism" found in the pages of Black history, but so is the term itself. See Ira DeA. Reid, "The Negro in the American Economic System" (A Research Memorandum for the Carnegie-Myrdal Study—*The Negro in America*), 1940, Book I, p. 170. In citing factors in the short business history of Blacks in America, Reid lists the restrictions of segregation on building economic power, lack of sufficient business education, and lack of adequate capital. His conclusion bears a striking resemblance to several current analyses. The above factors, he states, "have been submitted as *apologia* for Negro business, but they alone are not responsible for *Black capitalism's* low estate." (emphasis added)

19. For an excellent discussion of events related to the "Black capitalism" thrust, see John McClaughry, "Black Ownership and National Politics," in *Black Economic Development*, eds. William F. Haddad and G. Douglas Pugh (Englewood Cliffs, N.J.: Prentice–Hall, 1969), pp. 38–50. Two other reviews are Anthony Mason, "Black Capitalism: Rhetoric and Reality," (New York: Equity Research Associates, 1969); and Raymond L. Hoewing and Lawrence Finkelstein, "Minority Entrepreneurship: A Status Report" (Washington, D.C.: Public Affairs Council, 1969).

20. Robert Wright, "Viewpoint: Black Capitalism," *Negro Digest*, December 1969, p. 27.

21. Quoted in Milton Moskowitz, "Where It's At: Black Capitalism," *Business and Society*, December 17, 1968, p. 3.

22. William L. Henderson and Larry C. Ledebur, "The Viable Alternative for Black Economic Development," *Public Policy*, Spring 1970, pp. 429–449.

23. In reviewing this evidence, one observer concludes that even "to proclaim full integration as one's immediate goal is idle rhetoric." See Alan Altshuler, *Community Control: The Black Demand for Participation in Large American Cities* (New York: Pegasus, 1970), p. 21. Even the National Advisory Commission on Civil Disorders was insightful enough to conclude that "ghetto dispersal" was not a viable means to solving the problems of Blacks in America, but rather an ideal end to be reached through some combination of other means. See "The Future of the Cities," *Report*, chap. 16.

24. An analysis somewhat similar and of great relevance is one that came to my attention after the framework herein was formulated. See Glenn Dixon, "Outputs of Minority Entrepreneurship Programs," *The Review of Black Political Economy*, Spring–Summer 1970, pp. 3–17. His thesis is that traditional approaches to stating and defining goals of Black economic development activities are inadequate. "The inequities which define the problems of poverty are addressed, but the inequities which produce the dependence and powerlessness of Black neighborhoods in America are, for the most part, neglected" (p. 6).

25. Robert McKersie, "Vitalize Black Enterprise," *Harvard Business Review*, September–October 1968, p. 90.

26. For an elaboration of the concept of "institutional racism" see Stokeley Carmichael and Charles Hamilton, *Black Power: The Politics of Liberation in America* (New York: Random House, 1967).

27. James Boggs, "The Myth and Irrationality of Black Capitalism," *The Review of Black Political Economy*, Spring–Summer 1970, p. 28.

28. Black people in several countries are urging the adoption of Black economic and business activity along Afro-centric lines—based on principles of communalism, on *cooperation* rather than competition. Competition is seen as an unnecessarily wasteful luxury that oppressed Black America cannot afford. Clearly, this communal economic thrust calls for a new set of values among Black people in America. For an elaboration of the principles of "ujamaa"—cooperative economics or "familyhood"— the writings of The Honorable Julius K. Nyerere, President of Tanzania, are particularly relevant. See, for example, his *Freedom and Unity* (Oxford University Press, 1967), and *Freedom and Socialism* (Oxford University Press, 1968).

29. Although the National Advisory Commission on Civil Disorders may have popularized the notion for whites, Black folk have long been in agreement on the fact. Carmichael and Hamilton's assessment of the unwillingness of this society to deal with institutional racism because "the black community has been the creation of, and dominated by, a combination of oppressive forces and special interests in the white community" (p. 22) is illustrative of a sentiment among Blacks that predates a conclusion that was not even considered in the realm of possibility by most of white America until recently.

30. Lerone Bennett, "Liberation," *Ebony*, August 1970, p. 36.

# PART I

## *Recurring Themes: An Historical Overview*

# Introduction

The purpose of Part I is the presentation of readings which provide that historical perspective needed for a meaningful study of business enterprise in Black America. The first selection by Joseph Pierce is an excellent introductory essay. He provides insights into the role of business in American life and its relationship to the status Black businesses have been assigned within the American economy. He touches upon many themes that will appear throughout this book of readings. The second selection, by Kinzer and Sagarin, explores one of these themes in depth. They discuss the factors which furthered the drive for a separate Black economy and thereby heightened the separatist–integrationist conflict in the development of Black business enterprise.

The study of Black business in Chicago by St. Clair Drake and the late Horace Cayton provides a perceptive and realistic account of its status in the urban North. In the setting of a single city, the authors are able to illustrate the confluence of forces that made the thrust toward Black business development an inevitable one. In doing so, they provide insights into the causes of the discrepancy between the actual role of Black business enterprise in the economy of Chicago (or any urban city) and the status accorded it by the masses of Black people. The meaning of this discrepancy is critically assessed in the reading by E. Franklin Frazier, who describes it as a myth propagated by the Black bourgeoisie "to compensate for its feelings of inferiority in a white world dominated by business enterprise." Franklin's major criticism is that the advocates of Black business enterprise refused to consider such facts as the lack of a business tradition, the structure of the American economy, and the inherent limitations of a separate Black economy. It is somewhat paradoxical, therefore, that he claims the myth "was formulated . . . during the last decade of the nineteenth century when a legal system of racial separation and subordination was inaugurated and the hope of Negroes to attain equality in American life was crushed." The paradox is never resolved, for Franklin never adequately considers the impact on Black development of the racism that has pervaded the American social and economic system since its inception.

Harold Cruse has delved deeper in his analysis of the integrationist–separatist debate than any contemporary scholar. His call for "a new institutionalism"—one that can take advantage of the various motivations to Black business ownership for the development of the total community—is a succinct summary of the most promising movement today. The emphasis placed on the need to study and synthesize the various historical aspects of Black business enterprise was a primary consideration in the selection of the readings for Part I. It would have certainly been possible to use more statistical information in illustrating the points presented in this section. But such information would have only confirmed the obvious. And since the obvious (Black business underdevelopment) is not the desired state of affairs, analytical and evaluative material has been substituted.

# 1 ]] The Evolution of Negro Business

*Joseph A. Pierce*

Business has been defined as "the mechanism designed by man to satisfy his wants"[1] through the utilization of social resources such as natural resources, human labor, capital, and acquired knowledge.[2] This is a definition of business as it purports to operate generally in America, and it implicitly assumes the absence of racial restrictions in such activities.

It is a well-known fact, however, that the Negro, comprising the largest racial minority in the United States, is seriously limited by restricted economic and business opportunities. One inevitable result of such restrictions is to place the Negro in the position of feeling the necessity for establishing his own business—a circumscribed and virtually separate sphere of economic activity within the general American business economy —whatever the impediments or consequences involved. Within his sphere of economic activity the Negro business man is hindered by "giant financial combinations, cumulative business wisdom, cumulative wealth, mass production and marketing, marketing tricks and schemes,"[3] and he is circumscribed by geographical and population limitations, frustrated by knowing that there are certain types of businesses in which his chances of success are relatively small.

Many of his impediments naturally are those common to all small businesses, but, unless the Negro succeeds in gaining greater—and less restricted—participation in the production and exchange of goods and services on all levels, then Negro business is likely to continue to be peculiarly beset with special problems over and above those usually faced by businesses operated by whites. It is important, therefore, to determine the actual status of business among Negroes and its place and fundamental relationships in the national economy, to identify its problems and needs, and to offer suggestions for correcting defects, raising the levels of business practice, and increasing the extent of business operation by Negroes.

An examination of the beginnings and development of Negro business and of some of the trends and philosophies which have developed as a result of the experiences of Negro business men constitutes a fundamental approach to an understanding of the present status of business enterprise among Negroes. Also, to plan intelligently for the future, we must be able

From Joseph A. Pierce, "The Evolution of Negro Business," in *Negro Business and Business Education* (New York: Harper & Row, 1947), pp. 3–30. © 1947 by Harper & Row, Publishers, Inc. Reprinted by permission of the publishers.

to interpret the present status, problems, and needs of these enterprises in light of the nature and functions of business in American life and the place which Negro business has occupied in the general American economy.

## Functions and Nature of Business in American Life

Today our manner of living has multiplied our wants. Man no longer lives an almost self-dependent and self-sufficing life. We have developed levels of living the satisfaction of which has become necessary to the maintenance of human morale. Business in America today is concerned with meeting the wants, desires, and demands of 140 million men, women, and children, whose wants range from things connected with the existence of life itself to the many luxuries which enrich our standard of living. American business also contributes to the satisfaction of the wants of countless millions of foreign neighbors who desire to buy our products and services.

The social significance of business is revealed by the fact that it is interested not only in the production of goods but in the creation of desires. Our wants create the demand that keeps business going, and conversely we find that business frequently anticipates our desires and develops new products that we shall want as soon as we know about them. Thus business creates desires for more comforts and luxuries as well as supplies our present wants.

Business in America operates under what is known as the capitalistic system. Loosely defined, the capitalistic system is an economic system under which any person may operate or engage in any lawful business for personal gain or profit. It implies that individuals are free to work and make money where they will and that they are free to compete for jobs and customers with a minimum of governmental restrictions. Under the capitalistic system the great incentive to the establishment and growth of business is profit. Those who engage in business as profit seekers become known as "businessmen." To them the acquisition of profit is a major goal, because failure to acquire it threatens to eliminate them from the ranks of businessmen.

The businessman connects the processes of production with the processes of distribution. He either directs the techniques of trade, or does both together; but he is always engaged in buying and selling in one form or another for the purpose of pecuniary gain.[4]

Business enterprise cannot long exist in a competitive capitalistic system without profits.

The contemporary American businessman tends to operate in the framework of the traditional philosophy, "He who profits most serves best." His concept of the profit economy has not been greatly altered by pressure from either employees or consumers. There is, however, a growing appreciation among businessmen and women of the principle of service—

so much so that a new idea, "He profits most who serves best," is being more widely and seriously advocated.[5] This has resulted from a growing consciousness of the fact that "business itself is a social activity. It cannot exist without the approbation and support of society."[6]

Enterprises within the framework of American business organization reveal wide variations in the size, volume, and nature of their activities. Giant combines and large corporations hold a key position in this nation. One writer has declared that "businessmen who control large profit-making enterprises enjoy a greater prestige than any other group of economic functionaries in the United States."[7] The small businessman stands at the lower level of this prestige group. His ideals are closely allied to those of "big business," but his economic activities place him in more direct contact with the masses of wage earners.

Negro business enterprises, with few exceptions, fall within the following definition of small business:

Once a criterion is chosen there remains the problem of setting the points of division between small and large business . . . because of the way in which many of the statistics on this matter are presented, it is suggested that the upper limits for small enterprises be set at 250 workers employed, $250,000 in value of assets used, $100,000 in net worth, or $1,000,000 in business volume.[8]

The few exceptions fit into certain definitions of big business, but none of them could be referred to significantly as big businesses. A discussion of Negro business, therefore, involves an understanding of the problems common to small business as well as those peculiar to a minority group.

## Beginnings and Development of Business among Negroes

To understand Negro business as it is today it is necessary to know something of the beginnings and development of business among Negroes. Since the history of Negro business has been treated by a number of writers,[9] a detailed treatment of the subject is not necessary here. It is important, however, to understand the conditions of life under which Negro business has evolved and the social and economic forces which have operated on it and tended to assist or retard its development.

### NEGRO BUSINESS BEFORE 1865

The Negro as a participant in business activities is not new. Negroes in Africa had some business experience in trade with their own peoples and with outside commercial interests. The African, however, was not generally prepared to do business with European and American traders on an equitable basis, because his medium was barter and his natural environment made any new goods uniquely valuable.[10] Nevertheless, he had some contacts with commercial activity, and his transition to life in America under the institution of slavery did not destroy all his initiative for business.[11]

Prior to 1865, Negro business in America was circumscribed by slavery in the South and by Negro population scarcity and superior business organization in the North. Negro business operators in this period fell roughly into two groups. One group was composed of free Negroes who accumulated capital with which to set up businesses of many kinds through various means. The other group consisted of slaves who through thrift, industry, native intelligence, and the liberal paternalism of their masters managed to develop small businesses. The latter group was predestined to begin and remain small, because the slave system tended to destroy or inhibit business initiative in most of the slaves. Members of this group often used the proceeds of their efforts to purchase their freedom or that of their kinspeople.

The folkways of southern whites during slavery had much to do with the retardation of Negro business efforts after they had been initiated. The economic system of the South was such that only a small number of Negroes had opportunities for intelligent observation of, or practice in, the operation of businesses. The practice used is explained in the following statement:

To each position requiring the least manual labor were assigned two persons, a white man who actually held the position and received the income therefrom, and a Negro who did practically all of the work which the position required. The clerk in the store would meet the customers, politely inquire what they wanted, and discuss prices with them, after which the Negro would be told to measure the cloth or weigh the amount of flour or bacon required.[12]

Not all of the white merchants allowed this double expense to cut down their profits. Negroes were used in exceptional instances to perform tasks which required clerical qualifications. A historian[13] of that period has written that no objection arose to the use of Negroes in such capacities until about 1822, when the slaves began to indulge too freely in insurrections. It was found that Negroes, assembling at their own places of business, were formulating measures for their liberation. Consequently some of the states passed laws which prohibited the use or employment of Negroes in any business capacity which required a knowledge of reading and writing. These regulations, however, did not put an end to the Negro's participation in business. The master, in some instances, ignored the laws and continued to use slaves in business capacities. The free Negroes also, as a class, were handicapped by these regulations, but frequently their higher status, connections, and kinship with influential whites made it possible for them to conduct their businesses free from restrictions.

The patterns of slavery and racial separation were well-established and rigidly enforced in the South, but a number of business enterprises operated by Negroes managed to survive down to the Civil War in spite of restrictive legislation and uncertain status. Negro business was most profitable in such cities as Charleston, New Orleans, Savannah, and Richmond, where there were considerable concentrations of Negro populations. The lines of business in which Negroes met with greatest success were those which whites did not wish to operate. These were mainly of the labor and service types. Negro barbers, mechanics, artisans, and restaurant and hotel operators could be found in most southern cities. Negroes were also engaged in the manufacture of boots, shoes, and clothing on a small scale. The growth of these businesses was handicapped by a dearth of capital, severely limited credit, and a small and relatively poverty-stricken racial market. This limited market was further contracted after the whites saw its economic possibilities.

Even though the free Negro in the North had a better political status than his southern brother, several forces operated against his business success. The small and scattered Negro population in the North was one disadvantage; the increasing success of foreign immigrants in displacing Negroes from their jobs was another. The larger and more efficient businesses of the majority group in the North offered strong competition. The northern Negro, however, showed initiative and ingenuity in establishing many successful businesses in the face of these barriers. Some of the lines of business in which individual Negroes achieved considerable success were: lumber, tailoring, pickle making, sail manufacturing, coal, jewelry, catering, and bed manufacturing.

Negroes gained fundamental and important business experience through the organization and conduct of secret and beneficial societies. Available historical sources reveal that "church relief societies, crude but effective units," were first organized by free Negroes of the North in 1787.[14] In a definite sense, free Negroes of the North were as greatly in need of mutual aid as those living under the influence of the southern slave economy. Thus the precarious economic condition of the free Negroes led to the organization of many mutual aid societies in the North and South. These societies also served as centers of social activities and religious worship and were important factors in the social and economic life of the free Negroes and to some extent of the slaves. The leaders of these organizations had neither insurance knowledge nor training. They operated the societies on the basis of a small initiation fee and small periodic payments, both of which were arbitrarily determined. These rather uncomplicated efforts, however, laid the foundation for the structure of what is now the largest, most successful, and longest sustained business conducted by Negroes—life insurance. A successful Negro insurance executive explains this fact by the statement that "only those social and economic devices that are founded in the natural necessities of human existence find a permanent place in the progress of the human race."[15]

The beginnings of banking among Negroes are found in the practices of successful Negro businessmen who, early in the nineteenth century, loaned not only their own money but also the savings of their fellow men which were entrusted to their care. It is said that Thomy Lafon of New Orleans, who made his money in the dry-goods business, loaned it at advantageous rates and at his death left an estate of $413,000. Peter Vandyke of New York, reputed to have been worth $50,000 before the Civil War, and Stephen Smith of Columbia, Pennsylvania, who amassed a fortune of $500,000, also invested and loaned their funds at a profit.

Growing out of the conviction that real progress could be made by Negroes only by improving their economic condition, a convention was

held in New York, in 1851, for the purpose of making plans for improving
the Negroes' economic status. This convention recommended that a mutual
savings bank be established by Negroes. It was felt that a Negro bank
would encourage savings and thrift and might assist Negroes who wished
to enter business. The fact that Negroes had savings of between $40,000
and $50,000 in New York banks also encouraged the recommendation.
During this same period, suggestions were made for the establishment of
Negro banks in Cincinnati and Philadelphia. Nothing came of these
proposals.

Much of the energy used in promoting mutual aid societies and in
attempting the organization of banks was generated, at least in part, by
the need of concrete avenues of protest on the part of Negroes against the
pains induced by their minority status. This tenseness also found an outlet
in journalism.

The leading historians of the period agree that the first Negro newspaper was *Freedom's Journal*, established in New York in 1827 and edited
by John B. Russworm and Samuel E. Cornish. It was to be expected that
a pre–Civil War Negro newspaper would be confined to the North, because
obviously slavery in the South would in its own defense have to suppress
this type of expression. Then, too, the lack of appreciable literacy in the
slave South was a prime deterrent. *Freedom's Journal* and other Negro
newspapers established during this era were essentially organs of propaganda. The editors were not so much interested in printing news as in
publishing opinions about the evils of slavery. Myrdal has concluded that
in the struggle against slavery the Negro press was born as a Negro branch
of the Abolitionist propaganda organs of the North.[16] Negro journalism
has gained in scope, intensity, and diplomacy as literacy has increased
among Negroes. But the influence of the early newspapers is not to be
ignored. James Weldon Johnson testifies as follows:

It is astounding on glancing backward to see how well written and edited were
the majority of these periodicals. They stated and pleaded their cause with a
logic and eloquence which seldom fell below the highest level of the journalism
of the period. And yet it is not, after all, astounding—there was the great cause,
the auspicious time; and by some curiously propitious means there were, too,
the men able to measure up to the cause and the time. There were among the
editors of these papers, especially in New York, men of ability and men of
learning.[17]

This section would not be complete without special mention of the
catering business among Negroes. In the first place, the caterers were
pioneers in the field of Negro business; secondly, catering gave them an
opportunity to make a profit in a dignified way from their previous work
experiences which had once been considered menial; thirdly, it was a
"natural" opportunity for them to show capabilities for business operation.
The catering business was more profitable and meaningful to northern
than to southern Negroes because of the difference in the general status
of the former in a community of free as opposed to one of slave atmosphere. The late Booker T. Washington made the following comment:

From that time [1780] down to the present [1907] a considerable number of men and women of Negro ancestry have gone into the business of catering in New York and made fortunes. Sometimes these fortunes have been considerably increased by their children. In most cases, they have at least given to the children higher and better opportunities, in an intellectual and social way, than their fathers had.[18]

Even though catering is the one line of business in which Negroes have had a solid foundation of tradition and one in which the lack of capital is not a chief disability, Negroes have lost this monopoly. Possibly the real cause of Negroes losing their advantage in this business has been their almost frantic desire to lose identity with any occupation that might be considered menial.

NEGRO BUSINESS AFTER 1865

Although the legal emancipation of Negroes marked an epoch in their economic development and worked a radical difference in business relations between whites and blacks, the number of Negroes engaged in business for decades after 1865 did not greatly exceed the number in business enterprise before the Civil War. The mere grant of freedom did not obliterate the bald facts of the Negro's lack of capital, experience, and training or the long and effective conditioning brought about through the economics and sentiment of a slave regime. The few persons of color who set up business establishments in communities where Negroes had not been observed operating in this field did not succeed extensively.[19] Whites were loath to patronize Negro novices, and the belief was ingrained in Negroes that the white man could give them more returns for their hard-earned cash than could a Negro merchant. Years under the slave economy had educated both Negroes and whites along lines which doomed Negro business endeavors to partial oblivion for several decades after the Civil War.[20]

Yet Negro newspapers began to blossom forth in the South after the Emancipation. The earliest of them were organs of the Republican party. The fact that Negroes in the South could through such an effective medium join the protest of the North gave Negro newspapers a status and a prestige which have increased rather dramatically during each national or local crisis in which the disadvantaged Negro made "copy."

The whole South, impoverished by the devastating Civil War, found it increasingly difficult to raise capital for business enterprise during the Reconstruction Period. And the Negro found it even more difficult to accumulate the necessary capital for opening a business. This, among others, was a fundamental reason for his snail-like development in business.

The Negro church was the center from which basic and vital phases of Negro life unfolded. The church was the one institutionalized form which by many whites, even in slave days, had been given encouragement as good for Negroes. The whites had faith in its disciplinary power to help accommodate and maintain the Negro in an inferior societal status. Because of this license, Negroes used the church as a refuge and safety zone.

Consequently the church as an institution and the Negro preacher as an individual have gained leadership over large proportions of the Negro population and have contributed to the progress of the Negroes.

This foregoing statement is a reasonable explanation of why benevolent societies, the first serious Negro business, started under the leadership of ministers. The evident need of economic assistance, already cited, is a cue to why the nature of this business was mutual aid. As Harmon and his associates state the fact:

After the emancipation of the whole group the church in its new freedom gave ample opportunity for the unlimited development of benevolent societies among the Negroes. Inasmuch as these former bondsmen had been turned loose upon society without preparation to maintain themselves independently, large numbers of them easily fell as victims of poverty and disease. In some communities as many as twenty-five to forty percent of the Negroes died, and this so frightened their friends and pleased their enemies that some predicted the race would soon become extinct. . . . The Negroes in the final analysis had to learn to look out for themselves.[21]

A few Negroes had accepted solicitation for membership in actual insurance companies before 1896. As the benefits of life insurance became known, however, applications grew in volume. This stimulated the production of several publications tending to prove Negroes to be poor insurance risks. The best known and most damaging of these was Frederick L. Hoffman's *Race Traits and Tendencies of the American Negro*, which appeared in 1896. The author endeavored to show that, because of social diseases, living conditions, and other undesirable circumstances, companies would be unwise to insure Negroes.

As a direct result of these publications, especially Hoffman's, many of the white insurance companies cancelled policies held by Negroes, and the Prudential adjusted its rates upward. These actions, coupled with the sting of the insults, implied or expressed, reacted favorably toward the more rapid development and expansion of the insurance feature in Negro fraternal orders:

The first of these organizations to reach something like the insurance basis was the Grand United Order of True Reformers, organized [1881] in Virginia. This secret society emerged from the brain of a Methodist preacher, W. W. Browne, a native of Georgia. With a few persons who had the vision to see the wisdom of this effort he organized the society in his own residence in Richmond, Virginia. . . . The insurance feature of the organization was especially emphasized.[22]

As Negro business operators gained experience in fraternal orders and insurance companies they began to see the need of further economic expansion which called for credit that was too difficult, in the majority of instances, to obtain from the banks of the whites. Consequently Negroes entered the banking field. The first banks that were actually organized and operated by Negroes were the Savings Bank of the Grand Fountain United Order of True Reformers at Richmond, Virginia, in 1888, and the Capital Savings Bank at Washington, D. C., in the same year.

A striking example of the strong influence of the Negro church and the Negro minister on the integrative forces affecting Negro community life is again found in the early establishment of Negro banks. For example, the Rev. W. W. Browne was the founder of the True Reformer Bank, the Alabama Penny Saving Bank was founded by a preacher, and the Nickel Savings Bank was founded by the Rev. Evans Payne.[23]

Associated with the Negro's introduction to banking are other types of financial efforts initiated during the same period. They were in the nature of credit unions, industrial loan associations, and building and loan societies. The purposes behind their organization were basically the same as those which started Negroes in banking. They are significant in this framework because they have had, despite many failures, the strength of new life paralleling the renewed efforts of Negroes in banking. With reference to the establishment of building and loan associations among Negroes, Reid speculates:

It does not seem wise to conclude, however, that the building and loan program has been specially effective because of the Negro communities' great belief in the economic principle. It seems to be a more warrantable conclusion that the pressure of race and the attending disabilities of the race pattern have driven Negroes to this quasi-cooperative practice.[24]

The experiences of Negroes in such business fields as banking, insurance, credit unions, and building and loan associations between 1864 and 1900 were not notable successes when measured in terms of permanency and profit. Yet the courage, intelligence, initiative, and resourcefulness displayed by the organizers of these ventures served as experiential background and inspiration to the succeeding generation of Negroes with an inclination to enter business fields. The significance of the failures in Negro business is in the calamitous effect they invariably have upon a clientele that is habitually below par financially. The importance of the successes is that some Negro business organizers have the ability to restore faith in this same clientele for the support of identical or similar kinds of businesses after they have felt the effects of failure. An example of the latter point is the growth of Negro banking and life insurance organizations in Atlanta, Georgia, after the collapse of the Atlanta Savings Bank and the Standard Life Insurance Company.

Gunnar Myrdal, in his book *An American Dilemma*, has drawn certain conclusions with reference to the Negro-managed bank and insurance companies which because of the wide public reached by this book should be commented upon here. Myrdal writes:

The Negro-managed bank and insurance company will not get away from the fact that the Negroes are poor and the segregated Negro community cannot offer any range of investment opportunities such that investment risk can minimize.

Indeed, it is difficult to see a real future for a segregated Negro financial system. Basically, it is nothing but a poor substitute for what the Negroes really need: employment of Negroes in white-dominated financial institutions and more consideration for them as insurance or credit seekers.[25]

There is no logical reason upon which to base denial of Myrdal's statement that the limits of development of Negro business have been rather rigidly set by patterns of segregation. Techniques, however, must be developed whereby these limits may be extended, and even within these limits there is still a considerable range within which dignified Negro business might be developed into corporations of recognizable power. Negroes are poor people, but in the aggregate they constitute a sizable market, and the development of techniques for capturing this market should be of major concern to Negro business.

## The Setting for Negro Business

A clearer appreciation of the present status, problems, and needs of Negro business may be had if we examine the setting for Negro business. Negro business, like other business, operates mainly in urban areas, but, unlike other business, it is generally restricted to certain sections of the urban community. The forces of segregation and discrimination impose two distinct limitations on Negro business. The first arises from the fact that Negro business is, for the most part, solely dependent upon Negroes for its patronage and therefore must be located in sections of the country where large Negro populations are found. Consequently Negro businesses do not have the freedom of action of other businesses. They are forced to locate in urban areas in the South and in a few cities in the East and Middle West where large groups of Negroes have settled. The second limitation grows out of the practices of segregation and discrimination which are found in most sections of the country and to an aggravated degree in the South. To begin with, the Negro population itself is segregated into certain areas of the city, and this immediately results in the segregation of the businesses owned and operated by Negroes. Business enterprises operated by whites find no barriers which prevent them from entering Negro communities, but seldom are Negro businesses able to locate in white areas of the city.

Another factor here lies in the general nature of American business with its giant financial combinations, complex organizations, accumulated business wisdom, mass production and marketing methods, and other characteristics of "big business." Negro business must operate within the framework of American business, but seldom do Negro businesses partake of the characteristics which describe American business. Negro businesses are generally small in scale and possess the attendant points of strength and weakness of all small-scale enterprises.

It is important, therefore, that consideration be given, in this section, to the community in which Negro business finds itself and to the framework in which it operates.

### THE COMMUNITY

A large percentage of the Negroes who dwell in rural areas of the South rely on the landlord or the company store. The landlords "furnish" them either from their own commissaries or make arrangements with a local white merchant to supply their needs. As long as this system continues, this part of the Negro market will be lost to Negro merchants. Moreover, in villages and small towns where a considerable number of Negroes live, the same influence operates in varying degrees, and only businesses such as restaurants and barber shops—in which the great element is service— can expect to succeed. Thus it is in the larger cities, where the Negro is freed from his dependency on the landlord and where the concentrations of Negro population are large, that the best opportunity for Negro business exists. Even here, the composition of the population and the customs and traditions of the people, as well as their employment opportunities, must be considered.

Since the turn of this century Negroes have moved steadily into urban areas.

The great concentration of Negroes in cities is a new phenomenon. In 1870, only 75,000 lived in cities, and most of these were in the small cities of the South. As late as 1900, only 2,000,000 Negroes dwelt in cities; but from 1900 to 1925 this city population doubled. There was moreover a pronounced trend towards the larger cities—a concentration in metropolitan areas.[26]

Prominent among the causes are the increasing mechanization of farms, the need for industrial workers during World War I, the inability to get relief during the depression of the 1930s, and the industrial demands of World War II. In other words, social change has tended to render Negroes excess rural population.

Negroes in urban areas, in the majority of cases, are basically a rural people in the process of urbanization. This process has been described by Woofter as a series of experiences, the first of which—the migration itself —leaves certain classes of the population on the farm and shifts the more · ambitious into the business and industrial establishments of the city.[27] The next experience is segregation—a stratification of the newcomers into occupational, economic, and social classes, with an accompanying resi- dential segregation which is perpetuated by the development of neighbor- hood organization, institutions, and businesses. One of the serious handi- caps of the Negro migrants has been that only a few have had the types of vocational preparation capable of securing for them the income neces- sary to support a continuous process of urbanization.

The reenforcement of segregation, plus the handicaps of the migrants, have created that isolated social phenomenon known as the "Negro com- munity." Although there is some overlapping of Negro and white neighbor- hoods in urban places, except for borderline streets and areas in the process of transition from white to black the Negroes tend to live in Negro com- munities. Negroes usually dwell in the less desirable areas of a city, such as those bordering on railroad tracks, near factory and wholesale districts, and in residential areas abandoned by whites. The Negro community is frequently characterized by physical, cultural, educational, and economic poverty. Though Negroes are generally isolated from whites, their com- munities are usually not confined to any one section of the city but are widely scattered. According to Chivers, this isolation of Negro population areas, in varying degrees of intensity, tends to stereotype the local whites' concept of "the Negro's place."[28]

Naturally in these areas certain Negroes find themselves to be in leadership positions. Roughly such individuals fall into two major types: those selected, indoctrinated, and superimposed upon the Negroes by the whites; and those who arise out of the crises in community life. These two leadership types are the key to the psychological lives of the people resident in a particular community. They even serve as a gauge to the receptivity of the community to Negro business, the kinds and quality of such business, and the possible limits of its expansion.

The farther away from the metropolitan areas people live, the more conservative they are in their moral and social lives. The isolation of Negro communities tends to retard the changes in these factors. In fact, it is to the personal advantage of the superimposed leaders that change away from isolation be at a greatly retarded pace.

Divergences in culture have resulted from the segregation of Negroes in their own communities, but nevertheless American Negro culture is not a thing set apart from general American culture. It has been described as "a distorted development, or a pathological condition, of the general American culture."[29] As a consequence Negro business, similar to other areas of Negro life, finds itself confronted by special problems over and above those which confront the general American business. The relatively low purchasing power of its market, the difficulty of securing adequate investment capital, and the lack of opportunities for experience in certain lines of business are examples of the problems of Negro business which are induced mainly by caste pressures.

Within their restricted boundaries Negroes have social stratification. The bulk of them belong to the lower-middle and lower socioeconomic classes. These groups eye the Negro business man who comes into their community with equal or more interest than they do the marginal whites who are often their local business operators. An insight into the success of those non-Negro operators in Negro neighborhoods reveals differences in operational techniques. The white operator of a business in a Negro community tends to soften the caste lines between Negroes and whites by offering a partial identification of himself with the culture of the Negro neighborhood. He attempts also to render service which, though not up to the standards of white neighborhoods of the same type, is frequently better than that which many Negro operators in similar businesses offer their customers.

Some communities have traditions and superstitions which go far toward establishing their relationships with business men. A Negro undertaker in a small urban center stated that he had to close shop and move away from a nearby community because he had inadvertently referred to the body of a deceased man of prominence as a "stiff."

Furthermore, racial and religious prejudices may well be the deciding factor in the choosing of a location for business. Frequently the political administration will not permit Negroes to operate saloons or beer parlors in Negro communities. Other types of businesses are hindered because they offer competition to whites who wish to exploit Negro buying power. In many small urban communities in Alabama, Georgia, Mississippi, and Florida the religious lines are so rigidly drawn that business patronage is largely confined to the denomination of the proprietor.

The question of how Negro people make a living is certainly of fundamental importance to Negro business men. Negroes in urban communities are found in a broad variety of occupations, but the large majority of them are concentrated in the unskilled and semiskilled classes. This fact holds a great danger for the future security of the Negro worker and consequently for those who depend upon him. The Negro's low occupational status restricts his chances for advancement and increases the probability of his becoming unemployed.

The Negro has made occupational gains of consequence only in periods of national emergency. During World War II the movement of about 700,000 rural Negroes into northern and southern urban areas swelled the estimated total of Negroes employed in industrial pursuits to 1,500,000. This migratory movement received its basic stimulation from the unprecedented demand for labor created by the war urgency to maintain production schedules. The status of these Negro industrial workers has been raised, economically, socially, and politically. The occupational advantages which accrued to Negroes in this industrial crisis were largely due to the activities of federal agencies concerned with the utilization and control of manpower. A serious factor, however, in the prospects for continued employment of Negroes is the fact that large numbers of them were employed in war industries which have suffered, or may soon experience, severe curtailment in their activities.[30]

A second problem of major significance is that created by the thousands of Negro youths who have not yet entered the labor market. They find the mysteries of the machine, the airplane, and the motor more exciting than ever before. They are products of a society whose tempo has been so rapidly and suddenly speeded up by global conflicts as to prevent their acquiring the accommodation to life which their parents had achieved. Many of them are obviously chafing under the still existent barriers to their training and full integration in some field of industrial activity.

The grave emergencies created by World War II have served to give social status to a variety of new vocations for Negro women in industry and business which challenge their erstwhile thwarted ambitions. Before the war there were few occupations, socially acceptable to Negroes, which Negro women could enter in large numbers. Schoolteaching and dressmaking were the two occupations which offered the greatest employment opportunity. Social work and nursing had their status upgraded during the depression of the 1930s, but World War II on a large scale opened up to Negro women employment avenues which can be labeled as "firsts" and enlarged their opportunities in others. Reflections from the deprivations encountered during the depression and the emotionalizing strength of patriotism have tended to give these employment avenues social status.

Ample evidence of this statement is given by the hundreds of young Negro women who have gone into industry as skilled artisans, into the federal services as clerks, stenographers, and statisticians, and into other services, such as the OPA, which require specialized training in home economics and labor problems.[31]

A sharp increase in the development of small Negro business in the majority of urban communities reflects the improved economic position of Negroes. The future of such businesses, however, is dependent on the postwar concentration and distribution of Negro workers, the time consumed in reemployment, the grade of employment, and the wage scale. There is a strong probability that Negroes will become "stranded populations" unable to support the expanded Negro small business group, and the possibility that the established Negro businesses will be forced to make contractions due to the relatively sudden collapse of employment poses a serious question to Negro businessmen.

FRAMEWORK IN WHICH NEGRO BUSINESS OPERATES

A basic consideration in the establishment of any kind of business effort is an analysis of the framework in which it must operate. This is true in relation to individual or corporate businesses interested in serving economic or social class groups. It is just as true and possibly more fundamental in significance when these economic or social class groups are minorities. A deeper importance is attached to the need of such an analysis when the minority group is marked off by color and by its recent history of enslavement, as in the case of the American Negro.

The framework in which the American Negro business man operates is labeled caste. It is the Negro–white caste system. The whites are the majority in financial, political, social, and numerical strength. A virtual monopoly by the whites of police and military power makes caste lines almost inviolable. Religious practices tend to establish their "rightness." Prejudice is the fortifying agent of caste and has developed high moral status among whites as a collective unit. Because prejudice so thoroughly, persistently, and consistently permeates the entire framework in which Negro business operates, the progress of such business is dependent in a fundamental way upon the techniques which are developed to reduce its effectiveness.

The late philosopher of Negro–white relations, Booker T. Washington, writing in the first decade of the twentieth century expressed his opinion as follows:

More and more thoughtful students of the race problem are beginning to see that business and industry constitute what we may call the strategic point in its solution. These fundamental professions we are able to occupy not only without resistance but even with encouragement, and from them we shall gradually advance to all the rights and privileges which any class of citizens enjoy. It is in business and industry that I see the brightest and most hopeful phases of the race situation.[32]

It is understandable that leaders such as Booker T. Washington should express implicit faith in the effect of business and industry upon race

relations. Negroes were in such a weak position at that time that they did
not offer any semblance of a threat to the inviolability of the caste system.
Then too, the capitalistic system had not developed its monopolistic structure, which requires an even larger number of workers as its customers.
In other words, the overall business structure had not developed into the
great giant it now is, challenging the very existence of small business,
especially in urban areas. Negro business is essentially small.

The continuation of the philosophy of business and industry operation
as a major factor in the solution of the race problem without due consideration of the disabilities imposed by the caste system is, to say the
least, confusing in the face of well-known facts, the most important of
which will be set forth here. A thorough knowledge of these facts is essential to the development by Negro business of techniques of survival and
growth in face of "big business," which enjoys and utilizes the advantages
of the caste system.

A primary fact is that the ideological dilemma of Negro business is
chargeable to the evil genius, segregation. A casual perusal of the Negro
newspapers, attention to the proceedings of the National Negro Business
League, or a brief analysis of the teachings of Negro professors of business
education will, if objectively viewed, force agreement with the following
statement:

All Negro businessmen and professionals have to try to make as much use as
possible of racial solidarity as a selling point. This means that the entire Negro
middle and upper class becomes caught in an ideological dilemma. On the one
hand they find that the caste wall blocks their economic and social opportunities. On the other hand, they have at the same time a vested interest in
racial segregation since it gives them what opportunity they have.[33]

Neither ideally nor scientifically is this the desired solution for emotional
and intellectual conflict, but Negro business must operate at an increasing
profit under the American system in order to provide the funds and freedom necessary to fight for overall integration of Negro business into the
total American economic structure. The justification for a split ethics for
the Negro businessman is found in the succinct statement, "the tragedy
of race is that it does not spare the integrity of the soul either of the Negro
or of the white man."[34] For, as DuBois stated:

It is a peculiar sensation, this double-consciousness, this sense of always
looking at one's self through the eyes of others, of measuring one's soul by the
tape of a world that looks on in amused contempt and pity. One even feels his
two-ness; an American, a Negro; two souls, two thoughts, two unreconciled
strivings; two warring ideals in one dark body, whose dogged strength alone
keeps it from being torn asunder.[35]

Both the future and stability of Negro business are dependent, in no
mean way, upon facing the cold reality of this dilemma. The fact that it is
a dilemma means that Negro business is in a pathological state. The two
horns of this frustrating psychological phenomenon must be dissociated
rather thoroughly for practical purposes if Negro business is to increase
numerically and expand toward the caste limits or in some instances even
spill over the caste lines.

Some of the most serious handicaps of the Negro businessman, in this area of the framework, are his difficulty in getting credit, the low consumer income of Negroes, and the economic or opportunistic "social equality" offered by his white competitors.

Myrdal attached strong significance to the credit difficulties experienced by Negroes after he had evaluated his voluminous data on the American Negro. His conclusion is:

The Negro businessman, furthermore, encounters greater difficulties in securing credit. This is partly due to the marginal position of Negro business. It is also partly due to prejudiced opinions among whites concerning the business ability and personal reliability of Negroes. In either case a vicious circle is in operation keeping Negro business down.[36]

Herein lies a basic challenge to the schools of business in Negro colleges. What is the answer to the problem of credit for Negro business? Does its future lie in combining community resources by organizing a number of relatively small corporations or by creating, out of the meager incomes of Negroes, lending agencies which will make credit easier for individuals and partnerships? In attempting to study these questions dispassionately, full value must be given to the fact that prospective Negro businessmen must try in some manner to find opportunities to profit by the experiences of the majority groups in the operations of organizing and manipulating corporate structures. Again, there appears the need for cracking the caste wall, at least in certain strategic places.

A prime consideration for those interested in the development of Negro business is the very low percentage of the total consumer income enjoyed by Negroes. This is estimated to be considerably under 10 percent of the total consumer income of the United States. In fact:

Certain estimates made of Negro and white family income allow us to guess that the Negro's share in the national income does not exceed 4 percent, and probably is around 3 percent. As savings constitute generally a larger part of higher incomes, the Negro's share in total consumption is probably somewhat greater than his share of the national income, though not much. But even when the low level of Negro purchasing power is taken into account, Negro-owned stores and restaurants do not have more than 5 or 10 percent of the total Negro trade. The rest goes to white business.[37]

If Negro consumer income is so small and that is divided with white businesses, the student of Negro business is faced with the difficult problem of developing techniques for raising appreciably the family income of Negroes. Also, a sensitive but nonetheless fundamental problem is how to woo Negro business away from whites without causing retaliation from the majority group.

Would it be feasible to encourage Negro–white ownership of businesses the chief supporting trade of which is Negro? Might it not open up sizable cracks in the caste wall? White-owned and Negro-managed and -staffed businesses operating in Negro neighborhoods might be a partial answer to the competition of chain stores and the avenue through which needed experience can be obtained.

Frequently in Negro neighborhoods there are numerous businesses operated by Jews, Greeks, Italians, and other whites which cater to Negro patronage. These non-Negro business operators offer stubborn competition to Negro business operators in the following ways: (1) they have access to greater capital and easier credit; (2) they frequently give better service than their Negro competitors; (3) they tend to ingratiate themselves with their Negro patrons by appearing to be deeply interested in their welfare; and (4) because of their caste advantage they can buy a wider variety of standard goods.

There is a strong social and class conflict situation involved in the case of Negro businessmen operating successfully in Negro communities. It is an important part of the ideology which the framework encompasses. The Negroes as a whole do not recognize, objectively, class differences. They frequently give lip service and often concrete reality to a professed belief that no Negroes are of a higher social class than other people, but they often ask for and expect concessions from Negro businessmen which they would not dare request from whites. In this they base their arguments on the phrase "you're my color." Harmon and his co-authors sense this emotionalized situation as vital and expressed their thinking thus:

The Negro in business is faced with the difficulty of dealing with people who have been so influenced by the procedure of churches and lodges that they require Negro businessmen to deal with them on the basis of friendship rather than according to strict-up-to-date methods.[38]

## Trends and Philosophies in Negro Business

High prestige value has been assigned by Negro leaders to the participation of Negroes in business. In some instances this prestige value has been due to a faith in business as the avenue to a social status necessary for escape from the societal limitations of the wage-earning classes. Abram Harris says:

Like the white working men of the eighteenth century, the free Negroes were "men on the make" hoping to escape the wage-earning class through business enterprise and by accumulating wealth. "Let our young men and women," admonished the free Negro, Martin Delaney, in 1848, "prepare themselves for usefulness, trading, and other things of importance. . . . Educate them for the store and Counting House . . . to do everyday practical business." The advice of this black Benjamin Franklin is a typical expression of the ends to which a considerable number of free Negroes were directing their ambitions in pre–Civil War days.[39]

In other instances, Negro participation in business has been considered a strategic technique in the solution of the race problem, as being the means by which Negroes may "generally advance to all the rights and privileges which any class of citizens enjoy."[40]

As an indication of the persistence of the prestige value given to the participation of Negroes in business, the opening address of the 1941 meeting of the National Negro Business League included the following statement:

The respect of other Americans for Negro personality depends probably more on the economic and commercial advancement of the Negro than on all other factors put together. This respect cannot be gained unless Negroes become efficient conductors of commercial and industrial enterprises.[41]

Although this continuous preachment of the need for Negro business-men is a matter of record, the fact remains that the early Negro entre-preneur had little opportunity for business training, either through formal schooling or through apprenticeship. The lack of business training on the part of the pioneers in Negro business made for the development of busi-ness attitudes quite foreign to those considered by American business as fundamentally essential for conducting successful enterprises. The main concern of the early Negro businessman was the acquisition of sufficient capital with which to start. The operation of the business was then largely a matter of trial and error. Even the economic aspects of such items as rent, overhead, location of business, and depreciation were frequently ignored. Many of the failures and much of the retardation of Negro busi-ness may be attributed to these ill-considered attitudes.

It has been pointed out that the Negro businessman faces an ideological dilemma. On the one hand, he wishes to integrate his business into the general American economy but finds that caste walls block his efforts and hinder his economic progress. On the other hand, he has a vested interest in racial segregation since it gives him what opportunities he has. This dilemma has given rise to certain trends which may be listed in the follow-ing categories: (1) establishment of a separate and self-sufficient Negro economy; (2) establishment of a semiseparate Negro economy; (3) estab-lishment of a biracial economy; and (4) infiltration and integration into the overall American business structure. These trends are not mutually exclusive, and all are operating at the same time. Some of them, for per-fectly discernible reasons, are more dynamic and more clearly outlined in the states outside of the Deep South.

The trend toward a separate and self-sufficient Negro economy repre-sents a defensive philosophy calculated to counter the limitations growing out of the practices of segregation which are found in most sections of the country and to an aggravated degree in the South. In the past, therefore, a majority of the membership of the principal Negro business organiza-tions have favored, both in philosophy and practice, the establishment of a separate Negro business world. These Negro business leaders have insti-tutionalized the thinking of many business proprietors outside those or-ganizations as well as that of numerous Negro consumers. Their plea to their public has been, "Trade with me because I am a Negro and cannot expect trade from whites." This is essentially the doctrine of building business on the basis of "race pride." Now their philosophy is beginning to change, and the more progressive few are beginning to modify this statement by saying in substance, "Trade with me because I am a Negro

and can serve you as well as others can." A criticism of the separate
economy trend worth recording is voiced by Abram Harris, who states:

Although it is essentially the product of the revolt of the Negro middle class
against the ever increasing restriction of their economic opportunities, this
racial chauvinism is becoming the escape of the black masses. . . . The real
forces behind their disabilities and discomfort are masked by race, which prevents them from seeing that what the Negro businessman wants most of all is
to monopolize and exploit the market they provide.[42]

Some lines of business which have received larger shares of Negro trade
than others, because of the long-time ignorance of white businesses of the
buying power of Negroes and because of racial prejudice, are facing new
and ominous competition from white-operated businesses even in the Deep
South. Many of these Negro businesses have reenforced their stereotypes
with the race-pride argument. Too many of them have rested upon their
laurels and have not rewarded faithful Negro customers with quality
goods, customer services, competitive prices, and attractive businesses.

The selling argument of the separate-economy group is that they are
building businesses to give employment to other Negroes. They also
propagandize the value, to the race as a whole, of having capitalists. But
the proponents of a separate black economy fail to explain how it is possible for a small independent world of Negro business, erected within the
larger framework of general American business, to develop and function
in the midst of persistent industrial integration, business combinations,
centralization of capital control, and concentration of wealth.

The semiseparate Negro economy is an outgrowth of the separate
"Negro economy" stereotype and is evidence that it is definitely breaking
up. This trend represents an attempt to have Negroes employed in businesses operated by other races and catering primarily to Negro consumers.
Its slogan is, "Don't trade where you can't work." In its extreme form it
attempts to have all white help in these establishments displaced by
Negroes. In most instances it is effected by forming pressure groups. An
analysis of this trend shows the following:

Four different approaches are used in these pressure programs: (1) the organized boycott approach, most successful in Chicago; (2) the trade pact agreement approach, famous in New York; (3) the Black unit approach typical of the
St. Louis program; and (4) the picket approach, greatly stimulated by the
favorable Supreme Court decision.[43]

The milder form of the boycott movement attempts to get the ends
sought without risking actual conflict or promoting retaliation on the part
of white employees. The Negro Alliance of Washington, for instance, did
not seek the dismissal of white workers in businesses located in Negro
neighborhoods, but rather it sought the employment of Negroes during
the course of normal labor turnover.[44]

The boycott technique has had limited success in a few urban centers
located in the Deep South. As William Jones wrote in *Opportunity Magazine:*

One of the most significant pressure movements in the South occurred in Atlanta, Georgia, in the fall of 1935. It grew out of the alleged beating of a Negro customer, accused of stealing a pound of sugar, by clerks of a chain store located in a Negro district. An aroused community immediately began an unorganized boycott campaign in an effort to secure better treatment for customers and to have colored clerks placed in the store. The store still stands* in the same neighborhood selling groceries to the same community. It still employs no colored clerks. But its business has dropped away to nothing and nearby stores employing colored clerks have flourished and created new employment opportunities.[45]

The boycott technique has been critically analyzed by several Negro scholars and publicists. They generally agree that the argument that white employees should be replaced by Negroes in those businesses where large numbers of Negroes trade, if carried to its logical conclusion, might easily result in the dismissal of Negro employees of those businesses where Negroes spend little money.[46] This point of view is expressed by Johns and Schuyler, who state that "the boycott is too dangerous a weapon to be used in the campaign for jobs, especially by a minority as weak as the Negro American."[47]

The trend of a biracial economy is represented by biracial partnerships. These arrangements, though few in number, represent a technique which, if promoted extensively, might be used to secure greater capital and to break down the existing limitations of a segregated market. The newest development in this trend appears to be a proposal for the establishment, in a large southern city, of a bank that would be owned jointly by Negroes and whites and would be located in a Negro community.

The trend toward infiltration and integration into the overall American economy is attracting great attention. This is a newer trend, and its practical application up to this point gives reason for optimism. It utilizes principles from the two trends which have been labeled the semiseparate economy and the biracial economy. But its distinctive characteristic is that it envisages, as a long-range objective, the complete integration of Negro business into the general American business structure. This cannot be accomplished in a day. Perhaps it will take scores of years. But, however remote may be the complete realization of the objective of this trend, if the process continues active it will furnish wider employment opportunities, establish higher wage levels, and provide many of the types of business experience so badly needed by Negroes.

This trend is growing even in the Deep South. In Atlanta there is the example of a branch of a drug store chain where the soda-fountain restaurant is managed and staffed by Negroes and occupies over one-half of the floor space, whereas the drug department, operating on the other side of the store, is managed and staffed by whites. Other instances of infiltration are found in a hosiery chain's Negro-managed shops, chain laundry neighborhood stations, employment in white-owned five-and-ten-cent stores

---

* The store has closed. A variety store employing all-Negro personnel occupies the location.

located in Negro communities, and employment in the soda-fountain restaurant in one of New Orlean's largest variety stores.

This trend of infiltration and integration into the overall American business structure means more than added employment opportunities for Negroes in white-owned businesses. It means a complete change from a defensive philosophy based on race pride to a positive philosophy based on the realization that the only Negro business that can hope to expand and develop adequately in the American economy is one that partakes completely of the characteristics of American business. This proposed change in the thinking of Negro businessmen raises questions relative to an explicit formulation of a business philosophy as well as to the techniques of its promotion, which can be answered by businessmen and by educators only in the light of the present status and prospects of Negro business.

## Notes

1. Walter J. Matherly, *Business Education in the Changing South* (Chapel Hill: University of North Carolina Press, 1939), p. 5.

2. Leverett S. Lyon, *Education for Business* (Chicago: University of Chicago Press, 1931), p. 24.

3. M. S. Stuart, *An Economic Detour* (New York: Wendell Malliet and Company, 1940), p. xxii.

4. Matherly, *op. cit.*, p. 5.

5. Edward A. Filene, *Speaking of Change* (Washington: National Home Library Foundation, 1939), p. 196.

6. Percival White, *Business Management* (New York: Holt, 1926), p. 5.

7. Ira DeA., Reid, "The Negro in the American Economic System" (research memorandum prepared for the Carnegie–Myrdal Study, 1940), p. 3.

8. Theodore N. Beckman, "Large Versus Small Business after the War," *American Economic Review* 34 (March 1944), supplement.

9. J. H. Harmon, A. G. Lindsay, and C. G. Woodson, *The Negro As a Business Man* (Washington: Association for the Study of Negro Life and History, Inc., 1929). Abram L. Harris, *The Negro As Capitalist* (Philadelphia: American Academy of Political and Social Science, 1936).

10. Irene C. Hypps, "Changes in Business Attitudes and Activities of the Negro in the United States since 1916," (Abstract of thesis, School of Education, New York University, 1943), p. 47.

11. Harmon, Lindsay, and Woodson, *op. cit.*, p. 1.

12. *Ibid.*

13. *Ibid.*

14. M. S. Stuart, "Insurance, a Natural," *Crisis* 48 (April, 1941): 110.

15. *Ibid.*

16. Gunnar Myrdal, *An American Dilemma* (New York: Harper, 1944), p. 912.

17. *Ibid.*, p. 913.

18. Booker T. Washington, *The Negro in Business* (Chicago: Hertel, Jenkins and Company, 1907), p. 38.

19. Harmon, Lindsay, and Woodson, *op. cit.*, p. 7.

20. Reid, *op. cit.*, p. 26.

21. Harmon, Lindsay, and Woodson, *op. cit.*, p. 88.

22. *Ibid.*, pp. 94–95.

23. Harris, *op. cit.*, p. 47.

24. Reid, *op. cit.*, p. 84.

25. Myrdal, *op. cit.*, p. 318.

26. T. J. Woofter, Jr., *Negro Problems in Cities* (New York: Doubleday, 1928), p. 17.
27. *Ibid.*, p. 19.
28. Walter R. Chivers, unpublished notes (Department of Sociology, Morehouse College, Atlanta, 1945).
29. Myrdal, *op. cit.*, p. 928.
30. National Urban League news release, New York, April 13, 1945.
31. Walter R. Chivers, "Minutes of a Conference on Post-War Problems of Negroes," unpublished (Dillard University, April, 1945).
32. Washington, *op. cit.*, pp. 19–20.
33. Myrdal, *op. cit.*, p. 305.
34. *Ibid.*, p. 784.
35. W. E. B. DuBois, *Soul of Black Folk* (Chicago: A. C. McClurg and Company, 1903), p. 3.
36. Myrdal, *op. cit.*, p. 308.
37. Myrdal, *op. cit.*, p. 307.
38. Harmon, Lindsay, and Woodson, *op. cit.*, p. 39.
39. Harris, *op. cit.*, p. 3.
40. Washington, *op. cit.*, pp. 19–20.
41. J. B. Blayton, "Education and Negro Business," *Proceedings of the National Negro Business League*, August, 1941, p. 2.
42. Harris, *op. cit.*, p. 184.
43. William Jones, "Trade Boycotts," *Opportunity* 18 (August 1940): 239.
44. John A. Davis, "We Win the Right to Fight for Jobs," *Opportunity* 16 (August 1928): 230–237.
45. Jones, *op. cit.*, pp. 240–241.
46. Myrdal, *op. cit.*, pp. 802–803.
47. Vere S. Johns, and George S. Schuyler, "To Boycott or Not to Boycott," *Crisis* 41 (September 1934): 274.

# 2 ]] Roots of the
# Integrationist–Separatist Dilemma

*Robert Kinzer and Edward Sagarin*

Although the victory of the North marked a sharp turning point in the history of the American Negro in business, it is not to be thought that business enterprises were unknown among Negroes in antebellum America.* Chattel slavery, introduced into this country in 1619, became outlawed or withered away in most of the northern states in the early years of the republic, received its deathblow during the Civil War with the occupation of parts of the South by Union troops, the signing of the Emancipation Proclamation, and finally the passage of the Thirteenth Amendment to the Constitution. Prior to these events, a small but important section of the Negro population was already free, not only in the North, but also in the slaveholding southern states. A study of the Negro in business up to the Civil War will demonstrate that whereas only the free Negro could actually engage in business, the institution of slavery, with its restrictions on movement and education, and with the corresponding struggle for its abolition, dominated the Negro scene. The free Negro was thus able to engage in business, but all his activities were dominated by his brother in chains.[1]

## The Antebellum Period

The extent to which the antebellum Negro was engaged in business has been the subject of erudite research and previous summaries.[2] It is intended here to emphasize the sociohistorical forces that proved either encouraging or discouraging to such activities, that tended to channel them in certain directions but not in others, in an effort to find the roots of the problem as it now presents itself.

The Negro population in America has steadily and uninterruptedly grown in number while decreasing in proportion to the total American population.[3] Taking the year of the first census (1790), the year of the outbreak of the Civil War (1860), and the latest figures available at this time (1940), the Negro population of the United States has been 757,000,

From Robert Kinzer and Edward Sagarin, "Historical Roots of the Dilemma," *The Negro in American Business* (Greenberg, 1950), pp. 24–49. © 1950 by Robert H. Kinzer and Edward Sagarin. Reprinted by permission.
* The word "antebellum" is used throughout this book as referring to pre–Civil War. It is in this sense that the word is emphasized in historical literature dealing with slavery and related subjects.

4,442,000, and 12,800,000, respectively; and at the same time these figures represented 19.3, 14.1, and 9.7 percent of the total population in the country. Although the reliability of census figures on Negroes has been challenged, no one will deny the simultaneous growth in absolute numbers and decline in relative numbers, due to such influences as white European immigration, on the one hand, and high death rate among Negroes, on the other.

**TABLE 2-1\***

*Free Negroes and Slaves in the United States,*
*1790 and 1860*

| Year | Number of Negroes | Percentage of Negroes to United States Population | Number of Free Negroes | Percentage of Free Negroes to Negro Population |
|------|------|------|------|------|
| 1790 | 757,208 | 19.3 | 59,557 | 7.9 |
| 1860 | 4,441,830 | 14.1 | 488,070 | 11.0 |

\*Table based upon statistics found in *Negro Population 1790-1915* and *Negroes in the United States 1920-1932* (Washington, D.C.: Government Printing Office, 1918 and 1935, respectively), pp. 55 and 1, respectively.

As early as the Revolutionary War, a small number of Negroes had already attained freedom;[4] the official estimate is that they numbered almost 60,000. In Table 2–1, there are shown the total Negro population, percentage of Negroes to entire population, number of free Negroes, and percentage of Negroes who had obtained their freedom as of the time of the first census, and the year of secession. An examination of these data thus reveals the significant demographic trends; namely, growth in numbers and decline in proportion, not only of all Negroes, but corresponding growth in numbers and *increase* in proportion of free Negroes.

The distribution of the Negro population during this period to a large extent determined the business opportunities and possibilities.

In Table 2–2, one finds the number of Negroes in seceding slaveholding states, nonseceding slaveholding or Border states, and Union states, as of 1860. In this and the following tables, West Virginia population is included as part of Virginia, the state not being formed until secession. For all practical purposes, it can be said that the Negro population of the Union states was a free population, although there were both major and minor statistical exceptions. For example, the census figures indicate more than three thousand slaves in the District of Columbia, out of a total of more than fourteen thousand Negroes; and eighteen slaves in the state of New Jersey.[5] Of the slaveholding states, the percentage of free and slave Negroes in each state is shown in Table 2–3, and the geographical distribution of slaves and free Negroes by sections of the country in Table 2–4.

### TABLE 2-2*

*Negro Population in Various
Sections of the United States, 1860*

| | |
|---|---|
| Seceding Slaveholding States | 3,653,870 |
| Border States | 547,728 |
| Union States | 240,232 |

*Table based upon statistics found in *Negro Population 1790-1915* (Washington, D.C.: Government Printing Office, 1918), p. 57.

A study of these tables will reveal the inherent limitations of a business built around a service to the racial community. By the very nature of chattel slavery, the slave could not be a businessman, and therefore the overwhelming majority of Negroes were excluded from the possibilities of entering the business world. Furthermore, the slave could not be a customer at Negro-owned business enterprises, because the few needs of the slave, so far as food, clothing, and shelter were concerned, were taken care of through the purchasing by the master or his agent. Until the moment of liberation, many Negroes had never been in possession of any money; obviously, they could not be considered, under these circumstances, potential customers for business enterprises.

### TABLE 2-3*

*Free and Slave Negroes in Slaveholding States, 1860*

| States | Slaves | Free Negroes | Approximate Percentage of Free Negroes to Total Negro Population |
|---|---|---|---|
| Texas | 182,566 | 355 | 0.19% |
| Missouri | 114,931 | 3,572 | 3.01 |
| Delaware | 1,798 | 19,829 | 91.6 |
| Maryland | 87,189 | 83,942 | 49.05 |
| District of Columbia | 3,185 | 11,131 | 77.5 |
| Virginia | 490,865 | 58,042 | 10.57 |
| North Carolina | 331,059 | 30,463 | 8.43 |
| South Carolina | 402,406 | 9,914 | 2.40 |
| Georgia | 462,198 | 3,500 | 0.75 |
| Florida | 61,745 | 932 | 1.48 |
| Kentucky | 225,483 | 10,684 | 4.52 |
| Tennessee | 275,719 | 7,300 | 2.57 |
| Alabama | 435,080 | 2,690 | 0.61 |
| Mississippi | 436,631 | 773 | 0.16 |
| Arkansas | 111,115 | 144 | 0.12 |
| Louisiana | 331,726 | 18,647 | 5.32 |

*Table based upon statistics found in *Negro Population 1790-1915* (Washington, D.C.: Government Printing Office, 1918), p. 57.

In the North, the industrial possibilities of the Negro were extremely limited, but to the extent that he might enter business, overcoming resistance, prejudice, lack of education and training, it was almost inevitable that this be in the mainstream of American small business. Even if no other factor influencing the direction of Negro businessmen were present, the population distribution alone would have made the separate economy untenable. A retail or service enterprise that offered its products (or services) almost exclusively to other Negroes could hold out little hope for success, because of the fewness of clients in any area. There simply were not enough colored people in any one community to make possible the city-within-the-city method of conducting business.

## TABLE 2-4*

### Geographical Distribution of Slave and Free Negroes in the United States, 1860

| Section of Country | Slaves | Free Negroes |
|---|---|---|
| New England | 0 | 24,711 |
| Middle Atlantic | 18 | 131,272 |
| East North Central | 0 | 63,699 |
| West North Central | 114,948 | 5,592 |
| South Atlantic | 1,840,445 | 217,753 |
| East South Central | 1,372,913 | 21,447 |
| West South Central | 625,407 | 19,146 |
| Mountain | 29 | 206 |
| Pacific | 0 | 4,244 |

*Table based upon statistics found in *Negro Population 1790-1915* (Washington, D.C.: Government Printing Office, 1918), p. 57.

The distribution of the population was likewise an important factor in the South. There were only four communities—Charleston, South Carolina; New Orleans, Louisiana; Baltimore, Maryland; and Richmond, Virginia— in which there resided large enough groups of "free persons of color" to lay a foundation for a successful business along the lines of what later came to be the separatist economy.[6]

But the population grouping was not the sole factor militating against the entrance of the free Negro into the business economy. In the South, these men and women actually had only a half-free status. They lived in fear of being captured and returned to slavery, and were restricted in property and other legal rights, and in all their movements.

There was a mass of legislation designed to insure the white community against any threats or dangers from the free Negroes. Virginia, Maryland, and North Carolina were among the states forbidding free Negroes to possess or carry arms without a license. . . . By 1835 the right of assembly had been taken away from almost all free Negroes in the South. . . . Benevolent societies and similar organizations were not allowed to convene. . . . A number of proscriptions made it especially dfficult for free Negroes to make a living.[7]

In the northern states, discrimination was widespread, and sometimes took the form of terror against the businessman, particularly if he proved to be successful. In some cities of the North, the anti-Negro sentiment was perhaps less strong than in others; there was Philadelphia, with its large Quaker influence, and the acceptance by the white upper classes of the Negro as a caterer; and Boston, a center of the abolitionist movement; and finally Canada, where Negroes were often welcomed in a libertarian spirit as refugees from oppression. But even abolitionist sentiment and the desire for true equality were not interchangeable. Chicago, one of the outstanding centers of antislavery agitation, and a terminus of the underground railway, offers an illustration of the discriminatory attitudes of abolitionists, when an editor identified with this movement decried association with Negroes, comparing it to taking "felons to our embraces."[8]

The widespread illiteracy among antebellum Negroes, both slave and free, and the lack of normal educational opportunities, further affected the business possibilities of the Negro. Frequently the free man was either a runaway slave (particularly in the latter years of chattel slavery), or an exslave who had obtained his freedom in a legal fashion, known as manumission. If the slave was illiterate, the exslave was not less so. In many parts of the South, it was actually illegal to teach a slave to read and write. Fearful that knowledge of reading would lead to further dissemination of insurrectionary literature, the slaveholding legislators took drastic steps to conserve ignorance.

Believing that slaves could not be enlightened without developing in them a longing for liberty, not a few masters maintained that the more brutish the bondsmen the more pliant they become for purposes of exploitation. It was this class of slaveholders that finally won the majority of southerners to their way of thinking and determined that Negroes should not be educated.[9]

But it was not only the slave who was denied the possibilities of education. Inferior and segregated schools were the rule in the North, even in Boston; there were no compulsory education laws, little educational opportunity,[10] and frequently action was taken, particularly in the South, to restrict schooling for free Negroes.[11]

On the national scene, the most intelligent, the most advanced, the best educated, the most articulate of the free Negroes did not direct their attention to the business world. Negroes, free and slave, of the stature of Denmark Vesey, Frederick Douglass, and Harriet Tubman, placed their talents at the disposal of the insurrectionists, the runaway slaves, the underground railway system, the alliance with the white abolitionist. The leadership and initiative required for business were being directed elsewhere. With few Negroes free, and many of the free kept in ignorance, the outstanding minds that might have been available to sponsor a Negro business world were not thinking in that direction in the antebellum period. A few exceptions can be noted, such as David Walker, militant abolitionist, who became a successful clothing merchant in Boston.[12]

The industries in which Negroes were destined, at a later date, to play a role on a relatively important scale, as in banking, insurance, building and loan associations, realty, and newspaper publishing, had not yet come upon the scene, so far as the race was concerned. Except for the newspaper field, these industrial endeavors require a clientele of free people with sufficient funds to support enterprises requiring considerable capital investment. The Negro newspapers of the time were few in numbers, and could hardly be considered businesses; rather, they were clarion calls to struggle against the slave system and for aid to the free Negro.

Thus, the difficulties facing the Negro in business, the influences that made entry into or successful pursuit of industrial endeavors unlikely before the Emancipation Proclamation, can be summarized as follows:

1. Population distribution of slave and free Negroes.
2. Slave status of majority of Negroes.
3. Lack of education and business training, and lack of opportunities to obtain such education and training.
4. Restrictive laws and customs, and opposition and restrictive activities on the part of the white population.
5. Relative lack of interest in the business world on the part of the Negro leadership.
6. Lack of basis for the emergence of a national Negro banking, insurance, building and loan, or newspaper industries.
7. Depressed economic status of free Negro, involving lack of capital for investment, and poverty of market.

On the other hand, there were Negroes who entered the business world, and who achieved considerable success therein. The main factor that made possible the success of Negroes as businessmen likewise came about from the conditions of slavery and from the status of American business at the time. For if the Negro was denied the possibilities for formal education, if his main work was confined to agricultural pursuits of an unskilled and slightly skilled capacity on the cotton and tobacco plantations, nevertheless he was forced to accomplish all other tasks in the slave states for his master.[13] This meant that practically all crafts were taught to him, so that certain work would not have to be taken care of by the lords, and so that white labor would not have to be bought for pay. The Negro in the South was not only proficient as a carpenter, blacksmith, shoemaker, barber, tailor, and cook, but as a result of almost two and a half centuries of slavery, up to the outbreak of the Civil War, the knowledge of these skills was concentrated almost exclusively in the hands of the Negroes, free and slave. "Before emancipation," Rose has pointed out, "it was in the interest of slaveowners to use Negro slaves wherever it was profitable in handicraft and manufacture."[14]

Furthermore, a knowledge of reading, writing, and elementary arithmetic was not as important to the conduct of a small business a century ago as it would be today. If one were able to count the money, and knew how to give the proper change, the mathematics problem was frequently solved. Few of the smaller businessmen, Negro or white, kept books or records of any kind to aid them in the conduct of their businesses.

Actually, most of the Negroes who became owners of businesses at the time were self-employed artisans. They were skilled manual workers, sometimes employing an assistant, or even several, and in a few rare cases were even slaveholders. But above all they were workers themselves, and as such did not hold the respect of the southern white masters. The generally contemptuous attitude toward manual labor extended to the businessman, Negro or white, who engaged in such labor, even though it was for his own profit and benefit. "This use of Negro craftsmen," an historian has commented, "tended to run white men out of the trades, since it . . . cast a stigma on skilled labor."[15] There was, therefore, relatively little competition and opposition from the white rulers of the South:

The lines of business in which Negroes met with greatest success were those which whites did not wish to operate. They were mainly of the labor and service types.[16]

Summarizing, one finds the following factors advantageous to the Negroes in business in the antebellum period:

1. Widespread knowledge of craftsmanship.
2. Frequent lack of such knowledge among whites.
3. Relatively lesser significance of literacy and education for conduct of business.
4. Tolerant attitude of southern whites, arising out of general contempt for laborers.

Under these circumstances, and looking backward today with the wisdom of hindsight, the successes and limitations of the colored businessman become understandable. Outstanding among successful enterprises were sailmakers, shoemakers, barbers, draymen and liverymen, and caterers.[17] Few business enterprises were selling goods or services exclusively or primarily to Negroes, nor could they hope to, for reasons already pointed out. The separatist economy had not yet taken root, nor did Negro business function in a manner than can exactly be termed integration. Most of the successful Negro businessmen were making or selling products or services for the general consumer, regardless of color, but they were not yet engaged in the same type of business ventures, to any great extent, as were whites. A few Negroes were attempting to form professional businesses, as in the dramatic and entertainment fields, but such movements were premature.[18] There was already confinement to small business, but this was not as apparent at the time as it is in historical retrospect, because small and local business was then playing a major role.

Such was the situation when almost four million Negro Americans were declared to be slaves no more.

## The Origins of the Separate Economy

The period following the Civil War has come to be known in American history as Reconstruction. It was turbulent, confused, and fast-moving, and saw the Negro in the South, set free with neither property nor schooling, completely unprepared to meet the economic problem of earning a livelihood. The South was devastated by the war, deeply resentful against those who had achieved victory over them, and manifested this resentment against those who seemed to benefit by this victory, namely the former slaves.

Led by Frederick Douglass, who emerged as the outstanding Negro leader of the times, and allied with Stevens, Sumner, and other abolitionists prominent in national politics, the Negro made a bid for political and economic equality, and for integration into the mainstream of American democratic life. Over the veto of the President of the United States, Congress passed a National Civil Rights Law, and laid down stringent regulations governing the reentry of the former rebel states into the Union. The granting of citizenship and the right to vote was soon to result in Negro participation in all the lawmaking councils of the South, although no southern state gavernment, during the Reconstruction, was ever under the control of the Negroes.

Reconstruction sharpened the antagonisms between the races in the South, and was followed by a period of reaction, that saw the rise of lynching as a regional (and sometimes national) phenomenon, complete disfranchisement of the Negro in the South, and other legal and extralegal measures. Segregation into separate communities, in housing, in education, and in all social and political affairs, was reflected in a new economic outlook. It was impossible to have one economic world in the midst of two racial worlds.

The reaction taking place in the South did not meet the opposition in the North that one would have expected a few years earlier. The abolitionists, having gained their great victory when chattel slavery was outlawed, had been deprived of their rallying call and battle cry, and their influence was fast diminishing. The Freedmen's Bureau, the official governmental agency for taking care of the needs and protecting the rights of the former slaves, was looked upon in the South as the representative of the enemy:

The atmosphere in which the Freedmen's Bureau worked was one of hostility. Many northerners looked upon it as an expensive agency, the existence of which could not be justified in times of peace. In the South the opposition to the bureau was vehement.[19]

Finally, the Republican party, traditional champions of Negro rights, had abandoned a cause it had once espoused so militantly, making its final compromise in the presidential election of 1876, when it made important concessions to the white southerners in return for recognition of the disputed electors in the Hayes–Tilden battle.

For the majority of former slaves, the necessity of earning a livelihood meant turning to their erstwhile masters as employers, frequently under conditions no better than those of slavery. A few turned to business, but were hampered particularly by inability to obtain capital. The Negroes initiated lumber yards, drydocks, and many other ventures, several of which involved investments of $40,000 to $50,000, considerable sums for the period. Many of these businesses failed, states Franklin, because the Negro had "no knowledge of how to operate a business, and those who knew how were caught in the depression following the panic of 1873."[20]

At the first favorable opportunities, the white southerners turned upon the Negro, and laid the foundation for a system of segregation that was to go virtually unchallenged for several decades.

By the time that Frederick Douglass died in 1895, a new leader had arisen among the oppressed Negroes. Booker T. Washington was a former slave who believed that in the situation then prevailing in the South, there was a need for a program of gradualism which, though it may not have been more than a compromise to him, he nevertheless found practical and realistic.[21] His aim was to curry favor, to advance slowly through education and race improvement, to assure the whites that he neither sought nor desired integration for the Negroes:

In all things that are purely social we can be as separate as the fingers, yet one as the hand in all things essential to human progress.[22]

Between Douglass and Washington, the contrast was great, but it was more than a contrast of men. It was one of times. When the influence of Douglass was supreme, the struggle against slavery was the burning issue of the day; when Washington held millions under his sway, the struggle was to find a place in a world that had turned its terror and its laws against his people.

The Washington philosophy, which came to be known as accommodation, laid the foundation for the segregated outlook in American business, but the direction of the Negroes in business was determined by the conditions prevailing in the South (where almost the entire Negro population was then situated), and not by the influence of one man. Washington gave articulation, aid, leadership, but the direction was the sole possible one of the time.

The entry of Negroes into business, and support of that business by other Negroes, were given full encouragement by Washington. A conference was called at Tuskegee in 1900, and there the Negro Business League was formed. Among his other writings, Washington penned a book devoted to furthering Negro business,[23] in which every possible advance made by the colored people in establishing enterprises of their own was emphasized, but little was written of the limitations of an economy built along these lines. The entire educational program of Washington was dedicated to the vocational, rather than the academic, and that vocational program can be said to have been, in a limited way, the forerunner of modern business education among Negroes. In short, the outlook, the hope, and the illusions of Washington were summarized in his own words:

More and more thoughtful students of the race problem are beginning to see that business and industry constitute what we may call the strategic point in its solution. These fundamental professions we are able to occupy not only without resistance but even with encouragement, and from them we shall gradually advance to all the rights and privileges which any class of citizens enjoy. It is in business and industry that I see the brightest and most hopeful phases of the race situation.[24]

The fact is that the same social forces that were making necessary the creation of separate schools were at the same time laying the foundation for a separate business economy. Just as separate schools represented an advance during the dark days leading up to the end of the century, (the year 1900 represented, in the words of Rose, the "lowest level of the Negro position in the South")[25] so a separate business economy, small and limited though it had to be, was to play a progressive role. Integration was far beyond the reach of the Negro under the conditions of disfranchisement and Ku Klux Klan rule of the South, and in business, as in education, only separatism could yield worthwhile results at the time, in the form of accumulation and usage of capital, employment, utilization of talents, offering of services otherwise lacking, and laying a foundation for race improvement.

## Inevitability of Separatism

Thus, one can summarize that the separate economy that was to grow in the years that followed was inevitable for two main reasons:

1. The Negro was being excluded more and more from possibilities of employment, and was unable to find proper utilization of his talents in the general, or "white" business world. In business, the successes that had been tolerated during the pre–Civil War days became more and more repugnant to the white southerner, who fought any effort to uplift the race. Legal and credit difficulties were created against the Negro who sought to engage in business on the same basis and in competition with whites. Because of the racial appeal, Negroes in competitive businesses had to exclude whites as potential customers, and therefore had to seek a business world which appealed to their own race. Even in those industries and crafts which he had mastered as a slave, and which he had dominated as a free Negro during slavery, he was being driven out by the rising racial antagonisms.

2. Not only was the Negro unable to enter the mainstream of American business in the South, but as a customer he was unable to find goods and services available to him in many of the regular white business establishments. The "better" white stores did not seek or accept his patronage; the Negro was either deliberately and unashamedly excluded, or he was overcharged and made to feel unwelcome and unwanted in other ways. By law, by custom, and by practical usage, he could not obtain certain

desired goods and services except in separate institutions, thus laying the
basis for the formation of separate business. In the hotels, barber shops,
beauty shops, undertaking establishments, and elsewhere, separate Negro
facilities became mandatory throughout the South; otherwise, if not separate, there would have been none at all.

Toward the end of the century, the Negro was banned from white hotels, barber
shops, restaurants, and theatres, after the Supreme Court in 1883 outlawed
the Civil Rights Acts of 1875.[26]

The accommodation program of Booker T. Washington was challenged
by the more militant and younger intellectual leadership among the
Negroes, the most prominent of whom was W. E. B. DuBois. In the decade
previous to World War I, DuBois denounced the spirit of compromise,
and demanded that Negroes stand up and fight for their full rights as
human beings and as Americans. He called for the advance of Negroes in
business, declared that the separate economy was being forced upon the
race, but laid the foundations for a long-range program of integration
through militant struggle against all compromise.[27]

Nevertheless, it was not the philosophy of DuBois to ignore the need for
separate businesses and the progressive character of such institutions in
the situation then prevailing. Any road of economic advance had to be
exploited, no matter the difficulties, shortcomings, or temporary nature
of such advance.[28]

World War I, the growth of war industries, the democratic slogans
around which the people were being rallied, and the general industrialization that was taking place so rapidly in the North, opened new horizons
of hope to millions of Negroes, who saw a promised land above the Mason–
Dixon line. Large numbers, estimated as ranging from one and a half to
two million Negroes, began to move northward between 1910 and 1930,
to Chicago, Detroit, Philadelphia, New York, where major Negro communities were formed. Never before were so many Negroes centered in
one area as came to Harlem.

The growth of the Negro population in several important northern industrial states during the twentieth century is shown in Table 2–5.

This growth is all the more significant in that it took place at the same
time as the proportion of Negroes in the United States as a whole was
declining,[29] and in each of the above-mentioned states the migration resulted in the proportion of Negroes being increased. Furthermore, migration was part of the urbanization of the Negro; he came North and to the
cities of the North, and therefore in those cities he represented an important part of the total populace:

In practically all of the industrial cities Negroes have now built large colonies,
gained political and economic status, and proved that they are in the North
to stay.[30]

This urban growth is illustrated by Chicago population studies, which
reveal that the Negro population of that city rose from 30,000 to 277,000

**TABLE 2-5***

*Negro Population Growth in Northern
Industrial States, 1900-1940*

| State | 1900 | 1940 |
|-------|------|------|
| New York | 99,232 | 571,000 |
| Ohio | 96,901 | 339,000 |
| Pennsylvania | 156,845 | 470,000 |
| Illinois | 85,078 | 387,000 |
| Indiana | 57,505 | 122,000 |
| New Jersey | 69,844 | 227,000 |

*1940 population figures from Edwin C. Embree,
*American Negroes, a Handbook* (New York: John Day
Company, 1942), p. 22; 1910 figures from *Negro
Population 1790-1915* (Washington, D.C.: Government
Printing Office, 1918), p. 43.

and from 1.9 to 8.2 percent of the total Chicago population, from 1900
to 1940.[31] Comparing these figures with those for the state of Illinois in
Table 5, it is seen that Chicago had 34 percent of the state's Negroes in
1900, and 72 percent forty years later; further, that Chicago's colored
population had increased ninefold during the period of migration, whereas
that of the rest of the state of Illinois had merely doubled during this
same period.

With this migration, there came a sharpening of racial antagonisms in
the North, due to competition for employment, on the one hand, and also
caused by the fact that large numbers of the migrants were uneducated
and uncultured, and became easy subjects for a white population anxious
to find a foundation for stereotypes. "The sudden influx of southern
Negroes of low educational and cultural attainments during and after
World War I," writes Rose in this regard, "increased racial prejudice and
social discrimination."[32]

From the business point-of-view, the migration was extremely important.
It meant that large communities were formed of Negroes who were herded
together in ghettoes, and who would require goods and services obtainable
in their own neighborhoods. It laid the foundation for many Negro newspapers, and later magazines. Negro amusement and recreational centers
were opened.

In the North, the separate business movement, aided by the great
migration, did not have the hindrances encountered in the South. There
was pressure against the Negroes, and discrimination in the courts, but
seldom outright anti-Negro laws or property restrictions in the colored
areas. The terror was mild, compared with the South. The community
appeal was strengthened by the much-needed employment which Negro
enterprises were able, even in a small measure, to furnish.

By the time of the depression of 1929 and, shortly thereafter, the advent
of the New Deal, the evolution of Negro business, which had declined to

the point where it could be characterized as a semisegregated section, albeit rather small, of general business during the period of accommodation, was now at the end of an era. Integration was a far-off dream. Separate business, to the extent that it flourished at all, had failed to become a part of the general American economy. Migration, urbanization, and discrimination had combined to make separatism necessarily inevitable and, temporarily at least, advantageous; while at the same time the development and consolidation of large enterprises in the heavy industries placed the most severe limitations on the potential of this new and separate economy.

By and large, one can say that the separate economy consisted primarily of two sections. The first was the local businessman, usually retailer or service tradesman, grocer, barber, tailor, perhaps even small hotelkeeper; the second was the businessman participating in those national industries in which separate establishments were to play a significant role and which, considering the smallness of the entire Negro economy, were relatively important; more specifically, the banking and insurance fields. In these fields, and the related home loan organizations, segregated enterprises had taken hold to an extent that resembled a national movement, a phenomenon that was not apparent elsewhere on the American business scene.

During the many decades which we have so briefly summarized, beginnings were made in several businesses; successes were recorded and failures sustained. The social development of the country influenced Negroes in banking, insurance, and other enterprises. Ironically enough, however, it was a business venture that Negroes neither initiated nor conducted that proved to be the most disastrous event in their postbellum economic history.

## Notes

1. E. Franklin Frazier, *The Negro in the United States* (New York: Macmillan, 1949), chap. 4.
2. Joseph A. Pierce, *Negro Business and Business Education, Their Present and Prospective Development* (New York: Harper, 1947), chap. 1.
3. Edwin Embree, *American Negroes, a Handbook* (New York: John Day Company, 1942), p. 19.
4. Frazier, *op. cit.*, p. 60 ff.
5. U.S. Department of Commerce, Bureau of the Census, *Negro Population in the United States, 1790–1915* (Washington, D.C., 1918), p. 57.
6. Frazier, *op. cit.*, p. 64.
7. John Hope Franklin, *From Slavery to Freedom* (New York: Knopf, 1949), pp. 216–217.
8. St. Clair Drake and Horace Cayton, *Black Metropolis* (New York: Harcourt, Brace, 1945), p. 41, who quote from Bessie Pierce, *A History of Chicago* (New York: Knopf, 1937), vol. 2, p. 231.
9. Carter G. Woodson, *The Education of the Negro Prior to 1861* (New York: Putnam, 1915), p. 3.

10. *Ibid.*, chap. 10.

11. *Ibid.*, p. 151.

12. Vernon Loggins, *The Negro Author* (New York: Columbia University Press, 1934), p. 85.

13. Arnold Rose, *The Negro in America* (New York: Harper, 1948), p. 79.

14. *Ibid.*, p. 78.

15. Thomas J. Wertenbaker, *The Old South: The Founding of American Civilization* (New York: Scribner's, 1942), p. 232.

16. Pierce, *op. cit.*, p. 7.

17. J. H. Harmon, Jr., "The Negro As a Local Business Man," *The Journal of Negro History* 14 (April 1929): 121–127.

18. Carter G. Woodson, *The Negro Professional Man and the Community* (Washington, D.C.: Association for the Study of Negro Life and History, Inc., 1934), p. 13.

19. Franklin, *op. cit.*, p. 303.

20. *Ibid.*, p. 310.

21. Booker T. Washington, *Up From Slavery: An Autobiography* (New York: Doubleday, 1901).

22. Booker T. Washington, speech at Atlanta, Ga., quoted by Frazier, *op. cit.*, p. 545.

23. Booker T. Washington, *The Negro in Business* (Boston: Hertel, Jenkins and Company, 1907).

24. *Ibid.*, p. 19.

25. Rose, *op. cit.*, p. 314.

26. Franklin, *op. cit.*, p. 338.

27. *Ibid.*, p. 387.

28. W. E. B. DuBois, *The Negro in Business* (Atlanta: Atlanta University Press, 1899).

29. Embree, *op. cit.*, p. 22.

30. *Idem.*

31. Drake and Cayton, *op. cit.*, pp. 8–9.

32. Rose, *op. cit.*, p. 313.

# 3 ]] Negro Business: Myth and Fact

St. Clair Drake and Horace Cayton

## The Doctrine of the Double-duty Dollar[1]

It is Sunday morning in the "black belt." The pastor of one of the largest churches has just finished his morning prayer. There is an air of quiet expectancy, and then—a most unusual discourse begins. The minister, in the homely, humorous style so often affected by Bronzeville's "educated" leaders when dealing with a mass audience, is describing a *business exposition:*

The Business Exposition at the Armory was one of the finest achievements of our people in the history of Chicago. Are there any members of the Exposition Committee here? If so, please stand. [A man stands.] Come right down here where you belong; we've got a seat right here in front for you. This man is manager of the Apex Shoe Store—the shoes that I wear. . . . We can get anything we want to wear or eat from Negroes today. If you would do that it would not only purchase the necessities of life for you, but would open positions for your young folks. You can strut as much as you want to, and look like Miss Lizzie [an upper-class white person], but you don't know race respect if you don't buy from Negroes. As soon as these white folks get rich on the South Side, they go and live on the Gold Coast, and the only way you can get in is by washing their cuspidors. Why not go to Jackson's store, even if you don't want to buy nothin' but a gingersnap? Do that and encourage those girls workin' in there. Go in there and come out eating. Why don't you do that?

This is the doctrine of the "double-duty dollar," preached from many Bronzeville pulpits as a part of the weekly ritual. Church newspapers, too, carry advertisements of all types of business from "chicken shacks"[2] to corset shops. Specific businessmen are often pointed out to the congregations as being worthy of emulation and support, and occasional mass meetings stress the virtues of buying from Negroes—of making the dollar do "double-duty": by both purchasing a commodity and "advancing The Race." The pastor quoted above had been even more explicit in an address before the Business Exposition crowd itself:

Tomorrow I want all of you people to go to these stores. Have your shoes repaired at a Negro shop, buy your groceries from a Negro grocer . . . and for God's sake, buy your meats, pork chops, and yes, even your chitterlings,[3] from a Negro butcher. On behalf of the Negro ministers of Chicago, I wish to commend these Negro businessmen for promoting such an affair, and urge upon you again to patronize your own, for that is the only way we as a race will get anywhere.

From St. Clair Drake and Horace Cayton, *Black Metropolis* (New York: Harper & Row, Torchbook Edition, 1945), pp. 430–469. Reprinted by permission.

Residents of the Negro community rather generally approve of those churches and ministers who lend their support to Negro enterprises, and church members sometimes cite such actions as evidence that their pastors are "progressive." As one woman phrased it: "Reverend Moss is one of the progressive ministers. . . . He tells us that we are too dependent on other races for employment and that we must establish good sound business enterprises and at least give employment to the many youths that finish their education each year. His one principal subject is cooperation and racial solidarity, for in union there is strength."

Preachers who do not preach the gospel of the "double-duty dollar" are liable to such caustic criticisms as this:

God have mercy on our preachers! They are the supposed-to-be leaders of The Race. But all they are interested in is money for themselves. . . . We pay hundreds of thousands of dollars for churches, but when it comes to building Negro businesses, it seems that our people are not interested.

Some of the Holiness sects protest vigorously against this mixture of religion, business, and race pride, but they are definitely a minority voice in Bronzeville.

This endorsement of business by the church simply dramatizes, and brings the force of sacred sanctions to bear upon, slogans that the press, the civic organizations, and even the social clubs repeat incessantly, emphasizing the duty of Negroes to trade with Negroes and promising ultimate racial "salvation" if they will support racial business enterprises.

The efficacy of these appeals is difficult to measure. There is no way of knowing, for instance, how many of the hearers react like the person referred to in this (probably apocryphal) story told by a colored merchant:

A Negro came in here with five dollars worth of Jew stuff in his arms and bought ten cents' worth of salt pork from me. He said: "Every Sunday morning the Reverend wants all who bought groceries from a colored grocer to raise their hands. Now I can hold *mine* up with a clear conscience."

To the Negro community, a business is more than a mere enterprise to make profit for the owner. From the standpoints of both the customer and the owner it becomes a symbol of racial progress, for better or for worse. And the preacher is expected to encourage his flock to trade with Negroes.

That these ministerial appeals do have some effect is suggested by the rather general comments of white businessmen in the black belt, such as that of one man who told an interviewer:

There has been a great deal of propaganda created against the white merchants in this neighborhood, some of it coming from the ministers in the pulpits of their churches, advising the people to patronize Negro merchants whenever possible. And they are doing it!

The elevation of the double-duty dollar slogan into the realm of almost sacred dogma results primarily from the fact that Negroes participate in two worlds—the larger community of city, state, and nation, and the smaller, socially isolated, and spatially separate Negro world. As participants in the general American culture, they are exposed to a system that places a high premium upon business success and white-collar occupations. Financial power and economic control bring those political and social rewards which have traditionally been supposed to serve as incentives to thrift, enterprise, and hard work. Negroes, using the same school textbooks as whites, reading the same papers, attending the same movies, and in constant contact with the white world, tend to incorporate the general ideals of American life. Inevitably, they measure progress since slavery partly in terms of the positions of power and prestige which Negroes attain in the business world.

Objective reality, however, is at variance with the ideal. No Negro sits on a board of directors in La Salle Street; none trades in the grain pit or has a seat on the Stock Exchange; none owns a skyscraper. Negro girls are seldom seen in the offices and stores of the Loop except as maids. Colored traveling salesmen, buyers, and jobbers are a rarity. The largest retail stores and half of the smaller business enterprises in Bronzeville are owned and operated by white persons, and until recently many of these did not voluntarily employ Negroes.

## The Growth of a "Negro Market"

Chicago's first colored businessmen did not serve an exclusively Negro market. Most of the earliest colored businessmen were engaged in service enterprises catering to a white clientele. Reference has already been made to John Jones, the tailor, in the seventies. There were also barbers, hairdressers, wigmakers, masseurs, and caterers. A few Negroes ran livery stables and served as draymen. One Isom Artis made his living in the seventies by drawing water from Lake Michigan and selling it to the residents for eight cents a barrel. In the late seventies, another Negro opened a large lumber yard from which he later made a small fortune. While most of these had a predominantly white clientele, there were also less lucrative restaurants, barber shops, and small stores in the small Negro area.

Between the close of the Civil War and the publication of the first *Colored Men's Professional and Business Directory of Chicago* in 1885, the participation of the Negro in the business life of the city developed to the extent of some 200 enterprises in twenty-seven different fields. Most numerous were barber shops. Restaurants competed with "sample rooms" (combination liquor stores and saloons) for second place. Even as late as the turn of the century, however, the Negro market was relatively unimportant.

On the eve of the Great Migration, there were about 500 Negro businessmen concentrated either in the service occupations or in those enterprises calling for small amounts of capital and but little experience. Barber shops (now serving a Negro clientele) predominated, but it is significant that colored moving and storagemen (successors to the early draymen) serving both whites and Negroes were still numerous, for automobiles had not yet arrived in sufficient numbers to drive horses from the streets.

The Great Migration created the "Negro market." Both white and Negro merchants, as well as the Negro consumer, became increasingly conscious of the purchasing power of several hundred thousand people solidly massed in one compact community. The rapid growth of the Negro community between 1915 and 1929 was accompanied by expansion in all types of Negro-owned businesses, not the least lucrative of which was speculation in real estate.

The curve of Negro enterprise rose throughout the twenties.[4] Two colored banks and three or four insurance companies began to amass capital from within the Negro community and to lend money for the purchase of homes. As the population moved southward from the Loop, the business center moved with it. But there was little tendency among long-established white businesses (especially those on the main thorough-fares) to move away from these areas newly occupied by Negroes.

The depression of 1929 liquidated the two colored banks and wiped out many of the larger enterprises. Paradoxically, however, it stimulated an increase in the number of smaller businesses, as many people with some savings saw in the opening of a small store one means of insuring themselves against starvation. The impact of the depression combined with the fierce competition for good locations, for credit and capital, also resulted in an accentuation of racial antagonisms, including anti-Semitic manifestations.

The depression also revivified the dream of organizing the purchasing power of the Negro—not only for the salvation of Negro businessmen threatened with extinction, but also as a possible method of creating jobs for the thousands of persons who were going on relief and for the impecunious and unemployed white-collar class. Attempts to organize the economic power of the Negro have followed two main lines: (1) forcing white merchants to employ Negroes through the use of the boycott, and (2) urging Negroes to trade with Negroes. The latter has, of course, been the preferred objective of Negro businessmen.

That Negroes have not become fully integrated into the commercial life of the city and do not have a larger measure of economic control even within their own communities is due primarily to the fact that their normal participation in the economic life of Midwest Metropolis is curtailed by traditional attitudes toward colored persons and by the vested economic interests of white occupational groups. These factors are reinforced by the subtle, but none the less powerful, tendencies toward dispersal of effort which result from the conditions of life in the Black ghetto.

For Negro businesses to compete with white businesses in Negro communities, they must be able to "meet the price" and give equivalent service. Negro businessmen insist that they face five main competitive difficulties: (1) difficulty in procuring capital and credit, (2) difficulty in getting adequate training, (3) inability to secure choice locations on the main business streets, (4) lack of sufficient patronage to allow them to amass capital and to make improvements, (5) inability to organize for cooperative effort.

These circumstances have resulted in a situation in which Negroes have found it extremely difficult to compete with white businessmen in the same field as to prices and service. This, in turn, tends to reinforce the stereotype that Negroes are not good businessmen. In order to meet the competition, Negro businessmen and community leaders stress the dogmas of racial solidarity in an effort to amass capital and patronage. This results in a pattern of behavior in which both Negro customers and merchants are always on the defensive vis-à-vis one another, and often take refuge in mutual derogation. Despite these difficulties, some Negroes *have* been able to compete with whites for the Negro market, and some have even been able to develop businesses competing in the general city market.

## Odds Against the Negro

In the second year of the depression, Chicago Negroes were spending about $39 million annually—over $11 million on groceries and vegetables; $7 million on meat; a little over $4 million on wearing apparel; over $2 million on milk, butter, and eggs; nearly $2.5 million on shoes and over-shoes; a little less than a million dollars on millinery and haberdashery; over a quarter of a million on laundry and cleaning; and about $12 million on furniture. Four years later, the Department of Commerce estimated the purchasing power of Negroes in Chicago at about $81 million. Today, the figure must be somewhere near $150 million. This is the Negro market for which both white and Negro businessmen are competing.

In 1938, Negroes in Bronzeville owned and operated some 2,600 business enterprises.[5] Most of these were small retail stores and service enterprises on side streets, or in the older, less desirable communities. There were also about 2,800 white businesses within the Black Belt. *While Negro enterprises constituted almost half of all the businesses in Negro neighborhoods, they received less than a tenth of all the money spent by Negroes within these areas.*[6] The odds have been against Negro merchants, and their behavior reflects their plight.

Negro grocers and general retailers, matching wits and prices with the small white merchants and with the chain stores in Bronzeville and the Loop, appeal loudly to "race pride" and fulminate bitterly against white storekeepers in Negro neighborhoods. These Negro businessmen, quite naturally, dream of organizing the Negro market to corral the errant dollars. When they do not succeed in doing this, they are peeved with both competitors and potential customers. Out of this anger flow both bitter invective and a sigh of resignation. "No community can hope to thrive," insists one newspaper editor, "where people come from other communities and operate businesses in this community, and at the close of day you see the money taken out of the neighborhood never to return, except in the form of some more second- or third-grade goods to take the rest of the

Negro's money." Awareness of the potentialities of the Negro market has evoked many protests such as that of the Baptist minister who commented bitterly:

The Negro in Chicago spends billions on merchandise. All of that money goes into the white man's pocket and then out of our neighborhoods. It is used to buy white men cars and homes, and their wives mink coats and servants. Our money is being used by the white man to pay us for being his cook, his valet, and his washwoman.

In its most extreme form, the dream of controlling the Negro market visualizes a completely separate Negro economy: "The idea is to be able to support ourselves instead of being wholly dependent on the white race." Despite this dream, nine-tenths of Bronzeville's money is spent with whites, and this is why the Negro businessman complains that his own people do not support him.

## Businessman's Complaint

Bronzeville businessmen are convinced that one of the main problems facing them is the power of "the white man's psychology." "Negroes," they feel, "have never learned to patronize their own." Merchants are continually making such statements as the following (usually associated with one or two other complaints):

I think that colored people will have to be educated to trade with each other. I notice that even now what you would call the most substantial people on this street pass my store on their way to 31st Street to trade wih some Jew merchant. *Of course, the chain stores offer a deal of competition to any independent merchant,* but having come in close contact with Jews, as I did, I know they feel they can "jive" a Negro along and get his money.

A fairly well-educated and somewhat analytical merchant summed the matter up as follows:

Some Negroes do patronize Negro business. They are usually the laboring class, though—people who work in factories and do laboring work. The professionals and the so-called "big Negroes" spend nearly all of their earnings with the whites. The reason for this is simple: the professional group like the school teachers, doctors, and lawyers earn large salaries and get better fees. They have greater earning power and hence they open charge accounts and do most of their buying in the Loop. They buy not only clothes and furniture there, but also foodstuffs. They contribute very little to the success of the Negro merchants on the South Side.

One Negro merchant was so irritated by the alleged failure of Negroes to support business that he said: "Other businesses ought to force the colored man to patronize his own color by refusing to wait on him!"

With so general a feeling on the part of colored merchants that they do not receive the support of the Negro community, it might be instructive to turn to "the public" for its side of the case.

# The Negro Customer's Defense

### RACE PRIDE V. PRICES

Over and over, Negroes in Bronzeville reveal a conflict between the economic imperative of "making ends meet" and the social demands of "race pride." They insist that Negro merchants cannot give equivalent goods and services for the same price: "I'd like to do all my shopping— what little I do—with colored, but I can get things cheaper at the chain stores. I buy there for that reason."

### RACE PRIDE V. CREDIT

Poor people need credit. Negro merchants on the whole are unable to grant it. This forces the Negro housewife to avoid the colored grocer as well as the chain store. One woman who formerly shopped at the A & P, and who says she now goes to "the Jew," makes the following somewhat apologetic statement:

You see, I can get credit from him and I can't from the A & P or a colored store. I like to trade at the A & P because you can pick up quite a bit of fresh vegetables and stuff, but I tried to get credit there and couldn't.

### RACE PRIDE V. "SERVICE"

Colored storekeepers are also accused of general inefficiency and ineptitude:
The Negro does not know how to wait on customers; the clerk forgets his work and tries to sweetheart with you; our people are too slothful; they are behind the white man.
The Negro must learn to be independent and have the same type of goods the white man has for the same price. The Negro should not be expected to trade with another Negro because he is a Black man. People of any race should have some respect for their people, but any people naturally wants to get things where they can get the best bargains.

# The Merchant's Rebuttal

### NEGROES EXPECT TOO MUCH

Many Negro merchants have faced these criticisms frankly, and have studied the behavior of their customers. There is a general tendency to feel that Negroes "expect more" from a colored merchant than from a white, that they are "touchy" and constantly make comparisons with the type of service offered by whites.

One merchant said: "The public expects more of a colored man than it does out of a white man. It expects a better grade and prices, and more courtesy." He felt that Negroes should try to meet the competitive disadvantage, however, and accused most colored businessmen of "lack of courtesy." "The trouble with the Negro businessman," he observed, "is laziness, lack of energy, lack of stock, and ignorance of his public." Such a blanket indictment does not give sufficient weight to other factors, however.

WHITE COMPETITION IS KEEN

The more reflective colored businessman is likely to add that Negro businesses, on the whole, lack sufficient capital and experience to compete with the average white merchant. Thus they are often unable to provide the range of goods and services which a customer has a right to expect.

Some merchants feel that any accumulation of adequate capital is primarily dependent upon sustained support and that Negroes should "give their merchants a break." Thus, one woman who runs what she calls a "very high-class" beauty parlor and "has no serious problem" of her own, states this view at some length:

I think Negro business in Chicago is quite progressive, especially considering the experience our people have had in business and the small amount of money they invest in it. Negro business suffers, though, from lack of cooperation from the public.

The pooling of purchasing power is frequently mentioned as a possible competitive technique, as in the following case:

The Negro, on the whole, will try to patronize his own merchants, but the fact that they ask higher prices and often give poor merchandise causes him to stay away from them. The reason for this is that each merchant, no matter how small his place, buys independently of other merchants. This buying in small quantities makes him pay more for his commodities wholesale than the white customer asks of his customers retail.

We, as a group, are much more lenient with other groups than with our own. If we go into a Jewish store and ask for something and the Jew doesn't have it, we either buy something else in its place or go on without a murmur. Our own people could stock everything we want, but we fuss and carry on and say: "You see, that's the reason we can't patronize our own people; they never have anything we want." If they'd just buy from us, we'd stock all the things they want.

## The White Merchant's Verdict

White merchants in competition with Negroes will sometimes comment on the failure of Negroes to compete successfully with them. A few hold to stereotypes such as those of the real-estate agent who said: "The happy, carefree nature of the Negroes in seeking lines of least resistance in the conduct of their business is largely responsible for the high credit risk tabulated against them." Another white merchant thinks that "as long as Negroes have enough money to spend on booze and policy, they are happy," but concedes the point that "they haven't got the dough to invest in business." He is also sure that "they don't have the brains either" and "it takes brains to make a good businessman." A Jewish furniture dealer with years of experience in Negro neighborhoods thinks that "most of the colored people you find in business are failures," and observes: "I don't know what causes this, whether they don't grasp the principles of the business or whether they want to start right out on top as big shots. I'll bet that about all their failures are due to this fault. I really think they've got too much ego. That's the way they impress me."

Other merchants tried to take into consideration the basic factors which place Negro businessmen at a competitive disadvantage, as did the owner of a very large department store in Bronzeville's main business area, who analyzed the situation as follows: "There is no possibility of the Negro merchant ever predominating in this area because of his inadequate working capital, insufficient credit extension, and lack of experience in business."

## Odds to the Negro

Though the odds are against the Negro in the general merchandising field, Bronzeville's undertakers, barbers, and beauticians operate within a closed market, competing only among themselves.

### BURYING THE DEAD

Between 300 and 400 Negroes die in Chicago every month. They must be "put away right," whether in a pine box with a $75 funeral or at a $20,000 ceremony complete with couch casket and Lincoln limousines. Negro undertakers have a virtual monopoly on burying the colored dead, most of the white undertakers taking the position of the one who said: "I've been here for over fifty years and have seen this area change from all white to all black. However, I've never catered to the Negro business and at no time conducted a Negro funeral."

The undertakers, working as they do in a closed market, have little personal reason to react violently against white businessmen. As Negroes, however, they do share the general ideologies of race pride. One rather successful undertaker with a annual turnover of about $70,000 and a profit of 17–20 percent on his investment is proud of the fact that he buys "fluids and quite a number of caskets from Negroes," but regrets that he is "compelled to buy from whites when better qualities are selected." He does not approve of a racial business monopoly, however, insisting that he "should have the right to operate a business anywhere in Chicago and not be confined to the Black Belt." He states that he has no objection to whites' entering business in Bronzeville. Negroes who bury the dead definitely have the odds in their favor.

### BEAUTIFYING THE LIVING

If colored undertakers have a virtual monopoly in burying the Negro dead, the colored barber and beautician have an even more exclusive monopoly in beautifying the living. In 1938, there was not a white beauty parlor or barber shop in the Negro community, a circumstance which impelled one colored beautician to comment that "they would have them if they knew how to work on Negroes' hair." The fact of the matter is that few white persons have had experience with the cutting of Negro hair, or with the exceedingly complicated preparations and processes used in "straightening" the hair of colored women (and some men) who have not been favored with "good hair."

Despite the intense competition in the field, some of the most successful business associations in Bronzeville are those of the beauticians. Composed of beauty-shop owners, operators, and apprentices, and beauty-school owners, these organizations have as their aims the standardizing of prices and the enforcing of state health regulations. They also function as pressure groups for "racial advancement."

## High Finance

### INSURANCE

The Negro businesses that have been most successful in direct competition with whites during the last twenty years are insurance companies. In significant contrast to entrepreneurs in the field of general merchandising, these companies have been able to amass capital, secure a trained personnel, and weather the depression. In 1940 there were four such companies with home offices in Chicago. They were valued at over $10,000,000 and employed over 2,000 persons.

Prior to 1912, white companies had a monopoly on the Negro insurance business in Chicago, and charged a higher premium than whites paid. They hired some Negro agents, however, and a number of these became familiar with this aspect of the insurance business. By the time of the "great migration," a dozen young men who subsequently became prominent in Bronzeville's business life had had some office experience with a white company. In 1918 and 1919 three Negro companies were organized by this group and one of these now has the largest amount of insurance in force of any Negro company in America. Organized in 1919, by 1938 it was operating in nine states outside of Illinois. In 1944 this company reported $3,843,408.20 in assets with a "legal reserve" of $2,967,588.00 to cover $71,003,778 of insurance in force.

### BANKING

The largest measure of control and the greatest prestige in the American economy are associated with banking. It is therefore natural that the successful operation of a bank would have high symbolic significance for Bronzeville. In the "fat years," Bronzeville had two colored banks, which held over one-third of all the combined deposits in Negro banks in the United States. The depression wiped out both of them, as it wiped out the four white banks in the Black Belt and sixty-six banks in other parts of the city.

## Of Fame and Fortune

From the days of Point de Saible to the present, there have been some wealthy Negroes in Chicago. Individuals here and there have been able to amass property and bank accounts valued in hundreds of thousands of dollars. But there has been little continuity in these fortunes, and little combination of them into large corporate holdings. A man able enough to amass a fortune is not likely to invest it solely according to the promptings of race pride. During the optimistic twenties, however, when real estate and insurance seemed profitable, they did invest in "racial ventures."

There are today two main types of fortunes in the Negro community: those that have come from some success in the total society, such as the rise to fame of Joe Louis; and those that have come from the so-called "protected businesses," notably policy or the numbers racket. The one significant exception among Bronzeville's wealthy is a young man who inherited some Oklahoma oil property. The largest aggregations of liquid capital during the depression were in the hands of the so-called "policy kings." Since they, without exception, also own legitimate businesses, they are "businessmen" as well as "racketeers."

## Notes

1. The term "double-duty dollar" seems to have been first popularized by a Negro minister, Dr. Gordon B. Hancock, who runs a column called "Between the Lines" in several weekly Negro newspapers. In Chicago, the term is frequently used by public speakers and writers.

2. Restaurants which specialize in fried chicken.

3. A southern delicacy prepared from the intestines of the hog.

4. For the first five years of this period, the center of Bronzeville's commercial activities was still in the northern end of the black belt at State Street and 35th. Negro-owned businesses jumped from forty-seven to seventy-seven within two years on 35th and State, and from nine to seventy-one on 31st Street. Many migrants who had been shopkeepers in the South, or who brought ambition or savings with them, opened small retail enterprises; and, except for a short period between 1924 and 1927, there was a steady increase in retail business. In 1920, the ranking five businesses from the standpoint of number of units were barber shops, 211; groceries and delicatessens, 119; hairdressing parlors, 108; restaurants, 87; cleaning, pressing and dyeing, 68; express and storage, 71; tailors, 62; real estate offices, 52; notions, 25; shoe-shine parlors, 26; dressmakers, 32; drugstores, 31; shoemakers, 26; undertakers, 21.

5. Bronzeville's merchants like to feel that Chicago leads the country in Negro business enterprise. The Nov. 27, 1937, issue of the Pittsburgh *Courier* carried an article headlined:

### CHICAGO ANGERED OVER RANKING OF UNITED STATES CENSUS BUREAU
#### WINDY CITY BUSINESSMEN DENY THAT NEW YORK AND PHILADELPHIA LEAD THEM IN STORES AND SALES

The Negro businessmen insisted that white census-takers never enumerate Negro areas properly. New York and Philadelphia had Negro census-takers. One Bronzeville businessman was reported as saying: "If Chicago's business census was taken now by Negro enumerators, the results would show us away out in front. . . . We ought to start now and lay plans for the 1940 census of Negro business, so as to regain our lost prestige." Another man said: "Those figures just issued by the Census Bureau are all wrong. Everyone knows that Chicago has more and better business places than New York, and always will have."

6. A business census of 1935 revealed that only 5 per cent of the $11,000,000 which Bronzeville spent on groceries was spent with Negroes.

# 4 ]] Negro Business: A Social Myth

*E. Franklin Frazier*

Here our purpose is to show how false ideas concerning the importance of Negro business have become a social myth and how this myth has been propagated among Negroes. This social myth has been one of the main elements in the world of "make-believe" which the Black bourgeoisie has created to compensate for its feeling of inferiority in a white world dominated by business enterprise.

## 1. Origin of the Myth

When did this myth first take form? It was formulated, it should be noted, during the last decade of the nineteenth century when a legal system of racial separation and subordination was inaugurated and the hope of Negroes to attain equality in American life was crushed. The myth was created by a small group of Negro intellectuals and Negro leaders who accepted racial separation as the inevitable solution of the race problem. From the 1880s on, as Professor Harris has pointed out in his *The Negro as Capitalist*:

. . . the Negro masses, urged by their leaders, were led to place increasing faith in business and property as a means of escaping poverty and achieving economic independence. Although ostensibly sponsored as the means of self-help or racial cooperation, as it was sometimes called, through which the masses were to be economically emancipated, Negro business enterprise was motivated primarily by the desire for private profit and looked toward the establishment of a Negro capitalist employer class. One of the clearest expressions of the growing tendency to look upon the development of Negro capitalists and business enterprise as the basis of racial economic advancement is to be found in the proceedings of the Fourth Atlanta University Conference (1898) on "The Negro in Business."[1]

At this conference, the best formulation of the myth of the economic salvation of the Negro through Negro business was presented by the late John Hope, who later on, after becoming president of the Atlanta University system (exclusively for Negroes), hoped to train the future leaders of "Negro business." He stated:

Industrial education and labor unions for Negroes will not change this condition [displacement of Negro workers by white workers]. They may modify it, but the condition will not be very materially changed. The white man will meet the Negro on the same ground and work for the same wages. That much we may

Reprinted from E. Franklin Frazier, *Black Bourgeoisie* (New York: Macmillan, 1957), pp. 129–145. Reprinted with permission of the Macmillan Company, © by the Free Press, a Corporation, 1957.

as well take for granted, calculate the consequences of, and strive by every means to overcome this falling off in our old-time advantages. . . . We must take in some, if not all, of the wages, turn it into capital, hold it, increase it. This must be done as a means of employment for the thousands who cannot get work from old sources. Employment must be had, and this employment will have to come to Negroes from Negro sources. This phase of the Negro's condition is so easily seen that it needs no further consideration. Negro capital will have to give an opportunity to Negro workmen who will be crowded out by white competition; and when I say Negro workmen I would include both sexes. . . . Employment for colored men and women, colored boys and girls must be supplied by colored people. . . .

We are living among the so-called Anglo–Saxons and dealing with them. They are a conquering people who turn their conquests into their pockets. . . . Business seems to be not simply the raw material of Anglo–Saxon civilization— and by business I mean those efforts directly or indirectly concerned with a purposive tendency to material development and progress, with the point in view of the effort bringing material profit or advantage to the one making the effort; and I would include all such efforts whether made in peace or war. I was saying, business seems to be not only simply the raw material of Anglo– Saxon civilization, but almost the civilization itself. It is at least its mainspring to action. Living among such a people is it not obvious that we cannot escape its most powerful motive and survive? To the finite vision, to say the least, the policy of avoiding entrance in the world's business would be suicide to the Negro. Yet as a matter of great account, we ought to note that as good a showing as we have made, that showing is but as pebbles on the shore of business enterprise. . . .[2]

Among the resolutions adopted at the conference was the following:

The mass of the Negroes must learn to patronize business enterprises conducted by their own race, even at some slight disadvantage. We must cooperate or we are lost. Ten million people who join in intelligent self-help can never be long ignored or mistreated.[3]

## 2. The Myth Becomes Institutionalized

Two years after the Atlanta Conference on the Negro in business, Booker T. Washington took the initiative in organizing the National Negro Business League, which held its first meeting in Boston, Massachusetts.[4] At this meeting, attended by 115 delegates from twenty states (mostly southern) and the District of Columbia, Washington was elected president of the permanent organization. The four sessions of the two-day meeting were characterized by much oratory and enthusiasm. In his opening address, Washington made the highly dubious generalization that wherever he had "seen a Black man who was succeeding in business, who was a taxpayer, and who possessed intelligence and high character, that individual was treated with the highest respect by the members of the white race."[5] Faith in the power of business enterprise and money to wipe out racial prejudice was repeatedly echoed by the delegates, one of whom stated, "Fortunately human selfishness, the desire of every man to get all he can with least effort or money, has banished all prejudice."[6] These sentiments, it might be noted, won the approval of the leading Boston (white) daily paper.[7]

By far, most of the oratory at this meeting was devoted to the achieve-ments of the Negro in business and the bright future for the Negro in the field of business enterprise. At one point during the meeting, the compiler or statistician interrupted the oratory to announce that according to in-formation provided by the delegates they owned personal and real property amounting to $781,900.[8] In the enthusiasm of the meeting, it appears that no one stopped to realize that even if the figures were true, they repre-sented a very small amount of wealth for 115 businessmen. Nor does it seem that anyone gave sober thought to the report which was presented on the character of Negro business and the amount of capital which it represented.

The report included the study presented at the Atlanta Conference[9] according to which 432 of the 1906 Negro businessmen who sent in reports had small grocery stores; 166 were general merchandise dealers; 162 barbers with $500.00 or more invested in their businesses; 80 undertakers; 68 owners of saloons; 64 had drugstores; and 61 restaurants. The study presented a fair idea of the character of Negro business, since the figures from the United States Census gave a similar picture. These 1906 Negro businessmen represented about a tenth of all persons reported in the census who, by the broad definition given to "business" by the National Negro Business League, were regarded as engaged in business. For ex-ample, the league counted as Negro businessmen the "boarding and lodging housekeepers," "hucksters and peddlers," and "newsboys" reported in the census.

But what else could be expected in a meeting which was designed to bolster faith in a myth? The delegates were urged to spread the faith in this myth in organizing local business leagues throughout the country.

## 3. Propagation of the Myth

The success of the exhortation to spread the faith in salvation by business is indicated by the fact that within five years more than 300 local business leagues were organized.[10] Then in 1907 there appeared a book on Negro business by Booker T. Washington, who was elected year after year presi-dent of the National Business League.[11] This book, which according to the author was written to "take note of the undoubted business awakening among the Negro people of the United States," contained a series of success stories concerning Negroes in various enterprises. The series begins with stories showing how "the Negro farmer often passes from agriculture into business." Outstanding among these farmers who had become business-men was a Negro farmer from Kansas who became known as "the Negro Potato King." There followed stories of Negroes who had succeeded as caterers, hotelkeepers, undertakers, publishers, and bankers. One of the leading bankers was a minister whose success, according to Washington, showed "how closely the moral and spiritual interests of our people are interwoven with their material and economical welfare."[12]

It was not strange that a minister was named among the successful Negro businessmen, since the membership of the league was composed largely of professional Negroes, many of whom could hardly have been regarded as businessmen. If one examines the list of members of the leagues, especially those holding the offices, it will be found that they represent the leadership of the Negroes without respect to their relation to business enterprise. In fact, the report of the Eleventh Annual Conference of the league, which was held in New York City in 1910, stated as one of the notable features of this convention that a "diversity of interests" was represented.[13] Stated otherwise, it was notable in the sense that the crusade to gain supporters for the faith in business enterprise as the salvation of the Negro was gaining adherents among Negroes in all walks of life. The religious nature of this crusade was indicated in the annual address by Booker T. Washington which was delivered in the form of a "Business Sermon" based upon the Biblical text, "To him that hath shall be given."[14] According to Washington, "these lines spoken by the Master strike the keynote for individual success and equally so for racial success." He exhorted his hearers to go out from the meeting "determined that each individual shall be a missionary in his community—a missionary in teaching the masses to get property, to be more thrifty, more economical, and resolve to establish an industrial enterprise wherever a possibility presents itself."[15]

In this same annual address, Washington also stated that "before the starting of the Business League, there was not a single Negro bank in the state of Mississippi. At the present time, Mississippi has eleven Negro banks. When this Business League was organized in Boston ten years ago there were only four Negro banks in the United States; at the present time there are fifty-six Negro banks."[16] If Washington were living today he would probably be saddened by the fact that there are no Negro banks in the state of Mississippi and that there are only eleven Negro banks in the United States, with total assets amounting to less than a single white bank in many small cities.[17] But at the time that the myth of Negro business was being propagated, little concern was shown for the real economic position of the Negro and his experience in business. At each annual meeting of the league, the delegates were exhorted to spread the faith in business enterprise and were told of the golden opportunities to reap wealth by supplying the needs of the Negro masses. At the thirteenth annual convention in Chicago in 1912, Washington asked in his annual address, "If the white man can secure wealth and happiness by owning and operating a coal mine, brick yard, or lime kiln, why can not more Negroes do the same thing? If other races can attain prosperity by securing riches on a large scale from our seas, lakes, and rivers in the form of fish and other sea foods, thousands of Negroes can do the same thing. Activity in all these directions finds no races or color line."[18]

Two years later, when the League met in Muskogee, Oklahoma, Washington stated that "when the 2 million Negroes in the Southwest have made the most of their opportunities . . . and brought up the riches contained in the earth they will be able to support . . . 1,000 more grocery stores, owned by Negroes, 500 additional dry good stores, 300 more shoe stores, 200 more good restaurants and hotels, 300 additional millinery stores, 200 additional drug stores, and 40 more banks."[19] These fantastic dreams of business enterprise were applauded by the delegates who attended the annual meetings. Moreover, the delegates themselves engaged in oratory about the progress of the Black bourgeoisie in obtaining wealth. They related stories of the acquisition of wealth in business enterprises which, when coldly studied, were really of little significance. Nevertheless, the crusade to win believers in the myth of Negro business continued after these conventions closed. It was preached during the pilgrimages which Washington made through the South.[20] During these pilgrimages he constantly pointed out to the Negroes the opportunities which they were overlooking for gaining wealth through business enterprises and he invited Negro businessmen to give testimonies of their achievements in gaining wealth.

After the death of Washington the league continued to carry on the crusade to instill in Negroes faith in business enterprise as the way to economic salvation. Under the influence of the enthusiasm and oratory which characterized these meetings, the participants continued to relate all sorts of fanciful stories concerning their wealth. Myths grew up concerning Negro millionaires that had no basis in fact. The participants, who were drawn from many fields of professional activities, were often led to describe their activities as being inspired by the spirit of business enterprise. For example, at the meeting in Chattanooga, Tennessee, in 1917, Eugene K. Jones, the executive secretary of the National League on Urban Conditions of Negroes, a social work agency, declared that his organization was "a business organization" which made "a business of social welfare work."[21]

While the myth of Negro business was being propagated, the hard realities of the Negro's insignificant achievements in business were apparent to anyone who was not under the spell of the oratory of the conventions of the league. In order to create a substantial basis for the myth, the National Negro Business League undertook to establish the Colored Merchants Association (CMA) grocery stores throughout the country.[22] According to the CMA plan ten or more Negro retail stores in any city were to buy a share of stock in the CMA in which they paid weekly dues and buy from a wholesale dealer selected by the league. The first CMA organization was established in Montgomery, Alabama, in 1928, and soon thereafter organizations were set up in about eighteen other cities. The organization of the CMA was hailed as a new and realistic approach of the League to the promotion of business enterprise among Negroes. *The Chicago Whip*, a Negro newspaper, stated that the establishment of the CMA stores marked the end of the period of oratory and added, "It is well known why now that flamboyant oratory makes no lasting impression, gives no deep insight into the manner in which things are done, nor does it convey the information that the untrained businessman is so badly in

need of."[23] The establishment of the CMA stores was marked by much fanfare. In Harlem, in New York City, the opening of the CMA stores was celebrated by a parade which included men and women from business,
fraternal and church circles. Despite the fanfare and hopes of the bourgeoisie, the CMA movement failed after a few years. Those who had bought
stock in the CMA lost their money, if not their faith in Negro business
enterprise. Those who maintained their faith are still not sure whether the
failure was due to the lack of support by Negro retailers or that Negro
consumers preferred nationally advertised products.[24]

The failure of the CMA adventure did not affect the faith of the Black
bourgeoisie in the myth of Negro business, since the faith was constantly
being strengthened by the expansion of business education among Negro
colleges.[25] The number of Negro colleges giving business education grew
from six in 1900 to more than twenty in 1940. The majority of the
students pursuing courses in business receive a technical education in
such subjects as typewriting, bookkeeping, and shorthand. In five of the
Negro colleges the students are given professional courses in management
and other functions exercised by the owners and officials in business enterprises. A small number are prepared to teach the business courses which
they have studied. Of the thirty-five graduates of Atlanta University who
received the master's degree in business, five were teaching business and
eight were employed in Negro colleges as treasurers, business managers,
bursars, and one as a registrar.[26] Although twenty-nine of the thirty-five
were employed in fields related to the business courses which they had
taken, it does not appear that business education had enabled them to
become entrepreneurs. The vast majority of students who take technical
and business courses in Negro colleges could acquire the same technical
competence in some commercial business school. But in the Negro college,
business education is given profession status and is glorified because of the
myth of Negro business as a way to economic salvation for the Negro in
American society.

Beliefs in regard to the myths surrounding Negro business are not
affected by the facts [regarding the actual scope of Negro economic
activity.] For example, it has always been claimed that despite the oppression of the Negro in the South, there was a compensatory fact, namely,
that the South offered an opportunity for the development of Negro business. This claim is still made today by those who believe in the myth
despite the fact that in proportion to population there are more retail
stores in the North than in the South, and that the stores in the North have
a larger number of full-time employees and a greater volume of sales.
Moreover, despite the fact that there are less than half as many stores in
the North as in the South, the total payroll in the North is greater than
in the South and the sales three-fourths as great as in the South. Nor has
the belief in the myth been affected by the fact that the attempts of Negro
businessmen to establish industrial undertakings have constantly resulted
in failures. Even when they have had the support of northern white
philanthropists, Negroes have failed to establish industries of any im-

portance. For example, Julius Rosenwald was persuaded by Booker T. Washington to invest $30,000 in a cotton oil mill in Mound Bayou, an all-Negro town in Mississippi. This venture failed, as other such business ventures, and the oil mill was converted into a dance hall.[27] Negroes appealed again to Julius Rosenwald in the 1920s to salvage the wreckage of the manifold undertakings of a Negro banker in Atlanta who attempted to build up a large financial empire on the basis of stores and real estate holdings. But on this occasion, Rosenwald evidently did not think that his philanthropic contributions to Negroes should include the salvaging of their unsound business undertakings.

Nevertheless, northern philanthropy has been sympathetic to the efforts of Negroes to create business enterprises. This has been manifested especially in their financial support of the study of Negro business. Despite the myths surrounding the importance of Negro business, the obvious fact that Negro businesses have failed to become important has continually haunted the minds of the most ardent believers in Negro business as a solution of the Negro's problems. Hence, there has been a constant interest in discovering why Negro businesses have failed so often or have not become important in the economic life of the Negro. A quarter of a century ago, the Spelman Fund, established through Rockefeller contributions to social research, made an initial grant of $15,000, which was supplemented by $5,000, for the study of Negro business. The chief results of this study, which comprised less than fifty pages, were to show that almost all Negro businesses were small retail businesses and undertaking establishments serving Negroes, that they were conducted by their owners, and that they were in Negro neighborhoods. Once again, in 1943, the General Education Board was requested by Atlanta University and the National Urban League to contribute $25,000 to a study of Negro business. The cooperation of the National Urban League was sought by Atlanta University because the league had "become convinced that Negroes might help themselves by improving and expanding the business enterprises which they control."[28]

Neither of these studies revealed the fundamental causes of the failure of Negroes to carry on successful business enterprises on either a small or a large scale. They did not deal with the simple but fundamental sociological fact that the Negro lacks a business tradition or the experience of people who, over generations, have engaged in buying and selling. Neither the tradition of the gentleman nor his peasant heritage had provided the Negro with this outlook on the world. Nor did these studies deal with the relation of the efforts of Negroes to establish factories and business enterprises to the structure of the American economy. To have presented such facts these studies would have tended to destroy the Negro's faith in the myth. I have heard Professor Harris criticized by the president of a Negro college because in his book, *The Negro As Capitalist*, he showed that one of the fundamental causes of the failure of Negro banks was the impossibility of the Negro banks to function in a segregated Negro economy which lacked sound businesses requiring credit. The college president's criticism was not directed against the facts presented in this study but against its effect upon the Negro's faith in business enterprise as a solution to his economic problems. The myth concerning Negro business, from the standpoint of many Negro leaders, is more important than the facts of American economic life which determine the fate of Negro business enterprises.

The myth of Negro business is tied up with the belief in the possibility of a separate Negro economy. It has constantly been proposed by those who believe in a separate Negro economy that the Negro can build his own manufacturing plants, stores, and banks with the earnings of Negro workers who, by patronizing these Negro enterprises, would create more capital and give employment to Negroes. Of course, behind the idea of the separate Negro economy is the hope of the Black bourgeoisie that they will have the monopoly of the Negro market. They state that it is a sacred obligation of Negroes to patronize Negro business and that they should not complain if they pay higher prices for goods and cannot buy exactly what they want so long as they buy from Negroes. During the depression years, the black bourgeoisie in northern cities began to sponsor a campaign with the slogan, "Don't Buy Where You Can't Work." The result of this campaign was the growth of anti-Semitism which expressed itself during race riots when Jewish businessmen in Negro neighborhoods became the targets of Negro mobs.[29]

The idea of a separate Negro economy was given an odd turn by a Negro college professor who taught and popularized the theory of the "double-duty" dollar.[30] According to this theory, the Negro worker would not only purchase with his dollar the necessities of life, but he would provide with the dollar he spent the wages for Negro workers. Anyone who opposed this fanciful economic theory was called an enemy of Negroes. As the result of the faith in the myth of Negro business there have sprung up all over the country fanciful schemes, such as one recently started in the national capital which proposed that each Negro, man, woman, and child contribute one dollar to a fund to establish manufacturing plants which would make shoes and clothes for the Negro market.

## 4. The Myth and the Changing Status of the Negro

The changing status of the Negro in the United States, which has resulted from World War II and the world crisis, has not failed to influence the myth of Negro business. Paradoxically, on the surface at least, the increasing employment of Negroes desiring business careers by white business enterprises has not shaken faith in the myth of Negro business. The reason for this becomes apparent when one considers the relation of the myth to the world of make-believe which the Black bourgeoisie has created.

The Black bourgeoisie derives its income almost entirely from white collar and professional occupations which give it a privileged status within the isolated Negro community. Since the Black bourgeoisie has rejected identification with the masses, its isolation has been further intensified. In escaping from identification with the masses, the Black bourgeoisie has attempted to identify with the white propertied classes. Since this has been impossible, except in their minds, because of the racial barriers those identified with this class have attempted to act out their role in a world of make-believe. In the world of make-believe they have not taken over the patterns of behavior of the white-collar and professional white workers, but the values and as far as possible the patterns of behavior of wealthy whites. With their small earnings, their attempt to maintain the style of living of the white propertied classes has only emphasized the unreality of their way of life. Faith in the myth of Negro business, which symbolizes the power and status of white America, has been the main element in the world of make-believe that the Black bourgeoisie has created.

The prosperity which the United States enjoyed as the result of World War II and the war economy during the cold war has trickled down to the Negroes, especially since some of the barriers to the employment of Negroes have been lowered. The increase in the earnings of Negro workers has brought increased prosperity to Negro businesses, especially to Negro insurance companies and the Negro publishers of newspapers and maga-zines. Also, the lowering of barriers to the employment of Negroes in white-collar occupations has increased the proportion of Negroes able to main-tain a middle-class standard of life. Despite these improvements in the position of the Black bourgeoisie, there were some misgivings about the continuance of their prosperous condition after the war. The feeling that it was necessary to assess the economic improvement in the condition of Negroes in white-collar and professional occupations was the chief moti-vation for calling a conference at Howard University in 1946.[31]

At the opening session of this conference, the president of Howard Uni-versity declared that,

The Negro people, just a bit over eighty years from slavery, are a child people in their ability to organize the ordinary things that have to do with effective existence. Take the simple things that engage the attention of a community and involve the major activities of human beings in a small town—the gathering together and the distribution of food in a grocery store, a butcher shop, or a restaurant. In the little one-horse town or your Harlem or your Los Angeles, you miss Negro faces in this fundamental business of assembling and dis-tributing food products. We have a handful of men engaged in the grocery business, a handful in the butcher business, and a handful in the bakery busi-ness—although we have some of the best bread bakers in the world. We have nobody in the pastry business. There is also the question of clothing. Any group of 10,000 human beings will naturally require a certain amount of clothing of all kinds. Go into the communities where we live. Enterprises and persons engaged in the effective distribution of these things—to say nothing of their production—are practically missing among us. Then there are some of the service activities connected with clothing—for example, the laundry business. There are practically no Negro-operated laundries, even in the southern area, where we used to monopolize the washing of clothes. We have so few tailor shops or millinery shops. Yet none of these things are beyond our power. We just simply have not focused our attention upon them.[32]

Much of the discussion at this conference was of the same nature, deal-ing with the failure of the Negro to seize the opportunity to organize businesses which would thrive on the Negro market. Scarcely any attention was given to the organization of American economic life and how this fact affected the prospects of Negro business. Nor was any discussion directed to the fact that Negro white-collar and professional workers could not assemble the capital and organize the managerial ability necessary for large-scale production and distribution. There was in this conference, as in the conferences of the National Negro Business League, much exhortation to Negroes to engage in business, which revealed a continued faith in the myth of Negro business as providing a solution to the economic problems of the Negro.

When the National Business League celebrated its fiftieth anniversary in 1950 at Tuskegee Institute, the league rededicated itself to the achievement of the aims of the founder, Booker T. Washington. The president of the league announced that the philosophy upon which the league was founded was "as potent today as it was when it was first given. From the very beginning of the league," he added, "its preachments, propaganda and programs have been directed towards alerting our minds to the importance of entering into and building business of all kinds and to the necessity of becoming business minded on a national scale."[33] However, only two years later, when the president of the league reported on the results of his attempt, during his travels amounting to 172,000 miles, to develop faith in the importance and future of Negro business, he had to meet the objection that the league's program really provided for a separate economy. The president said that it did not take him long to convince the person who raised the objection "that a separate economy was a myth." Then he explained, "The customer of the Negro-owned grocery may work for and get his money from employment at General Motors—or General Electric, or at the Ford Automobile Plant, or in department stores owned by other groups—that fact alone eliminates the possibility of a separate economy."[34] Then the president attempted to show how other minority groups, especially the Jews, had become important in the economic life of various countries through their separate business operations.

That the president of the National Negro Business League felt that it was necessary to repudiate the myth of the separate economy, while defending the myth of Negro business, was due to the fact that Negroes were beginning to secure employment on an unprecedented scale in the marketing branches of white businesses. White firms have found it extremely profitable to employ Negroes in advertising products for Negro consumers, in establishing public relations with the Negro community, and as salesmen. Negroes have been employed on a large scale by the distributors of liquors, beers and nonalcoholic beverages, cigarettes, gasoline and automobiles. The employment of Negroes by large corporations has overshadowed even the exaggerated achievements of Negro businessmen. The importance of the employment of aspiring Negro businessmen in white enterprises stimulated the department of Business Administration at Howard University to hold a "Career Conference in Marketing" in February

1954. At this conference, the new careers which were opening up to
Negroes were discussed and the successful examples of Negroes in these
new occupations were presented to students who wanted to become businessmen.

The employment of Negroes in the field of marketing or distribution by
large American corporations is a phase of the integration of the Negro into
American life. The National Negro Business League, which has proclaimed
since its establishment that business success would break down racial
barriers, has been compelled to go along with this new development. In
fact, some of the younger members of the National Business League, many
of whom are not really engaged in *Negro* business, have proposed to delete
"Negro" from the name of the league. But this has not met with general
acceptance because the leaders recognize that "integration" means the
ultimate disappearance of *Negro* business. Some Negro businessmen have
pointed to cities where Negroes have recently been accepted into "white"
restaurants, theaters, and cinemas to show how integration has meant the
decline in *Negro* business. Moreover, as the increasing economic welfare
of the Negro has produced all sorts of extravagant claims about the purchasing power of Negroes, Negro businessmen have sought a share in this
market.[35]

The myth of Negro business has also been strengthened by the encouragement which the white community has given to the belief of Negroes
that the accumulation of wealth through business will solve their problems.
Negro salesmen, who are employed by white business and are only senti-
mentally attached to *Negro* business, are meeting at luncheons with white
salesmen; and Negro salesmen are being featured in the public relations
literature sent out by corporations. Yet no Negro businessmen are taken
into the white business groups which own and control the life of the
American community. The white community is assured, nevertheless, that
the Negro leaders who propagate the myth of Negro business are uncom-
promising enemies of any radical doctrines. The myth that Negroes were
spending $15 billion in 1951 was widely circulated by whites as well as
Negroes since it served to exaggerate the economic well-being of Negroes
in the United States and to whet the appetites of the Black bourgeoisie,
both Negro businessmen and Negroes employed by American corporations,
in their efforts to reap benefits from the increased earnings of Negroes.

The myth of Negro business thrives despite the fact that Negro businessmen can best be described as a "lumpen-bourgeoisie."[36] The myth of Negro
business is fed by the false notions and values that are current in the
isolated social world of the Negro, a world dominated by the views and
mental outlook of the Black bourgeoisie. The extent to which these false
notions influence the outlook of Negroes cannot better be illustrated than
by the case of the Negro Pullman porter who owned his home and four
shares of stock, valued at about eighty dollars, in a large American corporation. He declared that he was against the policies of Franklin D. Roosevelt
and the New Deal because they taxed men of property like himself in

order to assist lazy working men. Such delusions are created largely . . . by
the Negro press.

## Notes

1. Abram L. Harris, *The Negro As Capitalist* (Philadelphia: The American
Academy of Political and Social Science, 1936) pp. 49–50.
2. *Ibid.*, pp. 51–52.
3. *Ibid.*, p. 53.
4. *Proceedings of the National Negro Business League* (First meeting held in
Boston, Mass., August 23 and 24, 1900). (Copyright 1901).
5. *Ibid.*, p. 26.
6. *Ibid.*, p. 129.
7. *Ibid.*, p. 259.
8. *Ibid.*, p. 200.
9. W. E. B. DuBois, ed., *The Negro in Business* (Atlanta: Atlanta University Press,
1899), p. 50.
10. Booker T. Washington, *The Negro in Business* (Boston: Hertel, 1907), p. 275.
11. *Ibid.*
12. *Ibid.*, p. 136.
13. "Report of the Eleventh Annual Convention of the National Negro Business
League" (Nashville: A. M. E. Sunday School Union, 1911), p. 11.
14. *Ibid.*, pp. 78–85.
15. *Ibid.*, p. 81.
16. *Ibid.*, p. 83.
17. See Joseph A. Pierce, *Negro Business and Business Education* (New York:
Harper 1947), p. 152.
18. "Report of the Thirteenth Annual Convention of the National Negro Business
League" (Washington, D.C., n.d.), p. 52.
19. "Report of the Fifteenth Annual Convention of the National Negro Business
League" (Washington, D.C., n.d.), pp. 83–84.
20. Albion L. Holsey, *Booker T. Washington's Own Story of His Life and Work*
(Washington, D.C., 1915), pp. 407–409.
21. *National Negro Business League* (Washington, D.C., n.d.), p. 124.
22. Pierce, *op. cit.*, pp. 210–211.
23. Quoted in "Annual Report of the Secretary's Office, National Negro Business
League, for the Fiscal Year Ending August 15, 1929," p. 2.
24. Pierce, *op. cit.*, p. 211. See also Harris, *op. cit.*, p. 178.
25. See Pierce, *op. cit.*, "Book Two," concerning the development and character of
business education in Negro colleges.
26. Pierce, *op. cit.*, p. 277.
27. "The Post-War Outlook for Negroes in Small Business, The Engineering Professions, and Technical Vocations," (Papers and Proceedings of the Ninth Annual
Conference of the Division of the Social Sciences, Howard University, Washington,
D.C., 1946), p. 29.
28. Pierce, *op. cit.*, p. vi.
29. See St. Clair Drake and Horace Cayton, Black Metropolis (New York: Harcourt,
Brace, 1945), pp. 430–432.
30. Harris, *op. cit.*, pp. 182–184.
31. See *The Post-War Outlook for Negroes*, op. cit.
32. *Ibid.*, pp. 8–9.
33. See *Program of the Fiftieth Anniversary, National Negro Business League*
(Tuskegee, Ala., August 29–September 1, 1950).
34. *Ibid.*, p. 3.
35. Without any basis in available statistics on the purchasing power of Negroes,
an advertising magazine, *Tide*, July 20, 1951, made the statement that Negroes were
spending $15 billion in 1951. This same unfounded statement was repeated in an
article entitled "The Negro—Progress and Challenge," in the *New York Times Magazine*, February 7, 1954, by Chester Bowles. Although I wrote a letter to the *New York*

*Times* showing that, on the basis of available statistics, Negroes could not have spent more than $6 billion in 1951, the letter was never published.

36. After the writer had used the term "lumpen-bourgeoisie" to describe the Black bourgeoisie, he discovered that C. Wright Mills in his *White Collar* (New York: Oxford University Press, 1951, pp. 28–33) had used this term to designate the multitude of white firms "with a high death rate, which do a fraction of the total business done in their lines and engage a considerably larger proportion of people than their quota of business."

# 5 ]] The Black Economy

*Harold Cruse*

. . . The lack of clearly defined integrationist goals inexorably drives the northern integrationist back to the pressing reality of economic fundamentals. In the North this crisis lies precisely *inside* the Negro ghettoes—not in integrated housing projects or integrated classrooms or any other of the multitude of integrated externals over which Negroes rend the atmosphere with racial discord. Such externals are, in effect, the main social province of professional civil righters and civil writers: the province of Negro individualism as opposed to the social province of the group. When the Negro individualist–integrationist runs into trouble over the externals he reverts back to the group—sometimes. Thus, Paul B. Zuber in his article on economics returns to group considerations.[1]

The integrationists have always said that a separate Negro economy in the United States is a myth. But is it really? The reason that the debate on the black economy has gone on back and forth for years, with no conclusions reached, is because the idea is closely linked with nationalism, and the integrationists would rather be tarred and feathered than suspected of the nationalist taint. This was the great weakness of W. E. B. DuBois—the only real flaw in the man's intellectual equipment. DuBois upheld the idea of a separate black economy as "not so easily dismissed" because "in the first place we have already got a partially separate economy in the United States."[2] Yet he remarked in 1940 that his economic program for Negro advance "can easily be mistaken for a program of complete racial segregation and even nationalism among Negroes . . . this is a misapprehension."[3] It seems not to have occurred to DuBois that any thorough economic reorganization of Negro existence imposed from above will not be supported by the popular masses unless an appeal is made to their nationalism. In our times Malcolm X had the nationalist appeal but *not* the program; DuBois had the program but *not* the nationalist appeal. This explains, in part, the tragedy of the Negro and his luckless leadership in the twentieth century. For notice how long it took for an avowed integrationist like Paul B. Zuber to admit, even by implication, either the reality or the potential of the black economy. The black economy is a myth only because a truly viable black economy does not exist. It does not exist simply because Negroes as a group never came together to create one, which does not mean that it would be a simple matter to create a Black economy. But it could be done—with the aid of attributes the Negro has

From "Black Economy—Self-Made Myth" and "Capitalism Revisited" in *The Crisis of the Negro Intellectual* by Harold Cruse. Reprinted by permission of William Morrow and Company, Inc. © 1967 by Harold Cruse.

never developed, i.e., discipline, self-denial, cooperative organization, and knowledge of economic science. But let us examine how Zuber approaches the question: "The Black economy in this country suffers for the same reasons that other phases of social action are lost to the Black American. We are sold out before we have an opportunity to shift into high gear."[4]

. . . At the very outset, to create the proper basis for a Black economy, one must go back to the writings of Booker T. Washington and W. E. B. DuBois and update their economic thoughts. In pursuing the Black economy the integrationists are caught in the coils of the American economic status quo. Instinctively they know that upholding the idea of the Black economy means confronting and challenging white economic exploitation and rule *inside* the Harlem community. It does not mean smuggling a handful of handpicked Negroes into Wall Street offices or opening up bank branches in downtown Manhattan or in Brooklyn, for capitalistic economics alone is not the answer to the Black economy. It involves much more than sheer economics; it requires a point of view that the Stevenses and the Zubers do not possess. It takes a certain community point of view, a conditioned climate, in order to exert impact (political, economic, and cultural) on the white economy. It means the studied creation of new economic forms—a new institutionalism—one that can intelligently blend privately owned, collectively owned, cooperatively owned, as well as state-sponsored, economic organizations. It means mobilizing the ghetto populations and organizing them through education and persuasion (if not through authoritarian measures from above). In Harlem one cannot seriously talk about the Black economy until the main business artery of 125th Street is turned over to Negro business administration and economic control. One cannot have a Black economy until the day comes when the bulk of profits accrued from commercial enterprises in Harlem are poured back into the community for further development. When the day comes that Harlem Negroes are willing to sacrifice and discipline their buying and having habits to the extent of a total boycott of white business control and exploitation, by buying elsewhere, then one can talk seriously of creating the Black economy. If the Birmingham Negroes could use their feet to win dignity on the buses, Harlem Negroes should be able to use their feet and the subways and self-organized buying pools to break up economic exploitation in Harlem.

The Black economy idea is neither myth nor concrete reality. The ingredients exist and merely await skillful organizational use and application. America is a nation that abounds in many myths and many realities. The greatest myth is that of democratic capitalism, which has never existed for *all* groups in America. Minorities could not have won their way into different levels of economic status if it were not through some form of group economics—either capitalistic or cooperative. Some added group politics (the Irish), and others even used group crime (the Mafia) and its rewards as the key to economic respectability. The American Jews could not have won their way into the economic power they now possess if not through various forms of group solidarity. For many reasons too numerous to explain here, the American Negro, especially in New York, has failed to learn and practice his economic group responsibilities in the promised land of the North. Because of inadequate, selfish, and imperceptive leadership, the American Negro has been forced to play the impoverished foil for the white liberal conscience, while being blinded to the fundamental realities of political, economic, and cultural survival in America. As a result, the real tragedy of the economics of the ghetto is avoided by integrationists because they are hoodwinked into playing the game of American capitalism by the rules established by those in control of the economic exchange processes of the ghetto status quo. Thus they cannot possibly win much beyond one degree of tokenism or another. But even job tokenism means very little to the Negro ghettoes today. The job market is just about saturated outside the ghettoes and the future is endangered by automation. Consequently, the economic problems of Negro ghettoes can be tackled only by dealing with the bedrock realities of the whole premise of private property. This must be challenged wherever it is found to be in conflict with the democratic group needs and aspirations of Negroes inside the ghettos. It comes down to the basic question of who owns the ghetto and profits from it. Wherever this *ownership* and profiteering become the stumbling blocks to the economic rehabilitation and social and cultural revitalization of Negro ghetto life, these encumbrances must be removed. Toward this end, every means, every organizational, political, and economic approach, every institutional and group resource, must be coordinated and intelligently applied. And it goes without saying that such a radical and thoroughgoing changeover in the racial composition of property ownership presupposes the assumption of independent political power on the part of Negroes in ghettoes. In this regard, Harlem becomes the pilot ghetto wherein this radical overturn of property relations must occur. Harlem, once called the cultural capital of the Negro in America, has become, if not the most economically depressed and retarded of all northern Black enclaves, the most politically backward and the most racially irresponsible.

Determining where to put the blame for this state of affairs is one of the purposes of this article, and the special Harlem issue of *Freedomways* becomes a prime exhibit in our investigation. There, in black and white, is a panoramic view of this all-important community, as interpreted by a broad segment of Negro intellectual opinion. Since all of the issue's articles could not be transcribed and criticized here, I have chosen those on nationalism and economics because they deal with the bread-and-butter aspects of Negro ghetto life, and the ideological questions surrounding the issue of integration. They furnish a key to understanding what is positive, negative, effective, profound, superficial, enlightening, or simply clichéd about Negro integrationist leadership and Negro intellectual opinion.

There are many who will disagree with the critical conclusions presented here, on the problems of economics—or *the race factor of economics* —in the exploitation of Harlem by whites. If what I deem must be done about Harlem's condition seems radically impossible (within the context of our accepted morality about private property rights, etc.), let me stress that my outline is merely schematic and requires elaboration before being considered a comprehensive economic plan for ghetto rehabilitation. However, as I see it, given the impasse that race relations have reached in America, especially in the northern cities, anything *less* than this offers not the slightest hope for eventual ethnic democratization.

There comes a time in the relentless war of poverty v. profit when many ideas about economic reform become nothing but empty platitudes. The old rules of the game must be thrown overboard, and new ones adopted and enforced by every means possible within the range of the social intelligence and the economic resources of this nation. Capitalism (particularly the American brand) is highly touted as the best economic framework for political democracy, individual rights, and personal freedom. If true, it must, itself, uphold the rights of ethnic groups to participate democratically in the economic processes wherever it is patently shown that ethnic groups, economically insolvent and nonwhite, are subject to economic exploitation by solvent white Protestants, white Catholics, or white Jews. America, to repeat, is a collective of ethnic groups. *There is more disequilibrium in the economic, cultural, and political status of ethnic groups than there is class warfare in America.* The race question or the civil rights movement or racial integration or racial equality, etc., merely reflect this long-standing social condition. It has been brought to the fore by the Negro movement simply because of the Negroes' unique position vis-à-vis the American white world. In reality, Indians, Mexicans, and other nonwhite hyphenated-Americans at the bottom of the ethnic totem pole are also involved.

The Negro (or any other ethnic minority) cannot simply drift aimlessly, or hope by seeking constitutional redress of grievances to integrate into a secure status of ethnic group democracy, because the Constitution as it now stands, does not recognize the legal validity or the rights of groups *but only of individuals.* Hence, not only must the American Constitution be brought up to date in terms of mirroring the basic group reality of America, but it is the American Negro who must press the fight for this amending. For the Negro to continue to be trapped in the unstable no-man's land of more protest, more ghetto riots, more subsequent drift will lead to social and racial chaos in America of such degree that the nation as a whole may not survive on a racially democratic basis. Hence, of all the ethnic groups in American society, that of the Negro becomes, of necessity, the pivotal American ethnic group among all others. It will depend to what degree the articulate Negro leadership comprehends its group's innate potential for enforcing democratization of ethnic group status through federal-sponsored measures, whether the Negro will hope to survive the complicated and difficult future that lies ahead in American race relations.

Overall, the 1963 Harlem issue of *Freedomways*—a magazine which in 1961 asked "which way will we go?"—revealed but a scant awareness of the social complexities implied in the answer to that question.

. . . The gradualistic economic philosophy of a Stevens, a Zuber, a

Schuyler, sums up the total economic philosophy of the Black bourgeoisie. Politically, it is the economics of imitation and intellectual sterility. It is the economics of time-serving opportunism and theoretical incompetence. It is a philosophy that, under tutelage, will play at socialism and then turn and uphold capitalism with a straight face. It will adopt the partisan politics of Black conservatism against the traditions of the New Deal era while avidly accepting all the benefits of the same New Deal traditions. Taken as a whole, the Black bourgeoisie in the United States is the most politically backward of all the colored bourgeois classes in the non-Western world. It is a class that accepts the philosophy of whites whether radical, liberal, progressive, or conservative, without alteration or dissent and calls it leadership. It is a class that absorbs very little from the few thinkers it has produced—Martin R. Delany, W. E. B. DuBois, Booker T. Washington, E. Franklin Frazier, and Carter G. Woodson—men who left something behind them. It is the one nonwhite bourgois class in this world that fears to express its own legitimate nationalism, waiting on the benevolent nod from the power structure before it moves to achieve its limited social aims. Eschewing its own nationalistic birthright the Negro bourgeoisie compromises itself and undercuts its own political potential in advance. Hence, this class is sold out by none other than itself, not by white industrialists in civil rights organizations. Because it refuses to be assertive about its Afro–American heritage, this class fails to be revolutionary on any social front in the United States, not even in civil rights. It is a class whose social policies are so inept it seeks civil rights without seeking group political power, and then demands economic equality in the integrated world without having striven to create any kind of ethnic economic base in the Black world. It is a class that could not have the motivations to achieve these things because it fears to be nationalistic. Because of its refusal to break with the American two-party system this class lacks independent political power, and cannot even exert a commanding role in the federal antipoverty programs beamed into the Negro ghettos. Here in the rundown ghettos are the accumulated results of years of Black middle-class social irresponsibility. But federal intervention should *not* come only through the benevolence of enforced social necessity from without, but should also be forthcoming under the pressure of political power applied from within the ghettos themselves. That this kind of power was never cultivated is a Negro leadership default stretching back over several decades. It has robbed the Negro movement today of the powerful kind of cutting edge it ought to have. The historically true, native American radicalism is Black radicalism, but the history of this radicalism's bourgeois conformism is also the history of its emasculation. Therefore it becomes understandable why a Hope Stevens (a "real leader" of the Negroes in Schuyler's book) could not speak his piece about the economics of Harlem without mentioning Garvey; no more than could Stevens' great personal friend, Paul Robeson, offer up *Here I Stand* without arguing with Garvey's ghost. Is it not remarkable that these Negro capitalists, conservatives, leftwingers, and exradicals have so much in common?

The previously quoted allusion by Stevens to Garvey's economics is very interesting because it is highly doubtful that the NNC, during its heyday in the 1930s, had anything at all to do with the remnants of the Garveyite movement. In fact, there was no reference at all to this unique nationalistic trend in the first batch of NNC resolutions. Of course the NNC could not visualize its responsibilities in reconsidering Garvey's implications because the Communists had already relegated Garvey to political Hades back in the 1920s. Moreover, A. Philip Randolph, the president of the NNC, like many other Black intellectuals of that period, was leery of overt nationalism. This fear of nationalism is rooted in that manifestation of the Negro psychology that inhibits many Negroes from telling all white people exactly what they think of them as oppressors. This breaks down in various ways: There is the fear of losing the support of white liberals through criticizing them; there is the concomitant fear—an ingrained conditioning of Black America—of criticizing American Jews because they are an important segment of the liberal establishment and themselves oppressed by European history and Hitlerism; more than that, the fear of nationalism on the part of many Negroes is also a reflection of the fear of being forced to be self-critical of their own incompetent and shoddy intellectual role in American society; lastly, there is the fear of having a real confrontation with the dominant Anglo–Saxon Protestant in terms of his native, institutionalized nationalism that is today willing to sacrifice positive national purpose in subjecting the entire nation to international disgrace—in order to maintain group supremacy. These fears of nationalism are what give the lie to the claims of the integrationists that they are confronting the realities of racial discrimination. Racial integrationism that evades a confrontation of nationalism confronts nothing at all, because it deals with neither Black nationalism, white Anglo–Saxon nationalism, nor Jewish nationalism and their various implications. Hence Hope Stevens dealt with Garvey's capitalistic economics but not Garvey's nationalism, which is another way of saying that Stevens was merely indulging in economic platitudes.

Was the Garvey movement organized only to get Negroes to invest money? If so, then it was Stevens' business to give his views on why such an appeal to capitalistic "economics" could not have been made without the added ingredients of nationalism and back-to-Africa dreams. Why was Garvey's attempt to get investment money not successful in the British West Indies? What was the connection between Garvey's coming to the United States and Booker T. Washington, who was Garvey's American inspiration? It is a matter of record that Garvey came to the United States in 1916 for the express purpose of linking up his movement with Washington's movement in Tuskegee, Alabama, but that Washington died before Garvey arrived. Garvey himself admitted that "it is from America that I get most of the money from my work."[5] Garvey got the money, the risk capital, as Stevens calls it, but people invested it and lost. E. Franklin Frazier maintained that Negroes fail in business because of lack of business experience plus "a predatory view of economic activity." Was this the reason Garvey's investment ventures in his Black Star Line failed? W. E. B.

DuBois says it was because of business incompetence: "I begged his friends not to allow him foolishly to overwhelm with bankruptcy and disaster 'one of the most interesting spiritual movements of the modern world.' "[6]

It was estimated that over a million dollars of Negroes' money was lost investing in Garvey's schemes, of which some $800,000 went for the purchase of four rundown ships, plus $70,000 to $80,000 for repairs to make them seaworthy. What were the implications of all this? What was wrong was that Garvey's nationalism was more bourgeois than it was revolutionary; thus he fell into the error of trying to fight capitalistic imperialism solely with capitalistic methods of economic organization. Hope Stevens is repeating the same error (from another standpoint) in visualizing Harlem's economic resurrection through the accumulation of risk capital. Curiously enough, neither the old Garveyites, nor the new-wave Black nationalists, nor the Negro leftwingers (old or new) have made a single new contribution to the American Negro situation in terms of economic theories. The Garveyites are still, in 1967, discussing Africa in terms of capitalistic enterprises (Black banks, Black private enterprises, Black private entrepreneurs) when African nations are wrestling with problems of the socialist economies along African lines. The socialism of the American Black leftwing, however, is strictly utopian talk, while the young, new-wave Black nationalists have no economic theories, and do not even study economic thought with any seriousness, if at all. Hope Stevens himself declares that there is no special economic theory that even applies to the Harlem ghetto. This economic "know-nothingness" is the fundamental curse of the Negro movement's ideology today. Thus the connection between the state of affairs in the 1960s and the 1920s era of Garvey is much closer than Hope Stevens suggests. Not since Garveyism collapsed through Garvey's own personal economic ineptitude has a single Negro leader with the exception of W. E. B. DuBois, presented a creative economic idea—good, bad, or indifferent.

In his autobiography, *Dusk of Dawn*, DuBois outlined a whole new concept of what he called the "cooperative commonwealth" for the American Negro. Yet this very important aspect of DuBois's thinking is never even mentioned today by the various black intellectual worshippers of the DuBois tradition. In the W. E. B. DuBois Memorial Issue put out by *Freedomways* in the winter of 1965, thirty-four Black, (and not so Black) intellectuals were brought together to pay homage to the memory of DuBois's achievements. This lineup presented a united front of Communists, pro-Communists, anti-Communists, ex-Communists, white liberals, an African nationalist, and an African antinationalist. They discussed practically everything about W. E. B. DuBois except the real essentials of the man's thinking in politics, economics, and culture that might conceivably relate to Negro masses in American ghettos. This list of writers, from Herbert Aptheker through Roy Wilkins, all skirted the essentials of the DuBois–Washington–Garvey triangular dispute over politics, nationalism, economics, and culture and how it applies to the ghetto explosions today.

They even refused to reexamine what DuBois himself had to say about his own mistakes in dealing with Washington and Garvey. The *Freedomways* DuBois issue recalled nothing about DuBois's economic theories. Yet from all of this history Stevens's mind can conjure up no "theory." When the assertion was made earlier in this book that the influence of the Communist leftwing on the thinking of the Negro intellectual has been disastrous, it was no extravagant charge. Men like Stevens have been conditioned (directly or indirectly) by American Marxism to think only on either of two economic levels—pure capitalism or European socialism. When they depart from the left they revert to conformist capitalistic free-market thinking, while socialism remains only a dream, something that is supposed to exist in the Soviet Union. Negro intellectuals produce, therefore, no original economic theorists who can cope realistically with either capitalism or socialism from a Negro point of view. This is the failing not only of ex-leftwingers such as Stevens and the whole integrationist–civil rights school (left or reform), but is greviously evident among both the old and new nationalists as well.

Not for forty-odd years have Garveyites understood that Garvey, even at the start of his movement, began with economic ideas that, for him, had been rendered obsolete by World War I. Garvey properly belongs to the early-twentieth-century, bourgeois nationalist leaders that arose in the colonized world. One of the greatest of these was China's Dr. Sun Yat Sen. But Sun Yat Sen understood in 1911 what Marcus Garvey did not, and never grasped, about nationalist movements and their concomitant economic platforms. Sun Yat Sen understood that the Kuomintang of China could not utilize only capitalistic–free enterprise economic forms in the Chinese revolutionary movement. For Sun Yat Sen, nationalism in China had to be based on three essential principles: (1) Nationalism meant racial eqality with the rest of the world. Nationalism in China required the end of imperialism. (2) Nationalism in China meant socialism but not Western forms of socialism as propagated in the ideas of European Marxists. It meant that Chinese economic theorists had to create economic forms that would apply to Chinese problems of poverty in the cities and the countryside. (3) Nationalism in China meant new forms of democratic political rights applicable to the Chinese situation.

As a bourgeois nationalist of the Sun Yat Sen era, Garvey's nationalism was, by comparison, handicapped by numerous theoretical and conceptual flaws. Thus it was doomed to failure in the United States not only because its West Indian motivation was too pro-British for American race realities, but also because it did not meet the demands of twentieth-century developments. But the chief flaw of Garveyism was its capitalistic economies. The American Black bourgeoisie had made its initial bid for capitalistic class power—and failed—long before Garvey arrived. Booker T. Washington had established the National Negro Business League in 1900. By the time Garvey arrived with his program, the entire colonial world was passing from anti-imperialism to anticapitalism as a way of economic organization. Yet Garvey's program remained procapitalistic during its 1920s era, and the Garveyites have remained unbendingly, inflexibly procapitalistic ever since. Their nationalist speeches on Harlem streetcorners, in favor of creating Black capitalistic enterprises here and in Africa, have never been changed one iota in any aspect of economic theory.[7]

In 1940, W. E. B. DuBois advanced far enough in economic theory to deal differently with what he called the inner economy of the American Negro community—and here is *the* important phase of his thought that his most vociferous supporters never discuss. DuBois admitted the partial existence and the possible development of the Black economy in America. Certain of DuBois's detractors, such as Abram L. Harris, called the idea of the Black economy a manifestation of self-segregation. But DuBois attempted to deal with this reality in a theoretical way: "There faces the American Negro, therefore, an intricate and subtle problem of combining into one object two difficult sets of facts—his present racial segregation which will persist . . . for many decades, and his attempts by carefully planned and intelligent action to fit himself into the new economic organization which the world faces."[8]

DuBois then outlined a vast program which covered the whole gamut of planned cooperative consumer and producer enterprises that were to be initiated and engineered by Negroes themselves. This economic program was never carried out because of many factors, not the least of which was the advent of World War II. What is important, however, is that DuBois demonstrated, contrary to Stevens' thinking, that there are other economic theories applicable to Harlem besides the accumulation of risk capital. What is really lacking are Negro intellectuals who are economic theorists, or who are social theorists about anything else but racial integration.

W. E. B. DuBois outlived both of his antagonists—Booker T. Washington and Marcus Garvey. Out of this amazing historic, triangular feud came everything of intellectual, spiritual, cultural, and political value to the American Negro. Even today, the views of Washington v. DuBois v. Garvey are still being debated; but no one attempts to systematize the essential ideas of these pioneering leaders, for the Negro generations who came after these men can not hold a candle to their predecessors in intellect. The generation of Negro intellectuals born between the two world wars are, on the whole, an empty and unoriginal group. Their creative pretensions are mere grandstand polemics that conceal the most thorough brainwashing that Western civilization has ever perpetrated on the non-white colonized mentality. For all of DuBois's shifts, changes, and intellectual permutations, he clearly saw what the end product of his life's work amounted to and wrote of his great efforts:

I formulated a thesis of socialism for the American Negro in my *Dusk of Dawn.* The Second World War sent all my formulations a-whirl. . . .

Before this, he said:

We must admit that the majority of the American Negro intelligentsia, together with much of the West Indian and West African leadership, shows symptoms of following in the footsteps of western acquisitive society, with its exploitation of labor, monopoly of land and its resources, and with private profit for the smart and unscrupulous in a world of poverty, disease, and ignorance, as the natural end of human culture. I have long noted and fought this all too evident tendency, and built my faith in its ultimate change on an inner Negro cultural ideal. I thought this ideal would be built on ancient African communism, supported and developed by memory of slavery and experience of caste, which would drive the Negro group into a spiritual unity precluding the development of economic classes and inner class struggle. This was once possible, but it is now improbable. . . . The very loosening of outer racial discriminatory pressures has not, as I had once believed, left Negroes free to become a group cemented into a new cultural unity, capable of absorbing a socialism, tolerance and democracy, and helping to lead America into a new heaven and new earth. But rather, partial emancipation is freeing some of them to ape the worst of American and Anglo–Saxon chauvinism, luxury, showing-off, and "social climbing." . . . I have discovered that a large and powerful portion of the educated and well-to-do Negroes are refusing to forge forward in social leadership of anyone, even their own people, but are eager to fight social medicine for sick whites and sicker Negroes; are opposing trade unionism not only for white labor but for the far more helpless Black worker; are willing to get "rich quick" not simply by shady business enterprise, but even by organized gambling and the "dope" racket.[9]

When DuBois wrote these words in 1952, however, he had finally linked up with the Communist leftwing, even though many of the young, postwar generation in Harlem were leaving the Communist left in utter disillusionment. DuBois said at that time:

Without the help of the trade unionists, white and black, without the progressives and radicals, without Socialists and Communists and lovers of peace all over the world, my voice would now be stilled forever.[10]

It must be clearly understood here that, whatever were DuBois's motivations for his belated joining of the Communist Party, his status in the party was, among other things, not that of a Negro rank-and-filer. There is a great distinction to be considered here. Regrettably, the winning over of W. E. B. DuBois was a grand feather-in-the-caps of the incompetent Communist Party leadership. Yet as an individual, DuBois's intellectual reputation stands above and beyond the influences of Marxist Communism—a philosophy which added nothing to his historical stature—but abused and disoriented the thinking of countless other Negroes whose potential for positive achievements in society were negated by the intrusion of Communist machinations.

It is against the background of all this that one must judge the economic philosophy of a Hope Stevens. His unqualified procapitalism is typical of most Negro integrationist thinking, once one cuts through their civil rights verbiage to the core of their social philosophy. When the integrationists go left, they thoughtlessly swallow the European economic theories of Marxist–Communism whole, and secondhand, without the least qualification. Then when they abandon the left, they revert to their essential integrationism, and just as thoughtlessly reclaim pragmatic capitalism. And in both these guises they claim to speak for the downtrodden Negro masses—for whom Marxist Communism never meant a positive thing of any duration, and for whom American capitalism never fulfilled its promise of democratic abundance. As P. J. D. Wiles points out in a rather important book on modern economic thought:

The social sciences are full of unspoken, because unperceived, premises. . . .

This book is informed by the belief that there is no such thing as the logic of institutions: that an economic model will function in the way it does, and have the political effects it has, partly for internal, purely economic reasons inaccessible to the sociologist or historian. It is claimed, therefore, that a new institutionalism is possible, neither purely descriptive nor purely bogus like the old, so justly discredited among the economists, and independent up to a certain point of other disciplines, yet drawing upon them and flowing back into them, and in its own right vigorous and respectable. . . .

It is in countries of any type which show no capacity for institutional change that there are revolutions.[11]

What America needs at this perilous juncture in its history are new economic institutional forms, lest its unsolved racial problems explode on a grander scale than heretofore and rend the society into a disorganized chaos. However, the initial ideas on the nature, content and forms of these new institutions must emanate from the minds of an advanced type of Negro intelligentsia, or they will not emerge.

# Notes

1. Paul B. Zuber, "The Economic Plight of the Northern Negro," *Freedomways*, Summer 1962, pp. 245–252.

2. W. E. B. DuBois, *Dusk of Dawn*, New York: Harcourt, Brace and Co., 1940, p. 97.

3. *Ibid.*

4. Zuber, *op. cit.*, p. 251.

5. Amy Jacques-Garveys, *Garvey and Garveyism*. (Published by the author, 1963), p. 185.

6. DuBois, *op. cit.*, p. 278.

7. See Abram L. Harris, *The Negro As Capitalist* (Philadelphia: The American Academy of Political and Social Science, 1936).

8. DuBois, *op. cit.*, p. 199.

9. W. E. B. DuBois, "In Battle for Peace," *Masses and Mainstream*, 1952, pp. 154–155.

10. *Ibid.*, p. 155.

11. P. J. D. Wiles, *The Political Economy of Communism* (Cambridge: Harvard University Press, 1962), pp. 1, 18.

# PART II

*Black Capitalism:
Will (or Should)
It Work?*

# Introduction

The phrase "Black capitalism" should need little or no introduction to anyone who followed the general news of the late 1960s. Its rise in popularity as a cure-all of problems that have faced this country since its founding has been meteoric. The amount of rhetoric and controversy if not the resources being allocated to it merit the serious consideration of Black capitalism as a viable model for Black economic development.

*Harvard Business Review*, recognizing the significance of the problem, published a series of articles that provide a basis for a debate over the viability of Black capitalism. Robert McKersie makes the claim that despite the efforts of major corporations to hire and train unemployed Blacks, they will remain out of the mainstream of economic life until some meaningful degree of ownership is attained. He looks at the status of Black ownership and its causes and suggests what steps should be taken in correcting the situation. The second selection by Frederick Sturdivant critiques the Community Self-Determination Bill introduced in the Senate in 1968 and designed to foster community ownership and control of productive economic resources. Sturdivant suggests that the bill would increase the isolation that characterizes the ghetto economy and that economic development would be greatly retarded.

Richard F. America departs from the usually accepted parameters of American business practices. He advocates government sponsorship of transfers of major U.S. corporations to Black ownership and operation if the achievement of collective economic and commercial parity is the goal. Louis Allen returns the *Review* to its expected leanings by asserting that "the need is to adopt the old-fashioned, no-nonsense approach that has always been used by successful capitalists" to the ghettos.

The commentary of Blacks regarding "Black capitalism" has been a blend of cautious optimism and outright rejection. The author of a position paper originally prepared for the Black Economic Development Conference in 1969 asserts that any "color" of capitalism will lead to an exploitative situation similar to the one in which Blacks now find themselves. If this is indeed the case, as Robert Wright argues in the selection following Boggs, Black capitalism must be rejected in favor of some form of ownership that benefits masses of Black folk, and not just a few. An article in which Andrew Brimmer supports his contention that full participation in an integrated economy is the solution for Black folk with an appraisal of the prospects of Black business ownership follows. A most interesting critique of Brimmer's position by Charles Tate concludes Part II. These two pieces are important to note for they again reiterate variations on the integrationist–separatist theme in this section. Black powerlessness, its causes, and its cures are the major issues under discussion. Tate strongly claims that Brimmer's analysis places the blame on the "victims" and not the victimizers. Brimmer thus renders himself unable to grasp the significance of control of the ghetto as, in Tate's words, "a crucial determinant of the success of the Black economic development strategy."

# 6 ]] Vitalize Black Enterprise*

*Robert McKersie*

In the outpour of current discussion of the problems of our cities, little mention has been made of the importance of Negro entrepreneurship. The voluminous Kerner Commission report on the 1967 riots, for instance, devoted only three paragraphs to the subject, and the gist of its recommendations was merely to strengthen existing programs.

In the public and private programs recently launched to solve our racial predicament, the stress has been on housing, education, and, particularly, jobs. The objective of putting the so-called hard-core unemployed to work is certainly essential. But it is a question whether providing jobs for everyone in the ghettos will eliminate poverty or even end urban disorder as long as ghetto dwellers still feel helpless to control their own economic destiny and that of their communities.

It is difficult—no, impossible—for whites to appreciate fully the hopelessness and helplessness of Blacks in their awareness that everything they have or want for themselves is granted at the pleasure of "whitey" or handed out, at the expense of their self-esteem, by a faceless government representative.

The importance of business ownership and management in helping a minority group to achieve pride and influence cannot be overstated. Consider this description of the modest but personally significant achievements, decades ago, of members of two minority groups which eventually joined the mainstream of this country:

The small shopkeepers and manufacturers are important to a group for more than the greater income they bring in. Very often, as a matter of fact, the Italian or Jewish shopkeeper made less than the skilled worker. But, as against the worker, each businessman had the possibility, slim though it was, of achieving influence and perhaps wealth. The small businessman generally has access to that special world of credit which may give him for a while greater resources than a job. He learns about credit and finance and develops skills that are of value in a complex economy. He learns too about the world of local politics, and although he is generally its victim, he may also learn how to influence it, for mean and unimportant ends, perhaps, but this knowledge may be valuable to an entire community.[1]

White businessmen control the commerce of the Black ghetto. Though white businessmen may be providing satisfactory services in the ghetto

From Robert B. McKersie, *Harvard Business Review* (September–October 1968): 88–99. © 1968 by the President and Fellows of Harvard College; all rights reserved.

* This article reflects the cooperation and sharing of experiences by scores of businessmen, students, agency officials, and civil rights leaders. While I cannot mention them all by name, I would like to express my appreciation to them as a group and to Lawrence M. Horwitz specifically, who served as a research assistant during the field work period and is currently associated with the Cambridge Research Institute.

(the charges of high prices and poor quality notwithstanding), Negroes bitterly resent what they perceive as the continuation of the "plantation system." A Black resident of Newark made that point quite poignantly during the riots there in 1967:

One woman, guarding a family business along Springfield Avenue with a "soul brother" sign, told a stranger who had been chased from the street by police shotgun fire that she defended the looters of white stores. "These stores have been robbing these people for years and Negro businessmen can hardly beg, borrow, or steal their way to renting a place . . ." she said.[2]

This article will examine the condition of Black entrepreneurship, describe what is being done to improve it, and show how white business and white businessmen can help to alleviate this largely ignored, but very serious, problem in our large cities.

## State of Black Business

The Negro finds himself more underrepresented in business activity than in any other occupational category. Whereas more than 11 percent of the white population work as "managers, officials, and proprietors," the comparable figure for nonwhites is less than 3 percent. Entrance into white-collar positions has been increasing faster for Negroes than it has for whites, but this is not so in business management. If anything, Negroes appear to be losing ground there as a result, according to one observer, of "the attrition of Negro-owned firms that once served the now-disappearing segregated markets."[3]

Although the census category is "nonwhite" Negroes constitute more than 90 percent of that group. Economic development is, of course, a critical problem for other minority groups—Mexican–Americans, American Indians, and for that matter, certain elements in the white population, such as the residents of Appalachia. Because of the extent and immediacy of the urban Black problem, I am focusing my discussion on it, but much of my diagnosis and prescription should be applicable to minority groups generally.

For instance, the segregated market has been disappearing in insurance, where some sizable Black companies have prospered. But the Black companies' share of the Negro market is declining in the face of aggressive selling by large white companies. Since most Black-operated businesses are limited to serving the needs of the segregated communities—carry-out stores, barber shops, and "mom and pop" type grocery stores—they are small and likely to remain so. Manufacturers and distributors that might try to branch out from the ghetto markets are few.

The number of Negro businesses is about 45,000, out of a total of some 5 million businesses in the country. In Philadelphia less than 10 percent of the companies are Negro owned; and, even in an almost entirely Black area like Harlem, the figure is not above 20 percent. In the important commercial activity of food retailing, for example, no more than 3 percent of the Negro food bill is spent in Black grocery stores.[4]

## CONTRIBUTING FACTORS

Some of the causes of the low state of Black entrepreneurship can be laid to the problems of small business generally; others result from conditions of life in the ghetto.

Most Negroes hold business in low esteem. Abraham S. Venable, a Department of Commerce official, described their attitude this way:

More often than not, many Negro businessmen are a symbol of frustration and hopelessness rather than an example of achievement, success, and leadership. As a result, "business" per se is not a polite word in the Negro community, and Negro parents as a rule tend to discourage their children from pursuing business careers either as employees or as entrepreneurs.[5]

Lack of capital and necessary contacts with financing institutions and customers also have contributed to the situation. A type of vicious circle operates to keep Blacks out of the business system. A Negro construction company that has built only garages may want to bid on a government contract or handle a major renovation project in the ghetto. But it lacks the necessary capital, it cannot secure adequate bonding, and it cannot convince the customer that it has the capacity to perform the job. (Negro-owned banks, incidentally, suffer from lower profitability than the rest of the industry—though deposits have grown faster—reflecting the greater costs of making smaller loans and dealing with higher risk situations in the inner cities.)

A further complication is that *all* small business is undergoing challenge and change, especially in the city. As a result of urban renewal, concentration of retailing into shopping centers, and dispersal of industry to the urban perimeter, small-business opportunities in the city are diminishing regardless of whether the would-be entrepreneurs are white or Black.

The most significant factor in the underrepresentation of Negroes in business is their lack of managerial skills and attitudes. Negroes as a race have been little exposed to business operations and lack the technical experience and entrepreneurial values that are necessary for succeeding in business. Indeed, the historical position of the Negro in the South— the forefather of today's ghetto dweller—has prevented cultivation of these values:

The plantation system offered the Negro no experience with money, no incentive to save, no conception of time or progress—none of the basic experiences to prepare him for the urban money economy. Instead, it indoctrinated him to believe in his own inferiority, to be resigned, while it held him in a folk culture dominated by a spiritual, other-worldly, escapist outlook.[6]

## Responses to the Problem

While the efforts to stimulate and develop Negro business have not been overly extensive or effective, enough programs are in operation to permit some enumeration and evaluation.

ROLE OF NEGRO GROUPS

Apparently because of their growing realization that self-determination in business is as important as self-determination in the political arena, if they are to enter the mainstream of U.S. economic life, Negroes have increasingly begun organizing to promote Black enterprise. These fledgling groups have taken their place at the side of organizations like the Urban League and Operation Breadbasket, which have been active in this endeavor for several years.

. . . Too often in the past, successful Negro businessmen have preferred to adopt white middle-class coloration, figuratively speaking, and have remained aloof from the problems of the struggling Negro in the ghetto. Clearly, they must play a substantially larger role in the development of their communities, and they are becoming more active. In several cities they have formed organizations to pool their capital, provide counseling services, and act as liaison between the white communities and the ghettos.

OPERATION BREADBASKET

Since none of these efforts can be called typical and since most of them are still in their infancy, it is difficult to gauge their prospects for real achievement. Let us examine one organization that has a record and therefore may produce some clues.

The Southern Christian Leadership Conference, formerly headed by the late Dr. Martin Luther King, Jr., has devoted considerable energy to strengthening Black business and has recently inaugurated a nationwide program under the title of Operation Breadbasket. This organization's approach is mutual assistance with a militant twist; it attempts to inspire, persuade, or pressure the "establishment" into facilitating Black economic development. Whites are not excluded from the movement, but they are given no authority to make decisions and are permitted to play a role only if they fully subscribe to the principle of Black control.

The program has had its greatest success in Chicago, where at least a dozen large companies, mostly in the retailing field, have signed covenants with Breadbasket. The companies agreed to provide more shelfspace for goods produced by Negro manufacturers and to use the services of Negro-owned companies in such businesses as garbage removal, extermination, banking, and construction.

Breadbasket has accomplished some substantial gains. One company, Argia B's Food Products, has grown from virtually zero sales to a volume in six figures. Before it received help from Breadbasket, this company sold its only product, barbecue sauce, to a very limited market made up of small restaurants and independent stores in the ghetto. Now, however, it has 10 percent to 15 percent penetration of the entire Chicago market. Two Negro banks, which several years ago together counted assets of no more than $5 million to $6 million, have quadrupled that amount thanks to business Breadbasket brought in. Approximately 3,500 blacks have been hired by the companies that have agreements with the organization.

Have these gains been large in terms of the problem? The answer is *no*; Operation Breadbasket's achievements have hardly scratched the surface of Black unemployment and poverty in Chicago. The real significance of what Breadbasket has been doing is not in the economic statistics but in the pride and the feeling of community which the program has instilled in its adherents. Breadbasket must also be viewed as a staging area, rather than as a permanent state. Jesse Jackson, national director of Breadbasket, has expressed its ultimate aims:

We have to recognize that either we will live constrained and racially congested in a neighborhood or some of us will rise and participate in a brotherhood where men will be redefined and subsequently rerespected. And where the Steward Bleaches and the Bolles Waxes and the Joe Louis Milks will be on everybody's counter. Where we can own franchises and we can participate. And where you will not be able to determine the color of a man's skin by his address.[7]

## ROLE OF THE FEDERAL GOVERNMENT

In passing the War on Poverty legislation in 1964, Congress endorsed a greatly expanded program of assistance to small businessmen. Title IV provided for economic opportunity loans and established a number of SBDCs to process loan applications and render assistance to the recipients. Under the revised War on Poverty legislation, administrative control for the loan program was placed in the SBA, whose rate of disbursement in fiscal 1968 for this activity (about $3 million per month) compares favorably with the average distribution when the Office of Economic Opportunity had control over it (about $1.1 million a month). By comparison, the SBA distributes approximately $300 million per year under its other loan programs.

The shift of the Economic Opportunity Loans (EOL) program to the SBA meant that more attention would be paid to making sound investments and less attention to supporting persons considered to be high risks. Indeed, under the first phase of the EOL program, when it was under the aegis of the Office of Economic Opportunity, the delinquency and default experience was quite high by any standard; after the first two years of operation these rates in many cities were in the vicinity of 20 percent. Some experts estimated that the eventual liquidation level would reach at least 40 percent.

. . . The significance of the government program cannot be measured in statistics or individual case histories; it lies in the broader question of whether pumping federal funds into new business ventures in the cities represents a sound investment in business education and in overcoming attitudes of alienation. Unfortunately, such effects are difficult, if not impossible, to measure; and Congress, in its deliberations over the extension of the War on Poverty, adopted a banker's outlook, with the resulting revamping of the program.

Congress was also influenced by the conviction that had developed in certain interested federal agencies that a loan program for black business was not necessarily a direct route to creating substantially more urban employment. Rather, agency officials felt that the thrust of the program should be at developing more *viable* businesses which over the long run could create more employment and more income for the entrepreneurs and their communities. In an interview after the SBA had assumed responsibility for the program, an official of that agency expressed the policy this way:

In our evaluation of the economic opportunity loan program we attempt to make two estimates: the number of people who have been established at a decent income level—that is, how many marginal businesses have been converted into viable operations; and what kind of impact the loan program has had on the environment within the community—in other words, has the racial pattern of business been changed and have the expectations of the residents been altered in positive directions?

From our viewpoint in the SBA we have to evaluate the benefit of this loan program (aimed at impoverished people) against other programs that attempt to help small business generally, even though the individuals may not be operating businesses in or near depressed areas.

Congress and the administrative agencies may well have been correct in taking a more conservative view of financing Negro business, but it has resulted in a deemphasis on cultivation of business opportunities in the ghetto and the grooming of talent to exploit those opportunities. It was perhaps inevitable that these activities would take a back seat to federal efforts encouraging big business to hire the hard-core unemployed and influencing corporations to locate plants in the ghettos.

ROLE OF WHITE BUSINESS

The emphasis on jobs no doubt has much to do with the fact that large companies have shown little initiative so far, individually or jointly, in stimulating black enterprise. But as more business leaders come to realize that curtailing unemployment does not answer the Negro's need for self-determination, they will increasingly look for other ways. In adopting programs to further Negro business, they will likely favor corporate combinations. Such a program was announced last spring in Boston and another is in operation in Rochester, New York, to name two cities. (I shall discuss the Rochester venture in more detail later.)

As for individual company action, the performance record is difficult to assess, since much of the activity is carried on quietly. But the problems a company encounters when it ventures into this frontier can be so frustrating that relatively few have attempted it. I shall dwell on them later also.

Many corporations that shy from formal and overt action have encouraged their supervisory level employees to volunteer to advise black entrepreneurs. And in many cities white entrepreneurs have done the same. In New York City the Interracial Council for Business Opportunities has mobilized the talents of several hundred businessmen to provide counseling. The Chicago Economic Development Corporation has similarly tapped the services of executives of "establishment" corporations.

Corporate assistance programs, and particularly the more formal ones, are not without their critics. Consider a more or less typical case:

A large retail chain in Chicago made its staff services available to several small Negro-owned food products manufacturers, with the idea of providing an outlet for their goods. The quality of the products was uneven, and they were poorly packaged. The chain helped the manufacturers solve these problems, and now some of the products are appearing on the supermarket shelves. Moreover, when the corporation was planning to build a store on the South Side of Chicago, it awarded the construction contract to a black-owned firm. But first it provided the firm with engineering assistance and worked out bonding arrangements with several financial institutions.

It has been argued that such efforts represent discrimination against white companies, since retail chains do not usually extend this kind of assistance to suppliers. The justification for it is twofold: (1) the problem is severe and additional energies must be brought to bear on it by either the government or the business community, and it might as well be the latter; and (2) no *individual* suppliers have been discriminated against. So this form of "affirmative action" is acceptable as a short-run effort toward the long-run goal of increasing business opportunities for minority groups in this country.

Critics have also claimed that not much can be done to close the Negro entrepreneurship gap other than allowing the natural processes of education and competition to improve the situation. The factors that caused the underrepresentation of Negroes in business cannot be eliminated by any crash programs, they say, pointing to the folly of the government's program of putting money in the hands of inexperienced persons and expecting them to succeed. If the cultural and motivational problems are so severe, then outside groups, including the government, cannot instill in Blacks the drive and enterprising spirit that are necessary in establishing successful ventures. So the argument goes.

While this point of view has merit (and was responsible for the federal government's shift in emphasis), it settles for easy and riskless attacks on the problem and fails to reckon with the high cost of relying on a laissez-faire approach; urban disaster, perhaps. While the cost of expending great effort will be high, it is not necessarily relevant to perform a cost–benefit analysis on this problem, just as it is not appropriate to subject programs for preventing future military conflicts to cost–benefit calculations. If the efforts now under way or being planned to alleviate conditions in our large cities succeed in decreasing the chances of disaster by some small but significant amount, they will have been worth the doing.

## Strategies for Development

Vitalization of Black enterprise could help tip the balance in favor of stability and economic progress in the ghettos. The strategies of economic development should encompass three elements: the opening of new business opportunities, the infusion of sufficient capital, and the application of managerial know-how.

### OPENING NEW OPPORTUNITIES

As I indicated earlier, the underdevelopment of Negro-operated business is in part due to its narrow spectrum—Blacks selling only to Blacks. Not enough Black entrepreneurs, for instance, are manufacturers or marketers of hard goods which would afford them the potential for winning white customers. There do exist some promising programs, however, for widening the spectrum.

. . . But only a beginning has been made. Since the Negroes themselves usually lack the experience and resources to identify and exploit market opportunities, help must come from elsewhere. White business, having control of who its distributors, dealers, and suppliers are, is in the best position to provide that help.

### INFUSION OF CAPITAL

Negro businessmen frequently complain about their inability to obtain financing. And with some reason; in the view of financial institutions, the risk associated with lending to a small business is compounded by the greater risk associated with the potential borrower's Black skin.

Extending credit to Negro entrepreneurs, however, does not necessarily result in a high rate of delinquencies and defaults—if the lender exercises great care. In its loan program the First Pennsylvania Banking & Trust Company has minimized the risk by thorough investigation and screening and, once a loan is granted, close surveillance. Though it admittedly is accepting loan applications in the Negro community that would be rejected if they came from other parts of Philadelphia, the bank reports that the default rate has been less than 1 percent.[8]

Of course, such extra effort costs the banks money. One big-city institution even proposed to several of its large corporate depositors that they accept one percentage point less in interest in order to underwrite the administrative and reserve requirements of its loan program for Negro business.

Most financial institutions, however, would not touch Negro business with the proverbial ten-foot pole because of the gulf between their standards and the reality of the Negro community. The SBA has had little success in persuading banks to participate in the EOL program, whereas in its regular loan activities it has been able to achieve bank participation of about 20 percent. It is not surprising that the insurance companies that have pledged to President Johnson a billion dollar program for investment in the cities are having some difficulty in locating suitable candidates. They have even found themselves competing with one another for the few loan "plums."

Similarly, pledges of funds to banks promoting Negro economic development—as Southern California Edison Company is doing with Los Angeles' Black-operated Bank of Finance and New York City is doing with the Freedom National Bank in Harlem—will accomplish little unless the depositors are willing to accept some losses, in the form of either lower interest rates or allocation of some of the money to special reserves.

The use of equity capital shows some promise of helping Black businessmen over their financial difficulties without the constant burden of meeting interest or repayment schedules. In this connection, the formation of SBICs in several large northern cities is significant. Two of these, Accord in Detroit and Businessmen's Development Corporation in Philadelphia, sold stock at low prices for reinvestment in fledgling businesses. They also incorporate a vital element, the need for self-determination.

APPLYING KNOW-HOW

Development of managerial competence is the most critical need of Black enterprise, and that is where U.S. business can be most helpful.

Initially, the entrepreneur usually needs assistance most in bookkeeping and establishing the basic financial controls. Once his enterprise appears to be viable, he will need advice on more specialized concerns, such as gauging his market and tapping sources of capital.

The counselor's role often shifts during this time from that of a professional giving technical help to that of a confidant providing support on a wide range of topics. The most successful relationships have involved a close association between the "insider" and the "outsider." Of course, the danger exists that the Negro may become too dependent on the counselor. For this reason, management assistance programs give priority to creating the capacity within the client to identify and solve his own problems.

. . . Ignorance and suspicion on both sides can make the first few sessions between counselor and client tense and very disappointing. They may spar in an Alphonse and Gaston routine, with the counselor asking the client to "show me your wounds," and the client responding with "heal me." If the counselor is on assignment from his company, he may have difficulty convincing the Black of his sincerity in wanting to help—particularly if the counselor intimates that he hopes for recognition from his company. If the counselor is a high-level corporate executive or an entrepreneur himself, the Black may find it hard to believe that someone would volunteer his services purely for the love of helping. Proof that the advice improves the efficiency of the business or brings in more customers is the best way to put the relationship on a basis of mutual trust.

The presence of some kind of organization in the Black community that brings counselor and client together can smooth the path immeasurably. Operation Breadbasket, the Harlem Commonwealth Council, and the National Business League are examples. Through groups like these, counselor meets client not merely because white businessmen want to help but also because Black businessmen seek assistance. The atmosphere of cooperation that such an organization of Negro businessmen promotes makes them appreciate the fact that they are all weak and struggling, and the acceptance of aid together from "successful" white managers does not shame them.

. . . A word should be said here about the function of schools of business. Their location in urban areas and influence with the business community put them in a position to provide a meeting ground for corporate talent and would-be entrepreneurs. Training programs and workshops for Black businessmen have been set up by some leading business schools, such as Columbia, Stanford, Chicago, and Harvard—formally and informally— with the instruction and counseling provided by faculty members and students. On their part, corporations can use their influence to spur laggard business schools into action.

OTHER FORMS OF ASSISTANCE

Counseling, of course, is only one avenue of direct aid that corporate enterprise can extend to Black businessmen. Others I have cited earlier in the article.

Still another is a corporation sponsoring a new business involved in its industry during the shakedown period, then spinning it off. U.S. business so far, however, have not taken up this partnership idea to any extent because of lack of interest or perhaps because they are unwilling to establish competitors, however small. But if the federal government would provide sufficient enticements in the form of tax credits, large companies might become more interested, as they appear to be in government-subsidized, on-the-job training.

A corporation that feels uncomfortable in setting up Black businesses can find other valuable projects. The marketing staff could conduct a market analysis for a community organization, for example, or the company could handle the legal and other work involved in establishing a trade association or a nonprofit development corporation.

## Prescription for Action

The crucial ingredient in all successful efforts to promote Black entrepreneurship is a sound organization on both sides.

Without one on the Negroes' side, assistance bears the stigma of paternalism. Such an organization can provide the setting for feeding back analyses of the companies' progress. In Chicago, for instance, under the auspices of Operation Breadbasket, white and Black businessmen come together and discuss the consultants' reports.

A structure on the corporate side helps the participants over the hurdles of developing a close relationship with their clients. This requires close supervision and auditing. In one city volunteers were assigned to their clients through a sponsoring institution. When the institution checked back several months later, it learned to its chagrin that no consulting was being carried on. Corporations can furnish the impetus for a viable program by assigning executives for short periods of time—say, from three to six months—to nonprofit organizations coordinating assistance.

In the larger cities national groups, such as the Urban Coalition, the Urban League, and the newly formed Negro Industrial Union, are providing the mechanism. Recently, the New York Urban Coalition announced the establishment of three economic development corporations: one to channel managerial and technical assistance to Black businesses, a second to help finance them, and a third to start new ventures. In smaller cities the organizations are more likely to be strictly local in character. But in all cases the brokering structure must have both the respect of the Black community and the support of the business establishment.

### THE RBOC

Because it enjoys such respect and support and also because great care and thought went into its formation, the Rochester Business Opportunities Corporation is one of the most promising organizations for furthering the economic independence of that city's minority groups, which represent about 15 percent of the population.

. . . While it is too early to tell whether RBOC and its offspring will prosper or fail, all the necessary ingredients for success are present:

It is fostering minority-group enterprise not only in the traditional segregated businesses but also in manufacturing and service fields, where the entrepreneurs have a chance to overcome their historical market barriers.

It has broadly based support from the white business community, led by the major banks and corporations which have always supplied leadership in the city.

It has large financial resources, furnishing seed money for bank and government loans.

Because respected minority-group organizations are participating, it bears no taint of white paternalism.

It has an adequate and permanent administrative structure, which provides at the same time a meeting ground for the groups and individuals involved and an auditing mechanism for the new businesses.

Before it grants approval, it makes sure that the venture has a sustaining market that can produce a profit.

It provides technical assistance and consulting help through volunteers who, if necessary, are given time off from their duties by their employers.

It requires the entrepreneurs to contribute their own equity money when they can, and encourages them to offer profit-sharing and stock option plans to their employees, thus promoting self-respect and economic independence.

## Conclusion

A key attribute of any program aimed at increasing the extent and effectiveness of Negro business must be its ability to mobilize resources in the black community. In view of the feelings of Negroes about what they conceive of as white imperialism, outsiders must make sure their influence is not overwhelming. In their involvement they must exercise restraint.

White institutions are rushing into the ghettos to form new businesses for the "benefit" of the Negro. But they are not always welcomed. In New York City several finance companies decided to establish jointly a credit facility in Harlem, only to be told brusquely that ample channels for lending existed in most churches and the program was unnecessary.

In another city recently, during a meeting with spokesmen for several Negro groups, some white bankers suggested a plan to help a white retailer (in the Negro area) transform one of his store facilities into a light manufacturing enterprise capable of employing sixty to seventy workers. The response of a Black militant was: "We don't need any more Cohens in the ghetto."

We have entered a new era in race relations. Old approaches no longer serve the purpose; yet new ones are scornfully repudiated. The white businessman often feels that he is damned if he doesn't, but damned as well if he does. If he ignores the struggling black businessman, he is alleged to be callous, if not racist; whereas if he plunges into the ghetto with offers of assistance, he is advised to return to his carpeted office and to direct his energies toward solving the white problem. So it is not surprising that most white businessmen hesitate to volunteer their services in this charged atmosphere for fear of perpetuating the old colonial syndrome. Similarly, Negro businessmen, out of pride and determination to succeed on their own, may hesitate to seek help.

This situation of no contact sadly fails to exploit the great opportunity that exists. In city after city what is most needed for Negro economic development is a catalyst to put the pieces together—the capital is available, the markets are waiting to be tapped, and the individuals with entrepreneurial potential are on hand. Obviously, U.S. corporate enterprise possesses the managerial capability to be that catalyst.

While in these matters the white businessman is an expert, in race relations he is typically an amateur. When he decides to make his expertise available to the ghettos, the white businessman must be ready to learn and to adopt a new role. This role could be a strictly subordinate one. For example, a group of businessmen in a large northern city have pledged $1 million to stimulate Negro entrepreneurship, but strictly on a "no strings attached" basis; and they will offer assistance only if asked.

A white executive initially may be uncomfortable, if not angered, when in his sincere desire to help he is asked to defer to the wishes of inexperienced Black businessmen or to the policies of militant civil rights organizations. Nevertheless, some whites have been able to overcome their misgivings and develop a partnership of equals. Consider this scene:

It is the weekly gathering of Operation Breadbasket, and some 300 Negroes are assembled for the usual business meeting, complete with sermon and jazz session. A vice president of a large Chicago retail chain is on hand to sign an agreement with several entrepreneurs, whose business is scavenging, for the collection of garbage at several of his company's stores located in the ghetto. In some respects the incident is comical. But it also attests to a new dimension that is increasingly present in relationships between Blacks and whites.

## Notes

1. Nathan Glazer and Daniel P. Moynihan, *Beyond the Melting Pot* (Cambridge: M.I.T. Press 1963), pp. 30–31.

2. *The New York Times*, July 15, 1967.

3. Dan Cordtz, "The Negro Middle Class Is Right in the Middle," *Fortune*, November 1966, p. 174.

4. Eugene Foley, "The Negro Businessman: In Search of a Tradition," in *The Negro American*, eds. Talcott Parsons and Kenneth B. Clark (Boston: Beacon Press, 1965), p. 559.

5. "Mobilizing Dormant Resources: Negro Entrepreneurs," *The MBA*, May 1967, p. 28.

6. Jeanne R. Lowe, *Cities in a Race with Time* (New York: Random House, 1967), p. 283.

7. Address delivered at the first annual business seminar of Operation Breadbasket, Chicago, March 1, 1967.

8. See "Where Negro Business Gets Credit," *Business Week*, June 8, 1968, p. 98.

# 7 ]] The Limits of Black Capitalism

*Frederick D. Sturdivant*

Unlike Black power, the concept of Black capitalism has received widespread support from business and political leaders since it gained general currency recently.

Many of the larger corporations with operations in northern cities have undertaken or joined programs to further entrepreneurship in the ghettos.[1] In the 1968 political campaign, the presidential candidates of both major parties applauded, with equal fervor, the idea of giving Negro communities "a piece of the action."

One of the most significant outgrowths of this sudden interest in Black capitalism is the Community Self-Determination Bill, which was introduced in the U.S. Senate last July. Its sponsors ranged from Jacob Javits to John Tower, with twenty-five other Senators scattered between these two extremes on the ideological continuum. Its chances for passage on being reintroduced during the ninety-first Congress appear excellent. Such broad support for the bill is surprising, since it represents a radical change in public policy and, if enacted, would have a profound effect on the welfare of our northern cities that have heavy minority-group populations.

The objective of Senate Bill 3876 is to facilitate the creation of what amounts to community-owned and community-directed conglomerate corporations that would control the economic and social development of the areas where they exist. Drafted by representatives of the Congress of Racial Equality (CORE), together with associates of the Harvard Institute of Politics, the bill has these main features:

A federally chartered community development corporation (CDC) could be created by the residents of any disadvantaged community where at least 10 percent of them have agreed to buy at least one share of $5 par value stock. At least 500 residents sixteen years of age or older must pay in a total of at least $5,000 before issuance of the charter.

A local election of stockholders determines the makeup of the board of directors and officers of the corporation.

The CDC would acquire, create, and manage all businesses in its area; other companies entering the area could operate there only under "turnkey" contracts. Under agreement with the CDC an "outside" company would be permitted to develop an enterprise, with the proviso that it would be sold to the CDC as soon as it was capable of operating on its own. (The "outsider" would be given a tax advantage in the sale.)

From Frederick D. Sturdivant, *Harvard Business Review* (January–February 1969): 122–128. © 1969 by the President and Fellows of Harvard College; all rights reserved.

The capital for the acquisition of turnkey facilities and other corporate needs would be made available through a series of community development banks. These banks, supervised by the comptroller of the currency, would fund themselves by selling debentures guaranteed by the federal government.

The CDC and its subsidiaries would receive tax incentives determined by a formula based on an index of area unemployment and median income compared with the national average.

A portion of the CDC's profits would be used to help finance housing, education, recreation, and health services in the community.

Few would question the desirability of finding avenues toward greater participation by disadvantaged minorities in our society. The merits of the CDC concept in furthering that goal are many. On balance, however, the community self-determination program represents a dangerous and short-sighted approach to the solution of the domestic crisis.

In my view, the program would virtually force the community development corporations to perpetuate the inefficient and fragmented retail structures of the slum areas. In addition, it would not stimulate the involvement in entrepreneurial efforts so badly needed in minority communities. Also, the plan would block many avenues of escape from the ghetto that are beginning to develop.

Most important, the bill ignores the great challenge that confronts this nation, which is to find ways to surmount the racial barriers erected by the dominant society and create a truly pluralistic democracy. Any legislation that ignores this objective and enforces a concept of "separate but equal" economic development moves the nation toward apartheid. It would further the aims of the Black power advocates, who, the Kerner Commission Report warned, "have retreated from a direct confrontation with American society on the issue of integration and, by preaching separatism, unconsciously function as an accommodation to white racism."[2]

If *economic integration* involving communitywide participation is to be viewed as a step toward the goal of equal rights and opportunities for all citizens of this nation, then this approach to Black capitalism is not the answer. In this article I shall use this dangerous and regressive legislative measure as a springboard for a discussion, with examples, of what I think is a better answer to the problem of ghetto economic development.

## Dangers in the Bill

The chief dangers in the community development corporations, as the bill would establish them, are their potential effects on ghetto retailing and manufacturing enterprises, on their owners' independence and freedom of action, and on the opportunities for employment and advancement in "white" businesses.

### BARRIERS TO GROWTH

Community development corporations would perpetuate the inefficient, fragmented commercial and industrial structure of slum areas. Most low-income urban areas are characterized by the virtual absence of a manufacturing base and by a retail community made up largely of small, independent stores.

While the CDC plan might lead to the creation of a small manufacturing base, the bill offers little promise for progress in the retail sector. The articles of incorporation restrict the activities of a CDC to the boundaries of its community, thus greatly lessening the possibility of developing chain organizations capable of reaping the advantages of quantity purchasing, centralized warehousing, management specialization, multiple-unit advertising, and other efficiencies of this form of organization. (Even branches of a community development bank would be restricted to the defined area of its affiliated CDC.)

Since the population of a CDC area may not exceed 300,000, the opportunities for development of chains are quite limited. Not only would the development of efficient merchandising by a CDC itself be impeded, but the entry of "outside" companies with these efficiencies would be discouraged—despite the attractive capital gains tax forgiveness available to them when they sell their ghetto operations to a CDC. The only way for J. C. Penney Company, for example, to do business in a CDC area would be under a turnkey contract. But since Penney's involvement would be restricted to the period required to establish the business and put it on a sound basis, the company would have no prospects for long-range growth in that market.

### Tax Advantages

In addition, community development corporations and their subsidiaries would enjoy important tax advantages over outsiders. While both a "normal" tax and a surtax would be imposed on CDC operations, the rates for both would be reduced by application of the so-called development index. The components of the development index for a community would be:

The ratio of the percentage of national unemployment, or that within the community's metropolitan area (whichever is lower), to the percentage of the labor force unemployed in the community area.

The ratio of the median family income in the community area to the median nationally, or in the community's metropolitan area, whichever is greater.

The development index, expressed as a whole number, would be the lesser of these two ratios.

Those companies operating in areas with the highest index would be taxed at a maximum of 22 percent of taxable income, while those companies with the lowest index would be assessed nothing on the first $50,000 of taxable income. The surtax would equal 26 percent of the amount by which the taxable income exceeded the surtax exemption, which also would be based on the development index. The lowest exemption would be $25,000, while the maximum would equal $200,000.

By restricting the geographical scope of CDC subsidiaries' operations and by erecting tax barriers against outside competitors, the Community Self-Determination Bill promises to perpetuate the inefficient and fragmented business structures in ghetto areas.

### LOSS OF FREEDOM

Enterpreneurs and would-be entrepreneurs in the ghettos, Black or white, would be penalized if they refused to join the CDC and would forfeit their independence if they did join.

The operator of a machine shop or the owner of a men's clothing store would not be eligible for the liberal tax advantages unless he sold a majority interest in his business to the local CDC. Moreover, if he sought funds from the local community development bank, consideration of the loan application would be conditional on his willingness to sign a contract agreeing not to dispose of his interest in his business without first offering it to the CDC.

The bill also would amend the Economic Opportunity Act of 1964 so that, under its provisions, no loan could be made to any small business located in an area served by a community development bank unless it had unsuccessfully applied for a loan from that bank. In effect, therefore, if the machine shop operator should be unwilling to sign the agreement calling for offering his business interest to the CDC in the event he should decide to sell, he could not have his loan application considered and thus would also cut himself off from OEO funds.

If an entrepreneur wanted to sell his business, he might have trouble finding a buyer, as long as the tax incentives were limited to CDC subsidiaries. The bill makes no provision for determining an equitable purchase price in such a situation. The independent businessman faces the prospect of competing in a game where all of the rules favor the CDC.

On becoming the operator of a subsidiary of the local community development corporation, the entrepreneur would face more threats to his independence and freedom of action. The bill would require that each CDC board of directors elect a business management board made up of nine residents of the community. One can imagine the frustrations that would be encountered by a once-independent operator who is now forced to answer to a committee of nine persons trying to manage a corporation for the benefit of the community.

Pressure on the independent businessman to affiliate with a CDC and curtailment of his freedom of action would be especially unfortunate at this time, when encouraging progress is being made in stimulating entrepreneurial activity in Black communities. Such groups as the Interracial

Council for Business Opportunities and the Negro Industrial and Economic Union have given impetus to this movement by offering capital and advice to Black-owned companies. Since the appointment of Howard Samuels as administrator, the Small Business Administration has been trying to speed up the flow of available funds to aspiring Black entrepreneurs. And the Ford Foundation has launched a program to help Negroes establish their own companies and acquire businesses formerly owned by whites.

Clearly, these efforts would be blunted by the passage of legislation granting privileges like tax advantages to community-owned monopolies.

### HAMPERING ADVANCEMENT

An important part of the social revolution of the 1960s has been the increasing efforts of business to recruit Black employees. One important pool of talent in the future could be persons who have gained experience through ownership or management of businesses. Some chain stores operating in ghetto areas, for example, have local residents as managers. This opens the prospect of moving up through the organization's hierarchy.

Few have followed this Horatio Alger path to date, but if the presence of large businesses in these areas is allowed to increase, the opportunities for Blacks should multiply rapidly. By blocking entry of such companies, however, the CDC plan would close this narrow, but potentially important, path away from dead-end jobs.

## Meeting the Problem

There are three alternatives in dealing with the problem of the Black slums of this nation:

1. Try to disperse their population—that is, achieve total integration.
2. "Isolate" the ghettos from the rest of society, with provision of certain resources and encouragement to develop into prosperous, peaceful, and semiautonomous entities.
3. Try to improve the social and economic welfare of ghettos and increase interaction with "outside" communities, with a view to eventual elimination of the conditions of deprivation prevailing in the ghettos.

However much appeal the first alternative may have to Americans' traditional impatience to deal quickly and decisively with a problem, it obviously is impractical. Our remaining racial and social barriers (against which it is difficult, if not impossible, to legislate) preclude such a move. It also would be enormously expensive. And many, if not most, Blacks do not want to integrate in that fashion.

The second alternative is the approach of the Community Self-Determination Bill. Creating separate, estranged communities smacks of apartheid and would, I believe, have little appeal to the majority of Black or white Americans. It is antithetical to our often violated, but central, idea of this nation as a great melting pot. It runs counter to the dream that Dr. Martin Luther King had for the United States. Perhaps the most damning testimony to the bankruptcy of this concept is the fruitless and wasteful reservation system created for the American Indian.

The third alternative holds the only promise for solving this domestic crisis. Some initial steps have been taken to engage the dominant society in assisting ghetto residents in their efforts to improve their environment. This alternative offers both effective action and the reinforcement of community pride. Notwithstanding the claim that has been made that "whitetown" would oppose programs such as the CDC because of whitetown's obsession with efficiency,[3] I believe that efficiency and self-determination are by no means mutually exclusive. Two examples will illustrate the point:

### 1. El Mercado de Los Angeles

Few ghettos in the United States rival the Mexican–American community in East Los Angeles in size or in the extent to which poverty affects the lives of its residents. But an important development in the commercial life of East Los Angeles—created from community spirit and action, combined with outside assistance—has given grounds for hope of improvement in its lot.

Early in 1968, El Mercado de Los Angeles opened. El Mercado ("the marketplace") houses forty small businesses under a single roof. Designed to appeal to the Mexican heritage of the area's residents, it features Spanish architecture, mariachis strolling and playing in the patio, and a wide assortment of Mexican wares.

The idea for El Mercado originated with two brothers, Benjamin and Arturo Chayra, who sought the advice of the Small Business Administration. They were able to obtain partial funding under a section of the Small Business Investment Act of 1958 that provides for loans to local development corporations.

Such a corporation uses the funds, along with money raised within the community, to erect facilities for small businesses that participate in the project. Normally a minimum of 20 percent of the required capital must be raised by the corporation, but in some cases the proportion of funds required from the community may be lower. All the corporation's stockholders must be from the community, and they may not purchase more than $1,000 in stock apiece. Federal loans to El Mercado totaled $1,040,000, while $260,000 was raised in the community.

El Mercado represents an admirable model for the economic and social development of ghettos. The project was community-inspired; it was conceived, planned, and supported locally; and it met a need. Of equal importance, outside involvement was kept in balance; outsiders were used only in a few cases where special resources or training was required.

Because of careful planning of stores and close identification with the local consumers, the marketplace has been very successful. Indeed, although it did not aim to attract shoppers from elsewhere, El Mercado's reputation as an unusual and exciting place to shop has spread beyond East Los Angeles, and it even has become a tourist attraction.

### 2. Progress Plaza

Located in North Philadelphia, Progress Plaza represents a somewhat different approach. The plan for the shopping center was originated by the Reverend Leon Sullivan, a minister well known there for his efforts in behalf of Black self-development, and his administrative assistant, Elmer Young, Jr. First they conducted a study to determine the feasibility of, and desire for, such a venture in the area and to obtain the residents' preferences as to types of stores. On the basis of the study it was decided to move ahead with the project.

The trading area has a population of about 200,000, of which 95 percent are Black. Many of them were very hostile to the existing white-dominated business community, and the idea of a retail center under local direction had great appeal. Less than 2 percent of those with whom the project was discussed, however, expressed a preference for keeping it all Black. In fact, when asked if they wanted outside stores represented in the center, they overwhelmingly favored including units of certain chain stores. Only a relatively small number of militants objected to inviting white businesses to participate in the center.

Progress Plaza has sixteen tenants, including an outlet of a large super-market chain, a bank, a savings and loan office, and a district telephone office. All the units are managed by Blacks, and ten are Black-owned. Of those ten, two were ongoing businesses that relocated in the center; the other eight are new. Funds for the center were obtained from First Pennsylvania Banking & Trust Company and the Ford Foundation.

The founders of Progress Plaza are establishing similar centers in other black ghettos and are diversifying into manufacturing activities and apartment buildings. Their confidence in Progress Plaza is based on careful study of the needs of the trading area and awareness of the wishes of the community. Like El Mercado, Progress Plaza draws on the resources and talents of the outside community when necessary, but is otherwise strictly a local endeavor formed in response to local conditions.

#### ALTERED ROLE FOR THE CDC

These examples demonstrate that economic development in the ghetto based on community involvement is possible without creating local corporations that have pervasive economic power in their neighborhood. Such a position for the CDC not only is unnecessary, but also violates the avowed purpose of the Community Self-Determination Bill: "to mobilize the talents and resources of the people of this 'nation within a nation' to help them play a more meaningful and rewarding role in building a better, stronger, and more confident America."

To make progress toward achieving these goals, reasonable limits must be placed on this approach to Black capitalism. I do not suggest that the concept of community development corporations is devoid of value and should be ignored; community involvement obviously is crucial, and the need is great for locally controlled institutions to direct and coordinate the social and economic development of the ghetto. They can be made effective in this manner:

Barriers to business development should be lowered by offering tax incentives to *all* businesses opening new facilities or expanding existing facilities in the ghetto.

Investment capital should be made available through established channels as well as through the community development banks prescribed in Senate Bill 3876.

Development funds should *not* be restricted to the local CDC and its subsidiaries.

A national body charged with uplifting the ghettos should be created for the purpose of stimulating and coordinating private and public programs designed to achieve this end.

The high cost of doing business in the ghettos is a main reason why "outside" corporations have shied away from establishing operations there. From many quarters has come the sensible proposal that the federal government offer tax incentives to stimulate investment in deprived areas.[4]

As I have suggested in an earlier *Harvard Business Review* article, these incentives should be coupled with an investment guarantee program like that used to encourage corporate ventures in developing countries.[5] These provisions could be terminated if a company were found guilty of violating its community trust (defrauding customers, for example) or at such time as the area's development index reached the national norm.

The entry of outside companies would have to be consonant with the needs and wishes of the local population. Stripped of the stifling and potentially abusive powers now given them in the bill, community development corporations could serve this role effectively. They would stimulate entrepreneurship in their communities, purchase and create their own subsidiaries, and serve as coordinating groups for planning and development.

The national coordinating body would operate as a clearinghouse for the governmental agencies, foundations, businesses, universities, and communities interested in engaging in ghetto projects. There is no reason why carrying out this task would create what is so loathsome to businessmen, a bureaucratic governmental office.

## Conclusion

Our slum areas show very little evidence of realization of the promises and hopes that were held out for their residents in the early 1960s, when America rediscovered poverty. In Watts, for example, more than three years have passed since the riots, and, except for the Watts Manufacturing Company, White Front (one large discount house that was rebuilt), and a few small stores that have reopened, the business community is more stagnant and inadequate than before.

Clearly, there must be more action. Tax incentives and investment guarantees must be offered; capital for business ventures must be made more readily available; and a more vigorous and better coordinated effort must be made to deal with the crisis. The growing momentum of the activities of the Small Business Administration, the National Alliance of Businessmen, the Negro Industrial and Economic Union, and other groups offers greater promise than ever before that the social and economic conditions of the ghetto can be improved through peaceful revolution.

But our public and private institutions must respond more effectively if this momentum is to mount into a truly revolutionary force. The architects of Senate Bill 3876 rightly envision the community development corporation idea as an engine to increase that momentum. But the scheme they have chosen to implement the idea is a sure way to slow the momentum.

There is an aspect of political expediency involved, too. The bill offers a radically new approach to the problem—Black separatism—without altering the social and economic status quo outside the ghettos. Further, creation of CDCs and their affiliated banks would be relatively inexpensive by Washington's standards: estimates for the first three years of operation indicate annual expenditures of no more than $1.5 billion. The tax incentive and capital availability program that I recommend would doubtless be more expensive.

It would be unwise, indeed dangerous, to pass legislation that stifled efforts within and outside the ghettos to improve the lives of the disadvantaged. Aspiring entrepreneurs within the ghettos must have the chance not only to establish their businesses, but also to enjoy the freedom of action to which they are entitled. "Outside" companies that see an opportunity to make a profit as well as fill an unmet need in the ghettos should be encouraged to join, rather than restrained from joining, in the rebuilding effort.

The essential community involvement can be obtained—as it was in the Bedford–Stuyvesant area of New York, where a local development corporation and outside companies have worked together, and as it was in the cases of Progress Plaza and El Mercado. Community involvement, however, should not be equated with separatism and monopolistic power.

Who opposes self-determination? The vision of poor communities pulling themselves up by their bootstraps with little outside help is in conformance with the American dream. Black capitalism, the label that has been placed on the bill, is an appealing concept. When one moves beyond labels, however, it becomes apparent that this legislation could well deter the economic and social development of ghetto areas and delay by many years fuller participation of their residents in our prosperity. And there is a better way.

# Notes

1. See Robert B. McKersie, "Vitalize Black Enterprise," *Harvard Business Review*, September–October 1968, p. 88.

2. *Report of the National Advisory Commission on Civil Disorders* (New York: Bantam Books, 1968), p. 235.

3. See W. H. Ferry, "Whitetown and Blacktown: A Case for a New Federalism," *The Saturday Review*, June 15, 1968, p. 15.

4. See, for example, Robert F. Kennedy, *To Seek a Newer World* (New York: Bantam Books, 1968), p. 40.

5. Frederick D. Sturdivant, "Better Deal for Ghetto Shoppers," *Harvard Business Review*, March–April 1968, p. 130.

# 8 ]] "What Do You People Want?"*

*Richard F. America, Jr.*

In its November 19, 1967 issue *The New York Times* printed an editorial with the title "What Do the Negroes Want?" It said in part:

> Dr. Martin Luther King, Jr. . . . refers vaguely to [the Negroes' claim to] "fulfillment of the rights to share in the ownership of property." Mr. [James] Farmer declares that the Negro wants not merely jobs but "jobs that bear his individual stamp and in industries where he commands power and a measure of ownership." This is a hopelessly utopian claim that the United States has never honored for any other group. Impoverished Negroes, like all other poor Americans, past and present, will have to achieve success on an individual basis and by individual effort.
>
> American society is likely to accommodate Negro aspirations only as they express themselves in individual terms. It cannot be otherwise in a society that honors personal effort as its highest value and looks toward integration as its goal. Race, unlike poverty or the city, is a cultural or psychological concept, not one that can become a comprehensive basis for law or government policy.

The belief in the myth of rugged individualism; the espousal of Black individualism while forgetting the history of public support for whites' special economic interests; the general ignorance of U.S. history—these attitudes, as reflected in the editorial, are widely held by white Americans. Many of them seem to have a weakness for suspending judgment and retreating to such shibboleths when contemplating the changes necessary to sustain the nation's growth and realize its full potential.

What do Black people want? Jobs, housing, and education, certainly. But, beyond that, the Black community wants a secure economic base. Black people themselves, collectively and individually, must and can build much of that base, in profit-seeking and nonprofit forms.

Contrary to *The New York Times*, I maintain that race can indeed be made a basis for government economic policy explicitly favorable to Black people, as it has long been favorable implicitly to whites. The fundamental inequities are collective and not individual, and must be dealt with collectively.

No program conceived to meet major domestic problems has been ade-

From Richard F. America, Jr., *Harvard Business Review* (March–April 1969): 103–112. © 1969 by the President and Fellows of Harvard College. All rights reserved.

* Dean Michael Winston of Howard University, Mr. Stephen Levy of the Stanford Research Institute, and Professor Edwin Epstein of the School of Business, University of California at Berkeley, offered very helpful critical comments on this proposal, for which I am grateful.

quate. This is so because, among other reasons, none, not even the Freedom Budget and Domestic Marshall Plan, has sought to reallocate corporate power. No one has offered a program bold enough (however unsettling) to get at the fundamental inequities which even the most conservative voter and businessman, though he might deny it, must sense lie at the root of the country's present instability and disunity.

## Program Rationale

Now, it will be argued in protest that some steps have been taken, and that is quite true. The movement to eliminate poverty and substandard health, housing, and education for 15 million Black Americans seems destined to succeed if legislation already enacted is fully implemented. But the time elapsed between legislation, appropriation, and implementation of programs to full effect can be as long as a decade. If poverty is largely eliminated by, say, 1980, will the principal economic and political causes of urban unrest and racial conflict have been eliminated? Or are there other, currently secondary, considerations that will then assume primary importance?

There are many persons (Floyd McKissick and Senator Eugene McCarthy, for example) who define the Black–white problem in the United States as a colonial problem. The colonial analogy is central and illumines a policy question that may prove even more intractable than the poverty question; indeed, in retrospect, by 1980 the latter may even appear relatively simple by contrast.

The colonial analogy permits perception of the Black community as a "nation," systematically deprived of an opportunity to save and invest. It therefore can claim control of very little capital wealth. My basic assumption in this article is that, to treat the economics and politics of the race problem properly, this deficiency must be corrected.

The establishment and nurturing of small businesses, now being undertaken on an increasing scale, does not satisfy the need for significant economic independence and self-determination, which all emerging colonies require in order to prosper. Only large enterprises will satisfy that requirement, and they take a long time to develop.

All large businesses in the United States, with two or three exceptions, are owned and operated by whites. If relative economic parity is to be reached in one generation, some of these must be transferred to Blacks. There are two additional elements in the rationale for corporate transfer:

### 1. Influence in Policy Making

It can be expected that Black people will increasingly feel that white people, especially white businessmen, have had a disproportionate influence on the domestic and foreign affairs of this country. White businessmen have simply had too much to say about what goes on in this country. Domestic policy—including policy on problems in which the judgment of

Blacks is increasingly understood to be relevant, if not primary—is directly related to foreign policy. An example is domestic segregation and South Africa. U.S. foreign policy has always been made by the white establishment.

Black people, with certain exceptions like Senator Edward Brooke, have had no direct line of communication with the decision-making echelon. No Black leaders of large businesses have such access, since there are virtually no such leaders. And on many of the critical world issues facing this country, new views are badly needed.

One orderly way to change this situation is to accelerate the belated development of comparably powerful groups of Black businessmen whose perspectives on foreign and domestic questions would in all likelihood be somewhat different simply because of the racial difference.

It is reasonable to assume that Black corporate leaders will introduce new variables and place new weights on old variables in the decision equations of industry and government. That may strike some white businessmen as a terrible prospect, but thoughtful consideration should lead to the conclusion that the introduction of this new element would be in the pluralistic tradition with which many historians credit the relatively consistent stability of the American economic and political experiment.

In short, Black corporate leaders may be able to make a valuable contribution to high policy councils in the last quarter of this turbulent century. The entire nation would benefit from their presence.

### 2. A "Countervailing" Force

The Black–white problem in the United States can be framed in terms of John Kenneth Galbraith's concept of countervailing force. It may be necessary and desirable public policy from the white viewpoint, as it is already implicit Black "policy," to foster the development of Black corporate power as a force against continued mistreatment of Blacks by white corporate and labor power, and against the continued political, social, and economic instability which such mistreatment produces.

Massive mutual distrust is a factor between the races. Better economic and social conditions may reduce the level of distrust. But it is dangerous to assume that rising incomes and educational levels alone will be sufficient to dispel historic antipathies. On the contrary, they may just as easily inflame them, for we know that cultural, psychological, and political expectations will rise just as surely as economic expectations. A sense of relative collective political deprivation may persist when individual economic deprivation has been eliminated.

Secure and powerful Black economic institutions, rather than simply mass individual affluence, would be the surest safeguard against feelings of collective powerlessness and against manifestations of continued white supremacy. Creating such institutions would be in the public interest.

For these reasons, a workable mechanism is required for the transfer of some major national corporations to Black control.

### PRECEDENTS FOR THE PROPOSAL

U.S. history does not lack for examples of the use of public resources in support of private activities when the results were expected to be in the public interest. There are ample precedents of public encouragement leading to private wealth.

Construction of the western railroads, for example, was deemed so important to the development of both the western region and the nation that private citizens were given extraordinary incentives to build the roads. Land was practically given away.

Examples of the transfer of technology from public to private hands are of course equally common. The development of commercial aviation benefited from publicly sponsored research and development. Currently, the government's aerospace research program is creating products and techniques for private exploitation, and the public is providing a substantial windfall to corporations in the process.

In each of these activities the public treasury has directly supported the development of large private enterprise; and, in the last two cases, the government has removed much of the development risk by turning over to corporations proven products and protected markets. The private benefits accrued after public subsidy of the substantial early costs.

The case of the aluminum industry is also pertinent. After World War II, the federal government concluded that the Aluminum Company of America was too big according to certain objective and subjective criteria. The federal approach, simply stated, was to force Alcoa to divest itself of some of its holdings or face direct competition from a corporation to be founded by the government. Alcoa chose to divest. The important point here is that the government considered the public interest to be sufficiently threatened by the monopolistic situation that it was determined to commit public resources to restore a measure of competition in the industry.

The white monopoly represented by *Fortune*'s 500 largest companies might be similarly viewed. The total absence of any large Black corporations in the United States is, to some extent, due to a kind of restraint of trade and "collusive" behavior over the years by almost all white institutions, including the government and the legal system. This has resulted in a situation contrary to the public interest.

### Urban Renewal

Perhaps the most relevant precedent for a transfer mechanism exists in the federal urban renewal program. The power of eminent domain has been relied on to secure land for restoration of certain areas and for essential public projects. A series of court tests has established that eminent domain may further be used to change a land use while title to the property passes from one private party, through the government, to another. The courts have ruled that such changing uses are sufficiently in the public interest to justify the exercise of eminent domain.

The process normally proceeds after extensive public hearings and with numerous safeguards and checks against abuse, although abuses are not unknown. The mechanism essentially consists of three elements:

1. The owner is compensated at full appraised fair market value for his property. This payment is made from the public treasury.
2. The property thus acquired is prepared for transfer. The preparation in the case of a new use for the land usually consists of clearance of structures, preparation of the ground for new construction, and placement of infrastructure, such as utility lines, street realignments, and curbing.
3. The property is sold to the developer, who ordinarily agrees to certain tenure, use, and design controls which are imposed by the developing authority.

The total cost of acquisition and preparation usually greatly exceeds the final sale price to the developer; indeed, it is not uncommon for property to be disposed of for as little as 5 percent of that total cost. This price, of course, is an even smaller percentage of what a developer might have had to pay to assemble the parcels in the open market without benefit of the public intermediary, assuming that the assembly could have been accomplished at all. The "net project costs" amount to roughly the difference between total acquisition and the disposition price. The public treasury absorbs the net project cost.

I propose that a variation on the mechanism used in urban renewal be employed to accomplish the transfer of major corporations or portions of them from white to Black management and control.

ALTERNATIVE APPROACHES

It might be argued that a better, or at least a somewhat less bureaucratic, approach to developing large Black industrial institutions should be developed.

Why not, for example, simply give the full purchase price to a group of Black capitalists and let them proceed on their own toward acquisition? The problems of developing safeguards with that approach might be overwhelming. Or why not let the government directly set up large corporations in selected industries and turn them over to a Black management group? The problems of altering industry structures and distorting existing competitive situations would be formidable.

While both approaches, or others, might be made operable, my proposed solution appears to be applicable with the least departure from precedent and the minimum disruption of normal financial and production arrangements for all parties directly or indirectly concerned.

It might be argued that Black control could be achieved simply by bringing in Black managers and accelerating their movement to the top, without disturbing ownership. This approach would probably not work. It is unlikely that the relationship between Black management and a board of directors representing white interests would remain as harmonious as that between Black management and a Black-dominated board. Normal conflicts between management and the board would over time become exacerbated in the former case, in which racially based conflicts of interest, policy differences, and social objectives would be always potentially present, to the probable eventual detriment of the enterprise.

In transferring ownership of corporations, eminent domain, while not confiscatory, would not be a preferred method even if legal objections could be overcome. The process would require a congenial atmosphere and a high level of cooperation on the part of the original white owners and managers. The potential for obstruction or even sabotage is obvious, so proper incentives, indeed very attractive incentives, must be provided.

A brief aside is in order here. The process of Black community development has two facets, one internal and the other external. If the external aspect were completely satisfactory—that is, if the white community moved to reform itself and initiate the needed programs—much of the benefit would be lost unless the Black community were unified and able to carry out its part in the process.

For Black people, then, the solution of certain internal problems is crucial. One of them is the degree of separatism which they should practice. Few in the Black community would dispute that Black people—not the white world, governmental or corporate—have the responsibility for internal planning. But the proposal in this chapter will be viewed as a much too conservative, perhaps even dangerous, step by some significant Black analysts and activists who are separatists.

The converse of my statement about internal and external facets is not so. If internal problems are resolved and a high degree of unification is achieved, much white resistance will be effectively countered and eventually overcome. Black progress will not end if my proposal, or even others less far-reaching, is not put into action. Black self-help will accelerate and succeed; it will not be allowed to depend on white approbation.

## Transfer Mechanism

The process of corporate transfer should, if possible, be initiated by the candidate. An agency of the federal government created to facilitate such conveyances would issue a standing invitation to divest. Let's call it ACT (Agency for Corporate Transfer). It could be established in the Department of Commerce or the Office of the President.

The program should begin with a trial run, with perhaps three large companies transferred, one a year for three years. After the last transfer, two years of demonstration operations would be undertaken. At the end of the five-year test period it should be clear what program modifications would be required to improve the chances of success with subsequent transfers.

Two assumptions are implicit here: (1) there is a sufficient number of

Black capitalists with access to \$1 million to \$10 million to accomplish the program; and (2) there is a sufficient quantity of Black managerial talent to run the transferred concerns. These assumptions are sound, in my view; the money could be found, and the experience of personnel and management recruiting firms in the past five years suggests the existence of a sizable pool of unrecognized talent, particularly in government, education, and the military.

In each *Fortune* industry category (the 500 largest industrials, plus the 50 largest banks, utilities, and life insurance, merchandising, and transportation companies) might be set an ultimate target of 10 percent to come under Black ownership and control by 1990. Adding 10 percent to the next 500 largest industrials makes a total of 125 companies to be transferred.

If there were no takers despite very attractive tax and other financial inducements, then, theoretically at least, criteria could be developed for identifying candidates for acquisition. Conglomerates, for example, might be approached to determine their interest in selling off portions. In the event of such an impasse, the initiative for opening discussions would fall to the government.

A climate in which no corporations would be interested in voluntary divestiture for purposes of simple liquidation or to take advantage of very attractive financial inducements would be a negative climate in any case. With such a total lack of interest prevailing, the necessary legislation for this program obviously never would be enacted in the first place.

So, discussion of a program requiring government initiative leads to a dead end for all practical purposes. Corporate transfer requires that the white business community understand its advantages, accept its premises, and concur in its objective. Otherwise, the program is dead. But in that direction, as I have tried to suggest, lies severe uncertainty and social instability.

CORPORATE CANDIDATES

A difficulty might arise if the only offers of transfer come from marginal corporations or those whose prospects are dimming. It might be very tempting for a company with top management problems, or severe and chronic financial or labor problems, or obsolescent plant and equipment, or grim marketing problems to seize the opportunity to unload, perhaps even at a premium price. If offers from such companies are abundant in the early rounds, negotiations on selling price could be difficult.

Rejection of a few companies because of unsoundness or low potential, however, would cause them considerable embarrassment and would probably discourage offers from seriously troubled companies.

In seeking to develop Black industry, the problem of competitiveness will be primary. There is little point in accomplishing the transfer of corporations whose activities are in no-growth or declining areas. On the other hand, companies on the technological frontiers like aerospace, ocean exploitation, and nuclear energy are unlikely to offer themselves. The first rounds of negotiations with manufacturers therefore are likely to involve stable, moderate-growth producers of consumer and industrial goods.

ACT might want to concentrate on industries at both ends of the competitive spectrum. An industry that is relatively "competitive," such as paper products or petroleum, will suffer less dislocation from a transfer of one or two of its major companies. Similarly, utilities and other monopolies should be readily transferable, since they are already heavily regulated and not in such delicate competitive balance as more oligopolistic industries, like autos and aircraft.

The opportunity of acquiring large businesses, incidentally, should certainly be extended to other groups in the United States whose situation vis-à-vis the white business world is similar to that of Blacks: Puerto Ricans, Mexican–Americans, American Indians, and, to a lesser extent, Orientals. The government would have to have assurance first that the associates seeking transfer are qualified and would put the corporation to good use. This is the same as my suggested procedure with Black groups, which I take up next.

## BIDDING PROCEDURE

ACT would acquire a divesting corporation by paying a negotiated price for 51 percent of the common stock, after acceptance of a tender offer, with monies from the public treasury.

The availability of the corporation would then be made known to all interested parties through public media, and offers would be invited. In the case of a large manufacturer in which controlling interest could be purchased by ACT for $100 million, an offer of $1 million to $5 million should be sufficient to acquire that interest.

The net acquisition cost—the difference between what ACT paid for the 51 percent interest and the purchasing group's offer—would be absorbed by the government. The portion of the majority interest not held by these entrepreneurs would be assigned by ACT to a nonprofit organization, which I shall describe later.

Initially, the competition from groups of eager entrepreneurs would be keen, but as bidding continued, the field could be expected to dwindle. When a small number of bidders, say three, remained, a set of rigorous criteria would be applied to determine the winner.

The principal criterion would be the ability of the bidding group to produce a management cadre with the potential for successful management of the company. The groups would be required to put together a team of Black businessmen with the requisite training, background, general and specialized experience, and potential to fill the key management positions within a reasonable period of time, say five to ten years. This would mean a team of twenty to one hundred men with expertise in functional areas including marketing, finance, production, personnel, and so on. A typical team might average thirty-five years of age, with ten years of business or noncommercial experience per man.

Objective tests of the team's capacity to enter the divesting company and industry and to learn the business within ten years would be required. Perhaps more difficult, some subjective analysis would be necessary so that the interpersonal dynamics between the divesting management group and the acquiring group's managers could be anticipated.

Obviously, the introduction of a group of Black "fair-haired boys," taking over from white managers during a period of years, has the potential for triggering a variety of generally bad vibrations. The organizational behavior specialists would have their work cut out for them. It must be assumed, however, that in this situation—with a willing buyer, a willing seller, and competent managers, both Black and white—these problems can be overcome.

Administrative and legal safeguards of a high order of effectiveness would be required because of the very large sums of money involved. Particularly important is a procedure for restraining the level of bidding. It might be tempting for competing bidders to seek outside capital in support of their 1 to 5 percent bids. In the case of a corporation in which controlling interest can be acquired for $100 million, white entrepreneurs might find it worthwhile to provide $50 million, $75 million, or even more to a Black bidding group. In short, the price could be driven up to a level near the market price.

In that event, the Black capitalists would become hardly more than a front for the whites, which would defeat the purpose of the program. A technique for certifying the source of all money must be employed, and full disclosure would be essential.

## Transfer Safeguards

The mechanism will also have to protect the legitimate interests of minority stockholders who want to dispose of shares. ACT should stand ready to purchase their shares at the market price immediately before the announcement of the sale. On announcement, the stock market would probably discount the company's future earnings to take account of general uncertainty, the incoming and relatively inexperienced management, and similar factors. Small stockholders should not be penalized in this situation.

After the winning bidder has been selected, the stock would be immediately transferred. At this point, or perhaps even earlier, disgruntled minor stockholders might behave in such a way as to upset the management and the market. The government, through the Securities and Exchange Commission, would have to act to protect the corporation's securities from malevolent operators. Suspension of trading in case of panic selling or other abnormal market activities should be left to the judgment of the boards of the exchanges and the SEC.

The market's reassessment of the company's prospects is to be expected. Within a short time, if earnings hold up and operations continue normally, the market price should reflect the diminished uncertainty, and recovery should be complete.

## RESTRICTIONS ON THE BUYERS

The purpose of this program is to contribute to the achievement of economic and political parity, not transform certain Black capitalists into instant multimillionaires at public expense. But the purchase of, say, $100 million in stock for $1 million to $5 million would appear to have that effect. So the transfer mechanism must take care of that problem.

The safeguard likely to be most effective would take this form: members of the purchasing group would personally hold only that portion of stock which could have been acquired in the marketplace with the same amount of money as they actually expended. They would receive dividends only on those shares. The balance of the stock purchased by the government would reside in a nonprofit corporation with a community base, similar to the kind envisioned in several recent proposals advanced by Black community groups, Black spokesmen, and many politicians. It is commonly called a community development corporation (CDC).[1]

Dividends, if any, on these shares would be paid to that corporation and could be used to fund a variety of public benefit projects in housing, health, recreation, and so forth—much as the Ford Foundation does with its Ford Motor Company dividends. If, however, in management's judgment the interests of the corporation would be best served by retention of earnings, that judgment should not be subordinated to the CDC's desire for cash; funding local public projects must remain secondary to the goal of sustaining competitive businesses.

The location of these nonprofit corporations and the communities to be benefited would be jointly determined by the new controlling group, by expressions of interest and capacity from local organizations, and by relevant government departments, such as OEO, Commerce, HEW, and HUD. As the controlling group desired, it would be free to purchase stock from the CDC within certain limits designed to prevent abuse or price manipulation.

Some provision would have to be devised either to make this large block of stock nonvoting for a period, to prevent interference from that quarter, or otherwise to restrict direct participation by the CDC in the direction of the company until a transitional period, perhaps two to three years, has been completed.

The entrepreneurial group should be allowed to exercise effective control through its shares at least until the success of the transfer is assured— probably five years in most cases. But the nonprofit corporation should have some representation on the company's board of directors at an early date.

It would be undesirable, however, to protect the directors of the corporation from any of their shareholders for any great length of time. Two or three years of nonvoting status might be suitable, but the CDC should be permitted to express its wishes prudently on some proportionate basis after that transitional period. Mutual respect between company and community corporation should ensure that no harm comes to the company's commercial interests from the CDC's pursuit of its noncommercial objectives. It can be predicted that the community group would not interfere unduly with the company's operations if interference threatened to harm its investment and dividend position.

Members of the acquiring group might be tempted to take advantage of market opportunities and withdraw at an early time. They should be permitted to do so, but since the overriding purpose of the program is social, it seems reasonable to impose some limits on their freedom to trade their shares. Perhaps a moratorium of three years would be sufficient to prevent any manipulations.

## Operational Questions

So far as the company's operations are concerned, the period of accomplishing the transfer could run, as suggested earlier, five to ten years. The transition will introduce numerous uncertainty factors for the old management, for original board members who are phasing out, and for minority stockholders. Some means of reducing this uncertainty must be provided.

It will be necessary to allow the company to maintain normal operations while the old management is training the new. So the government should guarantee a minimum rate of return for the corporation and some negotiated level of sales and net income. This can be done through a government offer to purchase some quantity of the company's product (if it is a manufacturer) or through tax concessions.

The former approach is similar in intent to agricultural price supports, which are designed to maintain and protect certain economic activities in the belief that their continuation is in the public interest. Guaranteed markets or returns are also an element in U.S. government attempts to stimulate industrial development or investment in developing countries.

Tax concessions have been suggested recently by almost every nationally prominent politician as a means of inducing the participation of white private corporations in the solution of urban racial problems. Such a policy is undesirable because it would perpetuate the power imbalances that are at the root of these problems. Some kind of tax concessions are probably unavoidable, however, since private industry does have a role to play in treating physical and economic deterioration.

Tax incentives, if used at all, should be applied at least as extensively to the power problem as to the poverty or material deprivation problem. Indeed, the use of tax or other economic incentives to provide only housing, jobs, and so on, without using them to transfer corporate power, rewards white corporations for their past and current economic exploitation.

BLACK AND WHITE MANAGERS

The terms of transfer will provide for the recruitment and employment of a potential senior management cadre of Blacks. I do not envision that the important lower-and middle-management levels would be entirely Black. Even if that were desirable, it would be virtually impossible in a complex, multidivision corporation. But the recruitment of management trainees and young accountants, engineers, and technicians should focus on Black candidates having the potential for quick development. Many will be found in MBA programs at Black and white universities.

Young whites should also be recruited. They would, of course, have to be men and women with special social orientations, but such persons are increasing in number.[2] They of course would have to understand that, for good reason, the presidency and most other top management jobs would be filled by Blacks after five to ten years and for the foreseeable future beyond that. This is not unlike the unspoken understanding that Black MBAs and engineers have when entering large white corporations, and with less justification.

The problem with recruiting is not likely to be the absence of good white candidates. On the contrary, the problem is likely to be the attraction of droves of candidates with strong social motivations who anticipate an exciting five or ten years in an unusual, and therefore more interesting, industrial situation before making their normal career moves. Some screening out of young candidates with missionary motives may be necessary. There may be more of a problem with headhunting for white middle managers, because of their perceptions of risk; but, again, at this early conceptual stage we must rely on the organizational behavior specialists to work that problem out.

Since the program is designed to produce large corporations that are Black-controlled and led, some whites (perhaps many) will find these circumstances uncongenial and leave. The effort will be better off without them. The policy of the program, however, must be that whites are welcome to participate in the operation of Black economic institutions.

## SOURCES OF OPPOSITION

Employee relations will obviously be a delicate area, but success here could make the companies models of innovative human relations programs. And, as I mentioned previously, passage of the enabling legislation presupposes a national climate favorable to the transfer program. Resistance in the white business and labor communities would be assumed to be moderate.

Even so, the first corporations transferred are likely to encounter displays of displeasure by employees, by the general public, or in the market. Boycotts, work slowdowns, strikes, even sabotage are possible.

Negotiations with unions and with all employees in candidate companies should precede transfer, and these groups should have a voice in the decision to transfer. The same should be true for other affected parties, such as financial counselors and bankers, manufacturers' representatives, dealers, suppliers, and principal customers. The involvement of all relevant groups would reduce the risk of direct resistance everywhere, except perhaps in the marketplace.

For this reason, it may be prudent to select, as the first companies transferred, manufacturers of producers' goods with relatively few customers and those with heavy government contracts.

After five or six years of experience beyond the demonstration stage, and with twenty-five or thirty large companies in the transfer pipeline, a manufacturer of cars, soaps and cosmetics, or household appliances might be chosen. When the housewife is ready to choose Brand X (Brand Black over Brand White) on its merits (or for whatever reasons housewives make those decisions), then the entire program may be considered to be a success.

Opposition from organized labor, particularly from craft unions, might pose serious problems if the transfer process were allowed to look like an attempt to break union power. A number of craft unions have been targets recently of Black displeasure because of union resistance to entrance and ungrading of Blacks. General union reaction would probably depend largely on which industries appeared to offer the earliest opportunities for corporate transfer.

## Conclusion

After about eight corporations have been transferred to Black control each year for fifteen years, the procedure would be discontinued, since by then Blacks will have achieved economic parity roughly equivalent to their proportion of the population.

At an average purchase price of $100 million each, the total annual cost of the program, including administration and profit supports, should not run above $2 billion. In some years, however, it would exceed $2.5 billion if a giant or two should be transferred. A program with an annual cost of $2 billion that has the potential to contribute greatly to economic and social equality and stability is an effective program indeed.

Quantifiable benefits would presumably include most of those usually cited in assessing traditional social programs in housing, welfare, transportation, education, employment, and so forth. Such benefits are often realized from savings in public and private expenditures, and such savings might be realized from this program in a variety of ways.

But when the budget analysts have concluded with the cost–benefit arguments, the value of the program should rest on the political judgment that social progress depends on a reallocation of existing institutions— hence a redistribution of power—not merely on reallocation of resources in the form of educational dollars, or guaranteed income checks, or even job opportunities.

Only in this way can anything approaching economic parity be achieved in a satisfactory time—that is, in one generation. All other approaches are based implicitly on a policy of gradualism, which has been rejected by Black people. Such a policy includes efforts of private enterprise to stimulate the growth of small, Black-owned businesses in the Black communities, which President Nixon (it appears at this time of writing) intends to concentrate on.

Would conservative and liberal politicians today support a plan going beyond the limited objectives of legislation promoting a self-development, and designed to provide a measure of countervailing power to the Black community? The answer is probably *no*, but in time the wisdom of such a course will, I think, become clear.

Meanwhile, the search for low-cost, supposedly nonthreatening solutions will continue with the implicit hope that somehow white economic supremacy can be maintained and no one will notice that the gross power imbalance remains despite the proliferation of new, small, Black-controlled businesses.

A recent report by the Institute for Social Research at the University of Michigan contained the finding (according to a newspaper editorial) that "most Black Americans are seeking reform, not revolution," and the "changes they have in mind are essentially conservative in nature."[3] It may be true that the changes most Black people seek are conservative in principle.

But from the point of view of apprehensive white taxpayers and business leaders, the changes sought apparently are seen as very radical. Initially, the corporate transfer proposal may also be regarded as too radical by some, but its fundamentally conservative thrust should be obvious in light of the strong precedents.

In the 1930s much of the white business leadership, following the basically conservative direction of Franklin D. Roosevelt, supported stabilizing public and private policies that yielded a measure of power and wealth to labor. Though the circumstances are fundamentally different now (race rather than class being the basis of conflict), with enlightened conservatism a measure of institutional power will be yielded in order to secure for the nation the benefits of continuity and stability.

## Notes

1. For one view of CDCs, see Frederick D. Sturdivant, "The Limits of Black Capitalism," HBR January–February 1969, p. 122.

2. See Harold J. Leavitt, "The Company President is a Berkeley Student," HBR November–December 1967, p. 152.

3. *Palo Alto Times*, August 11, 1968.

# 9 ]] Making Capitalism Work

## in the Ghettos

*Louis L. Allen*

During a recent month, at least two dozen meetings, conferences, seminars, and orientation sessions were held in New York City on the subject of entrepreneurship and small business in the ghetto areas. Despite my interest in the subject, I did not attend a single one of the meetings. This was not because I knew all about the problem (I did not) but because I knew I would see the same faces, hear the same questions, and listen to the same answers that had long since become familiar to me from earlier meetings. Also, I was convinced that the ballroom of a plush midtown hotel was not the place to study or work on the problems of new business in disadvantaged areas.

In trying to help the ghettos, we have followed the time-honored approach to business problem solving that was started fifty years ago with time and motion study—breaking a task down into its smallest, irreducible parts in order to analyze them further. This approach has led us to:

Make an already difficult task much more complex by trying to "engineer" a magical, quick solution.

Adopt labels for the problem and solution that direct our attention along false and misleading lines.

Look in the wrong places for someone or something to blame for the problem.

Fail to talk with the people actually involved in ghetto business problems, while consulting with those who, though not directly involved, consider themselves spokesmen for the disadvantaged.

Forget what are known to be the basic rules of capitalism.

The purpose of this article is to clear away the logjam in thinking about the economic development of slum areas. I shall elaborate on the points just mentioned, recount some experiences I have had with ghetto entrepreneurs, and summarize some of the practical lessons I have learned about investing in ghetto businesses. I call for a moratorium on conferences and meetings until we in management have something *new* and relevant to talk about. Such methods as decision trees, PERT, and planning models are not applicable to the problems at hand. What we are testing is the entrepreneurial spirit, which means that successful capitalists must go one at a time into the ghetto, find entrepreneurs, and work with them one at a time in the small businesses they seek to build.

From Louis L. Allen, *Harvard Business Review* (May–June 1969): 83–92. © 1969 by the President and Fellows of Harvard College; all rights reserved.

## Epiphany of Capitalism

We are a jingle-writing and "sloganeering" people, we Americans. We like to tag everything with an acronym or a label, and this frequently gets us thinking along lines that we did not intend. Worse, with our aptness for phrasemaking, we sometimes mesmerize ourselves into assuming that since we have cleverly labeled something, we have somehow magically solved the problem it presents.

On occasions, the problem *does* go away. For example, as long as one fish product was called "horse mackerel," it could not be given away; now that it is called "tunafish," it's a very big seller. But the reverse can happen; the problem can be aggravated. For example, consider the label "Black capitalism." Although it is in current use, it is not appropriate to the circumstances, and its continued use will be dangerous. For "capitalism" is a word which describes a concept, a complex concept of many inter-woven threads. Capitalism is an economic system in pretty much the same way that Christianity, Judaism, or Mohammedanism are religious schools of thoughts; that is, basic appeal is that it can be universally applied, and the truths can withstand the closest scrutiny.

Capitalism can no more be adequately described by stating the color, racial origin, or religion of its practitioners than it can be described by the locality of its implementation—for example, Ohio capitalism as compared with New York capitalism. Its greatest strength is that it is, or should be, available to anyone, anywhere, anytime as a means to participate in an economic system, in the same way that Christianity, Judaism, or Mohammedanism can be practiced by all who want to believe in them. To use the term "Black capitalism" is to demean those of its practitioners who are Black.

It is true that there are many who have been and still are deprived of the opportunity to practice capitalism. But those who believe in this system, who have practiced it, and who have prospered from it must remember that there is no exclusivity in it. Exclusivity will change it—drastically and unfavorably.

The Epiphany is an annual feast celebrating the coming of the Magi with news for the Gentiles. What capitalism needs now is an "epiphany" of its own—many wise men who will bring its principles to those who need to know about them and who will remain with the initiates to make the principles work.

#### ILLUSION OF QUICK SOLUTIONS

Basic to a working understanding of capitalism is that it is built one step at a time by practitioners—not handed to them fully constructed. To talk about quick solutions is a terrible mistake because there are none.

An article in the March–April 1969 issue of *Harvard Business Review*[1] proposes that the government take over selected large corporations by eminent domain and give control of them to the Black man. The author goes to some lengths to outline the ways in which this approach could be implemented, how payment could be made, how transition to Black control could be effected, and so on. All of this explanation misses the point. My six-year-old son learned how to swim last winter at the local YMCA. But this summer I will still insist on his wearing a life jacket when he goes in a small boat. I will bet Richard F. America would do the same. Of course, the child may say he knows how to swim and does not need the life jacket.

Exactly the same principle holds in running a big business. No one can know how to manage a large corporation without experience in doing just that. Certainly experience in small company management is no substitute. America has outlined plans for an orderly transition of a few months time. I doubt how "orderly" the transition will be under the circumstances, and, in any case, the best of men could not learn to manage a big company in less than two years.

But the greatest oversight America has made is to give no thought to the customer. How many Ford customers would be lost if that company were turned over to Blacks to own and manage? How many Maxwell House buyers would switch to other brands if that organization were one of the ones selected for Black control? The problem with being a dictator and arranging things by decree, as America suggests, is that the decrees must cover all ramifications. America's proposals, I take it, ambitious as they may be, stop short of decreeing how many people are required to buy Fords and no other make, or to purchase only Maxwell House coffee.

Like a religion, capitalism can be practiced only on an individual basis. It is a matter of one man working at his task or working with a few or many others at an assigned or a selected task. If their work is to be successful, it must be done according to the rules. Capitalism cannot be legislated as suggested by America, nor does it offer any easy answers or comfortable compromises. To suggest that Blacks take over a large corporation on a ready-made basis is very much akin to suggesting that the fox be placed in charge of the henhouse.

Capitalism can be made to work for the economically disadvantaged in our urban centers; it is working there now in many instances. But it requires new approaches, new commitments, and new efforts by everyone who has been a recipient of its great promises.

## Getting Started

What are the requirements of making capitalism work in a depressed urban area? My experience in financing new and small businesses for the economically disadvantaged has led me to conclude that we have been asking the wrong questions of the wrong people. The people who want to know about small business and capitalism in the ghetto are the people who live there and are trying to make decent lives for themselves and their families there. They do not attend the meetings at the Waldorf; they probably never have talked to anyone who has. Hence the first mistake we have been making is not listening to the right people. We have been listening instead to banquet table speakers.

And the questions we have been asking are wrong—for example, questions such as "What needs to be done?" If one has to ask that question, he will not understand the answer, which is simply that the knowledgeable businessman must go into a ghetto area and begin to work with a person there who aspires to something better than what he has.

. . . The tragedy of our citizens that live in the ghetto is that they have no chance to save. The society in which they live does not permit saving, either implicitly or explicitly. They barely subsist on their low incomes and pay high prices for what they get. Because of the expense and lack of mobility, they are effectively denied the opportunity of going elsewhere. Since saving is the basis for accumulating capital, they simply cannot be expected to be in a position to provide any but the smallest part of the financial resources needed to get into business.

Would-be backers must make up their minds that they will have to relax or waive entirely the traditional requirement that an entrepreneur contribute part of the equity himself. If anyone wants to foster the start of capitalism in the economically disadvantaged areas, he must be ready and willing to put up all the money himself. There are no substitutes for this approach, in my experience. A lot of time is wasted and needless involvement undertaken looking around for "front money" to protect the investor's interest. That money is never there.

Bear in mind, too, that while the entrepreneur has no funds to get started, he has always faced very great odds. The level of his aspiration is high; yet he recognizes his prospects for achievement as low. If there is to be any chance for the success of such a venture, it must be constructed at the outset so he and any other principals will be the largest beneficiaries of any profits.

## FALLACY OF THE GIVE-AWAY

Yet what we are discussing here is not a giveaway program. This is one of the points where I disagree most vigorously with America's proposal. As I stated earlier, if the game is capitalism, it has to follow the rules. The only change is that here, because of the special circumstances, the investor must recognize the essential requirement of putting up all the money.

The investment should be made in capitalist terms. For instance, our typical financing at Chase Manhattan Capital Corporation is a ten-year loan with a five-year to seven-year moratorium on principal repayments. We form a corporation, issue *all* outstanding stock to the client, and take a detachable stock warrant for between 10 to 15 percent of the total capitalization.

At the same time we enter into a "put and call" arrangement with the founders according to which, after our original investment has been fully paid and discharged, they can "call" our warrant back for the prorated percentage of posttax profits earned during the period of time the warrant has been outstanding. In other words, we will sell our right to, say 10 percent of the stock, for that amount of the company's net earnings. Under other circumstances we can "put" the warrant back to the founders at one half the rate of the "call"; or if there should be an underwriting, merger, or sale of the business, we can exercise the warrant and go along for the ride.

This is fair to all parties, it is businesslike, and it puts the founders in the driver's seat with respect to how the profits will be taken.

## An Investor's Commitment

If we drop the requirement that the principals "come to the party" with some assets of their own to contribute, we must face some hard questions. One such question is inextricably involved with the general nature of business, especially small business. I regard it is an inalienable right of a businessman to be wrong—not stupid or careless, but just plain wrong. The uncertainties of business are such that the best plans can be laid waste regardless of the competence of the men who made the decisions.

Normally, however, the investor can protect himself. If he sees a decision going sour, he will turn to second lines of defense and commence working on them. But in the case of the typical small business in the ghetto, there is not going to be any second line of defense. To aggravate the matter, there will be no capital base which might absorb some of the trouble. All losses are going to come out of the funds provided by the investors. In this respect, a ghetto firm is a glaring example of a rule which impresses me more and more: the largest disadvantage of small size in business is the inability to absorb error.

This means that the investor must be willing, before he makes his original investment, to support the venture through at least one and probably many periods of crisis when all losses are in effect taken against funds provided by himself. All the deficits will come "out of his hide." It is a very discomforting thought!

How can anyone make a commitment like this? What must be considered, what weaknesses overlooked, what questions asked during the investigation and analysis of a loan or investment request? Indeed, what type of organization should even think about becoming involved?

### NEED FOR A BROAD BASE

It seems to me that any organization formed for the exclusive purpose of assisting the establishment of capitalism in the major urban centers and in other economically disadvantaged areas of our country is doomed to failure from the start. It will certainly fail economically, and this in turn will cause it to fail in its objectives. The usual rule is that an investor should "go hunting where the ducks are," and, take it from me, there are no "ducks" in the ghetto. There are enough problems in running a business profitably if it is located in the best of places. When you add the additional problems found in the ghetto, the compound effect is often devastating.

This fact suggests the basic weakness of Senate Bill 3876—the proposed Community Development Corporation (CDC) Act. It would have an isolating effect. It will virtually eliminate participation by groups not centered in the areas (in other words, it will keep "whitey" out). This bill is a manifestation of the gap between aspiration and achievement that its backers are trying to fill. In their frustration the Blacks think they need only money to bridge the gap—but in truth money is only part of their need. Those who would assist with financial aid cannot let the matter rest at that. They must not merely put up the cash, and, then, in the manner of Pilate, "wash their hands" of these people. Ongoing counsel and direct assistance are cardinal to success.

To whom, then, should they be able to turn for help? I suggest that those who can help the disadvantaged gain a measure of self-control over their affairs by assisting them in starting businesses of their own are precisely those who have already had some success in doing this—that is, the "swimmers" of the capitalist world. Such help is the best possible way for the "swimmers" to direct some of their surplus profits and energies. My greatest fear is that if adequate help comes too late, or if we do not follow through with all our resources other than cash, those of us who did not take time to work on these matters may become like Barabbas and wander from place to place always wondering what will be the ultimate price of our oversight and how it will be exacted.

Companies that have a broader base of operations and are making profits in more fertile ground are the ones that can and should devote their energy, skill, and understanding to developing a new capitalism among the worthy people in disadvantaged areas. For example, at Chase Manhattan Capital Corporation we have gone ahead as we have, not because the fellow across the street was doing it—he was not—but simply because we have felt that the work has to be done.

Our objective is to have one third of the accounts in our portfolio vested in ghetto businesses. That may not be the right percentage, but it should give us a workable balance. We make good to very good profits in our general assignment of financing small businesses around the country. We are reasonably confident we can break even in our ghetto program. Although the latter requires a great amount of time in proportion to the dollar amount of investment, the results are exciting and seem to confirm the validity of our approach. We now have approximately 25 percent of our clients in this category.

## ONE COMPANY'S APPROACH

We look at each investment opportunity with the hope that we can correctly identify and appraise the following:

1. The individual—his resourcefulness, his self-discipline, and his technical expertise.

2. The proposed business—its appropriateness to small size, the activities it will undertake to add value to its costs, its trading area, and its usefulness and social value to the neighborhood where it will be located.

3. The ability of our organization to give support in all areas, particularly during hard times, regardless of the size of investment.

There is no importance to the order of the list. Each category is part of the whole and adds either strength or weakness as the case may be. The list represents what we have found to be the important aspects of the failures and successes we have seen.

Our experience has been that when we find a person or group that meets the individual tests, has a proposition that meets the tests for the business, and leads us to feel reasonably confident that we will not lose faith, then we should go ahead with the support we can give in the way of capital and direct assistance; we believe we will not fail. We can provide the business with the resources needed to get over any periods of crisis or slowdown.

## Lessons and Guidelines

Now let me try to generalize from my company's experience and single out some of the things we have learned about backing a ghetto enterprise. These lessons may be useful to other investors who are new to this area.

### DON'T OVERLOOK THE OBVIOUS

We have been surprised at how little can be taken for granted concerning an entrepreneur's business know-how. The following story will illustrate:

One man we financed seemed to meet all the tests. He was working very hard, and his receipts were right on target. Yet after several months there were nothing but losses for his business. We could not understand.

Since the young man on our staff who was working with this small businessman was as puzzled as we, it was decided that we would work up a complete audit of the business. As the work progressed, we continued to be perplexed because we could not pinpoint anything of sufficient magnitude to account for the poor results. After some more digging, we finally discovered the cause: our client was not adding anything to his costs to cover overhead!

You might think this such a simple error that it would be immediately apparent. But we had blinders on. On several occasions since then I have wondered how many other blinders we are wearing—how many other established concepts of business are so basic and routine that we are overlooking them. Why should we presume that our client will know these things as intimately and instinctively as we do?

## SEEK TO BE TRUSTED

The next problem is extremely difficult in some cases. I have no easy answers for it—I know only that the investor or consultant must be alert to the danger of not being trusted.

It is easy for us to explain the theory of business practices to our clients. We can help them in planning a sales campaign, in recordkeeping, in determining plant or office location, and in almost any technical aspect they may encounter. We have these services available either on our own staff or elsewhere.

Sometimes, however, our clients *do not believe us*. They doubt whether we are really interested in seeing them succeed even though we go to such great lengths to arrange the financing satisfactorily. We tell them that we want them to be successful because that is the only way we can make a profit.

. . . I have no idea how anyone can assure himself that he will be believed, that his partner will trust him. Yet this trust is cardinal to success; without it, no positive results can be predicted, and very probably the project will end in failure. It can be most difficult to gain the entrepreneur's trust if he comes from a background that will have conditioned him to expect the opposite. Such difficulties notwithstanding, a number of our clients have voluntarily told us that while they first approached us with distrust, they became convinced later that we were interested in their progress because they got help when they stubbed their toes. They realized that what we had told them was true—we could not prosper unless they first prospered. They saw that the way we constructed our financings effectively put the initiative in their hands and prevented us from making any real profits until *after* they had made profits for themselves.

## DEAL IN TWO WORLDS

Related to the problem just described is the matter of appearances. The world of tall office buildings may affect the Black entrepreneur from the ghetto in an unexpected way. For example:

One young man was highly recommended to us by several of the businessmen who had taught the first sessions of the local Workshop in Business Opportunities. I called him, and we set a date. It was not kept. We set another date and still another. Finally I reported all this to one of the business executives who had recommended the young man. The executive made several phone calls which did not give him the answers he wanted. Finally, he paid a visit to the young man's mother. He found out that the young man had only an old pair of blue jeans and a torn jacket. Each time he rode down on the subway and walked up to our building, he could not make himself go in. My executive friend helped the family get some new clothes for the young man, who then kept his appointment. We are working with him now, and I hope we will be able to help him get started.

The lesson is that those of us who have "made it" are far removed from the world these applicants know. We must expect that as simple and obvious a fact as our physical surroundings will get a response (even though it may not be as pronounced as the one I have recounted). I think, on balance, that it is better to know this and be prepared to deal with it than to rent a shabby store and wear work clothes. It is essential that we be believed, and one cannot expect much belief if we start off with theatrics designed to put the client at ease.

### GIVE DIRECT, PERSONAL HELP

Some problems lend themselves to all-encompassing solutions. For instance, mass programs have dealt effectively with such things as polio, chicken pox, anthrax, social security, and housing. But other problems must be solved on, a one-to-one basis; that is, one problem-solver working with one client. A cardiac patient needs this kind of attention; so does a small company president. When he runs into problems, his need is for direct help, usually of a consultative nature. He needs *individual* advice and guidance, not a management course.

A man who has gone into business for himself has in effect picked the president of his company. The chances of this selection being made according to any of the established percepts of personnel policy are remote. The selection has been made completely subjectively, by a man who is usually not qualified in executive selection and personnel practices. Yet it is the most fateful of all decisions that will affect the future of his small business.

### INSIST ON REALISM

We decline some applications for help on the basis of inadequate preparation by the principals. Sometimes an applicant says he has heard we are helping men to get into business. We tell him that is correct. But when we ask what type of operation he is going to start, he replies that he does not care what it is, he just wants to be in business. Instead of rejecting such an applicant at the outset, we invite him in for a talk. Usually the meeting is not productive, but every now and then we can suggest something constructive. For example:

We once talked to a man who had been a mechanic and filling station attendant. He had gone to work at the age of 12 in the South to help support his mother. Later, he moved to New York and found similar employment. At our suggestion he attended a school run by a major oil company and also joined the Workshop in Business Opportunities. Now, after nearly a year, he is ready to try something on his own.

We also turn down proposed enterprises that do not seem to lend themselves to small size. For example, we have had a number of inquiries about starting businesses such as garment manufacturing companies. In this day and age, a competitor in such an industry has little chance if he lacks a well-trained labor force and topnotch facilities. Of particular importance, the investor should insist that the entrepreneur "*start small.*"

The aspiring Black businessman may want to go all the way in one jump (as Richard F. America proposes). He may think he can build a large market all at once. I feel that the investor should resist such tendencies. Let me illustrate:

In one case we considered, the principals of the new business had a potentially fine program, but they would not agree to start small; they insisted on forming a company that would immediately employ fifty people. Moreover, the market potential, in our view, was limited. The type of high fashion clothing the Blacks proposed to make was a risky venture. The projected sales were far above what we considered attainable goals. Therefore we turned down the application.

The men went elsewhere and got their financing. The results were predictable. Overhead "ate them up," and the results were so poor that the investors refused to go further. The enterprise collapsed.

The failure of this business, in my view, did more harm than if it had never started. It will unquestionably hinder those investors from going ahead again soon, and it put a lot of people back on welfare after building up their hopes for something better. All the parties in the transaction were either unaware of, or chose to overlook, one of the most basic rules of the game of capitalism: one can have the most capable management, the best possible plant and equipment, the finest products, and adequate financing, but unless there is a customer there is no business. This is true with our largest and more successful corporations, and it is true with the small business in the ghetto.

### TRADE OUTSIDE THE GHETTO

We encourage small businesses to trade outside the area where they are located. A case in point is a furniture and carpentry business we financed. It is located in the poorest section of Brooklyn near Flatbush Avenue. The few men who work at this business live within a block or two of the small shop from which they operate. Yet most of their jobs are done for homeowners and industry located in the well-to-do areas of Long Island. It is a struggling small business, but it brings fresh money to the ghetto area.

As long as the business located in the ghetto have their customers, or a majority of them, also located in the ghetto, capitalism will never reach its fullest potential. Could Detroit be so prosperous if most of the cars and trucks made there were sold only in Detroit? In this connection, it is worth noting that the Community Development Corporation legislation would very effectively eliminate any chance of trading outside the ghetto. This is one of the most urgent reasons why the whole program should be reevaluated. The history of industrial development has always shown a heavy incidence of "foreign" investment as the basic capital on which a country has built its economy. It is going to be just as true with our urban ghettos.

Of course, exceptions should occasionally be made to this rule, as the following case indicates:

A group of about thirty mothers who were on welfare in the Fort Greene area of Brooklyn determined that they wanted to be free of welfare payments (on which they had been depending). The mothers formed a family day-care center where they and other mothers could leave their children and try to find work.

Seven were employed by the day-care center, which was funded by the appropriate state and local agencies. Eight found other work. Then the mothers at the day-care center and others who had not found work started to cook food for take-out orders. These take-out foods were an immediate success; the demand was greater than the supply. At this point the mothers came to see us.

There was a vacant luncheonette for rent in their neighborhood. We put up all the funds required to start the restaurant proposed by the women. It specialized in "soul food," which was especially popular with the people who live in that area. The mothers working at the restaurant remained on relief and drew no pay until the business was doing a volume sufficient to support them. We forecasted a period of about eight weeks for this volume to materialize. But business was so good that within three weeks the receipts were running nearly three times those expected. The business continues to thrive.

What an appropriate way for small capitalists to get started. In any case like this the investors know their funds will be used to establish the business, but not to support an overhead of payroll until the firm can make it on its own. The welfare authorities, on the other hand, continue to support the would-be entrepreneurs during the time they are building something that will eliminate the need for public support. I hope we can duplicate this procedure many times over.

### EDUCATION IS CRUCIAL

Much of the frustration that undoubtedly results in the militancy and revolutionary fervor of many educated Blacks can be traced to their inability to achieve anything meaningful despite their aspirations. After the Civil War and after World War I their hopes rose but their achievements did not. Again today, after the passage over the last eight years of sweeping civil rights legislation, the Blacks have had their hopes built up only to find that they are still excluded from decision making at important levels. They still do not have the means for exercising an entrepreneurial spirit.

Indeed, with industry turning more and more to automation, with the widespread use of computers, and with the development of sophisticated techniques, the disadvantaged of our urban centers find it more and more difficult to prepare themselves for any kind of satisfying participation in significant affairs. We seem to have failed to develop adequate public schools in our urban centers. Up to about fifteen years ago, the working class could sell its muscle with only a low degree of skill or specialized training being required. Now employment of this kind is growing less and less available. But we have taken only a few of the necessary steps to provide the required schooling facilities.

If members of the disadvantaged class are to be given the chance to work toward better positions, schooling must be considered an absolute essential of the process. A negative income tax and massive direct support would undoubtedly be very helpful. However, they would not provide for the acquisition of capital or help directly to establish a climate conductive to it. Know-how is required for that—and know-how requires education.

## Conclusion

There have been enough conferences and meetings. We know right now all we need to know about the problem of developing entrepreneurship in the economically disadvantaged areas of our urban centers. Now there is just one great big pile of work to get on with.

Helping small businesses in these areas to get started and to prosper is no cure-all. It will not directly improve health standards, schooling, or housing. What it can and will do, if practiced broadly, will be to provide a significant number of deserving and aspiring individuals with the opportunity to try their hands at the capitalist game.

Those who would practice giving this help as investors and advisors should be the very ones who have themselves prospered as players in the capitalist game. It is true they will have to bend some of the rules a bit to fit special circumstances. But not very much bending is necessary. Moreover, the ghetto entrepreneurs themselves will be stronger and better qualified to "go it alone" if they are coached soundly and realistically.

Any program that would isolate small business in the ghetto or separate it from the mainstream of business affairs will fail. Any effort to donate capitalism ready-made must also fail. The best economic tool we have ever had is good, old-fashioned, no-nonsense capitalism. It is up to those of us who have learned it and prospered from it to pass it on to those who would use it if they could but learn how. Repeatedly, in the past, people succeeded and prospered if help was available when they needed it. It is time now for all of us to extend helping hands to our disadvantaged citizens.

## Note

1. Richard F. America, Jr., "What Do You People Want?" *Harvard Business Review*, March–April 1969, p. 103.

# 10 ]] The Myth and Irrationality
## of Black Capitalism

*James Boggs*

I cannot account for why many of us are here, but the fact that we are here indicates to me that the Black movement has now reached the stage where it compels us to seriously confront the question: What kind of economic system do Black people need at this stage in history? What kind of economic system do we envisage, not as a question for abstract discussion, but as the foundation on which we can mobilize the Black masses to struggle, with the perspective that their future is at stake?

It is now nearly fifteen years since the present Black movement started out with the intention of achieving civil rights via integration into the system. Year after year the movement has gained momentum until today millions of Black people in all strata of life consider themselves part of the movement.

At no other time in our 400 years upon this continent have Black people sustained such a long period of activity. Up to now, what we have had are rebellions and revolts of short duration. But it is now quite apparent that what we are engaged in is not just a revolt, not just a rebellion, but a full-fledged *movement* driving towards full growth and maturity and *therefore* requiring a serious examination of the fundamental nature of the *system* that we are attacking and the *system* that we are trying to build.

It is also now quite clear that Black people who have been the chief victims of this system which is under attack are the ones who have to make this examination—because for us it is a very concrete and not just an abstract question.

Up to now we have evaded this question because in reality *we* recognized that to tamper with the *system* is to tamper with the whole society and all its institutions.

*Now we cannot evade the question any longer.*

When we talk about the *system*, we are talking about *capitalism*. I repeat. When we talk about the system, we are talking about capitalism. Let us not be afraid to say it.

And when we talk about capitalism, we are talking about the system

From James Boggs, *Racism and the Class Struggle* (New York: Monthly Review Press, 1970), pp. 133–145. Written as a working paper for the National Black Economic Development Conference, Detroit, April, 1969. Reprinted by permission of Monthly Review Press. © 1970 by James Boggs.

that has created the situation that Blacks are in today! Let us be clear about that, too. *Black underdevelopment is a product of capitalist development.* Black America is underdeveloped today because of capitalist semi-colonialism, just as Africa, Asia, and Latin America are underdeveloped today because of capitalist colonialism.

We cannot look at the underdevelopment of the Black community separate from capitalism any more than we can look at the development of racism separate from capitalism.

The illusion that we could resolve racism without talking about the economic system came to an end when we arrived at the point of talking about power to control and develop our communities. Now we are forced to face the question squarely of *what system to reject and what system to adopt.* This has forced us to face squarely the relationship of racism to capitalism.

Capitalism in the United States is unique because, unlike capitalism elsewhere which first exploited its indigenous people and then fanned out through colonialism to exploit other races in other countries, capitalism in the United States started out by, first, dispossessing one set of people (the Indians) and then importing another set of people (Africans) to do the work on the land. This method of enslavement not only made Blacks the first working class in the country to be exploited for their *labor* but made Blacks the foundation of the *capital* necessary for early industrialization. As I pointed out in the *Manifesto for a Black Revolutionary Party*:

Black people were not immigrants to this country but captive, brought here for the purpose of developing the economy of British America. The traffic in slaves across the Atlantic stimulated northern shipping. The slave and sugar trade in the West Indies nourished northern distilleries. Cotton grown on southern plantations vitalized northern textile industries. So slavery was not only indispensable to the southern economy; it was indispensable to the entire national economy.

At the same time the land on which American southern plantations and northern farms were developed was taken from the Indians. Thus Indian dispossession and African slavery are the twin foundations of white economic advancement in North America. No section of the country was not party to the defrauding of the red man or the enslavement of the Black.

What white people had achieved by force and for the purpose of economic exploitation in the beginning, they then santified by ideology. People of color, they rationalized, are by nature inferior; *therefore, every* person of color should be subordinated to *every* white person in *every* sphere, even where economic profit is not involved. The economic exploitation of man required by capitalism, wheresoever situated, having assumed in this country the historical form of the economic exploitation of the Black and red man, this historical form was now given the authority of an eternal truth. Racism acquired a dynamic of its own, and armed with this ideology white Americans from all strata of life proceeded to structure all their institutions for the systematic subordination and oppression of Blacks.

I said earlier that Black underdevelopment is the result of capitalist development. At the bottom of *every* ladder in American society is a Black man. His place there is a direct result of capitalism supporting racism and racism supporting capitalism.

Today, in an effort to protect this capitalist system, the white power structure is seeking once again to reenslave Black people by offering them Black capitalism. Now, scientifically speaking, there is no such thing as Black capitalism which is different from white capitalism or capitalism of any other color. Capitalism, regardless of its color, is a system of exploitation of one set of people by another set of people. The very laws of capitalism require that some forces have to be exploited.

This effort on the part of the power structure has already caused certain numbers of the Black race, including some who have been active in this movement, to believe that self-determination can be achieved by coexistence with capitalism, that is, integration into the *system*.

In reality, Black capitalism is a dream and a delusion. Blacks have no one underneath them to exploit. So Black capitalism would have to exploit a Black labor force which is already at the bottom of the ladder and is in no mood to change from one exploiter to another just because he is of the same color.

Nevertheless, as residents and indigenous members of the Black community we recognize its need for development. Our question, therefore, is how can it be developed? How *should* it be developed? To answer these questions, we must clarify the nature of its underdevelopment.

The physical structure and environment of the Black community is underdeveloped *not* because it has never been at a stage of high industrial development, but because it has been devastated by the wear and tear of constant use in the course of the industrial development of this country. Scientifically speaking the physical undevelopment of the Black community is *decay*. Black communities are *used* communities, the end result and the aftermath of rapid economic development.

The undevelopment of Black communities, like that of the colonies in Africa, Asia, and Latin America, is a product of capitalist development. At the same time there is an important difference between the economic undevelopment of a colony in Africa, Asia, or Latin America and the economic undevelopment of the Black community inside an advanced country like the United States.

The economic undevelopment of a colony is the result of the fact that the colony's natural and historical process of development was interrupted and destroyed by colonialism, so that large sections of the country have been forced to become or remain preindustrial or agricultural. For example, many of these societies once had their own handicraft industries which were destroyed by Western economic penetration. Most were turned into one-crop countries to supply raw materials or agricultural produce to the Western imperialists. In struggling for independence from imperialism, these societies are fighting for the opportunity to develop themselves industrially.

On the other hand, the physical structure of Black communities inside the United States is the direct result of industrial development which has turned these communities into *wastelands*, abandoned by industry as it has undergone technological revolutions. The physical structure of Black communities is like that of abandoned mining communities in Appalachia whose original reason for existence has been destroyed by the discovery of new forms of energy or whose coal veins were exhausted by decades of mining. It would be sheer folly and naivete to propose reopening these mines and starting the process of getting energy from their coal all over again. When one form of production has been rendered obsolete and a community devastated by an earlier form of capitalist exploitation, it would be supporting a superstition to propose its rehabilitation by a repetition of the past. You don't hear any proposals for white capitalism in Appalachia, do you?

Secondly, the Black community is not technologically backward in the same sense as the majority of communities in an undeveloped nation in Asia, Africa, or Latin America. In these countries the vast majority of people still live on the land and until recently had had experience in using only the most elementary agricultural tools, such as the hoe or at best the plough. In these countries a revolution in agriculture must accompany the industrial revolution. By contrast, the mechanization of agriculture has already taken place in the United States, forcing the Black people (who were this country's first working class on the land) to move to the cities. The great majority of Blacks have now lived in the city for the last generation and have been exposed to the most modern appliances and machinery. In the use or production of these appliances and machines, they are no less developed than the great majority of white workers.

The undevelopment of Blacks is primarily in two areas:

1. They have been systematically excluded from supervisory, planning and decision-making roles which would have given them practical experience and skills in organizing, planning, and administration.

2. They have been systematically excluded from the higher education which would have given them the abstract and conceptual tools necessary for research and technological innovation at *this* stage of economic development when productivity is more dependent on imagination, knowledge, and the concepts of systems, i.e., on mental processes, then it is on manual labor.

From the preceding analysis we can propose certain fundamental guidelines for any programs aimed at developing Black communities:

1. Black communities are today capitalist communities, i.e., communities which have been developed by capitalist methods. Their present stage of decay, decline, and dilapidation, i.e., their present stage of undevelopment, is a product of capitalist exploitation. They have been used and reused as a means to produce profit by every form of capitalist: landlords, construction industries, merchants, insurance brokers, bankers, finance companies, racketeers, and manufacturers of cars, appliances, steel, and every other kind of industrial commodity.

*Development for the Black community means getting rid of these exploiters, not replacing white exploiters by Black ones.*

2. *Any future development of the Black community must start from the bottom up, not from the top down.* The people at the very bottom of the Black community, who are the chief victims of capitalist exploitation, cannot be delivered from their bottom position by Black capitalist exploitation. They are the ones in the most pressing need of rapid development. They are also the fastest growing section of the Black community. These are the Black street force, the ADC mothers, welfare recipients, domestic servants, unskilled laborers, etc. These are the people who must be given an opportunity to exercise initiative, to make important decisions, and for higher education, if the Black community is to be developed—not the relatively small Black middle class. The creation of a middle class of Black capitalists would make the distribution of income inside the Black community *less equal, not more equal.* It would be the source of *greater* chaos and disorder inside the Black community, not *more* order and stability, because the layer at the bottom of the Black community, far from seeing these Black capitalists as models and symbols to be admired and imitated, would be hostile to and strike out at them.

3. *Struggle should be built into any program of Black community development* in order to stimulate crisis learning and escalate and expand the sense of civic right and responsibilities. The struggle should be on issues related to the concrete grievances most deeply felt by the lowest layer of the Black community, i.e., on issues of education, welfare, health, housing, police brutality, and *should be aimed at mobilizing this layer for control of these institutions inside the Black community as the only means to reverse the manifest failure of these institutions to meet the needs of Black people.* It is only through struggle over *such* grievances that the largest and most important section of the Black community can be involved in decision making. The most important obstacle to the development of the Black community is the lack of power on the part of Blacks, and particularly on the part of this section of the Black community, and therefore the lack of conviction that anything they do can be meaningful. It is only through struggles for control of these institutions that they can achieve a degree of power and therewith an increasing awareness of their importance and their responsibilities. Only through struggle can a community be developed out of individuals and the leadership necessary to any community be created.

4. Any program for the development of the Black community must provide for and encourage *development at an extremely rapid, i.e., crash program pace and not an evolutionary or gradual pace.* Otherwise, in view of the rapid growth of the Black population, and particularly of its most oppressed sector, deterioration will proceed more rapidly than development. For example, in a community where there is pressing need for at least 10,000 low-cost housing units, the building of a couple of hundred units here and there in the course of a year does not begin to fill the need for the original 10,000 units—while at the same time another thousand or

more units have deteriorated far below livable level. The same principle applies to medical and health care. To set up a program for a few hundred addicts a year is ridiculous when there are hundreds of new addicts being created every week.

5. *The Black community cannot possibly be developed by introducing into it the trivial skills and the outmoded technology of yesteryear.* Proposals for funding small businesses which can only utilize sweatshop methods or machinery which is already or will soon become obsolete means funding businesses which are bound to fail and thereby increase the decay of the Black community. Proposals for vocational training or employment of the hard-core in Black or white businesses (on the theory that what Black people need most to develop the Black community is the discipline of work and money in their pockets) are simply proposals for *pacification* and for maintaining the Black community in its present stage of undevelopment.

There is absolutely no point in training Blacks for deadend jobs such as assembly work, clerical bank work, court reporters, elevator operators, craftsmen, clerks, meter readers, mail clerks, oil field or packing house workers, painting, railroad maintenance, service station attendant, steel mill or textile workers. There is little point in training Blacks for status quo jobs, such as accountant, auto mechanic, bank tellers, bricklayers, truck drivers, TV appliance repair, sheet meal workers. There is great demand for these jobs now, but new methods and new processes will make these jobs obsolete within the next decade. The jobs for which Blacks should be educated are the jobs of the future, such as aerospace engineers, recreation directors, dentistry, computer programming, mass media production, communications equipment experts, medical technicians, operations research, teaching, quality control. *There can be no economic development of the Black community unless there is development of Black people for these jobs with a bright future.*

At the same time the preparation of Blacks for these bright future jobs must not be confined to simply giving them skills in these jobs. In the modern world, productivity depends upon continued innovation which in turn depends upon research and the overall concepts needed for consciously organized change. *The only practical education for Black people,* therefore, is the education which increases their eagerness to learn by giving them not only a knowledge of what is known but *challenges them to explore what is still unknown* and to interpret, project, and imagine. *The only practical enterprises to develop the Black community* are those which are not only producing for today but which include research and development and the continuing education of their employees as an integral part of their present ongoing program.

Black youth, born during the space age, are particularly aware not only of the racism which has always confined Blacks to deadend jobs but of the revolutionary changes which are a routine part of modern industry. Any attempts to interest them in deadend jobs or in education for deadend jobs will only increase the decay and disorder in the Black community, because rather than accept these jobs or this education, Black youth will take to the streets. Any programs for developing the Black community must have built into them the greatest challenge to the imagination, ingenuity, and potential of Black youth. What you, and particularly Black youth, find hard to do are the "little things." What can mobilize their energies is "the impossible."

6. *Any program for the development of the Black community must be based on large-scale social ownership rather than on private individual enterprises.* In this period of large-scale production and distribution, private individual enterprises (or small businesses) can only remain marginal and dependent, adding to the sense of hopelessness and powerlessness inside the Black community.

The social needs of the community, consciously determined by the community, must be the determining fact in the allocation of resources, *not* the needs or interests of particular individual entrepreneurs. The philosophy that automatic progress will result for the community if enterprising individuals are allowed to pursue their private interests must be consciously rejected. Equally illusory is the idea that development of the Black community can take place through the operation of "blind" or "unseen" economic forces. The Black community can only be developed through *control by the community over the public institutions, public funds and other community resources, including land inside the Black community, which are in fact the public property of the Black community.*

Massive educational programs, including programs of struggle, must be instituted inside the Black community to establish clearly in the minds of Black people the *fact* that the institutions which most directly affect the lives of the deepest layer of the Black community (schools, hospitals, law-enforcement agencies, welfare agencies) *are the property of the Black community*, paid for by our taxes, and therefore that the Black community has the right to control the funds which go into the operation and administration of these institutions. This right is reinforced and made more urgent by the fact that these institutions under white control have completely failed to meet Black needs.

All over the country today the police are organizing themselves into independent *political* organizations, outside the control of elected civilian officials and challenging the right of civilian administrations and the public, which they are allegedly employed to protect, to control them. Community control of police is no longer just a slogan or an abstract question. It is a concrete necessity to overcome the increasing danger of lawlessness and disorder that is inherent in the swelling movement towards independent bodies of armed men wearing the badges of law and order but acting as a rallying point for militant white extremists.

In these campaigns special emphasis should also be placed on the question of *land reform and acquisition.* The federal government, over the last thirty years, has changed land tenure and agricultural technology through massive subsidies which have involved the plowing under of vast areas of land, rural electrification, agricultural research, etc. But all this has been for the benefit of whites who have become millionaire farmers and landowners, and at the expense of Blacks who have been driven off the land altogether or retained only as farm laborers, averaging less than $5.00 a day in wages or $800 a year.

In the South the Black community must undertake a massive *land reform movement* with the aim of forcing the federal government to turn these plowed-under lands over to the millions of Blacks still in the South, to be developed by Black community organizations. Black community development of these areas in the South should include not only the organization of producers' and distributors' cooperatives but also the organization of agricultural research institutions, funded by the federal government, where Blacks working on the land can combine production and management with continuing education, research, and innovation. The responsibility of government for funding research in relation to agricultural development is well-established. Nobody has a greater right to these funds than the Blacks now in the South and other Blacks who will be drawn back to the South to assist in community development of agricultural lands.

In order that the Black people in these agricultural areas do not fall behind their brothers and sisters in the cities, land in these communities should also be set aside for recreation, medical facilities, and for operation of advanced communication centers.

A similar campaign for *land reform and acquisition* should be organized in the urban areas of the North where the great majority of Blacks are now concentrated. The concept of "eminent domain," or the acquisition of private property for public use, has already been well-established in the urban renewal program. However, up to now, "eminent domain" has been exercised only in the interest of white developers and residents, and against the interests of Black homeowners and the Black community. Federal subsidies have been used, first, to expel Blacks from their homes, businesses, and churches, and then to improve the areas which have then been turned over to private developers to build homes for middle-class and wealthy whites.

The principle of "eminent domain" must now be employed to acquire land for the purposes of the Black community. Vacant land, land owned by whites which has been allowed to deteriorate, etc., must be acquired and turned over to Black communities to plan and develop under Black control and with Black labor, for the purpose of creating communities which will meet the all-sided needs of Black people for housing, health, education, recreation, shopping facilities, etc., and which will be a source of participation, pride, and inspiration to the Black community and particularly to Black youth.

The Black community cannot be developed unless Black youth, particularly, are given real and not just rhetorical opportunities to participate in the actual planning and development of the Black community. The feeling which Black youth have now is that the streets of the Black community belong to them. But without a positive and concrete program to involve them in the planning and construction of the Black community, they can only wander these streets angrily and aimlessly, each one a potential victim of white-controlled dope rings.

*The application of the concept of social ownership and control by the Black community is essential to the involvement of the Black street force in the development of the Black community.* These "untouchables" have no property which they can call their own and absolutely no reason to believe that they will ever acquire any. The only future before them is the prisons, the military, or the streets. They are the ones who have sparked the urban rebellions. Yet, up to now, after each rebellion, they have been excluded from participation, while middle-class Blacks have presumed to speak for them and to extract petty concessions which have uplifted these Blacks but left the "untouchables" out in the cold. The "untouchables" have not been organized into decision-making bodies with issues and grievances and aspirations and rights to development. Instead middle-class Blacks have been used to pacify them. The fact, however, is that these street forces will not just disappear. They are growing by leaps and bounds, threatening not only the system but also all those who stand between them and the system, including those Blacks who presume to speak for them.

7. Since pacification of these rebellious forces has been the chief purpose of all so-called development programs up to now, it is no accident that most of these programs have been single-action, one year or "one hot summer" programs, without any fundamental perspective for developing new social institutions or for resolving the basic issues and grievances which affect the largest section of the Black community.

On the other hand, it is obvious that any serious programs for the development of the Black community must be based on *comprehensive planning for at least a five-year period.* Piecemeal, single-action, one-year or "one hot summer" programs are worse than no programs at all. They constitute tokenism in the economic sphere and produce the same result as tokenism in any sphere, i.e., the increased discontent of the masses of the community.

*The purpose of these five-year comprehensive programs must be the reconstruction and reorganization of all the social institutions inside the Black community* which have manifestly failed to meet the needs of the Black community. Any programs for the development of the Black community which are worth funding at all must be programs that are not just for the curing of defects. Rather they must be for the purpose of creating new types of social institutions through the mobilization of the social creativity of Black youth, ADC mothers, welfare recipients, and all those in the Black community who are the main victims of the systematic degradation and exploitation of American racism. *Development for the Black community at this stage in history means social ownership, social change, social pioneering, and social reconstruction.*

# 11 ]] Toward Controlled Development
## of Black America

*Robert E. Wright*

It is politically correct to categorically reject "Black capitalism," but *only* if you define what you mean by the term. For example, if "Black capitalism" is the kind of capitalism that Richard Nixon is talking about, where Blacks merely exploit other Blacks or where Blacks merely become cogs in the traditional Western monopoly capitalist system, then we must oppose it without a doubt. But if what we mean by "Black capitalism" is the *primitive accumulation of capital* (i.e., land and material resources) by black people in a *collective* or *cooperative-ownership* fashion for the benefit of the *masses* of Black people and not just a few individuals, then we are speaking of a completely different animal, in that such a movement is fundamentally in *opposition* to Western monopoly capitalism, and we should support it. A good example of an attempt to primitive accumulation of necessary capital is outlined in the "Black Manifesto" which came out of the April 1969 Black Economic Development Conference in Detroit.

*We must discard the term "Black capitalism" from our vocabulary* because it only creates confusion: (1) it creates the illusion among many Blacks that the Black *masses* can be successfully integrated into the *present* U.S. economic system simply by our creating more "Black capitalists"; (2) but on the other hand it is a label with which "infantile leftists" often unfairly paint attempts by Blacks at achieving economic reforms in the Black community as "reactionary" or "counterrevolutionary." The most extreme example of this infantile thinking is the Progressive Labor Party, which regards *all* Black nationalism as "reactionary." We must learn to distinguish between *survival economics* (dealing with the *immediate necessary economic needs* of the Black community) and Western monopoly capitalism (which is based on profit for profit's sake, class and racial exploitation, and a dog-eat-dog value system).

We must begin to establish *guidelines* for the economic development of the Black community so that we don't end up enforcing the same old exploitative system that the European world has imposed on non-Europeans (and themselves) for the past five centuries. These guidelines must evolve from a *Black* theoretical framework based on *Black experience* and *needs* (and *not* mere mechanical application of "Marxism" or mere emotion against "capitalism"); only people who are fundamentally *Black*

From Robert E. Wright, "Viewpoint: Black Capitalism" in *Negro Digest* (December 1969): 27–33. Reprinted by permission.

*nationalists* in outlook will be able to build a "Black thing" (a Black political theory and apparatus), because what Blacks should really be involved in is building a Black nation. We must study and learn from *all* social theories and experiences, of course, but we must stop using terms like "capitalism," "socialism," and "communism," to define *our* economics and politics, because these terms only call up negative images in the Black community and sow confusion, misunderstanding, and sterile thinking. We should use only concepts originating from the *Black* American experience, such as "communalism," "survival economics," "Black power," "community control," etc.

The crucial fact to keep in mind in all our discussions about "Black nationhood," "Black liberation," and Black "freedom"—all of which imply *Black economic independence* or self-sufficiency—is that every "underdeveloped" nation—the whole "Third World," including Black America—needs above all else *economic* development, which is really *capital* development, or the *accumulation of capital resources*, in order to provide an economic base that will be self-sustaining in the future and allow for true political independence and free cultural development. Until we learn how to deal correctly with this cardinal fact—that the "Black colony" in America, as all the "Third World," needs *capital* as well as its own revolutionist culture and political apparatus in order to develop a "new order"— we will never break out of the quagmire of disunity and sectarianism, rhetoric politics practiced by the Black Panthers, the Republic of New Africa, the Progressive Labor Party, and most of the whole Black American left. We should all be able to agree that *Black America needs capital, but not the old Western monopoly capitalist system*, and work from there. Our only questions should be whether or not the economic or capital development program speaks to the needs of—and is responsible to—the *masses* of Black people rather than just a few individuals.

The most practical way to deal with the problem of Black economic development in North America (or anywhere) is to organize around the reality of *present Black economic needs*, such as, for example:

1. A Black cooperatively controlled communications system responsible to Blacks nationally.

2. A Black *urban* infrastructure of cooperatives linked up with a (southern) *rural* infrastructure of cooperatives, forming a *separate Black economy*.

3. *Land reform* (both North and South) and *redevelopment* and *collective* Black ownership of land resources to provide food, community services, and meaningful employment.

4. A *totally* Black-controlled network of research institutes and/or universities to deal with Black concerns on *all* of three fronts:
   a. The cultural
   b. The economic and technological
   c. The political (both domestic and international)

In other words, Blacks must begin to organize as if they were building their own separate Black nation—Black America. Black politics should be based on the (1) *survival*, (2) *development*, and (3) *preparation* of Black America for Armageddon—the race–class war that has existed and has been warming up ever since Blacks were first brought here from Africa and is apt to break out into a full-scale civil war at any time. In so organizing, Blacks should borrow or accept technical help and ideas from wherever they can, so long as Blacks always maintain control of their own movement. Again, Blacks need to acquire some basic *economic skills and resources*—by any means *necessary* (including nonviolent and conventional means where *possible*)—if they are to survive in this land and develop a common culture and value system that will unite, sustain, and prepare them for any situation that confronts them.

Blacks must create *their own "Black thing"* and not use terms like "capitalism," "socialism," and "communism" to describe what they are doing. Black people are a *spiritual* people, as Brother Ameer Baraka (LeRoi Jones) has said, and probably much of our confusion and disunity arises from our using "the man's" concepts to define ourselves and our enemies, and not developing our own "language" to relate to each other, i.e., to really *listen*, and create a dialogue (not a monologue) among ourselves and really try to understand where each of us is really "coming from."

Besides this *lack of group dialogue*, nothing has contributed more to our lack of historical perspective as to where we are and where we should be going than our hang-ups with the old radical and liberal dream of Black and white workers and poor people in general uniting together as *one class* to overthrow our capitalist rulers. But American society cannot be broken down simply into peasantry, proletariat, and *bourgeoisie* or "rich" and "poor." Nor is it simply "Black" people against "white" people, unless we consider all the oppressed people of this nation as "Blacks" and their enemies as "white." America is a nation of many smaller "nations"— "white" Anglo–Saxon Protestants (who are also divided *regionally*), Jews, Irish, Catholics, Italians, Puerto Ricans, American "Indians," Japanese–Americans, Chinese–Americans, Mexican–Americans, African–Americans, and others. Each of these groups has had its own unique experience in this country, as far as Black America is concerned, the extent to which Afro–Americans and other individuals in all these groups cut across class lines is virtually insignificant, because most Americans—including the few families who own and control America—owe their respective social, economic, and political status to the particular ethnic, religious, or cultural group they were *born* into. This is the reality that American Blacks must work from and study, not just Marx's theories about "class struggles," *or* Hubert Humphrey's "American Dream."

At this stage in history, the Afro–American struggle—and I think also the struggle of Puerto Ricans, Mexican–Americans, American Indians, Appalachian and other poor or alienated whites, and other domestic colonies dominated by the more powerful groups that rule America—must be mainly a struggle against *colonialism* and racism. Each colony must shape its own destiny. Insistence upon "Black and white workers together" and/or a premature coalition of "Black and white poor together" politics only obfuscates reality and holds back any real unity along radical lines among the various racial and cultural groups in the future. America needs *cultural revolution*, i.e., *ethnic and cultural democracy*, as well as it does economic and political revolution.

Once Blacks begin to work from this kind of perspective and disengage themselves from both liberal "integration" theories and "class struggle" politics they can better understand the true dynamics and revolutionary potential of Black economic and cultural nationalism, and end a lot of needless fratricide, for example:

1. Why are the Black Panthers, who call themselves *"revolutionary nationalists,"* so opposed to *"cultural* nationalists"? Isn't it possible for a *"cultural* nationalist" to also be a revolutionary? What kind of nationalist is Mao Tse-Tung, whom the Panthers are always quoting? Isn't there more to the dynamics of Black "cultural nationalism" than just wearing a dashiki or an "Afro," despite how confused the Panthers seem over the matter? Doesn't the conflict really boil down to the Black Panther's (as well as other so-called Marxists) apparent opposition to—and misunderstanding of—the role of Black economics and Black cultural development in the struggle?

2. Why is it that the Progressive Labor Party, in particular, is such a staunch opponent of "nationalism" among Blacks? Are all forms of Black nationalism, including Black economic nationalism, necessarily "reactionary" or "counterrevolutionary"? Or is it because Mao Tse-Tung in his 1963 statement in support of the Afro–American struggle, *incorrectly* characterized the *Black American* struggle as just part of the *general* "workers" struggle in the U.S.A., and the Progressive Labor Party is too subservient to "Mao's thought" to question him and too blind themselves to correct him? Why is it all right for every colonized people in the world to practice nationalism except American Blacks? Why have American "Marxists" traditionally opposed "nationalism" among Black people?— Because to accept "Black nationalism" as a legitimate political theory for Blacks would destroy their dreams of "Black and white workers together," and they don't want to deal with the present reality of the vast social and cultural differences and needs of the *masses* of *Black* people as opposed to the masses of the more dominant groups in America.

3. Why does the Republic of New Africa believe that it is all right for it to "negotiate" with the "white" U.S. government for reparations for Blacks but that it is (ideologically, and not just tactically) wrong for other Blacks to mobilize the Black colony for "reparations" from "white" churches and other racist institutions? Is it because the Republic of New Africa is too caught up in complying with European definitions of "nationhood"? Is there real ideological ground for the Republic of New Africa to oppose or refuse to support the demands of the Black Manifesto, or is the dispute personal? Is proceeding according to the Western-created rules of "international law" the only and best route to achieving "Black nationhood"? Is the Republic of New Africa anything more than a mechanical application of the Communist Party program of the 1930s for a Negro nation in the

Deep South; for example, what *historical* relationship does the R.N.A. have with any of the recent Black freedom movements in the Deep South (or anywhere else)? What makes the Republic of New Africa the only legitimate concept of "Black nationhood" to organize around? Has the Republic of New Africa jumped the gun? Similarly, are the Black Panthers "ahead of their time" or "too far out in front of the people"? Is it "time to pick up the gun" (because Mao and Che did) and merely brandish it before our enemies to prove how "bad" we are? (Haven't we graduated from that stage yet?) Isn't it perhaps time to teach our people to *hide* some guns, etc., before they're all outlawed and to exhaust other means of uniting and raising our people's consciousness?

Blacks must draw upon *all* historical experiences and ideas—*particularly their own*—in dealing with these questions. Above all, we must maintain a critical spirit and accept no solutions to our problems merely because they sound "militant" and "revolutionary" or merely because Che said it or Mao said it. As Ron Karenga has said, "The Red Book is better *read!*"—and so is Fanon, Malcolm X, and everyone else we call ourselves learning from. Blacks must see "Black revolution" as an *evolutionary* process as well as a cataclysmic one; we cannot skip stages, such as some minimal economic development of the Black community. We must use more historical perspective in our analyses.

For a start, Blacks who call themselves "nationalists" and "revolutionaries" in the same breath should reexamine the role of Booker T. Washington and put him (and themselves) in true historical perspective. Harold Cruse, for instance, points out that Booker T. Washington was Marcus Garvey's idol and that Garvey's *economic* program, as well as that of W. E. B. DuBois (in *Dusk of Dawn*), Mr. Elijah Muhammad, Malcolm X, and today's "Black power" people are not essentially different from Booker T. Washington's. If there is a common strain among all of these great thinkers—Washington, Garvey, DuBois, Elijah Muhammad, Malcolm X, Stokely Carmichael and James Forman—why is it that Washington is considered an "Uncle Tom" and the others are not? Mainly because most of us have accepted the myth perpetuated by August Meier and Herbert Aptheker that Washington's economic program was completely out-of-date but that DuBois's was *different* and was not out-of-date (since DuBois was more "militant" than Washington), and we are still trying to out-"militant" each other while not dealing with the concrete problems of "nation building." In short, we need to study our heroes and history closer, and stop throwing around terms like "Black capitalism" and "Black socialism," which have no real meaning to the masses of our people and prevent us from creating *our own* "Black thing", i.e., our own *political theory* about what we need and how we should go about getting it, and our own means and *institutions* for carrying out what we decide upon.

# 12 ]] Small Business and Economic Development in the Negro Community

*Andrew F. Brimmer*

I greatly appreciate the opportunity to share with the Select Committee on Small Business my views on the "role of small business in minority economic development." In responding to the invitation to testify, it occurred to me that I might be able to make a modest contribution to these hearings through an appraisal of the prospects for minority groups in business, based on an economic analysis of the market in which Negro businessmen are attempting to operate profit-making enterprises in the United States today. Thus, my efforts consist of an objective examination in which I set aside questions relating to noneconomic goals (such as enhancing pride of ownership) which other observers may find it worthwhile to pursue.

On the basis of my analysis of the economic evidence, I have concluded that we should be extremely cautious in encouraging Negroes to seek careers as self-employed, small businessmen. This is especially true if the expectation of success is based on the assumption that such a business can be conducted in a separate, all-Black environment, protected from the competition of firms doing business in a nationwide market. In general, if one wishes to restrict his efforts to small-scale neighborhood retailing and the provision of relatively simple personal services, it is quite possible that he can earn a living—although, it is likely to be a modest one. However, if the desire is to engage in manufacturing, construction, transportation, or wholesale trade, the prospects of success appear to be extremely dim—if the firm's output is to be sold mainly in the limited market provided by the Negro community. Between these extremes, the outlook for successful operation becomes less-and-less promising as the scale and technical sophistication of the enterprise increase.

## Economic Impact of Segregation and Desegregation

Before proceeding further with this assessment of the prospects for Negroes in small business, we should pause briefly to review the consequences of economic separatism which resulted as an historical legacy of

From a Statement before the Select Committee on Small Business, U.S. House of Representatives, July 25, 1969.

racial discrimination and segregation and the later consequences when some of these barriers were removed. In general, the effects were similar to those produced in international trade when a high tariff wall is erected between two countries. Separate markets prevail in the two areas for items subject to tariff control. For the Negro community in the United States, the greatest barrier imposed by segregation was not in the market for goods—to which they generally had relatively open access—but in the market for personal services, such as barber and beauty shops and funeral services. Consequently, a protected market evolved for the provision of these services within the Negro community.

Moreover, as one would expect, this wall of protection provided incentives for Negro professionals and entrepreneurs who began to specialize in activities servicing the Negro community. Negro professionals were highly concentrated in fields such as medicine, education, and religion—all hampered by segregation—but all of which also provided a protected market. In occupations which were dependent upon unprotected national markets, Negroes were conspiciously absent. For example, in 1960 (the last year for which we have detailed information) engineers, scientists, and technicians comprised only 3.8 percent of all Negroes classified as professional, technical, and managerial; the corresponding figure for whites was 10.5 percent. The fraction of Negro professionals who were architects was less than one-fifth the fraction for whites. Clearly Negro professionals were concentrating on servicing the Negro community.

In business the same pattern prevailed. Negroes were concentrated in enterprises servicing the protected Negro market. Life insurance provides probably the best example. For years, the major life insurance companies either did not sell policies to Negroes or did so on the basis of different actuarial tables which greatly increased the cost of protection to Negroes. The result was the creation of an environment where Negro life insurance companies were able to grow and prosper. In enterprises that sold to a more general public, such as hardware and department stores, Negroes have not made much headway.

The recent progress toward desegregation in the United States (symbolized by the opening of public accommodations) has eroded the position of many Negro businessmen who were dependent upon segregation to protect their markets. For instance, in many large cities in the East and Midwest, most of the hotels and restaurants which previously catered to Negroes have encountered hard times, and a few have actually closed their doors.

The trend towards desegregation in American life has influenced the Negro businessman in another important manner. Not only have many of his traditional customers deserted him to shop in the more diverse stores serving national markets but he has also encountered an increasing competition for his traditional supply of labor. Large national corporations for some time have been actively recruiting Negro personnel. Initially the aim was to help market their products in Negro areas, but more recently they have also been seeking manpower for their overall operations. Negro businessmen operating from much smaller economic bases are unable to offer competitive salaries or commensurate opportunities and are thus having a great deal of difficulty retaining qualified employees.

The adverse effects of these changes on Negro businessmen concentrating in those activities formerly protected by segregation is quite striking. This can be seen most clearly in the income trends among nonwhite men during the 1960s. For example, between 1959 and 1967, mean income of all self-employed nonwhite males rose by roughly 114 percent to about $7,200; among all self-employed white men, the rise was only 44 percent to approximately $8,500. In sharp contrast, income gains for self-employed retail merchants were much smaller for both groups (39 percent to about $7,400 for whites and 28 percent to about $4,500 for nonwhites).

Expressed differently, in 1959, average incomes of both white and nonwhite retail merchants were well above the average incomes of all employed men (13 percent above all whites for white retailers and 28 percent above all nonwhites for nonwhite retailers). By 1967, however, the averages for self-employed retail merchants showed smaller rises and were below the averages for all employed men—9 percent below all whites for white retailers and 12 percent below all nonwhites for nonwhite retailers.

## Economic Environment of Negro Business

The legacy of racial segregation is important because it has shaped the economic environment in which Negro businessmen are currently operating—and in which they are likely to operate for some time. The main economic characteristics of the Negro community are widely known and need not be reviewed in detail here. For example, in 1967, Negroes had a median family income of $4,939 which was only 59 percent of that of white families. These income figures are important because they clearly point up the differences in purchasing power in the two communities—a matter of fundamental importance to businessmen. However, when we examine the financial assets and liabilities of Negroes compared with other families, the differences in market potential are thrown into even sharper focus.

These differences are clearly marked in Tables 12–1 and 12–2, which summarize data on assets and liabilities from the Survey of Consumer Finances conducted by the Survey Research Center at the University of Michigan. The ownership of financial assets is presented in Table 12–1. As mentioned earlier, Negro life insurance companies emerged as a response to the failure of white life insurance companies to serve the Negro market. The results of this segregated market is that Negroes at all levels of income appear to have a slightly higher probability of holding life insurance than whites. The picture on other financial assets is quite different. Negroes at virtually all levels of income are less likely to have savings accounts or stocks. The lone exception appears in the over $10,000 income class where Negroes rely heavily on savings accounts but invest far less

**TABLE 12-1**

*Fraction of Population Holding Different
Financial Assets, by Income, Class and Race, 1967*

| Income Class | Life Insurance | | Savings Accounts | | Stocks | |
|---|---|---|---|---|---|---|
| | Negro | Non-Negro | Negro | Non-Negro | Negro | Non-Negro |
| Under $3,000 | 54 | 49 | 13 | 44 | 0 | 11 |
| $3,000-5,000 | 75 | 68 | 41 | 56 | 1 | 15 |
| $5,000-7,500 | 85 | 80 | 52 | 62 | 5 | 21 |
| $7,500-10,000 | 95 | 92 | 58 | 69 | 5 | 26 |
| Over $10,000 | 100 | 96 | 89 | 79 | 30 | 45 |
| Total | 73 | 80 | 38 | 64 | 4 | 26 |

*Source:* Survey Research Center, University of Michigan.

frequently in stocks. In fact, although not shown in Table 12–1, the Michigan Survey reported that in 1966 Negro families obtained only 2 percent (versus 6 percent for non-Negro families) of their total money income from dividends, rent, interest, and trust funds.

The most important data in Table 12–1 are for the income categories between $5,000 and $10,000. These two categories contain roughly 40 percent of all Negro families, and it is this range of income which provides the broadest foundations of the Negro market. The asset data for families within this critical income range show that Negroes have considerably less financial accumulation than white families. This finding implies that these Negro families would not be as good potential consumers as the income figures might suggest.

The other side of the financial picture is liabilities. (See Table 12–2.) One is immediately struck by the fact that Negroes at all levels of income are much more heavily burdened with installment debt. The repayment of

**TABLE 12-2**

*Fraction of Population with Different Financial Liabilities,
by Income Class and Race, 1967*

| Income Class | Installment Debt | | Mortgage Debt | | | |
|---|---|---|---|---|---|---|
| | | | Negro | | Non-Negro | |
| | Negro | Non-Negro | Owners | Debt | Owners | Debt |
| Under $3,000 | 49 | 19 | 40 | 10 | 52 | 8 |
| $3,000-5,000 | 59 | 39 | 29 | 8 | 54 | 18 |
| $5,000-7,500 | 84 | 52 | 37 | 25 | 54 | 27 |
| $7,500-10,000 | 71 | 60 | 50 | 39 | 68 | 46 |
| Over $10,000 | 93 | 53 | 70 | 66 | 79 | 55 |
| Total | 64 | 46 | 40 | 20 | 63 | 37 |

*Source:* Survey Research Center, University of Michigan.

this debt represents a sizable claim on disposable income and thus makes a Negro family a poorer potential consumer for additional goods and services than a family of similar income that is less encumbered by installment debt payments. The case of mortgage debt is a bit more difficult to analyze. The probability of home ownership rises substantially with income and is higher at all levels of income for whites than for Negroes. A single (not fully explained) exception to this general trend is the high tendency for Negro families in the lowest income category to own homes. In part this may reflect older retired families and in part it may represent impoverished rural southern Negroes whose home ownership may be quite modest. In general, it is safe to conclude that Negroes of similar income are not accumulating an equity position in housing at the same rate as white families.

The tendency to owe mortgage debt, however, appears roughly equal for Negroes and whites of similar income. Since Negroes have a lesser tendency to own a home at a given level of income, this similarity in the fraction of the total population owing mortgage debt suggests clearly that if a Negro does own a home, the chances are greater that he has a mortgage on it than for a white homeowner with the same income.

These data on the financial assets and liabilities shed new light on the economic achievements of Negro families. These data show that Negro families of comparable income have greater liabilities and fewer financial assets to meet these liabilities than whites. This finding suggests that the usually observed data on white–Negro income differentials actually understate differences in purchasing power, because the income figures do not indicate the relatively poorer net financial position of Negro families. The figures on assets and liabilities accentuate the problems of weak markets facing businessmen who limit themselves to the Negro community.

## The Structure of Negro Businesses and the Outlook for Economic Development

Having highlighted some of the limitations inherent in the Negro market, it might be helpful to see what types of enterprises have developed in this environment. For this purpose, only fragmentary information is available. One source relates to Negro-owned and -operated businesses in Washington, D.C., in 1967. (See Table 12–3.) These data show a heavy preponderance in the service area. The distribution of businesses within each category is also revealing:

Of the 1,249 businesses classified as services, 555 (or 44 percent) were barber shops, beauty salons, or beauty schools, while 146 (or 12 percent) were drycleaning establishments.

Of the 473 retail businesses 240 (or 51 percent) were carryout shops, delicatessens, grocery stores, or restaurants. There were only two used-car lots in this category and no new car dealers.

### TABLE 12-3

*Distribution of Negro-Owned and -Operated*
*Business in Washington, D.C., 1967*

| Type of Business | Number | Percent |
|---|---|---|
| Services | 1,249 | 60.5% |
| Retail | 473 | 22.9 |
| Contract Construction | 119 | 5.8 |
| Transportation | 82 | 4.0 |
| Finance, Insurance, and Real Estate | 84 | 4.1 |
| Manufacturing | 35 | 1.7 |
| Wholesale | 20 | 1.0 |
| Total | 2,062 | 100.0 |

*Source: A Directory of Negro-Owned and -Operated Businesses in Washington, D.C.* (compiled by Small Business Guidance and Development Center, Howard University, 1967).

Of the eighty-four businesses in finance, insurance, and real estate, there were two banks, one finance company, seven insurance companies, one title company, and seventy-three (or 87 percent) were in real estate.

Of the thirty-five manufacturing companies, twenty-eight (or 80 percent) were newspaper publishers, printers, or sign shops.

Thus, businesses in the Washington area are highly concentrated in areas such as barber shops, beauty salons, and drycleaning establishments where Negroes are servicing Negroes.

However, a second—and more important—conclusion emerging from these data is that these are not the types of enterprises which can serve as the mainsprings of economic development in the long-run.

This conclusion is also strongly supported by the results of a seven-city survey of Negro businesses conducted by the National Business League in early 1969. (See Table 12-4.)* Of the 564 businesses reported in the survey, 329 (or 58 percent) were concentrated in six out of sixty-seven industry categories. These six categories correspond closely to the local market–oriented service operations in Washington, D.C., described above.

A careful look at the employment patterns within the specific categories of Negro business is useful. Of the 329 businesses in the six-industry group, 268 (or 82 percent) had four or less employees, while the corresponding figure for the entire sample was nearly as high—80 percent. Thus, these six categories are a good representation of employment patterns for the entire sample. The obvious conclusion from these figures are that Negro businesses are very small indeed.

The small size of the average Negro business is, in part, due to a con-

* I am grateful to Mr. Berkeley Burrell, President of the National Business League, for permission to use data from the unpublished findings of this survey.

**TABLE 12-4**

*Distribution of Negro-Owned Enterprises by Number of Employees*

| Category of Business | Number of Employees | | | | | |
|---|---|---|---|---|---|---|
| | 1-4 | 5-10 | 11-20 | 21-30 | Over 30 | Total |
| Restaurants | 44 | 9 | 1 | 0 | 0 | 54 |
| Snack and Carryouts | 9 | 4 | 0 | 0 | 0 | 13 |
| Grocery and Supermarkets | 70 | 7 | 4 | 0 | 1 | 82 |
| Service Station and Auto Repairs | 29 | 10 | 1 | 0 | 0 | 40 |
| Laundry and Drycleaning | 24 | 8 | 3 | 2 | 1 | 38 |
| Beauty and Barber Shops | 92 | 8 | 2 | 0 | 0 | 102 |
| Total in Six Categories | 268 | 46 | 11 | 2 | 2 | 329 |
| Total, All Businesses | 452 | 83 | 21 | 3 | 5 | 564 |

*Source:* National Business League Survey, 1969.

centration in the types of enterprises which are traditionally quite small. Barber and beauty shops are small operations, and it is no surprise that ninety-two (or 90 percent) of the barber and beauty shops had four or fewer employees. What is more distressing is the tendency for Negro businesses to be small in operations which are not traditionally small. The category labeled "grocery stores and supermarkets" is a good example. Of the eighty-two businesses in this category, seventy (or 85 percent) had four or fewer employees, and only one had over twenty-one employees. Clearly the category labeled "grocery stores and supermarkets" refers to very small grocery stores serving limited markets.

Employment figures present only one dimension of Negro businesses, and more information is possible through data on income and profits. (See Table 12–5.) The income and profit figures reflect the same general trends as the employment data. Of the 329 firms in the six-industry groups, 279 (or 85 percent) expected gross income in 1967 of $20,000 or less, while 455 (or 81 percent of the total sample) expected to be in this range. For estimated net profits, the picture was equally poor—with 290 (or 88 percent of the businesses in the six categories) and 474 (or 81 percent of all businesses)—expecting a net profit of $5,000 or less. Of the fifty-four restaurants in the sample, forty-nine (or 91 percent) estimated net profits of $5,000 or less and the remaining five anticipated profits of between $5,000 and $10,000.

**TABLE 12-5**

Distribution of Negro-Owned Enterprises, by Size of Estimated Income and Profit, 1967

| Category of Business | Estimated Gross Income | | | | | Estimated Net Profit | | | | |
|---|---|---|---|---|---|---|---|---|---|---|
| | Under 20 | 20-50 | 50-95 | Over 95 | Total | Under 5 | 5-10 | 10-20 | 20-30 | Over 30 |
| Restaurants | 48 | 4 | 1 | 1 | 54 | 49 | 5 | 0 | 0 | 0 |
| Snack and Carryout | 11 | 1 | 1 | 0 | 13 | 13 | 0 | 0 | 0 | 0 |
| Grocery and Supermarkets | 62 | 10 | 2 | 8 | 82 | 75 | 4 | 2 | 1 | 0 |
| Service Station and Auto Repairs | 31 | 4 | 3 | 2 | 40 | 31 | 5 | 4 | 0 | 0 |
| Laundry and Drycleaning | 30 | 5 | 2 | 1 | 38 | 27 | 8 | 3 | 0 | 0 |
| Beauty and Barber Shops | 97 | 3 | 0 | 2 | 102 | 95 | 6 | 1 | 0 | 0 |
| Total in Six Categories | 279 | 27 | 9 | 14 | 329 | 290 | 28 | 10 | 1 | 0 |
| Total, All Businesses | 455 | 59 | 24 | 26 | 564 | 474 | 58 | 25 | 3 | 4 |

Source: National Business League Survey.

## Concluding Comments

From this analysis, we can conclude that the prospects for economic development through Negro-owned businesses dependent upon the type of infrastructure discussed above are not very encouraging. The asset and liability data presented above reinforce the already familiar income statistics, and together they show clearly that the Negro market is by no means a strong one. Consequently, entrepreneurs who limit themselves to these markets will be denied the economies of scale which are a precondition of long-run economic development. The small firms spawned by these markets offer a limited potential for an expansion in the total number of job opportunities. The high concentration of these firms in service areas does not provide a margin of profit large enough for the accumulation of new capital, and it inhibits the development of the types of skills needed to compete successfully for executive positions in large corporations operating in a modern high technology economy.

As mentioned at the outset, my purpose in testifying today is not to demean small businesses which I feel do offer modest opportunities for some potential Negro entrepreneurs. Rather, my purpose has been to point out some of the serious economic pitfalls of a strategy based upon separatism and segregation. Economic separatism has been tried in the past, and it has failed to provide genuine opportunity for Negro businessmen— and it certainly has failed to provide economic well-being for our Negro population. I am personally convinced that the most promising path of economic opportunity for Negroes lies in full participation in an integrated national economy. This holds for Negroes who want to be businessmen as well as for everyone else. The sooner we recognize this important lesson from the past, the quicker we can start to attack the real obstacles to the Negro's economic progress in the United States.

# 13 ]] Brimmer and Black Capitalism:
## An Analysis

*Charles Tate*

Andrew F. Brimmer, the sole Negro member of the Board of Governors of the Federal Reserve System, has written a number of papers and magazine articles and made several speeches over the past year attacking both the concept and the strategy of Black economic development through Black capitalism. "The Trouble with Black Capitalism" appeared in the May 1969 issue of the magazine *Nation's Business*. In October 1969, Brimmer presented a paper "Black Capitalism: An Assessment" at the fifty-fourth Annual Meeting of the Association for the Study of Negro Life and History in Birmingham, Alabama. "The Economic Potential of Black Capitalism" is the title of a paper prepared by Brimmer and Henry Terrell and presented at the eighty-second Annual Meeting of the American Economic Association in New York in December 1969.

Brimmer's attacks on Black capitalism have precipitated wide controversy among Blacks and whites with widely divergent economic and political views and interests in Black economic development.

What is the purpose and objective of these systematic, persistent onslaughts? At first glance, it might appear that Brimmer has elected to chastise the Nixon administration and various white capitalists for promoting what he considers the false doctrine of Black capitalism. Closer examination of his thesis and statements on Black capitalism, however, are illuminating and suggest other possible explanations.

### Brimmer's Position

Black capitalism is defined by Brimmer as the Black ownership of business located in the ghettos of major cities and totally dependent on the restricted, segregated ghetto market.

Historically, the small, Black-owned service and retail business located in the ghetto has been protected by a wall of segregation. According to Brimmer, now that the barriers of segregation are being removed and Black consumers have access to the broader marketplace, Black-owned hotels, restaurants, and similar businesses have been forced to compete with white establishments for the Black dollar. These mom-and-pop style

From Charles Tate, *The Review of Black Political Economy* (Spring–Summer 1970): 84–90. Reprinted by permission.

Black firms cannot compete successfully due to their size, inefficiency, and inability to expand sufficiently to realize the economies of scale that prevail in the larger more efficient operations of their white competitors. As a result, the traditional Black-owned business in the service and retail field is doomed to failure or highly marginal existence.

The economic environment in which these businesses are forced to operate is characterized by low incomes, heavy debts, high unemployment, and very small savings and financial assets. Moreover, Brimmer reasons, any increases in the income of ghetto residents will further stimulate white competition and penetration of the Black market.

Brimmer concludes that the general trend in the national economy is toward salaried employment rather than self-employment due to the higher earnings that prevail in the former category. Further, the earning differentials between salaried and self-employment categories have induced the expected rapid occupational shifts without the normally anticipated reduction in earnings differential. Stated differently, the demand for salaried workers in the manager, official, and proprietor classes continued to expand at a higher rate than the increases in the supply. This analysis suggests that Blacks have an opportunity to compete successfully in this labor market because of scarcities on the supply side.

In the *Nation's Business* article, Brimmer states ". . . the only really promising path to equal opportunity for Negroes in business as in other aspects of economic activity lies in full participation in an integrated national economy. It cannot be found in a backwater of separatism and segregation." In the Birmingham speech, he indicates that Blacks cannot develop the skills in ghetto enterprises that are required to enable them to compete for executive positions in large corporations. This position is restated in the paper presented at the AEA meeting in New York, in which he advocates that Blacks seek salaried positions in white firms rather than self-employment in ghetto businesses.

## Neglected Elements

The most striking feature of this assessment of Black capitalism is not what it says, but rather what it ignores and omits. To note that the "legacy of segregation" provided a wall of protection for the development of Black business in America presents an unusually sanitized, one-sided account of the economic history of Black people. It obscures the causal relationship between exploitative white capitalism, and the economic structure of the ghetto. Are Black businesses to be blamed for failing to grow and expand under the harsh political and economic restraints imposed upon them? Or should attention be turned to the political–economic system of white capitalism that imposed—and continues to impose—the restraints?

Black business is condemned as a concept in the Brimmer thesis because it has struggled to survive under adverse conditions. Yet, white capitalism, the real culprit, is never identified or charged. Is it bad for Blacks to own and operate a business or is it simply bad to be forced to operate that business under the restraints imposed by white capitalism? Is it a triumph or a tragedy if Black businesses, restricted to a ghetto market and constrained by economic, political, and social sanctions imposed by white capitalism, can still create 550,000 to 750,000 new jobs by 1980 (as Brimmer himself estimated)? If this can be accomplished under the worst conditions, it would seem to justify current efforts to break down the barriers to expanded growth and development of Black businesses rather than to urge abandonment of the concept of Black business ownership.

A second major ommission is the failure to mention or examine any of the numerous programs or proposals for Black economic development that reject the concept of Black capitalism. These alternatives promote the concepts of Black self-determination, collective or community ownership and control of large-scale capital instruments and industrial resources. The Community Self-Determination Act proposed by CORE, Dunbar McLaurin's Ghediplan, and Richard America's proposal for the transfer of major American corporations to Black ownership and control are a few of the proposals advanced as a strategy for Black economic development. Additionally, Brimmer ignores the activities and concepts of the Community Development Corporations, the Black Muslims, and the Zion Investment Program headed by Reverend Leon Sullivan. None of these proposals or programs advocate the development of mom-and-pop stores in Black ghettos as an ultimate goal.

Community ownership of worn-out white businesses now operating in the ghettos is not a basic tenet of either the Black militants or moderates. Generally, they seek a much larger share of the wealth and resources of America. A casual review of some of the current activities would have revealed that their strategy of business development is not totally ghetto-specific, nor totally dependent on the segregated market. The Muslims are buying land and are attempting to establish large, mechanized farms in white communities. Leon Sullivan has opened a plant that manufactures aerospace parts; Fighton in Rochester manufactures transformers and metal stampings; California Golden Oaks Products Company in Watts manufactures baseball bats, etc.

Of course, if you view the ownership and control of businesses by Blacks as undesirable a priori, there is no need to consider these forms of Black economic development.

The most glaring deficiency in the Brimmer thesis is the failure to explore the causal relationship between the conditions of Black poverty and powerlessness and the workings of the American political and economic systems.

Poverty among Black people is not an accident of history. It derives from a complex of decisions from the courthouse to the White House which Black people do not influence or control. Locally and nationally, America is ruled by organized interest groups. Whether these groups are elitist or heterogenous, the same results obtain for Blacks. If the needs of Black people are recognized at all, it is after the fact. This has been the

Black experience in Reconstruction, New Deal, Fair Deal, the Frontier, and the Great Society. Nixon's New Federalism portends a return to the Black disenfranchisement of the Reconstruction period.

In *Who Rules America*, G. William Domhoff identifies the elitist upper-class power structure and details its control of industry, foundations, educational institutions, the mass media, the White House, the Defense Department, and the CIA; and its domination and influence over the Congress, the federal judiciary, and the FBI. Similar interest groups and power blocs that patently exclude Blacks exist at the state and local levels. In his keynote speech at the National Black Economic Development Conference in Detroit in April 1969, Black economist Robert Browne noted that Black impoverishment derives from the fact that Black people do not have access to the levers of power in America; namely, (1) accumulations of private wealth; (2) some 200 major corporations, most of whose annual incomes exceed the budgets of most of the nations of Africa; (3) the military–industrial complex centered in the Pentagon and obviously overlapping with the 200 largest corporations; (4) the federal and state government apparatus; (5) the Congress; (6) organized crime, and (7) organized labor.

These groups mould public opinion and directly shape or indirectly influence both private and public policies in a manner that protects and advances their economic interests and power. Their success in influencing defense spending, agricultural subsidies, oil depletion allowances, airline and railroad subsidies, and similar benefits for the affluent and the wealthy is a matter of record.

It is important to recognize, as C. Wright Mills points out, that the exercise of power through decisions is two-dimensional. It is evidenced not only in the decisions made but in those decisions purposely not made.

Decisions made or not made relative to public policies in the fields of tax reform, education, welfare, housing, law and order, and health, to mention a few, are shaped by men who are members of these powerful interest groups or whose political ambitions depend on financing or other support from these sources.

Because of this hierarchial structure of the white decision-making apparatus, the masses of Blacks are the victims rather than the beneficiaries of the American system. St. Clair Drake explains that "the concept of victimization implies . . . that some people are used as means to other people's end—without their consent—and that the social system is so structured that it can be deliberately manipulated to the disadvantage of some groups by the clever, the vicious, the cynical as well as by the powerful." This manipulation, to the detriment of Blacks, can be traced from the refusal of the U.S. government to allocate forty acres of publicly held lands to freed slaves to contemporary programs in urban renewal, highway construction, rapid transit construction, a dehumanizing welfare program, and the hunger and malnutrition that prevails among Blacks is the most affluent nation in the world today.

A complete economic profile of the Black ghetto further highlights the powerlessness of its inhabitants. There are more than mom-and-pop stores in the ghetto economy. There are substandard overdepreciated housing units with inflated rents that absorb from 20 to 30 percent of the income of the tenants. There are overcrowded inefficient school systems that receive a disproportionate share of tax revenues; unequal law enforcement that creates and maintains a market for prostitution, narcotics, and criminal activity leading to reduced efficiency and productivity of the ghetto as an economic unit and depletion of its supply of human capital; and merchants who inflate prices when welfare checks are due.

If we subscribe to Brimmer's one-sided analysis, the "victims" are more responsible for the existence of the ghetto than the victimizers.

When Brimmer's statements and concepts are considered with his deliberate omissions, his purpose and objective in condemning Black capitalism is revealed as more than a gentle chastisement of Richard Nixon or an admonishment to misguided Blacks who cannot recognize the pitfalls and constraints of ghetto capitalism. The larger purpose and objective is to persuade students, intellectuals, and community leaders to abandon the concepts of Black power, Black nationalism, and Black self-determination that are gaining ascendancy in the ghetto and to pursue a strategy of integration instead.

The strategy of Black economic advancement through salaried employment in white firms is an unrealistic, integrationist concept. It "writes off" the masses of Black people who are excluded from competition for white-collar jobs, and condemns them to a marginal, subhuman existence. The riots and rebellions during the sixties revealed the explosive destructive potential of the ghettos. They cannot be written-off and will no longer remain quiet, peaceful, and invisible.

This strategy ignores the vulnerability of Blacks to white domination, exploitation, and racism. Even if more Blacks secure salaried management positions in white firms, it will not provide the leverage needed to influence or control the decision-making apparatus in either the public or the private sectors. As one observer has pointed out, "The political power of an individual is not significantly changed when his income rises from $3,000 to $10,000 or even $30,000—in fact, his political influence might actually be decreased, because he has more to lose and therefore will take fewer risks."

It is equally true that increased individual incomes do not substantially increase economic power. Higher incomes generally produce higher consumption. A house in the suburbs, two cars, and two television sets do not constitute economic power. Economic power in America today flows from the control and ownership of capital-producing instruments. A plant is a capital-producing instrument because it can be sold or used as collateral to secure money for development or expansion of economic enterprises. Individual income and equity in a home or automobile will not produce equivalent leverage.

Based on current employment trends, it is unlikely that Black gains in white-collar positions will produce more than a minimal impact on un-

employment and underemployment over the next decade. Harvard economist Otto Eckstein estimates that Blacks will comprise 12 percent of the
total work force by 1985, but will hold a significantly smaller percentage
of jobs in the professional, skilled, and clerical sales fields. Full economic
equality based on the Black percentage of the work force in 1985 will
require 1,330,000 Black managers and proprietors. Eckstein estimates that
there will be only 420,000; there will be only 410,000 in sales against an
equality ratio of 830,000; and only 1,510,000 clerical workers instead of
2,160,000.

Further, it is illogical to assume that white firms will continue to provide white-collar positions to Blacks at the same rate as experienced over
the past decade. The momentum for the hiring resulted from civil rights
demonstrations carried out by Blacks in the lowest income brackets who
are still denied access to white-collar jobs. It is unlikely that they will
support future actions of this type.

It is more reasonable to assume that the masses will use the power of
their numbers to secure higher wages and fringe benefits for themselves in
the unskilled and skilled occupations. The strikes of hospital workers and
sanitation workers in Charleston, Atlanta, Memphis, and other cities reflect
this trend.

In the final analysis, it is folly to argue the relative merits of Black
capitalism and salaried employment in white-owned firms as exclusive
alternative methods of Black economic development. It is analogous to
debating the relative advantages of occupational specialties within the
slave system rather than addressing the issue of abolition.

It is very clear that powerlessness, more than any other factor, is the
cause of poverty and other forms of oppression inflicted upon the Black
population. Black economic development, along with political, social, and
cultural development, must be viewed and evaluated in this context of
powerlessness to determine the proper methods and strategies for progress
and advancement.

The economic structure of the ghetto can be changed if the resources
are provided to accomplish the task. These resources must come from the
public sector. Farm subsidies, oil subsidies, the rural electrification program, the Marshall Plan, and numerous precedents exist for making the
required investment of public funds. Social benefits, rather than dollar
profits, fully justify the required expenditures.

It is unlikely that these resources will be provided voluntarily. The
pressure to secure these concessions resides in the masses who occupy the
ghettos. Hence, "control" of the ghetto will be a crucial determinant of
the success of the Black economic development strategy.

More than half of the Black population lives in the cities. Approximately
80 percent of these urban dwellers are concentrated in the inner-city areas
of these urban centers. By 1975, over a half-dozen major U.S. cities will
have Black majorities.

Control of the institutions of the ghetto could provide the resources
and potential for organization of the masses required to break the yoke of

white control and to enable Blacks to gain access to the levers of power. Roy Innis of CORE points out that Harlem schools purchase over $100 million in goods and services each year. Aside from the political implications, community control of Harlem schools could insure that Black community-owned firms benefited from these expenditures. Control of health and hospital services, sanitation, police and fire departments, and other municipally funded activities would promote the development of a Black political and economic infrastructure.

The real potential of Black economic development must be measured in terms of its capability to produce the leadership in the Black ghettos for organizing the human and capital resources to take control of local institutions. Neither mom-and-pop style Black capitalism nor token employment of Blacks in salaried positions in the white corporate economy constitute viable alternatives.

# PART III

## *Alternatives to Black Capitalism*

# Introduction

The amount of rhetoric surrounding business and economic development in Black America has been matched by the generation of many models and blueprints to guide practitioners. Perhaps the least surprising facet of the movement towards the economic liberation of Blacks is that there has emerged no meaningful consensus on the most viable among several alternate ends or means in our struggle. There are those who contend that this disagreement is much to our detriment. They espouse their particular view as the "only" means by which the chosen goals can be attained. To expect total agreement on how the struggle is to proceed is unreasonable. But to encourage a respect for a variety of means toward the same generally accepted ends is to display the intellectual maturity that is a necessary condition for a solution to the plight of Blacks in this country.

The models and guidelines presented in Part III cover a broad range of alternatives on the business and economic development continuum. The first two selections are efforts to apply the experiences of international development economists to less-developed urban communities. The "Ghedi-plan" is a rather innovative concept which details the tools and machinery needed to increase "GNP"—ghetto national product. The second selection is more an attempt to describe the planning process utilized in economic development activities centered in Harlem. Both the readings by Schucter and Cross are involved attempts to improve the development potential of concentrated urban communities. The first focuses on attitudes and institutional arrangements and the second concentrates on incentives needed to rejuvenate financial and commercial enterprise. Kelso and Hetter argue strongly for effective capital dispersal in the American economy. Their "second-income plan" is already used by several corporations to provide equity ownership to their employees and is the basis of an extensive economic development program formulated under the auspices of the Congress of Racial Equality.

Cooperatives represent an old but relatively untried approach to the economic development of Black communities. The article by Ulmer and the last selection are related to the notion of cooperative ventures. Community development corporations represent one of the few well-structured innovations in approaches to the developmental problems of urban and rural Black communities. The Community Self-Determination Bill introduced in Congress in 1968 is built around this notion.

Whether or not any of the models become more widely operational in the quest for Black economic freedom remains to be seen. But that the success of these models depends upon the resourcefulness brought to bear on strengthening their various weaknesses and synthesizing their strong points into workable programs cannot be gainsaid.

# 14 ]] Ghetto Economic Development and Industrialization Plan (Ghediplan)

*Dunbar S. McLaurin*

The events of the past several summers have produced convincing proof that traditional approaches to urban crises are woefully inadequate and that something new must be developed. It is equally clear that this something must be based upon creative economics, with a generous and imaginative application of the sociological lessons we have learned in the slums. The Ghetto Economic Development and Industrialization Plan, or "Ghediplan" for short, is an attempt to meet that need.

This plan has been written and developed against the compelling events of the last hot summer of 1967, and against the shadows cast by the impending summer. At this time, the nation has not begun to comprehend the full impact of the Report of the President's Commission on Civil Disorders. But what is apparent is that we cannot long provide the vast sums recommended by the Commission as a dole. Yet the nation itself cannot be sustained, it is apparent, unless something approaching the recommended order of magnitude is applied to the problem. The problem can only be solved by making the economies of the ghettos productive and self-sustaining. This is what the Ghediplan seeks to do.

The social agony of the slums is but the symptom of an underlying and basic pathology of economic sickness. Until the ghettos have a sound economic basis, the social service dollar is only a financial palliative at best—a Band-Aid, an aspirin, or a "Compoz" pill. It has taken a long time, and many hot summers, to reach this truth. The word "economic" in the Economic Opportunity Act has finally attained the respectability that it should have had all along.

Now, however, economic development of the ghettos is of the highest domestic priority. Poverty experts now realize that unless ghetto residents own their businesses and have a stake in the economy, it is easy for them to rationalize that what they are burning and looting belongs not to them but to absentee white owners and is fair game.

Senator Jacob Javits of New York has dramatically stated the case:

Though he is tragically mistaken, the slum Negro sees himself as having no stake in the economic life of his community and no realistic possibility of becoming part of it—hence there is no community morality against destroying it. (*Cong. Rec.* S10554 (1967).)

From Dunbar S. McLaurin, "The Ghediplan" (New York: Ghettonomics, Inc.). © 1968, Dunbar S. McLaurin.

The weakness in most ghetto economic development plans, which now abound, is that they do not view the ghetto as an entirety, and they therefore are basically piecemeal, sociological, and cosmetic in their approach to the problem. None comes to grips with the immediate economic problems of:

1. Transferring ownership from absentee owners to local minority owners in an orderly manner, thereby strengthening the local population.

2. Diversifying, strengthening, and expanding the economic base so that it can compete in the wider economic mainstream.

3. Increasing the "Ghetto National Product" by increasing the number of ghetto-owned industries that *produce*, as opposed to the present businesses that merely *distribute* "foreign" goods and services.

## Inadequate Philosophy of Other Plans

The failure to view the problems of the underdeveloped ghetto economy in the same way that we view those of an underdeveloped nation has led to several inadequate plans—all based upon an inadequate philosophy—about the requirements for true economic development of these areas.

There are five basic false assumptions underlying this philosophy:

*First:* That only research is needed to develop ghetto businesses. This false assumption has resulted in a rash of "plans" which, when distilled, provide for nothing more than the collection of data about ghetto businesses. Many of these businesses fail even before the statistics are compiled. Research *is* needed, but a study or a diagnostic survey does not produce economic development. It is, at most, a tool.

*Second:* That high unemployment is the real economic problem of the ghetto. This false assumption is bottomed on the belief that if more people worked there would be more consumers, and ghetto businesses would therefore flourish. What is overlooked, however, is that these businesses are rarely *owned* by ghetto residents. Hence another rash of "development plans," which are nothing more than programs to train, retrain, and break down employment barriers.

Full employment is a desired goal and must be vigorously pursued, but it alone will not insure a healthy, viable minority business community. The Negro had full employment on the plantation. Yet it insured only the economic growth of the white owner. New industry is needed in the ghetto. Manpower training is vital. Discrimination must end. But these are not the true routes to economic growth.

For without ownership and control of production and distribution, employment means little. The Negro remains a straight man for the flow of money through him directly back into the white community. The minority business community must be helped to diversify and develop its capacity to own and control the economic mechanisms; to retain the money once it is earned, and to circulate the money within the community.

In the "real" world outside the ghetto, a dollar that is worth only a dollar is a losing dollar. A plan to develop the ghetto economically must look beyond mere full *employment*. The goal must be full *self*-employment. The ghetto must not only help provide full employment, it must also determine the multiplier effect use of money in the community and participate in the basic economic decisions that underlie a sound economy.

*Third:* That ghetto economic development requires only the provision of long-term, low-interest loan money. The theory is that only the lack of capital prevents the survival and expansion of the otherwise marginal and high-risk ghetto businesses.

*Fourth:* That the provision of management training, together with sufficient capital, is a sure-fire solution to the problem. All that is needed additionally, the theory goes, is some professional guidance about tax practices, and in the maintenance of ledgers, inventory systematizing, purchasing, store layout, etc.

These last two assumptions constitute perhaps the oldest and most traditional approach: provide the ghetto businessman with capital and training, and, ipso facto, the problem is solved. This approach is the "old fur coat" theory, based upon the radio commercial: "Don't remodel your old fur coat; you will still have an old fur coat."

It is apparent that if every minority businessman was thoroughly trained in bookkeeping, inventory control, layout, etc., and if each was given a small loan, the economy of the ghetto would hardly move upwards an inch. The result would be a community of clean, neat, tidy—but still marginal—shopkeepers with a minimum economic output. In short, we would still have "an old fur coat."

The "old fur coat" approach has failed in minority economic development, largely because it itself is based upon a fifth false assumption.

*Fifth:* That the minority businessmen have the same problems as their white counterparts and that remedies and legislation designed for the white community can be applied intact to the ghetto small business community.

The small businessman in the white community operates within a framework of mutually supporting larger businesses and industry. Unlike the minority businessman, he is an integral part of a fluid and mobile economy, in which he can move upwards and outwards in response to the interactions of the free enterprise system, and according to his own entrepreneurial ability. He is a member of a network of business and social relationships that are alien and unavailable to his minority counterpart but that constantly stimulate and offer him happenstance unearned opportunities. He has a heritage of business tradition and of easy availability of capital and technical know-how unknown to the ghetto. Growth is a natural consequence of this heritage; it is expected of the white businessman. And the rules and regulations of the game are designed for and by him.

On the other hand, the ghetto businessman has no such advantages, and no such opportunities. He operates within the high-walled framework of a closed economy. His access to the outer and larger business and industrial world with its opportunities, challenges, and stimuli is as nonexistent as if he were in a remote, underdeveloped country.

And therein lies the challenge. As long as plans for the economic development of the ghettos are based upon the foregoing false assumptions, they will continue to fall far short of what is necessary. The problems of the ghetto economy must be viewed the same way as the problems of an underdeveloped nation are viewed: as an entity and as an interlocking whole. This is the basic approach of the Ghediplan and the essential distinction between this plan and its predecessors.

## The "Underdeveloped Nation" Philosophy of the Ghediplan

When the ghetto is viewed as an underdeveloped nation, an entirely different perspective of the problem is gained.

When the United States helps underdeveloped nations, it concentrates on extending the free enterprise system. The United States wants these nations to have a favorable balance of trade and applies hard and soft money theories in lending money at fair interest rates.

The goal is to create businesses and industries that will use local resources most productively. A central banking system, insurance networks, and other instruments of capital accumulation are established. Favorable tariff rates are set so they can trade with us, and production machinery as well as consumer items are sold. The goal, then, is to establish a balanced, diversified, and self-supporting economy that will generate capital and support a stable, friendly society. Enlightened and selfish dividends are sought, for only a stable economy can support a society that is free of political upheavals and friendly to us.

The parallel lesson for New York City is that ghettos are indeed impacted underdeveloped "nations." As long as their economies are unproductive, unstable, and unable to support their inhabitants in dignity, they, too, will breed riots and upheavals. To eliminate our Watts, Newarks, and Detroits, the cities' underdeveloped ghetto-nations must be given the economic tools with which to build stable, sound economies.

A final and fundamental similarity between the economic philosophy underlying both the Ghediplan and aid programs for underdeveloped nations is that of "nationalism," the local ownership of the economy and the control of its destiny. This concept reflects the universal feeling that dignity, opportunity, and a sense of economic independence are vital energizing elements for the development of a young economy, whether in the ghetto or in an underdeveloped nation.

This, then, is the philosophic background for the Ghediplan. It seeks to establish the machinery with which to restructure the ghetto economy as we would restructure an underdeveloped nation. The plan would diversify the ghetto, create new businesses and industries, and interlock the whole into a mosaic with itself and with the presently "foreign" outer white community. It is not a plan to attack one sector timidly. It seeks to look at the overall ghetto picture and to utilize available municipal resources to create a whole new economy in the ghetto. This economy will be strong enough to participate in, compete with, and become an integral part of the national economy, contributing its own part to the gross national product, instead of being a "colonial" underdeveloped appendage.

It is only by this method that the separate *economic* division of the nation—a serious division that is similar to the social and political division about which the Commission on Civil Disorders warned—can be avoided.

Against the backdrop of the times, nothing less seems worth trying. Nothing less will do. The fate of this nation depends upon the solution of the problems of the ghetto economy.

## *Summary*

Ghediplan seeks to end poverty by creating a strong locally owned economy. The prime target is not the small service business. Emphasis is placed on large-scale business and industry that will have a productive economic impact. Ghetto communities sadly lack indigenously owned businesses that are large enough to be productive and to provide significant employment. For example, statistics compiled by the Interracial Council for Business Opportunity show dramatically the absence of such large scale firms: New York City has a Negro population of about 1.1 million, yet only about twelve Negro-owned or -managed enterprises employing as many as ten persons.

Thus the creation of ten viable new enterprises, providing substantial employment and capitalized at $1 million each, would do more for the ghetto economies than 1,000 additional tiny businesses capitalized at $10,000. However, heretofore no machinery has existed for the broad economic development of the ghetto community through the creation of such large enterprises that require greater funds.

### THE BASIC REQUIREMENTS

In creating the plan, these following basic requirements were considered:

It must be able legally to use public funds to generate financing for developing private profit-making businesses with actually spending these funds.

It must be able to use the city's purchasing power as a generative factor without dislocating city procurement activities.

It must harness the ghetto's private initiative, profit motives, and business instincts.

It must be broad enough to be capable of real community improvement and central planning.

It must be designed to attract broad support from the community, the city, bankers, local and outside businessmen, and federal agencies, including the Small Business Administration and the Office of Economic Opportunity.

It must be self-generating, so the businesses and industries that are created will eventually become healthy enough to compete in the general economic structure, once the pump-priming process is finished.

## THE GOALS

The plan seeks to remove the causes of poverty in the ghetto, not only by creating or helping individual businesses, but by developing the community's entire economy as a working entity and as a whole. In short, the entire economy is treated like an underdeveloped nation as far as feasible. To achieve this economic growth without the need for large grants or at a great cost to the city, a new and creative use of the city's present fiscal, purchasing, and administrative resources is required.

The plan consists of the following components: two *tools*, and six *machinery* instruments. The tools are the guaranteed market and guaranteed financing. The machinery instruments are *administrative* (the Office of Minority Development); *operative* (Small Business Development Centers plus two "conduit corporations"—Local Development Corporations and Small Business Investment Companies); and *supportive* (the Private Economic Consultant Firm and the Small Business Administration).

## THE TOOLS

### Guaranteed Markets

The city would establish "guaranteed markets" for ghetto businesses and contractors by setting aside for the ghettos roughly 10 percent of its one-half billion dollar annual expenditures for purchases and small contracts. This would pump an additional $50 million in purchases of goods and services into the ghettos. This would trigger an additional $50 million from the private sector and from federal and state governments, for a total guaranteed market of $100 million.

As presently structured, however, minority small business communities cannot supply this demand, because they do not have the right type or the right size businesses. It is therefore necessary to diversify and restructure these economies by creating new businesses or expanding existing ones. Such a vast undertaking requires (1) ample capital and (2) technical know-how and management training. These requirements are supplied by the creative use of existing city resources, via guaranteed financing and the machinery components.

### Guaranteed Financing

Guaranteed financing would be achieved by using the city's aggregate $20 to $100 million day-to-day demand deposits to encourage banks to lend money to, or invest in, minority businesses and industries.

The city recently started depositing a portion of these funds in banks that agreed to lend to ghetto businessmen. But this system has not worked because the deposits are merely backed by general promises to lend, and these bank promises cannot be policed effectively. Moreover, this "un-linked policy" is isolated and provides no overall backup resources for the borrowing businesses such as the Ghediplan provides, and the banks are therefore hesitant to participate.

Ghediplan would extend and change the present unlinked policy. Each deposit would be *linked* to a specific commitment by the bank to lend or invest an agreed-upon amount. The line of credit thus established would be the ghetto's guaranteed financing, and the plan is designated the "link-posit plan."

### THE ADMINISTRATIVE MACHINERY

#### The Office of Minority Economic Development (OMED)

OMED would be the city agency that organizes and catalyzes the entire plan. It would represent the city in administering, implementing, and operating the plan, and would generate guaranteed financing and guaranteed markets with city resources.

### THE OPERATIVE MACHINERY

#### The Small Business Development Centers (SBDCs)

SBDCs are quasi-governmental, community-based economic development centers that will recruit, organize, and spawn the ghetto conduits. Initially operational and administrative, they will provide training, planning, technical aid, and community coordination. SBDCs now exist and are operating under HRA. There would be one SBDC in each ghetto area.

#### The Local Development Corporations (LDCs)

An LDC is a conduit to convert city link deposits into medium- and long-term "brick-and-mortar" capital. These conduits will gain leverage of up to nine to one by securing matching federal funds. They are private, community-based, and community-controlled. There would be one LDC in each community. Eventually, the LDC would be the economic planning center of the community, providing management and technical training and establishing businesses.

#### The Small Business Investment Companies (SBICs)

An SBIC is a conduit to convert city link deposits into equity or venture capital. By securing matching federal funds, it will gain leverage of up to three to one. SBICs are flexible enough to provide technical training and to be community-based, with one for each community, or it may be centralized with community branches and a common board.

### THE SUPPORTIVE MACHINERY

#### The Private Economic Consultant Firm

The firm would provide technical and professional know-how for establishing the plan. It would provide back-up for management and technical training and would design and establish the two community "conduit corporations," the LDCs and the SBICs.

*The Small Business Administration (SBA)*

The federal SBA provides monetary leverage to both the LDC and the SBIC conduits through matching federal funding of up to nine to one. It provides a wide range of direct and guaranteed loans and of back-up technical services, advice, and materials.

## OPERATIONAL CHRONOLOGY OF THE GHEDIPLAN

The city establishes an Office of Minority Economic Development (OMED)

OMED retains a private economic consultant firm for technical back-up, especially in designing the conduits.

The firm works with the Small Business Development Centers (SBDCs), under OMEDs supervision, to establish local conduit corporations and to plan the economic growth of the community.

OMED, aided by the consulting firm, establishes the procedure and machinery for the guaranteed markets and for the link deposits to provide guaranteed financing.

OMED, using link deposits, generates seed money for the embryo conduits.

The conduits draw the seed money, hire staff, and consult with an SBDC and the consulting firm to identify business opportunities and to organize the ownership structure of the proposed businesses.

The city's purchasing needs and link deposits are coordinated so that the new businesses are provided with guaranteed financing and guaranteed markets.

Under this chronology, the conduits are organized by OMED, experts from the consulting firm, and the SBDCs, each working together in an administrative, technical, and community operational capacity.

These conduits then identify opportunities and organize new businesses or expand the existing businesses, which are then backed up by management assistance and technical help from all levels. City purchases will provide their markets and city-generated funds their financing.

With this overall coordinated structure, chances for success of those ghetto businesses should be maximum.

## THE COST AND FINANCING OF THE PLAN

The plan's only foreseeable additional cost to the city is that of creating the Office of Minority Economic Development and of retaining the services of the private economic consultant firm, since the plan is designed to use the city's existing resources to generate up to $200 million in ghetto-financing and new markets.

The Office of Minority Economic Development would work directly with the Small Business Development Centers to establish the local conduits. These SBDCs already exist and are funded. Once a local conduit is operating, it will be self-supporting, and some will even be profit making.

The remaining cost is that of "start-up," or "seed money," for the conduits. Seed money could come from a foundation or government grant. But the plan prefers to avoid a grant, because it would diminish the objectives of self-help and self-sustaining private enterprise. Participating banks, therefore, would be asked for the seed money. Several banks have already agreed to supply this seed money as part of the link deposit plan. Their reasons for this contribution have been set forth by city administrator Roy Goodman:

The banks are eager to get the city's money. Each $1 million brings them $60,000 a year in interest, which they can keep. That's a pretty good deal. (*N. Y. Sunday News*, July 9, 1967.)

Each conduit corporation is tentatively budgeted at $30,000. Banks that have participated in a pilot link deposit project have already agreed to supply this amount of seed money in return for compensating link deposits.

# 15 ]] Economic Development Planning for American Urban Slums*

Central Harlem is a slum community in the city of New York. Its population of about 200,000 consists almost entirely of Black Americans whose annual median family income is only 57 percent of the citywide median. Its housing is crumbling, rat-infested, and overcrowded; at the density rate of parts of Harlem, the entire U.S. population could be squeezed into three of New York City's five boroughs. Nearly 30 percent of its participating labor force is unemployed or underemployed. Much of its property is held by absentee white owners, with consequent loss to the community of circulating income. Its infrastructure—roads, sanitation and power facilities—has deteriorated and is not being replaced. The community's educational facilities are so grossly inadequate that two in five high school students fail to receive diplomas, and attendance rates in general are far below national norms. Yet elementary school attendance exceeds capacity by 5,500 children. One index of the relative state of health facilities is the mean mortality rate; Harlem's 1962 rate of 49.5 infant deaths per 1,000 was almost four times greater than the New York City *white* average rate of 12.8 per 1,000.

Relative to the city, to the region and to the nation at large, then, Harlem—like most of the urban Black communities in the United States—is a depressed, underdeveloped area, sharing many of the attributes of the less-developed countries. For example:

The typical *vicious circles of poverty* are operative in the ghetto: "Improving a man's living conditions won't help him much unless he has a job. A job won't help unless he is trained to perform it. He cannot be trained without the basic conviction that he has a chance to succeed. But he is not likely to form that belief in the squalor of the slum" (*Newsweek*, November 20, 1967, p. 42).

Harlem may be said to have an *unfavorable balance of payments*. The bulk of the goods and services consumed in the area are imported from the outside, and due to the relative scarcity of retail and wholesale activi-

From Bennett Harrison, *International Development Review* (March 1968): 23–29 © 1968 by the Society for International Development.

* The research reflected in the present paper is support by funds granted by OEO pursuant to the provisions of the U.S. Economic Opportunity Act of 1964. The point of view expressed herein is, of course, that of the author, who does not presume to speak for OEO.

ties, much of the disposable income is spent "abroad," in lower Manhattan and in the other boroughs of the city. Harlem's only real export commodity is its labor, and for reasons to be discussed below, the rate of growth of exports is declining. These "leakages" of disposable income out of the community prevent the ordinary economic and employment multipliers from operating to the benefit of the residents.

The United States is entering its eighth straight year of continuous economic growth at an average annual product rate of 5½ percent. Yet the economy of Harlem, we think, continues to lag far behind. Between 1950 and 1960, median family income in the United States rose by 6.9 percent per annum, and in New York City by about 6.7 percent. In Harlem, it rose by less than 4 percent. In real terms, the gap may be even larger, to the extent that the "poor" really do "pay more."[1] Moreover, we have no evidence to indicate that this gap is closing. In fact, inference from national data suggests that it may be *growing*: The difference between the median family incomes of American Blacks and whites increased from $2,726 in 1959 to $3,346 in 1966. In such a situation, powerful *negative demonstration effects become operative.*

The Office of Economic Opportunity is the U.S. government agency responsible for the management of President Johnson's "War on Poverty." OEO, perceiving the similarity between conditions in Harlem and those obtaining in the less-developed countries, has assembled a team of international development economists, engineers, and architects. This team, acting as consultants to a community council consisting entirely of Harlem residents, is preparing an economic development plan for Central Harlem.[2] At the heart of the plan is our intention to establish a "development bank" *inside* the ghetto to coordinate and promote strategies for community economic development.

In this paper, I shall describe our initial formulation of the planning problem, the goals we hope to achieve, the instruments at our disposal, and our intended strategies for employing them. Although the project began in September 1967, this discussion must be considered primarily as a blueprint for action; as the planning period progresses, our strategies will undergo continuous modification as we receive outside advice, fresh insights, and feedback from our first projects. Moreover, we insist on our "plans" remaining sufficiently flexible to permit accommodation to as yet only dimly perceived government programs for direct investment in the core cities of America.

The "less-developed country" analogy of course suggests a policy of import substitution, to be pursued in conjunction with export development, both subject to an evaluation of the area's comparative advantages. This is, in fact, the overall planning strategy we have adopted. The decision to approach from slum planning in this way is based, however, on considerably more than the analogy we have been discussing. To this formulation of the problem we now turn.

## The Problem

The previous inhabitants of American urban slums came to the cities at a time when the structures of employment and housing were relatively more hospitable to the poor than they are today:

These new European migrants brought varied skills with them, frequently had some degree of familiarity with industrial–urban life, and (perhaps most important of all) had been legally free men and women having an unambiguous, homogeneous cultural history with which to identify.

The slum dwellings they inhabited were frequently only one or two generations removed from having been (sometimes fashionable) middle-class residences.

The urban economy provided them with nearly full (albeit difficult and usually unpleasant) secular employment, conveniently located near or even within the slums. *The kinds of jobs which the new migrants were capable of performing were in fact available.* And a critically important implication of the local location of these jobs was that these previous minorities were not *forced* to challenge the de-facto segregation typically imposed by the middle-class neighborhoods in and around the city.

The Black Americans living in the urban slums today face very different circumstances, only some of which are associated with their race:

These latest immigrants to the cities have come as former agricultural slaves, with virtually no industrial or urban experience, victims of an enforced loss of racial and cultural identity which they are only just now beginning to rediscover. "The Negro population, as late as 1940, was three-fourths southern and mostly rural; today, nearly half the nation's 22 million Blacks live in the North and two-thirds are clotted in and around the nation's cities. And they came to the cities a peasant class. . . ." (*Newsweek*, p. 38.) . . .

Slum housing which was relatively new for previous minorities is now entirely obsolete, yet it is still pressed into service by continuation of Black migration from the rural South and by the failure of business and government at all levels to provide significant quantities of truly low-income housing. In South Philadelphia, seven out of eight of the one-family dwelling units [were] built before 1919; on Manhattan's lower East Side, the figure is two-thirds. And yet we suspect, although we do not yet have reliable documentation, that the rent constitutes a significantly larger proportion of the Black urban slum dweller's income than it did for his predecessors, especially if we adjust the data for quality changes.

Far reaching transformations in middle-class residential preferences and in industrial technologies have taken place in the twentieth century (notably the substitution of horizontal space-intensive techniques for vertical "loft" space-intensive techniques). These changes have generated a net outmigration of industries from the core cities to the suburban rings around them. And this trend is especially pronounced for precisely those manufacturing and wholesaling industries which have historically been the most intensive employers of unskilled and semiskilled labor. The kinds of employment which have replaced these more traditional jobs in the core cities center around communications and central business office services. Within this group, the only class of jobs to which the private market has provided significant access (i.e., training and placement) for Black Americans is secretarial and clerical employment. But among New York City office employees, only about 25 percent are male. The inescapable conclusion is that the Black urban community—superficially only the latest of a series of urban minorities to inhabit the slums—is effectively the first to face a situation where full male employment in the free market economy is available only in areas *outside* the core city, areas to which the Black slum dweller can migrate (if at all) only at a personal and social cost far exceeding anything his predecessors ever had to face.

## The Objectives

Our overall planning objectives are to increase the per capita income and employment of our clients, the residents of Central Harlem. They will need greater and more versatile labor and management skills in order to be able to improve the quality of life in Harlem proper, and in order to be in a position to respond to government and private business offers of jobs *outside* the ghetto. This last point reminds us that important externalities will accrue to the city, state, and country at large from the successful implementation of the "Harlem Project."

Our understanding of the problem suggests that we can no longer rely on the private economy to create local employment. By any sort of estimate, the current social costs of rapidly relocating Harlem residents into the suburban communities to which the private economy *has* led new industrial and housing investments (assuming they wished to go, a point too infrequently considered), are simply prohibitively high, perhaps infinitely so. Therefore, while public policy *must* continue to address itself to lowering the barriers to residential and job integration in the suburbs, policy planning for at least the next decade has to emphasize the economic development of the ghetto itself. Harlem must be transformed into a kind of "greenhouse," a planned environment whose function is to provide its inhabitants, first with the basic amenities of a decent life, and secondly, with the skills needed to permit them to compete in the world outside the greenhouse. This, of course, is the (only legitimate) purpose of what development planners generally call "infant industry protection." If people —like industries—are able to compete, then they will be able to exercise free choice: choice of residence, choice of job. And this, in a way, is the most fundamental planning objective of all.

## The Instruments

There are four broad categories of expenditure (public and private) which might address themselves to our income, employment, and "ability-to-compete" goals:

1. Investment in new and/or expanded businesses
2. Investment in job-training programs
3. Renewal and rehabilitation of ghetto housing
4. Direct income transfer payments, e.g., increased unemployment compensation or a negative income tax

The latter is not an instrument whose employment is subject to the control either of any individual community such as Harlem or of any single government agency such as OEO, so we shall not consider it further.

With respect to the third instrument, our very scarce resources have forced us to think carefully about the jobs–housing sequence. It has frequently been observed (in many countries, including the United States) that newly constructed, low-income housing rapidly becomes deteriorated unless the tenants already have or are about to embark on new jobs. While we have by no means settled this question of sectoral sequencing, we have decided to act on the sorely inadequate data on hand (as planners everywhere are forced to do) which indicate concentration on employment-creation first.

Finally, it follows naturally from our formulation of the problem that instruments (1) and (2) ought to be combined. That is, we wish to invest in new and/or expanded businesses—retail, wholesale, manufacturing, and service—which will intensively employ Harlem residents which will be owned and/or managed by Harlem businessmen and which will, in effect, be *designed* to have joint outputs: Commodities (for import substitution and for export) and skilled Black workers and managers. These Black businesses *are*, then, our principal planning instruments.

Some of these businesses will be financed through the Harlem Corporation, a "development bank" to be established within the ghetto. Some will be financed by Black businessmen affiliated with this "bank." Others (especially in manufacturing) will be established under subcontracts or franchises from national and/or regional firms.

Some of these businesses may actually be physically located *in* Central Harlem. Others will locate in adjacent areas, according to space availabilities, transport access, availability of necessary "satellite" or ancillary services, and the general rule of thumb that, whenever possible, the "external economies" or "spillovers" generated by new industries should accrue to the residents of Harlem.

## Planning Strategies

There are three basic components in our planning strategy: (1) The study of the existing economic and demographic structure of Harlem, particularly with respect to labor force characteristics, land use, and income-expenditure behavior; (2) institutional development planning, focusing on the creation of a "development bank" within the ghetto; and (3) industrial development planning, the identification and programming of potentially profitable black businesses to be financed and/or coordinated by the "development bank."

### 1. THE EXISTING ECONOMIC STRUCTURE

The Development Planning Workshop of Columbia University is conducting several crucial diagnostic studies. Their *Food Price Survey* will establish whether there exist significant retail price differentials between Harlem and outside businesses of various size classes, and how much of the price dispersion (if any) could be remedied by a consumer education program. The *Consumer Attitude Survey* will identify nonfood purchasing behavior and intentions of Harlem residents. This information will be employed later in assessing community preferences for the ranking of alternative import substitution and other activities. A *Survey of Institutional Demand* will identify the kinds and quantities of goods and services which might be sold by Harlem businesses to major institutions in New York City, and particularly to those in and around Harlem. Institutions such as universities, hospitals, and government office buildings do exist in the area; since these constitute one of the city's leading growth sectors, business linkages to them are especially desirable. Other Columbia studies will deal with income, population, and education. But probably the single-most important of Columbia's special studies deals with *Employment, Unemployment, and Manpower in Harlem*. This will define the present status of the labor–management force potentially available for staffing the new and expanded businesses to be programmed. This study is, therefore, a major input into the industrial development plan.

Four kinds of physical facilities will be required to accommodate the proposed new economic activities:

1. Street level retail commercial space
2. Loft space for light manufacturing and wholesaling
3. Loft space for medium manufacturing with loading facilities
4. Modern, large span manufacturing space

The Architects' Renewal Committee in Harlem will survey existing facilities in Harlem and adjacent areas, categorizing them by size, location, cost, condition, and ancillary service availability. Other ARCH surveys will identify vacant land availability and renovation potential. These land-use surveys constitute the other major input into the industrial development plan.

## 2. INSTITUTIONAL PLANNING

During the planning period of nine months, the Harlem Commonwealth Council is serving as project center. More precisely, the functions of the council are to identify and bring together existing and potential Black businessmen in the community, to mobilize public support for the development and promotion of Black businesses, and to direct the research activities of the professional consultants. The council is the ultimate decision-maker in matters concerning the ranking and/or selection of candidate economic activities.

Within the first year, the council and OEO will create a wholly new institution in Harlem, a nonprofit investment corporation, qualified to receive tax-deductible gifts and grants, and governmental agency subsidies. The *Harlem Corporation* will, in effect, serve as a community "development bank." It will provide:

Loans and grants to new and existing businesses which create or maintain employment and/or ownership for the community.

Bondability to Black contractors engaged in housing construction and rehabilitation.

A brokerage service for Black businessmen seeking to procure loans from outside parties (e.g., government agencies, private banks) and sub-contracts or franchises from outside firms.

Technical and management assistance to Harlem businesses, through a permanent staff of local economists, engineers, and financial experts to complement the architectural staff already operating in the community. This "team," with occasional assistance from outside consultants, would provide technical assistance to Harlem businessmen *whenever and for as long as they are in need of it*. We all know that inadequate provision of permanent and continuing technical advice to producers is one of the most frequently encountered flaws in the development plans of the less-developed countries.

Continuing management and job-training programs for the residents of the community, both through its affiliated businesses and, if necessary, through special remedial programs.

A service for placing Harlem workers in local businesses and, over time, in outside firms, government agencies and public training programs.

The organization of "trading blocks" of local businesses for the purpose of obtaining lower-unit-cost business services such as insurance and credit.

In short, the corporation will function as a central planning and coordinating agency in the ghetto. From the national perspective, of course, such an institutional development represents a *decentralization* of responsibility. In time, networks of such "banks" may emerge, linking the urban slums with one another and with a coordinating agency in Washington.

## 3. INDUSTRIAL PLANNING

The Center for Economic Planning of The New School for Social Research has the responsibility for generating the industrial development plan for Harlem. The final plan, to be completed by June 1968 will consist of detailed cost–benefit studies of a number of individual business prospects and of "investment packages." Explicit calculations will be attempted for different institutional forms (e.g., cooperatives versus corporations). A general rule of thumb guiding the preparation of the plan is the "leap-frog" concept, according to which—even for a high unemployment area like Harlem—the programming of "best-practice" technologies is to be preferred, on the assumption that any losses in direct employment creation are more than offset by the "spillovers" (indirect demand generation) associated with industries which are at the leading rather than at the trailing edge of development.

The industrial development research is being conducted according to a dual strategy. Simultaneously, we are employing a *narrowing-down* and a *building-up* approach. Since the latter is easier to describe (but harder to do), we shall discuss it first.

According to the building-up approach, we start with several "bright ideas," generally (but not necessarily) based on existing business activities in the area. Following the suggestion of Albert Hirschmann, we then look for backward and forward linkages. That is, we try to identify those business activities linked to the "base activity" as suppliers of inputs or services and as demanders (intermediate and final) of the base activity's output. In this way, we develop an "investment package," and our cost–revenue analyses are conducted in terms of such *sets* of businesses.[3] For example, we might start with a hospital supply firm in the community, "integrate forward" into the management of hospital supply systems by computer, and "integrate backward" into the manufacture of pharmaceuticals. Ultimately, we shall generate a set of "built-up" industrial programs, which are then simply incorporated into the final plan.

The narrowing-down approach starts with the identification of a universe of commercial activities, which we call our PRELIST. In order not to miss any potentially profitable activities, we have chosen as our universe the list of all four-digit Standard Industrial Classification industries: the SIC system is a coding format developed by the U.S. Bureau of the Budget. An example of the detail available at the four-digit level of aggregation is code 3011: Tires and inner tubes.

A second major universe which we are generating is an inventory of all commercial establishments presently doing business in Harlem. For compatability, this too is arranged by four-digit SIC codes.

Both lists are then subjected to a prefeasibility analysis (sometimes called "market planning"). In our case, this consists of comparing two or, if relevant, three parallel statistical series for each four-digit industry:

1. National series
2. City or metropolitan area series
3. Harlem series

We are constructing series on employment, payrolls, value of shipments, capital expenditure, value added, and on several key ratios, notably *value added per production worker*, a good proxy indicator of capital intensity. We are also making (and borrowing existing) five- and ten-year projections of overall growth in sales and unemployment.

The objective is to assign priorities according to the probable "competitive potential" of the activities in an urban core location. With our forecasts it may be possible to actually construct quantitative indices, such as net expected present value, internal rate of return, or simple rate of return over cost. But, however they are determined, these priorities will refer *not* to investment, but to *resources to be allocated to further study*.[4]

Once this preliminary ranking is completed, and the two lists are permitted to "overlap," we are immediately presented with three reasonably distinct sets of four-digit activities:

*Existing Harlem businesses which are doing well* and ought to be expanded. We call this list EXIDEV, and expect to address further analysis of this sector only to the identification of such general business problems as cyclical shortages of working capital. This analyzed EXIDEV list will then be transferred directly to the final planning document.

*Existing Harlem businesses which are not doing well*, or EXIPROB. Activities on this list must receive a careful diagnostic analysis to identify critical bottlenecks such as credit availability, high cost of insurance, etc. The list, the analysis, and relevant recommendations will then become part of the final plan.

*New business to be developed*, or NEWDEV. This list constitutes the first of three "options displays" to be presented to the Harlem Commonwealth Council. All (rank-ordered) NEWDEV activities will be presented to the council which will then, in effect, establish a cutoff point, resulting in the reduction of the NEWDEV list to a smaller, more manageable subset of activities to receive further study (this is shown as Decision $D_1$ in Figure 15–1).

A full scale feasibility analysis must now be performed on the reduced NEWDEV list. This is the heart of the development project planning process. Feasibility studies (or "market research") consist of:

1. Detailed cost–revenue profiles for each candidate industry by scale and by diversity of products
2. Cost–benefit companion profiles, which attempt to capture (a) the employment—income effects generated by the project, and (b) the more important "externalities" not reflected in measures of private profit but

critical to the whole development program, e.g., smoke nuisance or, conversely, slum clearance effects of new construction

3. Alternative specifications of labor and management requirements

4. Considerations of the possible effects on net profitability of different modes of organization

The results of the feasibility studies now permit us to present HCC with the second options display, which we call PROFILES. The candidate industries in this display are less numerous, but far more exhaustively described than those in the first display.

At this point, the Columbia labor force studies and the ARCH land use studies are brought into use. Here, HCC and its consultants have two sequential decisions to take (Decisions $D_2$ and $D_3$ in Figure 15–1). First, we must compare the labor–management requirements associated with the activities on the PROFILES list to the existing labor tween the two yields order-of-magnitude estimates of job-training requirements. Here, the training programmers on the team will make the critical decision as to which PROFILE activities are infeasible by virtue of having too large a gap. Having thus reduced the set of candidate activities, HCC will now reduce it yet again by considering *other* factors than labor—notably the land-use study results, and the projected strength of the various markets we are considering: "Domestic" private, "domestic" public, "foreign" private, and "foreign" public demand.

The reduced set of cost–revenue and cost–benefit profiles which emerges from this process constitutes our third and final options display, the BUSINESS PROSPECTUS. These will be studied by HCC, and then submitted to outside firms, financial intermediaries, and government agencies for consideration. Availability of subcontracts and government subsidies, and the loan capacity of the Harlem Corporation are some of the considerations which will govern HCC's final decision ($D_4$ in Figure 15–1): *The selection of specific business prospects for implementation.* Once this selection is made, the entire planning team will conduct a *production planning analysis* (i.e., implementation study) with businessmen in the community and with outside business advisors. The result of this last analysis will be a program of specific projects which, taken together with the EXIDEV, EXIPROB, and "BUILT-UP PROGRAM" lists and studies, constitutes the final industrial development plan for Harlem.

Two final points: The planning document will also include two studies of some importance, produced as by-products of the dual planning strategies described above. These are:

1. Estimation of the *efficiency gaps*, the expected differences in unit operating costs between Harlem Project activities and similar businesses already operating outside the ghetto. These gaps will suggest the magnitude of the public subsidies necessary to complement private capital in the implementation of the plan.

2. We shall estimate the infrastructural requirements which will be needed in order to permit the project businesses to function efficiently.

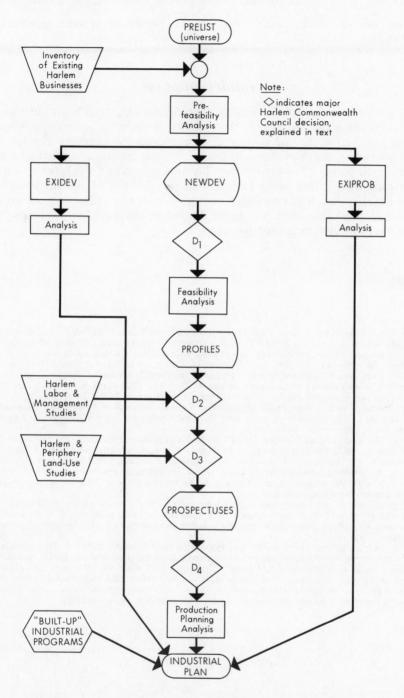

FIGURE 15–1. *Narrowing-Down Industrial Programming*

This "bill of requirements" will then be presented to local government officials.

## Implementation

At this point as in every planning venture, the emphasis must shift to the *implementing institutions*, to their ability to mobilize their client population into action. In our project the community development council and its off-spring, the "development bank," are the institutions without which the development plan cannot possibly succeed. While we believe that we have devoted rather more attention to the shaping of the implementing institutions than is normally the case in development planning, all we can do is to hope that they will make the commitments of will, energy, and resources needed to get the job done.

## Notes

1. An August 1966 *New York Post* survey indicated that "the price of a dozen eggs in Harlem was 20 cents higher than the citywide average and the price of butter was 20 cents higher per pound. The same meat sold in Harlem for $1.69 lb. is sold elsewhere for over $1.15." The U.S. Bureau of Labor Statistics concluded late in 1966 that: "For equivalent rents, poor families [the study included Harlem] get poorer housing than families with higher incomes. . . ." The BLS study also noted that "poor families pay more for credit." Citations are from: Herbert Hill, "Demographic Change and Racial Ghettos: The Crisis of American Cities," *Journal of Urban Law* (University of Detroit), Winter 1966. For the best detailed study, see David Caplowitz, *The Poor Pay More*, New York: Free Press, 1967.

2. The core citizens' group is the Harlem Commonwealth Council. Principal Consultants to HCC are the Center for Economic Planning of The New School for Social Research, the Columbia University Development Planning Workshop and the Architects' Renewal Committee in Harlem. Other consultants are being retained in connection with the programming of job training and as liaisons with American-business and government organizations.

3. Of course, we must also make these estimates for each of the individual component projects, where decomposition is meaningful and possible. A comparison of the two sets of statistics indicates the relative desirability of the "program" over the "project" approach.

4. In all our calculations, we use market prices, suitably deflated. The calculation of accounting or "shadow" prices is not only a nasty practical business, but is also theoretically questionable from both a "second best" point of view and in consideration of the fact that market prices in part *already* reflect the influence of phenomena "external" to perfectly competitive systems: dynamic, probabilistic, and strategic (oligopoly-type) factors and the averaging out of many nonconvexities.

# 16 ]] Conjoining Black Revolution

## and Private Enterprise

*Arnold Schuchter*

Hearings before the Senate Subcommittee on Executive Reorganization, the "Ribicoff Committee," dwelled on trying to find out from business-men what it would take to get them involved in creating jobs and housing in slum ghettos. The primary conclusion, reflected in subsequent legisla-tion by Senators Kennedy and Javits, was that the federal government must create a competitive, lucrative market in the slum ghettos, by in-creasing the yields on equity investment after taxes and by guaranteeing no risk of loss; in other words, guaranteeing a high profit yield after taxes for private equity capital. The Economic Opportunity Program (War on Poverty) was not altogether repudiated, but the consensus of testimony at the hearings, from both public officials and the private sector, was that the primary shortcoming of the antipoverty program has been its failure to involve *and rely upon* the private enterprise system. This viewpoint was strengthened by the strong prevalent opinion that negligible additional financial help will come from the federal government as long as national resources are being diverted to Vietnam and for cold war purposes.

Frequent references were made at the Senate hearing, by Senator Javits of New York and in testimony from private business persons, about the need for a Communication Satellite Corporation (COMSAT)-type corpora-tion to build new housing in slum areas and develop new industry to expand employment opportunities. It appears that the public has some-how been led to believe that COMSAT is a spaceage public service corpora-tion formed for social purposes. In fact, COMSAT is a private, profit-making corporation chartered by the federal government to hold a monopoly on U.S. development of, and participation in, the national and international communications satellite business. The social purposes of this type of corporation, if any exist, are in no way comparable to those required to undo the slum ghetto system. The profit potential of COMSAT is enormous. Here, *perhaps*, there is a valid analogy—in terms of the profit potential of corporate participation in slum renewal. Renewal of ghetto slums, however, cannot be compared to the investment attraction of COMSAT for the international communications carriers. This point should be elaborated further.

The international communications carriers were allotted (i.e., restricted

From Arnold Schuchter, *White Power/Black Freedom: Planning For the Future of Urban America* (Boston: Beacon Press, 1968), pp. 321–345. Reprinted by permission of the Beacon Press, © 1968 by Arnold Schuchter.

to) 50 percent of the outstanding voting stock of COMSAT. These corporations, especially AT&T, would have preferred 100 percent of the voting stock, but a compromise had to be worked out to placate congressmen outraged by a "no strings" billion dollar giveaway. For instance, AT&T was sold 2,895,750 shares of nonvoting stock at $20 per share, valued at $57,915,000. The price range for COMSAT stock in 1965 and 1966 hit a low of $35 and a high of about $65.

Thus Senator Javits' remark, at the Ribicoff hearings, about COMSAT, by way of analogy to his proposed Economic Opportunity Corporation,* was somewhat naïve and misleading: "We have seen in COMSAT that the people will invest in mixed government–business corporations." Furthermore, COMSAT is not, as Senator Javits described it, an example of "public–private financing" except in the sense that COMSAT benefited from over $470 million in government funds invested in space communications prior to COMSAT's inception. As David Rockefeller pointed out to Senator Javits at the Ribicoff hearings: "In the case of COMSAT, they [the public shareholders] have been led to believe, and there seems to be every reason to think that they are right, that this could be a profitable venture. In other words, a sound investment as well as a publicly desirable cause." Further aspects of this dialogue on the COMSAT model between Senator Javits and David Rockefeller, president of the Chase Manhattan Bank of New York, are quite illuminating:

.     .     .

SENATOR JAVITS . . . would you go along with us in a COMSAT-type corporation? By that I mean, public–private financing. Let's forget about the division, how much, but a public–private board of directors with some public standards which it is required to meet, as well as considerable freedom in private sector operations, and essentially private sector management? Would you go along with us with that kind of company, perhaps national, certainly regional, for the service function—all kinds of training, all kinds of management, all kinds of technical assistance?

MR. ROCKEFELLER. If you carry the analogy to COMSAT one step further, this would mean the investment of funds by the public. COMSAT has an enormous number of public shareholders [actually 148,056 in December 1966]. It seems to me that if they are going to be asked to put up their equity and their savings, many of them people of small means themselves, that they must understand clearly what they are getting into. . . . I think it would be a great mistake to launch a venture in the housing field [like COMSAT], trying to attract similar funds, and then have the investing public discover that in point of fact this was not economically viable, and they were perhaps helping a good cause, but they weren't getting tax credit for it, and they were losing part of their savings, so that I think there is a very serious public responsibility to make sure that it does have economic justification, and that the public understands clearly when they invest what they are getting into.

---

* A proposal for a federally chartered, mixed public–private corporation, with $600 million of stock issued to the public and $400 subscribed to by the federal government, for the purpose of financing any program designed to reduce urban or rural poverty approved by the directors and stockholders, with special emphasis on the application of business management techniques in the fields of job development, housing, and business development.

. . .

SENATOR JAVITS. Would you believe, in your judgment—would an important section of American business leadership back such a company or even initiate, set it up? Could you gather around yourself or some other business leader enough American business to do something like this? After all, this is the practical implementation of your testimony and for people like myself, who are sitting here and contending that this is the way it ought to be done, it sounds pretty ridiculous, unless American business is really ready to move in and do it on some basis, and that is really what I am asking you.

MR. ROCKEFELLER. I am sure that there are business leaders who would be interested and glad to give it a good, hard look and see what could be put together and whether or not a viable type corporation could be established. Yes, I am sure they would go that far. Now, whether their conclusions would in their judgment justify their going further, I wouldn't know until I had studied it a lot more than I have.

With all their curiosity about the profit prospects of "slum business," industry is still wary and hesitant about making investment commitments. Spokesmen for industry have indicated that they are prepared to work on a contract basis for a nonprofit, mixed public–private corporation, or a public corporation that has urban rehabilitation as its primary objective. The semipublic or public corporation would establish a public consensus on the objective, raise capital funds, establish an effective demand for industry participation, and then, screen the private corporation from criticism if performance fails to meet standards, much the way NASA has performed for prime contractors in the space business. On the other hand, business has indicated its willingness to participate individually, if corporate profits are guaranteed. Thus far, very little public debate has focused on this point—that private sector support of the public good requires substantial profit-making incentives created by government.

There is an ironical twist to the emerging consensus about the "necessary" role of the private sector in renewing slum ghettos, as follows: plans and proposals for private industry involvement in slum ghettos have been precipitated and accelerated by ghetto riots and the prospects of future violence; at the heart of the riots is rebellion against dominance by white economic and political power; most plans for business investment in ghettos, with Senator Kennedy's tax credit plans at the head of the phalanx, stress devising organizational and market mechanisms for slum ghetto redevelopment which guarantee profits to white economic power interests in order to intensify their activities in the rebellious Black ghettos. Thus, the aim of the latest thrust in the War on Poverty is "maximum feasible participation" of white economic power in the ghetto, and the result is likely to be reinforcement of the sense of dependency and powerlessness that provoked riots in the first place.

A further irony in the emerging business role in ghetto renewal is that the political leader who has shown the deepest understanding and most consistent regard for community development principles and practices in the ghetto areas—Senator Robert Kennedy—is the leading exponent of tax credit programs in ghetto housing and industrial development which tend to vitiate community participation and "self-government power."

In December 1966, Kennedy announced the establishment of two parallel and cooperating corporations in Brooklyn: the Bedford–Stuyvesant Renewal and Rehabilitation Corporation and the Bedford–Stuyvesant Development and Services Corporation. The creation of both evolved out of extensive discussions with community groups. The nonprofit Renewal and Rehabilitation Corporation is responsible for developing and carrying out a program for physical, economic, and social development in Bedford–Stuyvesant (about 400,000 population) and to be operated "on a business-like basis." This relatively new type of quasi-public organization seeks to become a parallel form of government in Brooklyn, New York, to function as the principal agent of community change in that area. It is in the process of drafting plans for housing, commercial and industrial development, education, health clinics, and so forth, all designed to consolidate and draw on self-help resources and federal grant-in-aid programs. Bedford–Stuyvesant is one of the areas selected by the city, and approved by HUD, for the Model Cities program.

The second corporation, the Development and Services Corporation, was created to assemble corporate leadership that could stimulate investment of private resources in program activities of the Renewal and Rehabilitation Corporation. The form of this second corporation apparently reflects several astute judgments: that the relationship of business resources to the community development corporation should be formalized and systematized through a parallel corporation, with specific commitments and responsibilities; that expert managerial advice for the community development corporation should be available when and as needed; and, for the foreseeable future, the community development corporation needed a powerful intermediator with the existing white economic and political power structure and its institutional resources.

Senator Kennedy's remarks before the Subcommittee on Executive Reorganization contain an excellent summary of the purpose of community development corporations: "The measure of success of this or any other program will be the extent to which it helps the ghetto to become a community—a functioning unit, its people acting together on matters of mutual concern, with the power and resources to affect the conditions of their own lives. Therefore, the heart of the program, I believe, should be the creation of community development corporations, which would carry out the work of construction, the hiring and training of workers, the provision of services, the encouragement of associated enterprises."

Against the background of this unique (for politicians) experience with creating community development structures in the ghetto and the remarkable perception of the purposes of community development, it is surprising that Senator Kennedy's proposed legislation for employment and housing development work *against* the community development concept. Senator Kennedy's "Urban Employment Opportunities Development

Act of 1967" is significant for three reasons: first, the use of tax credits
to spur economic and job development for ghetto inhabitants is feasible,
logical, and probably inevitable, regardless of which sponsors the tax
credit plan; second, his plan, as of this writing, is the most carefully
thought out and complete employment development plan utilizing tax
credits; third, if Senator Kennedy, with his experience and background,
sees no contradiction between his tax credit plan and community development approaches in ghettos, future public and private job development
plans are even more likely to reflect the same misconception.

First, a brief summary of highlights of Senator Kennedy's "Urban
Unemployment Opportunities Development Act of 1967." The plan would
benefit poverty areas in Standard Metropolitan Statistical Area's (SMSA's)
and persons living on Indian reservations. The program would be controlled, in terms of certification for eligibility, by municipalities. Federal
participation and control would essentially be reduced to administration
of compliance with standards set by the Department of Housing and
Urban Development, the Department of Commerce, and the Department
of Labor. The type of eligible industries would include manufacturers,
producers, distributors, and construction firms—but not retailers. The
industry receiving tax credits and subsidies would have to hire significant
numbers of unskilled or semiskilled workers from poverty areas, with
no income criteria or unemployment criteria included in the legislation.
Reflecting the intent to cater to enterprise with substantial investment resources, the legislation requires that companies must create at least fifty
new jobs ("as a safeguard against insubstantial or fly-by-night operators"),
and fill at least two-thirds of these jobs with residents of poverty areas,
or other unemployed persons. The company's investment must be maintained for at least ten years in order to retain the tax credits. Citizen
participation would consist of prior consultation with residents of the
poverty area in which the industrial facility is to be located, culminating
in a public hearing.

The provisions of the legislation are designed to create new jobs in
manufacturing and services in ghettos (the later through multiplier effect),
in part, by overcoming transportation handicaps, and to bring symbols
of entrepreneurial activity into poverty areas. In return for investing in
industrial expansion in poverty areas, the plan is designed to afford investors *a minimum of a 50 percent increase in their normal rate of
return.*\* The main tax credit benefits of Senator Kennedy's plan in relation to normal existing benefits under the tax code are summarized in
Table, 16–1.

Combined with existing corporate income tax and investment allowances, the above tax credits offer substantial inducements to corporations
with surplus equity to invest, and a market that justifies expansion.
Corporation income tax is high but tax and investment allowances have

---

\* Corporate earnings after tax on equity capital generally range between 5 and
10 percent.

**TABLE 16-1**

| Kennedy Tax Plan | Current Tax Code |
|---|---|
| A 10 percent credit on machinery and equipment | 7 percent investment credit |
| A 7 percent credit on costs of constructing a facility or leasing space | None |
| A carryback of three taxable years and a carryover of ten years on capital losses | Capital gains can be carried forward for five years to offset capital losses |
| A useful life for depreciation of 66⅔ percent of the normal useful life of real and personal property | Writeoff period for depreciation allowance geared to actual replacement of assets by firm (to encourage faster writeoffs) |
| A net operating loss carryover of ten taxable years | Net operating losses can be carried back three years or, if not sufficient, carried forward five years |
| A special deduction of 25 percent of salaries paid to workers hired to meet requirements of the Act | None |

tended to reduce the percentage of corporation taxes to profits-before-taxes. Between 1952 and 1963, when the general corporation tax rate was 52 percent, the percentage of corporation taxes to profits-before-taxes dropped almost ten points, from 37.5 to 27.8 percent.[1] For those who argue that corporation income taxes are still too high, Senator Kennedy's plan is a small step in the right direction; for those who argue that corporation profits are too high, the plan does not add much weight to their position. From the viewpoint of the have-nots in poverty areas, a good case might be made for the plan's amounting to outright bribery of the haves to share some of the leftovers with the have-nots.

For business and industry that stand to lose money in central cities if ghetto rebellion and rioting continue to grow, tax credit plans for ghetto investment at least offer a way to take positive action with a profit rationale. The assumption here is that altruism will not suffice even when supported by interests of self-protection. Frances Fox Piven, of the Columbia University School of Social Work, takes a much more cynical *realpolitik* view of the increasing political pressure to get corporations into the ghetto: "If Negroes were a powerful influence in city government they would be able to control redevelopment and all that it implies," Mrs. Piven says. "The corporate move into the slums is a way to sidestep the emerging Negro influence.[2] Mrs. Piven poses a problem that will increasingly preoccupy the strategists of ghetto renewal: the corporate "invasion" of the ghetto could result in the Negro being better off economically, but at the expense of Negro political self-determination. Stating the problem somewhat differently; how do you put together enough white power to do anything in slum ghettos without putting together too much white power to do too much?

It is possible, of course, that a strategy of "corporate colonialism" may indeed be developing in the inner sanctum of Washington bureaucracy, with corporate leadership and trusted White House aides plotting to restore order and control in the ghetto by feeding thousands of Black militants into the corporate machinery of subsidized jobs. It has probably occurred to HUD that its urban constituency is seriously jeopardized by the growing and turbulent hiatus between city hall and the ghetto. However, it is more likely that Mrs. Piven is both overstretching the "credibility gap" and overestimating the role of advanced political strategizing in Washington bureaucracy. Urban problem-solving has not yet reached the threshold of cold war planning, alternative retaliatory strike strategies, and so forth. (I hate to think that the day may come when HUD borrows Defense Department strategy teams and computer experts to simulate counteroffense strategies and ghetto "kill ratios.") It is unlikely, therefore, that corporations have either volunteered or been chosen for the mission of bridging the political control grap between city halls and the ghettos in major urban centers afflicted by ghetto revolts.

The political pressure for corporate involvement in the ghetto comes from a much simpler and less conspiratorial combination of sources: desperation in the private sector over the inadequacies of government planning and programs; determination by public and private sectors to create a stopgap program to avert intensified racial violence in the hot summer of 1968, or more realistically, in 1969 and beyond; efforts by the administration to avert serious preelection rioting in the cities, general recognition that, given the complex root causes of ghetto turmoil and urban decay, remedies are remote, and the lead-time for planning, programming, and staging, very extensive. Businessmen throughout the nation are in fact deeply concerned, for more than self-interest reasons; they want to act effectively, but they really do not know what to do—safely and inexpensively.

*          *          *

The partnership between ghetto-dwellers and both federal and local government that abortively emerged under the Economic Opportunity Program now appears to be shifting to a partnership between large corporations, financial institutions, and government. As expressed by Bruce P. Hayden, Vice President of the Connecticut General Life Insurance Company: ". . . any partnership approach to urban problems which involves government must be profit-oriented, if it is to do well and economically that which we want done . . . If we can create an atmosphere in which a thousand Rouses,* of greater or lesser capacity, can attack the problems of American cities, and can be driven on by the possibility of substantial profit, we will have those men on the job.

Congress and the citizens of the United States must be wary of overconfidence in the capacities of our planners, developers, and industrial problem-solvers, of a hundred or a thousand extraordinary "Rouses," to

* James Rouse, developer of the new town of Columbia, Maryland.

design and implement "solutions" to the social and economic problems of the Negro masses. There is no question that, given the political will and consensus, the financial resources and the time required for organization and tooling-up, the United States government could carve out attractive markets to "systems contractors," COMSAT's, and entrepreneur–developers to engage in large-scale city rebuilding and rehabilitation. However, in my judgment, this approach would prove unwise and disastrous, because it would ignore the basic "anticolonialism" message of the ghetto rebellion. *A way must be found to attract and utilize private and public capital in order to vastly increase our present institutional capacity to involve and develop the human capital resources in Negro ghettos.* Negroes need the opportunity to participate fully in creating and controlling new and re-habilitated communities around new forms of political, social, and economic institutions—new not only for Negroes, but new for urban society in the United States. Institutional change in this country is lagging far behind our capabilities and standards for improving the quality of personal, social, and community life.

Everything we know about life in the Black ghetto today demonstrates that, in the process of coping with social, economic, and other problems, the nature of the planning and development process itself is much more important than the end product, as far as ghetto-dwellers are concerned. Who provides the financial and technical assistance—public or private interests—is much less crucial than *how* that help is forthcoming. And it is not how efficiently the job is done that counts (when efficiency is judged by incomprehensible or alien standards such as intricate cost–benefit criteria); what counts is how many people benefit, and in what real and meaningful ways. (How many more people have freedom of choice today than yesterday? How many people exercised that freedom and did it actually pay off?) The question is not how many "Rouses" can be harnessed by profit and social purpose to bring about social and economic change in the ghetto. The question is how much Negro talent and human potential is rescued from ghetto oblivion through full participation in, and control over, community reconstruction.

Negroes know they have little or no inducements to offer to private investment in the ghetto. They have only two assets: their ability to generate fear of social disruption ("Burn, baby, burn") and the prospect of politically controlling major urban centers containing the centers of investment and trade. At the moment, these are the only "incentives" or bargaining tools that the ghetto market possesses. Political control through population growth is a bargaining tool that is relatively independent of Negro manipulation. As long as ghetto-dwellers possess no other significant bargaining instruments, no countervailing power, the threat of social disorder will not be discarded as a major bargaining weapon, and violence is likely to occur again and again. And fear of social disruption and violence may undermine even the best program for attracting private industry into the ghetto. In my judgment, even though private enterprise is becoming aroused to its social responsibilities, and even with congressional provision of a generous tax incentives program, private enterprise will choose to participate primarily through capital investment rather than through direct participation (such as construction of new industrial or commercial facilities within ghettos). This opinion is supported, for instance, by the dialogue between Gerald L. Phillippe, Chairman of the Board of the General Electric Company, and Senator Robert Kennedy, at the Ribicoff Committee hearings.

First, Mr. Phillippe made a prepared statement to the Ribicoff Committee, highlighting the urgency of the so-called urban crisis, and describing GE's proposal to enter the "new cities industry," announced by GE in the summer of 1966.

MR. PHILLIPPE. . . . . the quality of our whole national life depends on the quality of urban living. Neither industry nor any other segment of society can evade responsibility for doing its share to improve this quality. . . . The challenges we face are of massive proportions—reminiscent of the grim challenge of Pearl Harbor just twenty-five years ago today. . . .

.    .    .

SENATOR KENNEDY. For instance, you have in Bedford–Stuyvesant a population of some 400,000. You have in Harlem a population of perhaps 400,000 or 500,000. What would be required for you to decide that you were going to build a plant in Bedford–Stuyvesant or Harlem or South Side Chicago or Watts, you or General Motors or Ford or any of the other large corporations or companies in the United States.

(After discussing general location requirements, Board Chairman Phillippe and Senator Kennedy discussed the threat of disorders and violence as deterrents to industry's locating in ghetto areas.)

MR. PHILLIPPE. I do not know, I have not investigated it, nor have any of our industrial relations people investigated it, but the record, if you are talking about climate right at the moment, the record of Harlem would not be particularly attractive to us, I would think.
SENATOR KENNEDY. Are you thinking particularly about violence?
MR. PHILLIPPE. Yes.
SENATOR KENNEDY. And the fact that there would be concern about this?
MR. PHILLIPPE. Yes. We would not like to walk into one of those things knowingly if we could avoid it. Now there might be some other motivations. There might be, if we could make some contribution to it, why we might consider it.
SENATOR KENNEDY. What you have talked about . . . the central market, the transportation of builders' supplies, the labor market, and the cost of power . . . are not insurmountable problems as far as taking the kind of steps we are outlining.
MR. PHILLIPPE. Yes. They may not be.
SENATOR KENNEDY. I would think that if you could have some assurances, for instance, for the future. . . .
MR. PHILLIPPE. Did you have on your list the climate in which we would be operating?
SENATOR KENNEDY. I will put that down. If you could have some assurances in connection with the labor supply and the training of people by the federal government, and if you could have some assurances as far as transportation in and out of the area, by the city, giving you certain guarantees regarding police protection and the environment under which people were working, you

would have a market that really has been untapped as of the present time, first as far as workers is concerned, and, second, as far as purchasers are concerned.

MR. PHILLIPPE. A market for what, Senator?

SENATOR KENNEDY. All kinds of products.

MR. PHILLIPPE. For example, you could not make turbines in the middle of New York.

SENATOR KENNEDY. No, but I come back to this paragraph [in Mr. Phillippe's prepared statement] where you discuss the "more extensive market research into the needs of cities."

MR. PHILLIPPE. Oh, yes.

SENATOR KENNEDY. . . . let me ask you if anybody has ever asked you, across the country, to ever build a plant in any one of these areas?

MR. PHILLIPPE. Has anyone ever asked us to build a plant?

MR. SMITH (vice president for market and public relations). In any one of those areas?

MR. PHILLIPPE. In Stuyvesant?

SENATOR KENNEDY. Not just in Stuyvesant, but in any. . . .

MR. PHILLIPPE. In any areas?

SENATOR KENNEDY. Ghetto areas.

MR. PHILLIPPE. Oh, yes.

SENATOR KENNEDY. Not just in any area but in any of the ghetto areas.

MR. PHILLIPPE. No, I do not believe so.

It is quite apparent from the above testimony that between the rhetoric about an "urban crisis" of the magnitude of "Pearl Harbor" and the justification and commitment to act, and between the tax incentive for large-scale industrial development in the ghetto and actual job creation, there is a gap filled with ambivalence, ambiguity, contradiction, and plain nonsense. Furthermore, it should be apparent that guarantees and assurances of tractable workers harmoniously adjusting to their nice new ghetto work environments are an improbable dream.

There is no structure of authority in urban centers that can guarantee to any corporation a cessation of hostilities in the ghetto. The ghetto is a trap for lower-income and lower-class Negroes. With sufficient income and dissolution of discrimination in housing, large numbers of Negroes would leave the Harlems and Bedford–Stuyvesants, still leaving a vast black proletariat in the inner cities. The question becomes, how do you gainfully employ lower-income, lower-class Negroes, trapped for their lifetimes in one ghetto or another, in a manner that makes them content despite their lack of freedom? How do we make the Negroes' reservations under our apartheid system tolerably comfortable? If there is a rational answer to such fundamentally absurd questions, I suspect that major emphasis on direct investment by large corporations in industrial development in the ghettos is not that answer.

Let us briefly recapitulate the logic of the argument for industrial development in the ghetto up to this point:

Male breadwinners in the ghettos need jobs, especially jobs which pay decent wages. Industrial job growth has a multiplier effect, generating new service and retail jobs. Industrial jobs, therefore, should be a primary target in ghetto economic development. These new jobs should be located in the ghetto, so as to be easily accessible and also to generate new secondary employment in the ghetto.

It requires substantial capital investment and entrepreneurial skills to produce large quantities of new industrial jobs. Large industry has lots of both. The most effective way to tap large industries' resources is to provide incentives for such industry to locate new plants in the ghetto.

These incentives must be sufficiently strong to compete favorably with alternative investment opportunities. The best proved incentive system for business development is the tax code. In recent years it has increasingly been used as an incentive to induce investment by level, location, type, and frequency over time. Based on past precedents, the tax code system can be modified and augmented by amendment to provide special incentives to achieve a worthwhile economic and social objective—in this case, investment by industry in the ghetto.

These tax credit incentives must (1) induce the investor to take more economic *and* social risks, but minimize the economic risks (manipulation of the social risks is problematic); (2) subsidize the *possibility* of a lower rate of return, but if the return on equity is normal, subsidize the *possibility* of higher than normal profits; and (3) induce the investor to spend money that normally would not be spent (e.g., training the hard-core unemployed).

In contrast to housing development, which involves the production of a social utility, the risks to profits for industrial development cannot be eliminated altogether by a guaranteed return on investment in industrial development. Operating losses can only be offset by liberal tax credits, and not eliminated—a critical difference when compared to housing investment protected wholly by government guarantees.

The only weakness in the above argument is its underlying premise— that the number one need in the ghetto is jobs. In my judgment, this is a false assumption. *The number one need in the ghetto is freedom of choice and, more specifically, community reconstruction and development through a Black structured decision-making process,* a major by-product of this being a job for every person willing and able to work. One of the methods for community development is economic development, including the expansion of industrial employment. The method for expansion of industrial employment opportunities for Negroes within the territorial boundaries of the ghetto must be consistent with an economic development plan approved by the ghetto area's Community Development Corporation. The primary benefits of industrial development, capital accumulation, and profit benefits, as well as job benefits, must accrue to residents of the ghetto area.

Under Robert Kennedy's tax incentive plan for industrial development in the ghetto, private industry is being asked to play the role of an agent of economic and social change—beyond its capacity to support that role. Inspired by overconfidence in technology and power of "bigness," the Kennedy plan makes an assumption about the transferability of competence from production engineering to social engineering that is more workable in Pakistan than in Harlem. In Pakistan, for example, private incentives, spurred by direct and indirect government intervention, do not have to contend with the social consequences of ghettoization.[3] A pragmatic approach to the role of government and private enterprise, with good economic management on both sides, can produce significantly improved economic performance in an "underdeveloped" economy, such as we find in the ghetto or in Pakistan, if the powerful factor of racial segregation is not present. The existence of racial segregation, and the expectation that it will perpetuate for the foreseeable future, calls for a radically different approach to community and economic development: *a strategy designed for large, racially segregated Negro communities, convulsively seeking both self-government and freedom of choice to live beyond the ghetto.*

The overall elements of this strategy are discussed elsewhere. At this point it would be useful to describe one possible working model for industrial and business development in ghettos which conforms to the principles and operating requirements of a national, regional, and community development strategy focused on enlarging Negro power and freedom of choice. The working model, like the overall strategy, must reflect the character and pace of economic, technological, social, and broadly political forces at work in urban society, including the shifts in organization and control of power to and from public bureaucracies. At the same time, at the geopolitical level of the Negro ghetto, the working model must reflect and support *the need to build countervailing power and consumer choice close to the point of consumption of goods, services, and opportunities.*

First, on the whole, industrial development should be designed to create a substantially improved ghetto-based economy, compatible with the concept of the ghetto as a self-governing, underdeveloped (or "industralizing") territory. Industrial development, primarily small industry (roughly defined as one hundred or fewer employees), should be owned and managed by ghetto residents and employ, predominantly, ghetto residents. Tax credit and subsidy plans should be restricted to firms with majority Negro ownership, but, in contrast to Senator Kennedy's plan, should not be restricted by the size of the firm.

Second, the concept of a "development bank" at the national level is basically sound, but should be augmented by a similar institution at the state level, both of which could finance a broad range of economic and industrial development activities, as well as new cities development, from the sale of government-backed securities. Both national and regional financing, however, should be channeled through a Metroregional Development Corporation (MDC), the quasi-public, state-chartered regional development organization. Only at the metroregional level can sound decisions be made about economic development activities within the urban region. The MDC would review and finance industrial and business development projects in the ghettos and in new cities. This would be accomplished with participation of financial institutions and federal and state government. In the ghettos and new cities, the Urban-Grant University would act as the technical assistance and coordinating instrument, working with one or more Community Development Corporations to program and carry out economic development activities.

Third, since preparation of an economic development plan by a Community Development Corporation, in consultation with the Urban-Grant

University, should be a prerequisite to governmental financing of industrial and business development, funds to finance the administrative and program development costs of ghetto-based Community Development Corporations will have to be provided by federal and state sources, as a counterpart to economic development financing. These funds would be administered by the Urban-Grant University until legal incorporation of a nonprofit Community Development Corporation.

Fourth, the municipality would participate in such an economic development program at several levels: at the level of the Metropolitan Council of Governments (MCOG), which must approve MDC development plans and programs; as a participant in policy making within the local Urban-Grant Universities; by underwriting a small percentage of the loan funds for industrial and business development projects, and through the city's contracting system.

Cities have had the statutory authority to require companies submitting bids on city contracts to include in those bids specific plans for hiring the long-term unemployed. Until 1968, cities simply have not exercised this authority, even though in the twenty-five major cities in the United States, between 200,000 and 300,000 jobs could be created in this manner. In Philadelphia, for example, such a plan was announced in February 1968, following a similar announcement in New York City. Each city maintains a list of approved bidders, which is a potentially potent lever to get work for the unemployed. In Philadelphia, with some 50,000 chronically unemployed persons, 4,000 companies, doing a total business of $100 million annually in city business, are expected to provide between 7,000 and 10,000 jobs, an average of about two jobs per company or one job for every $10,000 worth of business. A city such as Philadelphia could reserve 10 percent of its annual business, or $10 million, for contracts with Negro-owned businesses employing double the number of hard-core jobless, or two persons for every $10,000 worth of business. The $10 million in city contracts would help to support training and work for 2,000 formerly hard-core unemployed in Negro-owned enterprises. Federal subsidies under various on-the-job training programs could offset the added costs of utilizing and training less productive workers.

Fifth, Senator Kennedy's tax credit program, as applied to small-industry development in the ghetto, should be expanded in its subsidy aids, possibly as follows: (1) raise the surtax exemption on corporate income tax to $50,000 from $25,000;* (2) a 7 percent credit on expenditures for constructing *multistory* industrial and commercial facilities (in addition to the 7 percent credit, proposed by Kennedy, on expenditures for constructing a facility or leasing space); (3) capitalization and depreciation of

---

* By raising the surtax exemption from $25,000, under present tax law, to $50,000 for ghetto small-industry, forty subsidiary corporations, benefiting from multiple surtax exemptions, with a net profit of $50,000, would each save $253,500 more than under present laws, or a total of $507,000 on a total net profit of $2 million. The surtax exemption over $25,000 could be made contingent upon establishing (1) a reserve fund against losses, (2) a fund for reinvestment, and (3) a profit-sharing program with employees and/or a matching retirement plan.

research and development expenditures over a ten-year period, instead of over a five-year period; and (4) a 50 percent deduction in wages and fringe benefits up to $2.50 per hour (with a sliding scale provision under and over $2.50 per hour) for previously jobless workers receiving on-the-job training or regular employment.

Sixth, the aims of modernization and development in newly industrializing countries are in several basic respects comparable to the economic development and job-creation needs of core city ghettos. Short- and long-range development policies and planning should take these similarities into account. In slum ghettos or in industrializing countries, the economic development objectives generally are as follow: (1) develop indigenous management capability; (2) reach and train members of the labor force, or labor force dropouts who have never worked steadily under modern production conditions; (3) provide vastly improved working and living opportunities for large numbers of families coming from a farm or rural nonfarm environment and trying to adapt to urban life; (4) modernize the existing small-industry sector by application of up-to-date ideas of planning, budgeting, organization, management, product design, and production, and create new small-industry with these management advantages; (5) overcome the lack of loans and credit from financing institutions through special types of credit and tax aids; (6) create a diversified economic base for the community as a component of a community development strategy; (7) create an enterprise structure which functions as a pipeline from the pool of unemployed and underemployed into higher grade semiskilled and service occupations; and (8) create a pool of entrepreneurs and technicians with a stake in fostering and servicing local economic and community development programs and projects.

In both newly industrializing countries and in large ghettos in the United States, capital is scarce and labor abundant. And modernization has to be adapted to the specific environmental and labor-force characteristics found in both settings. Viewing the ghetto—the Black rural–urban continuum—as a newly developing society within a more advanced society can prove to be a very useful frame of reference. Within this context, small business and industry in the core-city ghetto or in the urban hinterland can play an important socializing as well as economic development role. For low-skilled and semiskilled lower-class ghetto workers and nonworkers, the small enterprise can offer these advantages: (1) lower stress in adapting to the work environment than in a large factory ; (2) closer contact of the worker with management, and also closer supervision by management; (3) jobs closer to home, which reduces the transportation costs and travel time; (4) a context conducive to the development of entrepreneurship; and (5) easier adaptation to on-the-job training.

Even in the era of the giant corporation, there are technical and business factors that tend to favor small manufacturers. Location is the most significant factor for small plants serving local or regional markets and for those production facilities which provide customized or specialized services for local customers. Negroes are concentrated in the centers of major consumer markets offering a wide range of opportunities to exploit growing and diversifying consumer demands for goods and services. As indicated elsewhere, the Detroit urban area, for instance, has lagged behind other urban centers in diversification of consumer goods production and the development of its service industry. The development of Negro entrepreneurship should become part of a major effort to remedy this type of metroregional deficiency in economic development.

In constructing a small-industry development strategy as a component of ghetto economic development, the investment choices are between labor-intensive and capital-intensive production activities. The range of choices between labor-intensive and capital-intensive industries and products requires a careful analysis of local and regional markets. The initial scarcity of organizing resources—entrepreneurs, managers, and administrators—suggests the desirability of articulating the development of existing or new small industry with large industry in the metroregion. Deliberately developed linkages and complementarity between small ghetto industry (as supplier) and larger industry outside the ghetto will be essential components of a small-industry development strategy. Other elements of this strategy are as follows: First, small industry in the ghetto should be viewed as a vital *school of entrepreneurship*, an incubator of entrepreneurial, managerial, and technical skills. Second, small industry should serve as an incubator of other small industry and business enterprises frequently with the products or services of the "spin-off" enterprise consumed in part by the parent enterprise. Third, small-industry enterprise can be viewed as an incubator of economic, social, and political leadership within the ghetto. Fourth, small industry in the ghetto can serve as channels for workers, talented managers, and technicians to move into other types of economic activity in the larger metropolitan community. Fifth, small industry in the ghetto can be operated in a manner which also makes it a significant channel of social mobility and a source of status, especially via company-sponsored participation in community development activities, advanced training and educational programs (in part or wholly subsidized by the company), profit-sharing schemes based on performance, and so forth.

The objectives for a sound small-industry program, as outlined above, will not be achieved without careful planning and resourceful administration. With the assistance of existing industrial enterprises to plan and implement a small-industry development program built around knowledge of the market and the existing production system, with adequate loans and technical and managerial assistance, there is every reason to expect that small-industry development in the West Side of Chicago or in Boston's Roxbury could compare favorably with experiences in India and Pakistan. Private industry should be paid for its contribution by means of direct contract and tax incentives. But the primary purposes of luring private industry participation into ghetto small-industry development should be human and financial capital formation within the ghetto, both for reinvestment in community development. Without an indigenous enterprise structure that serves as a mechanism for capital assembly and transfer within the Black community, reconstruction of the social and economic environment of the ghetto will fail.

It should be clearly understood, however, that the development of small industry is not an employment-generating panacea for unemployment and underemployment in slum ghettos. The fundamental remedies involve public interventions and incentives designed (1) to control the scope, direction, and pattern of racial discrimination, metroregional development, labor mobility, housing construction, and educational institutions, and (2) to structure the whole community development process in ghettos for the purpose of educating, training, and job creation. Within this larger framework, and in the process of economic and social development of the ghetto environment, small industry can play an extremely useful role, as suggested above, in terms of skill training, capital formation and transfer, entrepreneurship incubation and growth, and leadership development, as well as job creation. However, in the overall long-term strategy for human capital development among ghetto Negroes, job creation is viewed as a by-product, rather than as the primary purpose, of small-industry development. Moreover, small-industry development cannot be regarded as a rapid route to job creation for the hard-core unemployed in the ghettos. More productive and direct routes to labor-intensive job creation are the formation of Community Service Corporations, the community reconstruction activities of the Urban-Grant Universities, the National Service Corps, the development of new cities in the metroregion and in underdeveloped regions, as well as the construction of major cities-within-cities of diverse urban activity within core cities.

For established industry, especially for those which want to learn more about ghetto life and needs in order to better define their own potential contribution, small-industry development, offers worthwhile opportunities, if not for substantial profits, then for learning, with possible profit payoffs. As suggested above, small manufacturers in the ghetto can do best in lines that complement rather than compete with large industry. Large manufacturing companies can help nascent small industries to find product lines which have a competitive advantage, by direct consultation and subcontract relations with the larger manufacturer. The largest corporations in the United States each depend on anywhere from 10,000 to over 50,000 suppliers. Few people are aware of the vast interlocking pattern of large companies and small suppliers, as well as the extent to which the policy of large companies has been oriented to provide technical assistance, training, and expert guidance to small vendors in order to enable them to met the company's procurement standards and requirements. This pattern of complementarity, cooperation, or symbiosis is company policy in foreign countries, too, among major American industries that for many years have been heavily involved in business and economic development in newly industrializing countries. While the United States government is providing incentives to induce many of these same industries to locate in its own underdeveloped regions and communities, rural and urban; the profit potential in numerous industrializing nations often holds still greater attractions.

Sears, Roebuck and Company, for example, has its headquarters in the North Lawndale section of the West Side Black ghetto of Chicago. In the North Lawndale and West Side area, Sears' sprawling *and* spreading complex is viewed as *the* symbol of white economic power and domination, the headquarters of white "colonialism." Most of the Negroes I interviewed in the West Side area viewed Sears' expansion plans and progress to date as part of a "downtown" conspiracy for a much larger land grab. Despite modest annual contributions to safe Negro causes, operation of its own YMCA, and the only remaining bank in the West Side area, the Sears image continues to deteriorate rather than improve. When, in October 1967, President Johnson announced that the federal government would test a program to reduce risks to investment for businesses *willing to build or expand* in ghetto areas, it came as no surprise (or joy) to the more aware North Lawndale residents that Chicago was named as one of the first five pilot cities, with Sears as the cooperating industry.

Sears Roebuck's hiring practices, with a low proportion of Negroes in the Chicago center and few in white-collar jobs, have been a major source of friction with West Side community organizations for years. Meanwhile, for more than a decade, during the period when the West Side was being transformed into a volatile ghetto, Sears' Chicago headquarters was sending substantial technical and financial assistance south of the border—as a matter of marketing and investment necessity. The barest outline of the Sears' role in Mexico is worth examining to indicate the extent to which the policy of a major industry toward its role in economic development can change drastically with the proper financial incentives.

A foreign exchange crisis in Mexico resulted in an embargo on imports for consumer goods. Sears was forced to seek and develop Mexican sources. Consequently, Sears provided loans, technical assistance, and training to Mexican small manufacturers; helped local factories design products and cut costs; laid out new plants; tested products; adjusted buying schedules to fit producer's schedules; conducted market studies; provided advances against sales for operating capital; and so forth. Sears devoted a major share of store earnings in Mexico to reinvestment, in order to stimulate growth in the stores' market areas. If, in 1968, Sears Roebuck in Chicago were to apply the same policies and methods to the development of small industry in the West Side area, the local impact would not only transform the Sears image but set a precedent for other manufacturers in Chicago and other major cities, in terms of a new model of participation in ghetto economic development. Without such an economic development and technical assistance program, Sears may be forced to move out of the West Side area in the next few years.

The various legislative proposals, aimed at training and job creation for the unemployed and underemployed, pending before Congress, most notably Senator Robert Kennedy's Urban Employment Opportunities Development Act of 1967, are designed to draw the Sears Roebucks and other corporations of lesser size into the ghetto with tax incentives and other subsidies. It should be clearly understood that tax inducements to attract industry into the ghetto, to generate direct and indirect employment, is an objective quite different from promoting the development of indigenously owned and managed small industry.

Small-industry development in the ghetto, as well as in new cities in the metroregions, in which Negroes have the incentives of ownership, entrepreneurship, and profit-sharing, will require much more planning than envisioned by tax incentive plans. Land within the ghetto is a scarce commodity. Industrial development will have to be land-intensive or high-density capital-intensive, to stimulate the greatest growth of secondary and tertiary jobs and service industries and retailing; and labor-intensive, to directly employ the maximum number of persons. Maximization of employment and capital densities per unit of land area, designed for increased social and economic "profitability" for ghetto residents, will not occur automatically with a tax incentive program.

Large modern industrial plants are seeking sites in suburban locations which offer ample room for future expansion, plenty of parking, loading, and storage space, and amenities which make the plant facility more attractive to prospective employees. As indicated in Table 16–2 below, for a representative cross section of industrial facilities,[4] the land-to-building ratio and the square footage of building per employee, if transposed to the ghetto, would consume huge amounts of acreage without a significant employment and income-producing payoff relative to the required displacement of housing. Moreover, ghetto-based small industry should employ a high percentage of males, and, in fact, give preferential treatment to employers of male workers.

Small-enterprise development in the ghetto should be housed in factory-fabricated multistory structures (up to ten stories) that can be built to

### TABLE 16-2

| Type of Industry (Typical Suburban Plant) | Land-to-Building Ratio | Sq. Ft. of Building per Employee | Ratio of Female-to-Male Workers |
|---|---|---|---|
| Metal Fabrication | 6:1 | 700 | 1:2 |
| Food Products | 1.4:1 | 836 | 1:1.2 |
| Paper Products | 22:1 | 925 | 1:10 |
| Home Products | 9:1 | 444 | 1:1.2 |
| Women's Garments | 7:1 | 106 | 10:1 |
| Consumer Electronics | 5:1 | 239 | 1:1.2 |
| Hardware | 6:1 | 212 | 1:1 |
| Industrial Electronics | 7:1 | 488 | 1:2 |
| Automotive Parts | 8:1 | 385 | 1:12 |
| Computer Components | 5:1 | 150 | 2:1 |
| Pharmaceuticals | 3:1 | 300 | 1:2 |

expand vertically and, if necessary, convert into commercial or office space, or even housing facilities. Buildings could be occupied by numerous types of small enterprises, training, and research facilities. The buildings could be constructed by a local public development corporation and leased to the Urban-Grant University for subleasing under a small-industry development plan. The leasing arrangement could provide for condominium ownership under a rent-with-option-to-purchase scheme. To reiterate, the primary purposes of the small-industry program are (1) to develop large numbers of achievement-motivated, competent, creative, innovative entrepreneur–managers and workers, who know how to organize to get things done; (2) to provide the highest income and work incentives for workers, compatible with the operation of a profitable enterprise, i.e., one which accumulates surplus capital for reinvestment in business improvement and expansion; and (3) to obtain the maximum multiplier effect, in terms or related training, education, and community development, from economic development activities.

The Urban-Grant University would be in the best position to coordinate the planning of outside industry, government at all levels, business guidance and counseling, research and evaluation, education and training, and local community development program activities. Under this approach to small-industry development, the tax incentives of an "Urban Employment Opportunities Development Act" would be provided to enterprises certified by an Urban-Grant University, and would *not* be limited to employers with fifty or more employees, as stipulated in the proposed Kennedy legislation. This latter provision was inserted in the Kennedy legislation "as a safeguard against insubstantial or fly-by-night operators." Certification by an Urban-Grant Univeristy would minimize this kind of risk.

In addition to indirect financing through tax incentives, small-industry financing could be patterned after the New York State Job Development Authority's (JDA) program. Founded in 1962, the authority has approved over $41 million in low-interest (average cost 3.75 percent) long-term second mortgages. The usual pattern with these loans has been for companies to obtain a first mortgage from a bank for half of the loan, 30 percent on a second mortgage basis from the Job Development Authority, and the rest from their own funds or from one of the more than two hundred local nonprofit development corporations in the state. These development corporations, moreover, are the conduit through which JDA funds pass to individual companies. The JDA money comes from bond-anticipation notes guaranteed by the state.

In the case of the small-industry development program under the joint auspices of the Urban-Grant University and the local Community Development Corporation, the latter would be the conduit for loan funds; the commercial bank's 50 percent could be guaranteed by the federal government, just as the JDA's money is guaranteed by the state; the federal government could make a grant of 5 percent of capital costs, and the city, a grant of 5 to 10 percent of capital costs; thus, the small industry's ownership would only have to invest 1 to 5 percent equity money. (JDA's loan program should be expanded to cover machinery and equipment.) Within the ghetto, the Community Development Corporation could form a business development corporation, comprised of the largest possible group of established Negro businessmen and Negroes who aspire to go into business. This corporation would act as a clearinghouse for loans, provide encouragement and counseling assistance to Negro businessmen and loan applicants, and sell stock to develop its own business ventures.

The National Urban Resources Development Corporation (NURDC) could establish a subsidiary special-purpose corporation, similar to Senator Javits' proposed Domestic Development Bank (patterned after the World Bank), to provide mortgage loans that cover up to 90 percent of the project cost, payable in thirty years at 7 percent interest. Today, loans to industries and retailers in the ghettos generally cover no more than half the cost of the project, with a mortgage term of fifteen years at a minimum of 9 percent interest. Under the Javits loan plan, Congress would authorize the "domestic development bank" to raise up to $10 billion through sales of stocks or bonds. Of this amount, $2 billion would be subscribed by the federal government, $400 million for use as loan funds, and the remaining $1.6 billion to be held as a reserve against defaults on the bank's loans. As Senator Kennedy's tax credit plan stands now, the Javits plan would mean more to the small ghetto businessman. But there is no reason why both programs could not be meshed to provide a major financial boost for small-business development in the ghetto and in new cities within the framework of the New Urban America program. Moreover, both the Kennedy and the Javits plans leave plenty of room for state participation, especially in view of the small-business and industry financing requirements generated by the development of new cities and industrial facilities in core city reconstruction programs.

As a general situation, local banks tend to serve established businesses with adequate resources to provide collateral and guarantees for loans. Small and marginal businessmen do not have access to public or private sources of capital. Moreover, the kind of small-business enterprises which predominate in the ghetto, many of which could survive and grow with help, would not generally be helped by conventional loans even if they were readily available. Conventional loans are most often for a short term, for inventory, or some other self-liquidating purpose. Most small businesses and industries operated by Negroes in the ghettos are so undercapitalized that they need long-term loans as a substitute for additional equity. This type of loan is generally beyond the scope of services offered by banks, even to acceptable credit risks.

The Economic Opportunity Loan (EOL) program, under the Economic Opportunity Act of 1964, was designed to help small businessmen with this kind of difficult credit situation. In 1966, after only about a year of operation and many loan defaults, Congress gave full control of the EOL program to the Small Business Administration (SBA), which formerly had shared responsibility for the EOL program with the Office of Economic

Opportunity (OEO). SBA took over loan-processing responsibilities from OEO-funded Small Business Development Centers located in poverty areas. SBA attributed a high default rate in the EOL program to lack of management skills on the part of loan recipients, and lack of adequate loan supervision and guidance. As a result, SBA changed its lending qualifications to increase emphasis on the borrower's past business record and his likelihood of success. Low-income and membership in a "disadvantaged" group still carry weight, but ceilings on family income and residence in specified poverty areas have been dropped as eligibility requirements.

The implications of these shifts are that federal business loans are a highly inefficient means for improving living standards of the poor in urban ghettos; that the small-margin businessman is not likely to provide employment opportunities in substantial numbers for the unemployed and under-employed poor; and that the costs for training and loan servicing of these types of businesses outweigh the benefits—in terms of viable business-enterprise development and, even more so, job creation. The truth of the matter, however, is that the inadequacies and failures of the EOL program on the whole resulted from an inappropriate business development strategy and weak, or nonexistent, administrative, evaluation, and research components. These weaknesses can be remedied (or easily duplicated) in new loan programs.

First, the guidance, counseling, and training components of the EOL program have not been designed to systematically and specifically assist minority group business being conducted at low levels of efficiency, organization, and profitability. The EOL program in each local area should have aimed for standardization of operational procedures and marketing techniques.

Second, the EOL program has been geared to a one-by-one approach to business development and loan servicing, instead of using loans as *an incentive and tool for promoting economic organization* among minority group businesses which produce or sell similar products or services. Organization of homogeneous self-help groups would have facilitated greater efficiency through combined purchasing, group advertising, maintenance of equality workmanship and attractive shop appearance in retail service trades.

Third, the EOL program was not designed especially to help Negro businessmen make greater use of the public and private resources available to assist business. As discussed below, the potential roles of trade associations and local university resources have not been adequately exploited.

Fourth, administration of SBA loan servicing has been under financed and alternative administrative approaches have not been adequately developed.

The key to small-industry and -business development in the ghetto is centralized planning and servicing by implementation of an *economic organization program*. Loans with liberal repayment terms and low interest rates, without a framework of economic organization which combines "wholesale" management servicing and quality control (including research), will inevitably result in very mixed and uncertain results, with an inordinate amount of time spent on policing loans. Since more jobs will result from secondary and tertiary service employment by-products of small-industry development than from industrial development itself, it is imperative that the economic organization approach be applied to small-business development simultaneously with small-industry development.

Firms in the same line of business in the ghetto should be formed into trade associations by an Urban-Grant University (with the cooperation of existing business organizations, local law school students and faculty, and the business and economics departments of local colleges and universities). Minimal operational standards would be established by the trade associations, with assistance coordinated by the Urban-Grant University. Minimal operational standards would include: rehabilitation standards for upgrading physical appearance; accounting, inventory control, and credit procedures; employee training; employee and employer benefit programs; cooperative buying of wholesale supplies; merchandising and sales promotion; group business insurance and other types of insurance; and so forth.

New business enterprises, established with the assistance of federal, state, and local loan programs, would conform to these minimal operating standards. The Small Business Administration and other governmental lending sources, as well as local lending institutions, would work closely with the ghetto's trade associations and the Urban-Grant University so that operational standards would meet their requirements for loan approval and servicing. Rather than SBA or other governmental agencies carrying the major responsibility for loan policing (with all the attendant problems of bureaucratic overload, rigidity, and remoteness from the problems), each trade association, in consultation with the Urban-Grant University, would carry the major responsibility for coordinating and supervising the guidance, counseling, and training components of the small-business development program. Moreover, trade associations formed within the ghetto should have an important role in loan-processing procedure. If loan decisions are contingent upon character, management ability, and other circumstantial factors, trade associations can be invaluable resources for recruiting and screening loan applicants, viz., existing or potential small businessmen unable to obtain assistance from conventional lending sources.

Any loan program aimed at small-business development must fully face up to the need for much more management training and counseling than has hitherto been provided. The training and counseling of very small businessmen is still a very new field. To date, the emphasis of training curricula has been on techniques of bookkeeping and record management—perhaps because financial records of loan applicants tend to be inadequate or inaccurate. However, the amount of effort, thought, and financial support devoted to designing and carrying out a management training and counseling program will have to be raised considerably to match the difficulties of the problem. The Urban-Grant University has a major developmental and research role to play in this area of management-training and business advisory services.

Within the framework of an Urban-Grant University, a broad cross section of metroregional industries would be coordinated to provide a small-industry advisory service, in effect, pooling the management-training and business development resources of each company, with tax incentives legislation providing tax bonuses for the companies to add full- and part-time company personnel to the advisory and support services. The staff would include personnel to prepare training aids, courses, and case materials oriented to local small-enterprise needs. These resource people would work out of small-industry facilities in the ghetto, to be in close contact with the needs and problems of small-industry and community development. One of the first activities of this group (aided by local schools of business education affiliated with an Urban-Grant University) would be to conduct a study and diagnosis of small-industry needs and potentials in the metroregion and in the ghetto—helping first the existing small entrepreneurs with real potential. It is imperative that management training methods and materials should reflect in-plant diagnoses conducted in existing ghetto small industries.

To a large degree, production and market factors will determine the type of small-industry enterprises developed under this program. For example: simple assembly, mixing, or finishing operations involving small products on light equipment; production of components for large firms, no one of which requires a volume sufficient to warrant its own production facilities; nonstandardized products, customized to consumer tastes; and so forth. The applied research and development function of the Urban-Grant University has a significant contribution to make to the "mix" and quality of work opportunities created under this program, and to the process of occupational mobility and related skill development. The Urban-Grant University will have to provide performance standards and guidelines to ghetto business and industry for control of the movement of workers through a progression of work-experience and training opportunities. A small-industry development program is only among numerous types of training resources, including: workshop enterprises, community service corporations, lighted cities training program, new cities development program, and so forth. All these should be coordinated by an Urban-Grant University in order to function virtually as a unified metroregional training-and-education system.

With respect to small-industry planning, ideally, the bulk of small manufacturing enterprises should fall into an intermediate range of industrial technology which incorporates and adapts existing and newly available science and technology into on-the-job training programs. Products and manufacturing processes may need to be broken down and analyzed for job-related education in the science and technology of materials and production. In order to accommodate training demand, specialized equipment will probably have to be operated on at least two shifts a day, with continuous classroom and informal workshop-type training activities. In a major city, with 200,000 or more Negroes, a reasonable target would be 20 percent of the Negro labor force engaged in such a small-industry and business development program at any one time. In order to reach this target in the shortest possible time, it will be necessary to create a consortium of business enterprises to provide management-training services under contract with the Urban-Grant University. The management-training program could take the following form: each participating business enterprise would agree to accept a minimum quota of Negro trainees for up to one year, to receive on-the-job training in management, administrative, and technical areas. After one year of such training and related education, in-plant and within an Urban-Grant University, the trainees would move into field-training situations under joint supervision of the sponsoring company and an Urban-Grant University. Field training would consist of working in existing or newly established small enterprises in the ghetto, including community service corporations, to apply and test their management, administrative, and technical skills, and also to meet the manpower needs of these organizations. Many of the trainees would work in storefront centers, established by each participating industrial and business enterprise for the following purposes: to disseminate equal opportunity employment information to people off the streets and in neighborhood groups; to publicize specific job and training opportunities available within the small-industry development program, as well as in sponsoring industries; to exhibit equipment and materials produced and used by the sponsoring company and local industries; to provide informal job and career guidance; to provide a limited library of nontechnical and technical materials related to the sponsoring enterprise and the developing small industries in the locality; to take job and training applications and to provide applicants with experience in job-application and interview procedures.

These storefront centers would operate as part of the ghettos' open-ended educational system, and would be treated by the Urban-Grant University as an important resource for experimentation with unconventional and informal educational techniques, especially those which utilize nonprofessional personnel. In this way, a continuous flow of Black management and technical skills can be fed into the ghettos' business, industries, community development projects, and activities. Many trainees probably will become producers and suppliers for former sponsoring corporations, under the financing and technical assistance schemes discussed above. Thus, coalitions of business and industry in each metro-region, working closely with an Urban-Grant University, would serve as incubators for Negro business, managerial, and technical skills which can direct Black economic development in the ghettos and Black economic participation in the development of new cities.

\*  \*  \*

One of the most remarkable aspects of the modern corporation is that for all the creativeness, daring, and drive required to organize and operate a large-scale business firm, corporate managers, as a group, exercise negligible social initiative both locally and nationally. The public increasingly hears of business expanding its role in the War on Poverty: of insurance companies committing billions of dollars to wipe out slum housing; of business coalitions planning strategy for anti–hot summer activities, holding conferences to castigate welfare bureaucracies, and moving into rural and urban backwaters of hard-core unemployment to create jobs. But close examination of each of these efforts reveals not only the most minimal financial and social commitment commensurate with sound public relations, but, more surprising, an unbusinesslike acceptance of the status quo as the framework of operations, even when the status quo framework is at the root of the problem. However, business ideology is changing, slowly but perceptibly, toward more aggressive leadership in public affairs affecting urban development. But corporate America still has a long way to go before achieving effectiveness in relation to the Black revolution evolving in major urban centers.

The separation of equity ownership and management has given to corporate institutions wide latitude for activities in the public interest, so long as these activities do not impede or impair profit-making operations. In the past few years, as the urban crisis became more visible as a result of ghetto riots, corporate rhetoric on social statesmanship has stressed its capabilities to operate effectively in the social sphere, with or without government partnership; but lately, there is increasing emphasis on the federal government as the marketmaker and guarantor against risk for private participation in social uplift. This corporate rhetoric has tended to support the rejection of political centralism, by advocating that decision-making power be decentralized and vested in the locality. To the extent that corporations are successful in obtaining major responsibilities for urban development, the opponents of centralization of governmental power will have won a victory, though perhaps a Pyrrhic one. The unlimited scope of corporate activity, the limitations of both centralized and decentralized federal control and regulatory mechanisms, the metropolitanization of the most urgent domestic problems, the great lag in state and local government management capabilities, and many other factors, will operate in favor of a much more powerful corporate role in urban and human resources development at the national, state, metroregional, and local levels, as against a more significant role for local government itself.

A new phase of public–private enterprise partnership is taking shape around the problems and needs of urban ghettos. Because of the pace, complexity, scope, and intensity of technological and social change in urban America, specially organized institutions will be required to cope with the consequences of urbanization and ghettoization. Urban development and management will require mobilization of a vast number of highly trained administrators, technicians, researchers, project managers, and planners—quantities of the kind of talented manpower who normally shun public bureaucracies. One of the most significant outcomes of the urban crisis, therefore, will be increasing reliance on private enterprise to plan and carry out what traditionally have been public functions. Indeed, if this trend is not redirected, private enterprise will move into the position of deciding how and where this nation will live in the twenty-first century. The seventies will mark the clear emergence of this quasi-public role for private enterprise.

Social critics like Michael Harrington take the extreme position that business methods and priorities are inapplicable to the crisis of the cities: ". . . when business methods are sincerely and honestly applied to urban problems, with very good intentions, they still *inevitably* lead to anti-social results" (italics mine).[5] Harrington is saying more than that the allocation of resources dominated by economic criteria inevitably is antisocial in consequences. He states that the profit-making motive and social purpose are inherently incompatible, leading "straight to private alliances between self-interested executives and ambitious bureaucrats."[6] Therefore, the duplicity and, possibly, dishonesty, of public and private management, according to Harrington, preclude public–private joint ventures to build and rebuild substantial portions of our metroregions.

No method of doing anything offers foolproof protection against anti-social institutional behavior. Even the collection of data can have anti-social consequences and certainly is not an ideologically neutral activity. Data collection for all governmental programs is politically biased in favor of the ideological interest of the data collection agency. The longer that an organization, like government, has been in the business, the stronger the vested interest in collecting data that can be interpreted favorably to the established institution, requiring no drastic adjustments in organizational structure or operating procedures. For this reason alone, the public domain should be opened to private enterprise, to force upon the public establishment systematic confrontation with its rationale and management system. Even if there were no poor people, no Negroes, Indians, or Mexican–Americans, "antimonopoly" action against federal, state, and local government is desperately needed.

There is an abundant history, including and highlighted by the Economic Opportunity Program, of good intentions harnessed to nonprofit motives by "indigenous" poor people's organizations and nonindigenous rich people's organizations, resulting in more democratic but still pathetic results. Had these same people operated under the profit motive (perhaps paid on a piecework basis for successful project activities, with performance measured by reasonably meaningful criteria), the results probably would have been little better. For another example, social and economic research unencumbered by the profit motive, under university or private foundation auspices, has made very little contribution to coping with the problems of urban living in a highly industrialized society burdened by a powerful legacy of racism. In fact, the latest badge of humility for "urbanologists" is to confess that they know very little about how our urban society actually works (and therefore, of course, millions of dollars more in applied research is needed, with some new innovative twists or "wrinkles," as they are termed by funding specialists).

The greatest menace to democratic control of planning in the ghettos is not the corporation seeking profit but inept and uninformed leadership and organization which result in continuous frustration and opens the way for exploitation and anarchism. Harrington does not give Negroes in the ghetto sufficient credit for becoming increasingly wiser about the diverse forms of economic and political "colonialism" to which they have been subjected. They are becoming well aware of the fact that, for example, "pilot" and "demonstration" projects in educational remediation and "enrichment" (so-called compensatory education) only serve to protect the school system from basic reforms in administration, teacher training, curriculum design, and so forth. However, there still remains among Negroes a huge gap between their increasingly sophisticated perception of underlying political power relationships and the lack of organizational, management, and programming skills to capitalize on this awareness. In my experience, Negroes in the ghettos, including incipient hard-core political leadership, would welcome the kind of technical and financial assistance that corporate enterprise could assemble, *if* the contractual terms and conditions of delivery and utilization can be satisfactorily established and then faithfully performed. These militant Blacks, including savvy gang leaders, see frustration-crazed agitators and massive riots as undermining the potential for political and economic organization in the ghetto. They know, and white society must learn, that unless economic and political Black power can be successfully organized in the ghetto to systematically direct ghetto manpower and profits into ghetto reconstruction, the social restraints on anarchic action will continue to disintegrate. *As of the moment however, there is no Black power movement in the ghetto, just as there is no civil rights movement. There are only diverse and multiplying perceptions of the need for sufficient control, knowledge, and tools to crystallize power out of futility and wasted humanity.*

Contrary to Michael Harrington's convictions, the so-called social industrialists, the corporate elite, are not incapable of grasping, intellectually and intuitively, the basic conflicts between corporate economic ideology, methods, goals, and processes and the Black power concept of planning and development in urban ghettos. If so-called democratic planning institutions in the ghetto can be analytically described and humanly experienced, they can be understood sufficiently by corporate planners to enable them to work out a flexible, adaptable, but "businesslike" work program—one that allows plenty of margin for uncertainties and unknowns, one that respects the ideology and dynamics of evolving Black power institutions. The critical prerequisites for the problematic matrimony between Black revolution and private enterprise are: first, a vision of where Blacks and whites are heading in urban America—one that can meaningfully encompass the aspirations of both races; and second, a new set of institutional vehicles, such as the Metroregional Development Corporation, the Urban-Grant University, and the Community Development Corporation, designed to pack a century of economic, social, political, and physical change into the span of a few decades.

# Notes

1. Joseph A. Pechman, *Federal Tax Policy* (Washington: The Brookings Institution, 1966), p. 111, table 5–2.
2. Quoted in an article by David Deitch, *Boston Globe*, November 2, 1967.
3. See, for example, Gustav F. Papanek, *Pakistan's Development: Social Goals and Private Incentives* (Cambridge: Harvard University Press, 1967).
4. See, for example, U.S. Department of Commerce, Economic Development Administration, *Characteristics of Modern Industrial Plants* (Washington, D.C.: U.S. Government Printing Office, 1966).
5. Michael Harrington, "The Social–Industrial Complex," *Harper's Magazine*, November 1967.
6. *Ibid.*

# 17 ]] Equality of Economic Opportunity through Capital Ownership

*Louis O. Kelso and Patricia Hetter*

"Men in Cadillacs meet at champagne lunches to plan our future while expecting us to stand hat in hand," a Negro minister from Chicago told a House Education and Labor subcommittee in April 1965, and in April 1966, Sargent Shriver himself was unceremoniously routed by the poor from a Washington, D.C., poverty conference where the keynote complaint was bawled into the microphones by Mrs. Johnnie Tillman of Watts. "When all this poverty money is spent," shouted Mrs. Tillman to applause, "the rich man is going to be richer and I'm still going to be receiving a welfare check."

These rumbles from America's poverty craters signify that the impoverished resent being rehabilitated by their "betters"—and even suspect that the poverty under attack in the Anti-poverty War is mainly their betters' own.

To understand such rank ingratitude, we must remember that the economic objective of the poor in an affluent society is exactly the same as everyone else's: to be *affluent*. The sociological jargon of the poverty investigator obscures this fact. It also obscures the special peculiarity of the poor, that unique characteristic of their caste that fatally distinguishes it from every other caste: namely, lack of money.

"There's One Thing Money Can't Buy: Poverty!" reads the legend on J. Paul Getty's paperweight. This great truth should be emblazoned on the shield of every poverty warrior. The poor lack money. They lack money because they do not know the secret of producing wealth. They know it is possible to be old, unemployed, uneducated, lazy—even halt, deaf, dumb, and blind—and still be excessively rich. But you have to be in on the secret, and the poor by definition are not.

What the poor man wants is an end to his poverty. Charity, handouts, even his own personal social worker, have no appeal. Even if humiliation has crushed his spirit, or he has learned that what he can produce in the economy on *its* terms is not worth *his* effort, he hates being dependent on the ephemeral good will of others. Experience has taught him that the bread of charity is not even bread, but crumbs, and that distribution when measured by need is, has been, and always will be niggardly.

In practice, charity is always niggardly because people are incapable of

From *Social Policies for America in the Seventies*, edited by Robert Theobald. © 1968 by Doubleday & Company, Inc. Reprinted by permission of Doubleday & Company, Inc.

judging the need of someone else to be as great as their own. This is true whether the dispenser of affluence is a Soviet commissar, an American politician, or one's own rich Great-Aunt Maud.

To be sure, the compassionate man is prepared to do much for the poor. He will feed them, clothe them, teach their children, bandage their sores. He will live for them gladly and die for them with grace. He will do everything under heaven for the poor except give them what they yearn for most—the secret of his ability personally to produce the wealth that enables *him* to serve *them*. At that juncture, the compassionate man—and the compassionate society—always back off. And this the poor man knows.

The theme of the government antipoverty program is "economic opportunity."

"I don't believe the government owes you a living," Vice President Humphrey told eighty trainees at the Camp Kilmer Job Corps Center dedication. "I don't believe the government owes you a salary. But I do believe the government owes you the opportunity to make something of your lives."[1]

Writes Sargent Shriver in *Point of the Lance*: "But no one connected with the poverty program proposes to equalize life's burdens. Helping the poor help themselves is the keynote of the president's program. It does not offer handouts; it offers opportunities. It is concerned with creating the conditions under which the child born into poverty can have the chance to help himself, to compete on equal terms with those lucky enough to be born into affluence."[2]

These are authoritative Great Society utterances. The burden of them and of the President's Message on Poverty transmitting the Economic Opportunity Act of 1964 is that economic opportunity is a responsibility of the federal government. It would be difficult to argue otherwise. The right *effectively* to participate in the economy would seem to be a corollary of the right to life and the pursuit of happiness. A citizen excluded from making his living, somehow prevented from taking a significant part in the production and distribution of goods and services, could not sustain life very long, much less live it. Therefore, economic opportunity would seem not only a constitutional, but a natural right, valid for all men, everywhere, at all times.

In practice, however, the question is local. The nature of opportunity depends upon the conditions in a specific economy—its resources, state of technology, physical development, and potential. It is a matter of how wealth is currently produced, of how the livings of substantial and honorable citizens are generally made. What represents opportunity in one economy (for instance, owning a herd of reindeer) would be useless or irrelevant in another. What represented opportunity in the past may be anachronistic in the present. No one connected with the antipoverty program suggests apprenticing young men as blacksmiths or harness makers, or providing them with thirty acres and a mule. In 1840, the slogan "6¼ Cents a Day and Sheeps Pluck to the Laborer under Van Buren—2 Dollars a Day and Good Roast Beef under General Harrison" helped elect a president, but it would hardly win any votes today.

Besides being temporally appropriate, economic opportunity implies favorable prospects for producing a reasonably good and dependable living. While many well-fed people deny that intellectual and spiritual life has any connection with such a vulgar organ as the stomach, or that culture has anything to do with the financial ability to buy and maintain, say, a grand piano, or to pay the music master, the fact is that living in "decency and dignity" is impossible without a stable source of income. Legitimate economic opportunity must offer at least a fair chance of providing it.

Thus, while the Goddess Fortuna rules all, enterprise counting too heavily on her favor is not genuine economic opportunity. Large sums are won all the time in football pools and horseraces, and many countries (and a few but growing number of our states) use lotteries to divert the people from the hopelessness of their situation; but the opportunity such events provide is illusory. So is the chance to "compete" for a job, for all except the winner, if too many persons want it. Not long ago, a San Francisco union ran a tiny classified advertisement announcing eight openings on its roll—and hundreds of men showed up. In London a few years ago, an industrial federation in need of an economist, found that the Ministry of Labour and the University of London alone could immediately supply forty economists theoretically capable of doing the job. No attempt was made to check the "human resources" on deposit in such institutions as Oxford, Cambridge, the London School of Economics, or the provincial universities. Instead, the thirteenth man interviewed was given the job—on the theory that at best the other twenty-seven would prove only equal to No. 13. The post paid £500 a year. That so many well-educated and qualified men should have been eager, indeed desperate, to compete for what they all knew to be a mediocre and deadend job, eloquently defined economic opportunity for economists in Great Britain at that moment.

Incidents like this are commonplace not only in Great Britain, but in Italy, the Philippines, Greece, Latin America, wherever the number of persons qualified by education and training is greater than the economy can support in a style commensurate with the social status traditionally associated with persons of their accomplishments. They show that education per se is not economic opportunity, although some professional educators toil mightily in the antipoverty vanguard to implant the notion that their speciality is the key to the golden door. Certainly, enough federal billions spent in support of this fallacy will keep the young off the labor market and the wolf away from the door of the professional educator.

But the poor man, let us remind ourselves once more, is not interested in being used to solve the poverty problems of others. He is interested in solving his own poverty problem. As a citizen of the richest and most fortunate nation in the history of the world, he is interested in learning how he can be rich and fortunate instead of poor and miserable. His hope is to find out how wealth is being produced in the United States in his time, so that he can produce some of it for his own benefit and enjoyment and that of his family and his heirs.

One might expect such valuable and relevant information to be at least touched upon in a congressional enactment entitled the "Economic Opportunity Act of 1964." But the poor man will search its fine print in vain for the secret of how "the well-being and prosperity of the United States have progressed to a level surpassing any achieved in world history."[3] About the source of this well-being and prosperity nothing is said. Indeed, in his Letter of Transmittal to Congress, the President of the United States is as coy about telling the electorate where affluence comes from as a Victorian parent telling his children where they came from. We just "grew" to be the richest and most fortunate nation in the history of the world; and what caused the growing, the Economic Opportunity Act does not confide.

While the words "job" and "work" stud the 19¾ pages of this document like raisins in a pudding, the word "capital" is not used once. A visitor from another planet could read the act from beginning to end without ever learning that there exists within the boundaries of this spanned continent any such thing as physical capital or the nonhuman factor of production. Much less would he suspect the presence of almost $3 trillion worth of it. Or that this aggregate might be related to the nation's historically unprecedented well-being and prosperity.

The Economic Opportunity Act neglects to mention that 180 years ago, when "we were a small country struggling for survival on the margin of a hostile land," Watt's first steam engine and the Wilkinson boring mill (the first basic machine tool) were still not a decade old, and Cartwright's power loom was on the eve of being announced. Even half a century later, though industrial technology was gaining momentum and breakthroughs in science, chemistry, metallurgy, precision measurement, and mechanics were remaking the face of England, and the winds of the Industrial Revolution were sweeping toward our eastern shore, Americans were still providing themselves food, clothing, and shelter with simple hand tools— essentially the same ones that their forebears brought from Europe. Axe, hammer, bellows, anvil, knife, plow, flax spindle, loom, spinning wheel— simple capital instruments like these had kept generations of Europeans fully employed. Unfortunately, the process hardly yielded daily bread. For the great majority of men, doomed to toil for others or to squander their labor on farms too small and poor to provide more than subsistence, life everywhere was a struggle for survival.

It might be salutary for a generation desiring to collect the scattered hopes of the American past to remember what kind of opportunity America once represented to the poor. At its best, it was something infinitely more precious and rare than a job. It was the opportunity of claiming title to some kind of productive property. The most violent hope of the American past, still ungathered and every day more scattered, is not merely the hope of using one's energies in productive work. It is the hope of freeing oneself from the compulsions and indignities of economic necessity by producing one's livelihood to a substantial extent through ownership of capital.

Economic opportunity in the American past was land—unclaimed, uncultivated, unexploited earth and forest—that would reward the resourceful and industrious for their hardship and toil, instead of breaking their backs and hearts for nothing. Our ancestors understood, as we apparently do not, the truth of the Russian proverb: "Work does not make a man rich, but roundshouldered." And beyond abundance, although secured by it, was the ultimate opportunity—the opportunity forever beyond the reach of the employee or tenant: autonomy. The pulled forelock, the doffed cap, the bent knee—most of our ancestors were well-rehearsed in these outward signs of economic subservience, and they wisely addressed themselves to repairing their dignity by improving their estates.

Not all of these ventures ended happily, nor did all of the immigrants achieve the independence of landowners or small proprietors. The New World was still a long way from Cockaigne, the folk paradise where fritters grew on trees and dropped into lakes of syrup. An old Latvian woman remembered her bitter disappointment as a girl to discover that for her the golden door of America led only to twelve hours a day of subsistence toil in a New York hat factory. For persons owning nothing but their power to labor, the outlook has rarely been enviable anywhere. The economic opportunity offered by America, Canada, South Africa, Australia, and other popular emigrant destinations of the last century, was strictly relative, and its terms were often cruel; but within the context of a primarily agricultural economy requiring large amounts of labor, it was fairly genuine and positive. If the door to the ultimate prize, land property, was not wide open, at least it was ajar.

But economic opportunity, we have said, is related to the way in which goods and services are produced. *If the means undergo a change, then the nature of economic opportunity must also change.* The agricultural economy of the last century was rewrought by the Industrial Revolution, and now the Cybernetics Revolution is recasting the industrial economy. In both revolutions, the agent of change is technology embodied in capital instruments. Productive wealth in the United States today is in the form of machines, structures, and land. Not "human capital" but nonhuman capital has transformed the quality of life. To it is owed those opportunities which have in fact expanded—opportunity for leisure, for education, for cultural pursuits, for travel. But at the same time, the triumph of the nonhuman factor has diminished economic opportunity as our forebears understood it. Predominantly, economic goods are most efficiently produced and distributed by large, incredibly expensive aggregates of capital instruments organized into appropriate patterns through large corporations; and within them, the labor power of human beings other than key management is of diminishing importance. Work cannot be pushed onto machines and still be performed by men. To coin a proverb, "You can't automate your job and have it, too."

Even if economic growth were to expand at a rate sufficient to provide real work for everyone who wanted or needed it, work is no longer the first step toward acquiring capital. The day of the self-made man is past. Every day the small farmer, the small businessman, the small proprietor finds it more difficult to exist. Saving one's way to capital ownership was never easy, but it used to be done just often enough to perpetuate the illusion that it could be done by anyone sufficiently toilsome and parsimonious. Today, only a few highly paid professions can save enough to acquire an income-producing capital estate. Indeed, if many citizens of an industrial economy should suddenly rediscover the old virtues of self-denial and thrift, the government would have to intervene to avert disaster. As for individual enterprise, it is probably harder to sell automobiles today than it was to found an automobile factory at the turn of the century. Henry Ford did it in a garage with a $28,000 investment. In 1903, his feat was merely spectacular. Today it would be insane.

For a long time now, the avant-garde of science and technology has been telling us—warning us—that in our lifetime we are witnessing five millennia of drudgery draw to a close. Even if we choose to ignore men like Dr. Richard Bellman (the Rand Corporation scientist who predicts that within twenty-five years our vast capital plant can turn out all the goods and services the entire economy can consume with the assistance of only 2 percent of the labor force), it is obvious that a revolution is going on. Not in our "manpower resources," as the Department of Labor pretends, but in our capital instruments.

In his open letter to the President, published in *Datamation*, Dr. Louis Fein, a pioneer computer designer, builder and consultant, tactfully inquires: "Isn't it plausible that U.S. science and technology is advancing at a sufficiently great rate that at some instant soon we will have just one more person that we need, then two more, then ten more, then thousands more, than 3.5 million more, then tens of thousands more . . . ? Is it not imperative that we start right now seeking alternative viable economic policies for coping with such contingent conditions—instead of gambling that the roof won't fall in?"[4]

But poor though the outlook for mass employment may be, the question of economic opportunity is not necessarily related to the number of jobs available, or even to employment. The decisive question, to repeat, is: *How is wealth actually produced?* While research that would measure the respective contributions of labor and capital remains unproposed and undesigned, we can deduce which of the two factors plays the dominant role.

We know, for instance, that the annual 3 percent increase in output per man-hour must be credited mostly, if not entirely, to capital instruments. We know that capital expenditure per employee is constantly rising —that it averages $10,000 in the gas and electric utilities industry, for example, and that in other industries the figure is as high as $300,000 per employee. We know that new plant and equipment expenditures have set records every year since 1961, and that projections for 1967 promise a new record of almost $65 billion.[5] We know also that while the estimated market value of land in the United States in 1964 was $16.8 billion, the value of structures (i.e., land improvements) and other reproducible assets was over $81 billion.[6]

And finally, we know from reading, from experience, and from observation which factor of production is being displaced by technological change. Not capital primarily. Technology is its lifeblood. Technology raises the productivity of capital instruments and paves the way for more to be performed. Technology thus favors the capital owner. Its effect is to make his economic role ever more secure.

Since technological change increases only the output of capital, and since every round of new plant and equipment spending only speeds up this process, genuine economic opportunity must be linked to capital ownership. A job will not unlock for its holder the full potential largesse of the economy. With rare exceptions, households entirely dependent on their labor cannot produce enough purchasing power to buy the things they want to consume—things the economy could produce with ease, but does not because of inadequate purchasing power of those with unsatisfied wants and needs. Economic participation through labor alone is inadequate and uncertain. Only families owning viable capital estates can drink the pristine waters of affluence directly from the source. The labor-dependent must wait, often hat in hand, for affluence to trickle down—and the farther down it trickles, the thinner it gets.

There is more to life than material well-being. Who would claim that the wholly wage-dependent family enjoys the dignity, the security, the range of choice, and the autonomy (not to mention the leisure and freedom) of the family even partially supported by capital ownership?

If employment no longer represents full participation in the production of goods and services (assuming it ever did), then economic opportunity cannot merely consist of job training. In a capital-dominated economy, labor-centered measures *are inadequate*. Creating jobs, training people for jobs, retraining people for different jobs, matching people and jobs—all of these miss the mark. The opportunity most appropriate to an industrial economy is the opportunity to acquire a viable interest in the increasingly productive factor: *capital*.

The Economic Opportunity Act of 1964, of course, does not provide—or even mention—any such opportunity. Although capital ownership is most emphatically a social opportunity (indeed, a socially created opportunity), it is evidently not one which society is prepared to share with those who are not already capital owners. All nonowners may share is the economy's toil. The message this act delivers to the plain man (by definition, one who owns nothing but his power to work) is something less than inspiring. It tells him that "economic opportunity" for *him* consists of a job, or the chance to train for a job. This is as high as he may aspire. He may not aspire to ownership of the capital instruments that are obsoleting his labor. His economic contribution must be made through labor, or not at all.

Even at best, assuming that its vocational training is successful and that all its graduates find employment, the Economic Opportunity Act dooms those "aided" to a life of low economic productivity, with its resulting semipoverty, insecurity, and dependence on organized corecion to force their employers to artificially elevate wages or salaries.

"*I had to forget my seniority and start all over again,*" said a Pennsylvania glass cutter after automatic glass-cutting machines converted him into an unemployment statistic. By going back to school for twenty-six weeks under the Federal Manpower Development and Retraining Act (while his family of six got by on a $33-per-week federal allowance, a little service pension and $15 worth of surplus food a month), this spunky and energetic man, "marvelling at his luck while sympathizing with 3,200 of his neighbors still unemployed," finally got a new job paying $20 a week *less* than his old one.[7]

In its summary of the so-called Manpower Revolution, the Clark Committee concluded: "The time appears near at hand when the average worker cannot expect to continue a single occupation for a working lifetime. Even if the occupational title does not disappear, the occupational content over time is likely to change completely."[8]

Let us consider, then, the fate in store for that fortunate fellow: the *employed* worker. This is what he has to look forward to—a lifetime of shedding his vocational skin, of periodically being stripped of his habits and skills, of being trained and retrained, advised and revised, remodeled, revamped, rehabilitated, doled, redoled, retreaded, rerouted, relocated, uprooted, and replanted. And behind him all the while that "untiring foe of all skilled manpower: obsolescence" pants hotly down his neck. Indeed, rather than providing him with economic opportunity, the act of that name seems designed to make the poor man do penance all his life for the sin of being born into a non–capital-owning family.

Meanwhile, the political and financial arrangements that visit the sin of the fathers upon the sons (i.e., nonownership of the economically most productive factor) go unchanged and even unchallenged. And yet the children of the capital owner come into the world as naked of property, as innocent of the ability to manage it, as the child of the lowliest pauper! It is the institutions of society, not parental genes, that bestow the blessings of ownership of productive capital. Yet Sargent Shriver has declared that the federal antipoverty program is concerned with "creating the conditions under which the child born into poverty can have the chance to help himself, to compete on *equal* terms with the child lucky enough to have been born into affluence."[9]

If we may assume with Aristotle that equality is for equals, let us analyze our richest and most fortunate citizens in the same detached scientific spirit that characterizes the dedicated poverty investigator. But instead of, "Why are the poor, poor?," let our question be, *"Why are the rich, rich?"* To our surprise, we discover that the hard-core structural poverty at the bottom of the social pyramid has a counterpart at the apex. Let us call it *hard-core structural affluence.* And then we discover something else: the existence of a profound causal relationship between hardcore structural affluence and ownership of sizable pieces of productive real estate or large blocks of corporate shares in such concerns as those listed on the boards of the New York and American Stock Exchanges, or other viable holdings of the nonhuman factor of production. This association occurs much too regularly for chance. Indeed, the connection is so common that affluence can be described as a *function* of capital ownership.

Moreover, our study of the rich and fortunate discloses a very close correlation between ownership of productive capital and the most gainful and rewarding employments. This finding is further substantiated by the Economic Opportunity Act. One searches it in vain for measures designed to provide economic opportunity to the capital owner. Nobody proposes to educate, train, or rehabilitate either him or his children, even when their "unemployment" is notorious. Evidently the capital owner's skills and talents are fully developed by the opportunities provided by capital ownership itself. The conclusion is corroborated by the large numbers of capital owners we find employed as corporate lawyers, stockholders, bankers, managing directors, corporation presidents, cabinet members, government department chiefs, ambassadors, governors of sovereign states, and presidents of united ones.

This being demonstrably so, it would seem that an effective antipoverty program, instead of seeking to share the poverty of an economy many times too small to provide the majority with real affluence (i.e., the standard of living enjoyed by the 10 percent of households at the capital-owning apex) would seek to (1) greatly expand the existing economy and (2) finance this "second economy" in ways that would enable those who own none of the existing assets to buy and pay for equity shares in the new or expanded industries. Instead of matching men and jobs, it would seek to match propertyless labor-dependent households with portfolios of corporate securities or other viable capital holdings capable of providing, in time, a "second income" from dividends. Within the context of private property, this means providing equality of access to ownership of the economy's newly formed capital. And unless we wish to perpetuate our economic double standard (one kind of opportunity for the rich man, another for the poor), families without capital *must* have the same "opportunity" to acquire capital ownership without tightening their belts and reducing their (already minimal) consumption. In short, means need to be found to enable the poor man, who cannot afford belt-tightening, to finance the acquisition of newly formed capital in the same manner as the rich man, whose consumption is not necessarily restricted by his capital-acquiring activities.

In comparison with the financial feats we are performing daily by the millions, such a policy would be child's play. An economy that has developed techniques to credit-finance a house, every kind of appliance, a holiday in Hawaii, even a weekend in Disneyland, will find it easy to finance the things that produce income. Productive capital is inherently financeable. Newly created capital instruments (plants, equipment, etc.) in well-managed enterprises, with negligible exceptions, in a few years produce net income equal to their cost and then go on to produce income for owners for years. Consumer goods, by contrast, produce no income.

Our remarkable credit techniques, developed to narrow the purchasing-power gap, in the long run only widen it. Service and interest charges reduce the spendable income of the consumer. How much wiser it would be to use these familiar and highly developed techniques to finance the acquisition of income-producing capital for every household in America, thus enabling them to consume the abundance our industries are ready, able, willing, and eager to produce, if only they could find enough customers with dollars in their pockets, or even unsaturated credit.

If, after embarking on this objective, the government still has time to engage in training, it might train the propertyless in one of the chief skills required in an advanced industrial economy: the care and management of one's productive capital, or in the art of selecting competent advisers and fiduciaries for this purpose.

As for *retraining*, we might well begin with those in our society who, though they already possess large capital estates, persist in setting examples of economic toil and greed for more accumulation, instead of inspiring the rest of us to a more noble use of wealth and leisure.

## Notes

1. *New York Times*, March 14, 1965.
2. Sargent Shriver, *Point of the Lance* (New York: Harper, 1964), p. 98.
3. *Economic Opportunity Act of 1964*, Section 2.
4. Louis Fein, "Dear Mr. President," *Datamation*, January 1965.
5. *Business Week*, February 11, 1967.
6. R. W. Goldsmith and R. E. Lipsey, *Studies in the National Balance Sheet of the United States*, vol. I, table 11, extended to 1964 by J. W. Kendrick, assisted by J. Japha, *The Morgan Guaranty Survey* (New York: Morgan Guaranty Trust Co., August 1966), p. 8. While about $25 billion of the reproducible assets were residential structures, a substantial portion of these are rental structures and thus properly classified as productive capital rather than consumer goods.
7. *Life*, July 19, 1963, p. 69.
8. Subcommittee on Employment and Manpower of the Committee on Labor and Public Welfare, U.S. Senate, "Toward Full Employment: Proposals for a Comprehensive Employment and Manpower Policy in the United States" (Washington, D.C.: Government Printing Office, 1964), p. 19.
9. Sargent Shriver, *op. cit.*, p. 98.

# 18 ]] Cooperatives and Poor

## People in the South

*Al Ulmer*

There are, at least, forty poor people's cooperatives in the South, fifteen or sixteen of which might be termed, because of size and strength, significant efforts. These co-ops are all in the rural areas of the South. They affect perhaps 15,000 persons, almost all of whom are Black. As yet, few of the co-ops have reached the poorest of the poor, the people without land, jobs, or adequate food.

In this report, nine of the cooperative efforts are examined to see to what extent they have helped poor people meet their basic needs—needs going unmet in today's rural South. The problems of co-ops are also discussed, those resulting from actions *outside* the co-ops, and those caused by events *within* the organizations. An estimate is made of what it will take to overcome these problems and to establish a number of strong cooperatives. Finally, there are suggestions for what might be the results of a good co-op movement in the rural South.

### Where Are Cooperatives Now?

Seven years ago, Father Albert McKnight, a Black Catholic priest in Lafayette, Louisiana, frustrated in his attempts to start a statewide credit union, organized Southern Consumers Cooperative. Members of the Lafayette area Negro community, both poor and middle-class, were urged to buy shares in the co-op. With the invested money, the co-op in 1964 opened a bakery and a loan company.

The same year, Jesse Morris, a SNCC organizer in Mississippi, and others established the Poor People's Corporation (PPC) as an investment cooperative. PPC made loans to worker-owned cooperatives producing handicraft items and toys.

Three farm cooperatives soon joined these initial efforts: West Batesville Farmers Association in Panola County, Mississippi; Mid-South Consumers Oil Co-op in Whiteville, Tennessee; and Grand Marie Vegetable Growers Association in Sunset, Louisiana. The Grenala Citizens Federal Credit Union in Hale County, Alabama, began operations about the same time. By 1968, there were thirty-eight poor people's co-ops and credit unions. They included farm marketing and farm machinery co-ops, buying

From Al Ulmer, *Cooperatives and Poor People in the South* (Atlanta: Southern Regional Council, 1969). Reprinted with permission from Southern Regional Council.

clubs, sewing co-ops, handicraft production groups, self-help housing units, bakeries, candy-making businesses, gas and oil retailers and wholesalers; grocery stories, and fish-processing associations.

Needs for technical and management assistance, for help in marketing, planning, and bookkeeping for these co-ops were partially met in July 1967, when the Ford Foundation gave $578,000 to Southern Consumers Education Foundation (an outgrowth of Southern Consumers Co-op) to fund the two-year Southern Cooperative Development Program (SCDP). Father McKnight left Southern Consumers to direct the four-state (Alabama, Louisiana, Mississippi, and Southwest Tennessee) program.

Ideas for this program came from members of existing cooperatives and workers from several civil rights and human rights organizations. Out of the thinking that went into the proposal, the awareness of the need of all the newly founded co-ops to learn from one another's mistakes and successes, developed the Federation of Southern Cooperatives, a southwide organization. The Federation, a co-op itself, is owned and directed by representatives of the various low-income co-ops. Charles Prejean has been director of the Federation since its inception in October 1967. The Federation provides technical and management assistance to those states not covered by SCDP. The Federation also sees itself as an eventual wholesale supplier and group marketing outlet for its member co-ops. Several foundation grants and a recent grant of more than $500,000 from the Office of Economic Opportunity finance the Federation's work.

Any attempt to assess the cooperative movement among poor people of the rural South has to take into consideration how nearly the co-ops come to meeting basic needs of the people they have touched. Are they helping poor people to obtain (1) more money; (2) decent housing; (3) land for farms, industry, and recreation; (4) adequate food; (5) education or the chance for self-development; (6) political and economic power; (7) adequate circumstances to keep young people from leaving the rural area; (8) strong, organized communities; (9) a measure of security in terms of such things as insurance against bad health, unemployment, and death?* A look at several of the co-ops indicates what they have been able to do in the few years of their existence. . . .


## Problems of Poor People's Co-ops

It is obvious that the cooperatives vary greatly in how they are attempting to meet their members' needs and in the degree to which they are succeeding. They all have problems. There are "outside" problems, the accumulative results of years of unheeded poverty in an oppressive political and economic system. There are "inside" problems, such as poor accounting

---

* Most of these criteria were included in a 1941 report by the National Resources Board called, "After Defense—What?" The answer during the years since 1941 has been very little meeting of these needs of the rural, largely landless poor.

procedures, bad management, conservative leadership, insufficient operating and development capital.

These involve the basic question of how many of the needs of poor people, as outlined in the list of nine critical needs, are being met by the cooperatives. Further, how many of these basic needs can or should be met by co-ops? And how many of the needs *must* be met by someone if co-ops are to have more than token success?

The co-op built about crop diversification and group buying and marketing has been the most successful of all the recent efforts. It has, however, with few exceptions, included only men who own their own land. The base upon which farm co-ops must build is small and getting smaller. Approximately 7,000 Black farm owners in the United States netted an average of $2,500 or more from their farms in 1960. Another 3,000 farm owners made slightly less. Thirty-four thousand other owners and renters had enough off-farm work to give them an annual total income of over $2,500. These 44,000 owners and renters represent only 17 percent of the Negro farm operators in the United States. The other 83 percent earn less than $2,500. It is the group making more than $2,500 that farm co-ops can realistically expect to involve, under present conditions. And even these, the elite of the rural Black poor, are in a desperate situation. They are old; more than one-third of nonwhites owning rural land in the Southeast were over sixty-four in 1960. This group owned two-fifths of the land owned by nonwhites. For all nonwhite landowners, the average amount of land owned is but fifty-two acres (as against 249 acres for whites). Fifth grade is about the median of educational achievement.

As for the remaining 83 percent of Black farm operators, they are without land, without money, and without much chance of getting either under present governmental programs.

If the majority of Black farmers still left in the rural areas cannot get land and money with which to develop the land, it is most uncertain what long-range success farm cooperatives can achieve.

If farm cooperatives are to have more than token success, it seems clear that the problem of land must be solved. Should co-ops try to solve the land problem? If so, how? One effort was underway in the summer of 1968 to start a land developing corporation in rural Alabama. The corporation planned to lease land to poor people or to cooperatives of poor people.

It is doubtful whether a private land-buying program can do more than prove the feasibility of poor people owning or leasing their own land. What is needed is land reform. The Mississippi Freedom Democratic Party at the Chicago Convention called for a program of land redistribution, citing New Deal programs as examples of what might be done today. From 1937 to 1941, the federal government spent $200 million in resettlement programs affecting 35,415 families. A portion of MFDP's suggested plank called for ". . . outright grants of land to poor people. The government should also sell acreage to low and moderate income people at a nominal fee and should offer low-interest, long-term loans. Land should be made available from federal- and state-owned acreage and from private land now being subsidized to lie unused which may be taken under the power of eminent domain. . . ." Unless *someone* can provide land, farm co-ops are incapable of reaching the very poor. There will remain only small, often conservative, struggling co-op businesses with limited futures.

On the other hand, what if land were made available to poor people along with technical assistance in growing cooperatively marketed crops, a share in a feeder pig or calf program on co-op owned land, part owner-ship in recreation facilities, day-care centers, adult education programs, etc., built with co-op and government funds (i.e., the transformation of rural farm co-ops into rural cooperative service centers); part ownership in an industrial enterprise or a processing plant? Would such a program possibly offer solutions to some of the needs of the rural poor? It would cost a great amount of money. How much is impossible to estimate accu-rately until it is tried. Ten thousand dollars per family might begin such an operation.

The outside problems weigh as heavily on nonfarm cooperatives and credit unions. Seventy-five percent of rural Black young men drop out of their inadequate schools; a majority of adult rural Blacks have not finished fifth grade; 90 percent of Negro farm houses have no indoor toilet or run-ning water; malnutrition and its effects have crippled the potential of thousands of poor people and, of course, whites own the land, control credit and employment opportunities, and administer justice.

Many of the co-ops presently in existence cannot be expected to continue to withstand these tremendous problems—over which they have no con-trol. They began with very little money, small numbers of people, and limited objectives. Limited objectives may prove the most debilitating factor of all, tending to keep the co-ops poor and small. If a co-op can achieve enough size, strength, and allied support, it can take on the system, the complex of outside problems, at least locally. Both SWAFCA and Southern Consumers have been able to push out a little space for themselves in which to grow.

The necessity for expansion and for forming strong federations and regional confederations cannot be overemphasized. Neither can the danger of centralization and the resultant loss in membership loyalty inherent in big impersonal organizations. A cooperative's strength is built upon twin bases, the degree of ownership, and, therefore, the loyalty its members feel, and the quality of service it can provide. For example, fertilizer is a highly competitive commodity; the only way to save farmers' money is to buy it in very large volumes. Even then a co-op's price on certain grades of fertilizer might run very close to (perhaps even higher than) local suppliers', especially if the suppliers are out to ruin the co-ops anyway. Unless the individual members of the large co-op have been in-volved in making the decision to buy the fertilizer as owners of the co-op, the cooperative is in the position of being just another business competing for the farmer's money.

Not only must the co-op member be involved in such a decision, but he must also understand that his savings through cooperative purchasing come in the form of quarterly or semiannual distribution of the co-op's profits. Such distributions (called patronage refunds) are made to member–owners on the basis of how much they used the services of the co-op. Since most of the cooperatives are paying back loans, the patronage refunds are paid as shares of stock in the business rather than as cash dividends, the cash going to pay the loans. It is difficult enough to get each member of a small group to understand all of this, even with weekly or monthly meetings. When co-ops get so large and centralized and attempt to do it at annual meetings, chaos is the result.

Decentralization means decisions will be arrived at more slowly. It also means lengthy and numerous discussions of policies and, probably in the beginning, concentration on easily understood unimportant items at the expense of the more important, more complex matters. Initially, decentralization will be expensive; without it, however, co-op members will once again be customers and clients—not owners.

THE INSIDE PROBLEMS

Co-ops lack money, long-term development capital, and short-term operating funds. An assessment of how much money they need depends on how many of the needs of poor people cooperatives can be expected to meet. The small, stagnant cooperatives need money to help them expand. The already sizable co-ops must have money for at least five years (mostly loan capital) to allow them to grow more and at the same time keep close contact with their members.

Money creates a problem even when present in adequate amounts. It has a tendency, when given as direct subsidy as in SWAFCA's case, to damage the feeling of ownership among the members. This is especially true when a large staff is hired from outside the area at big salaries "to develop" the co-op. As much of the co-op's money as possible needs to come from the members. Co-ops that have forced their members to invest until it hurts generally have members who realize they own the co-op.

Most co-ops lack good managers. Small co-ops usually cannot pay any salary the first two or three years. At present, almost every co-op in the four states in which the SCDP works receives a management subsidy. It is impossible for small (100 members or less) co-ops ever to think about paying their own manager. If one is hired on subsidy, he must expand the co-op to the point where in the reasonably near future the co-op can pay his salary. Local middle-aged poor people with very limited educations cannot usually be trained in six months or a year to be competent managers. Most co-ops have conservative leadership. Several co-ops have men with vision and the ability to set forth expansion plans and carry them out. But in most cases, the managers must force the boards to take the necessary risks to achieve expansion, to incur the debts, and to operate on other than personal financial management lines. This is not a surprising problem. Rural poor people are basically conservative in economics and often middle class in values. These are middle-aged and older people, many of whom have worked extremely hard for what little they have and are afraid of losing it. They have no experience in large-scale finance or in making decisions that will affect large numbers of people. SCDP and the Federation are carrying on training programs with the various boards of directors in an attempt to reorient them to see their communities and their co-ops in realistic new terms. The large majority of board members do not yet understand the potential of co-ops as agents of economic and social change. Many do not yet understand what a co-op is or might possibly be if given the right leadership.

Another internal problem is lack of membership support. Generally, this is caused by the members not understanding that the co-op belongs to them. Poor public relations, a proprietary attitude on the part of many boards, and the failure of most co-ops to see themselves and to work as community organizations are all responsible. Membership campaigns, radio broadcasts, posters in the community, and better trained boards can be applied to the first two aspects of the problem. The failure of members to understand the community-strengthening aspects of a co-op, regardless of whether every person in the community has bought a share or not, often gives the impression that it is just another business venture of benefit only to its owners.

At times it appears the present co-op efforts have become so wedded to the idea of co-ops as businesses for economic gain of their members that they have ignored their community responsibilities, a shortcoming which has made many of the large midwestern and northern co-ops, organized during the thirties, little more than economically successful defenders of the status quo.

Farm co-ops need to rent land for landless poor farmers, paying for it out of their patronage refunds, if necessary. This might be an excellent way to use subsidy money to help a near-dormant co-op expand. Consumer co-ops and credit unions could sponsor day-care centers, renovate rundown houses, give scholarships, sponsor athletic events, or initiate any number of other community projects.

## What Might a Strong Co-op Movement Do?

For people who must keep hoping, there is always the danger of thinking of the present co-op efforts in ways similar to W. O. Brown's description of the thinking of southern liberals in 1933, regarding race relations: "Every skirmish won appears to us a major victory. We are always in danger of becoming silly romanticists, mistaking gestures for action, our programs for achievements, our dreams for realities. . . . We believe because faith and hope compel, not because of the facts. . . ."

The facts of the rural South, and especially the Black, rural southerner, reveal a desperate poverty. The facts of the cooperatives owned by poor people reflect this desperation, with several exceptions, in struggling, underfinanced efforts.

Realistic hopes for rural co-ops are linked inescapably with the hope for reconstruction of the rural South. Co-ops, at present, are holding actions or "demonstration" programs. They are making it possible for a few people to stay in the rural South who otherwise would have no alternative but to starve or migrate. And, to a limited degree, they are proof to the 70 percent of Americans living in 2 percent of the land area of the United States that people can also live out in the country.

There are several misconceptions that existing cooperatives might help dispel about the rural United States. They can show that rural life is not necessarily dawn-to-dusk, backbreaking farm life, but can involve small industries, new rural communities, mechanized farming. William Crook says it well in a recent article ("Needed: A New Homestead Act") in the *Saturday Review*:

Most of history's recorded failures at rural relocation of population have one thing in common: They have consistently confused rural with agricultural, decentralization of population with country life, and nonurban employment with farming.

Co-ops of poor people require subsidy in order to continue and to expand to include the very poor. As businesses, co-ops can go a considerable way toward meeting many of their own needs out of their profits. In time, some co-ops might even prove to be self-sufficient. But if co-ops are to serve as community-owned tools through which flow power and influence, subsidy is needed. The subsidy might come in the form of long-term low-interest loans similar to the 2 percent money the Rural Electric Cooperatives receive from the federal government, or in direct payments such as the $6 billion a year private industry receives from Washington. (Agricultural subsidies alone last year amounted to $4 billion.) Subsidized cooperatives need to be large and as inclusive as possible in their membership. They would be democratically controlled organizations chartered to undertake a variety of business operations while charged with community responsibility —something subsidized private enterprise avoids religiously unless given cost-plus contracts (Job Corps camps) or 12 to 14 percent profit guarantees (slum renewal).

Such co-ops, large and decently financed, could compete in the very areas where much of the federal action is—federal contracts and subsidy. Large and controlling cooperatives could compete with Senator Eastland for his $157,000 subsidy for not growing cotton last year. They could run their own adult education and Head Start programs, be paid in the off-season to beautify highways and small towns like "Operation Green Thumb" in Arkansas two years ago. Co-ops could run Job Corps camps surely as proficiently as Litton Industries. Co-op members could receive payment for sharing their homes during the summer with city slum children. Co-op industries and processing plants could be given preference on certain types of government contracts. Tax incentives could be offered to low-income co-op industries. And, if and when reform programs like the guaranteed annual income become realities, cooperatives could help protect the consumer rights of their members from what will likely be increased exploitative efforts. If some type of land redistribution program should come into effect, co-op organizations could insure against the repeat of another Homestead fiasco by offering technical assistance, jobs, and credit, and by securing first option rights on their members' land so that if a member were forced to sell the land, it would not slip away from the community.

The results of a good co-op movement could mean a degree of control over their own lives for people who have no control at present. . . .

# 19 ]] Magnets of Profit: A Program for

## Categorical Corrective Incentives

*Theodore L. Cross*

## Injections of Leverage

### REDUCING THE RISK OF "SOFT" COMMERCIAL LOANS

"Adam Smith," the sage of Wall Street, tells us how to recognize a money crisis: first mortgages are either unavaliable or command interest rates of 12 percent, offerings of real estate move like molasses, business values crumble, risk capital evaporates, and finally grass grows in the streets. If these conditions described the national economy during the crisis of 1933, they describe as well conditions in the credit economy of Watts and Bedford–Stuyvesant in the late 1960s. The fundamental malignancy in Negro business has been its chronic failure to attract, hold, and use institutional credit. This has occurred because the risks of nonrepayment of slum-area business loans and the extra cost of servicing and collateralizing (and frequently salvaging) them are so massive that the banker faces the same dilemma as the businessman who would embark on programs for hiring or manufacturing in the ghetto. The ghetto economy has amassed such a pernicious array of risks, punishing any effort to introduce credit, that no interest rate is high enough to permit the banker to lend on a basis which is fair both to the ghetto borrower and to the owners of the bank. No liberalization of the banking laws to permit high-risk slum-area business loans can, in itself, alter this dilemma.[1]

A few innovative banks, such as the First Pennsylvania Banking and Trust Company in Philadelphia, have made important and creative efforts to move commercial business credit into the ghetto. But since Negroes rarely come into the branches of the First Pennsylvania Bank, the bank has found that the most effective method of implementing its Negro business-lending program is to work through a loan-clearing house which is located in the ghetto. In Philadelphia, this clearing house consists of a nonprofit association organized by a group of Negro businessmen who actively recruit potential businessmen who need credit. The local group examines these loans from the standpoint of feasibility and either recommends them to the bank or rejects them. The primary function of the

From Theodore L. Cross, in *Black Capitalism* (New York: Atheneum, 1969), pp. 159–202. Reprinted by permission.

bank is to supply credit, acting on the recommendation of people on the scene who understand the ghetto's special credit needs and risks.

This is a most effective program for forcing commercial credit into the ghetto. The program takes maximum advantage of the bank's economic power and, at the same time, negates the great disability which all banks share—an inherent reluctance of the loan officer to make a potentially soft loan. The bank assumes the credit risk, supplies the funds, and benefits in terms of greater citywide business with the Negro community. But, unfortunately, one bank cannot reverse the direction of a massive ghetto economy that banished all commercial credit many decades ago.

Negro businessmen need bank credit for all the usual purposes—business start-up expenses, equipment purchases, and seasonal inventory requirements. Often, too, the Negro business needs credit for a special purpose which no downtown banker has ever heard of.

Bankers in the main economy favor so-called special-purpose loans—loans for a new plant construction, acquisition of machinery, or expansion of markets. These are the loans that enrich and build the national economy and are therefore frequently exempted from voluntary credit restraints. However, loans to refund or pay off another loan do not create a net addition to the economy, and are looked on with less banking favor when credit is tight. In the ghetto economy, there is a special and legitimate need for refunding loans, since slum businesses are often started up with short-term and high-cost credit. In the ghetto business firm, the interest rate, as we have seen, may be 10 percent a week rather than 10 percent a year. Therefore, refunding or "clean-up" loans are especially enriching to the slum economy. The credits should not be viewed with the same skepticism that they receive in banks downtown.[2]

The importance of the refunding loan to the ghetto economy was illustrated a few years ago when most of the drugstores in Harlem were close to bankruptcy. A large proportion of drugs purchased in the ghettos of Harlem and the South Bronx are paid for under New York City's Medicaid or welfare program. At the time, the city was several months behind in its paperwork and disbursement, so the druggists were stuck with stale customer accounts four or five months old. They carried these accounts receivable by borrowing at exorbitant rates from local hip-pocket lenders. Through the brilliant work of McKinsey & Company, Arthur Andersen & Co., and James Talcott, Inc., a refunding-loan program was arranged, under which the loan sharks were paid off and reasonably priced commercial finance credit was substituted. This incident illustrates that often Negro businessmen need commercial credit, not simply to start a new business, but to save a perfectly sound existing business which is being strangled by a special and unusual credit need.

Another special credit need of the Black economy is for loans to finance the transfer ghetto business from white to Black control. This type of loan also does not add to the "net worth" of the Black slum economy. However, it satisfies a vital and urgent desire of the Black man to control the marketplace and commerce where he lives. This type of bank credit is a necessary part of the Black community's objective of working toward "decolonializing" the ownership of real estate and businesses in the slums. This program runs contrary to past—and, in my view, mistaken—policies of the federal Small Business Administration, whose rulings actually discouraged ghetto business loans to either repay pressing creditors or to buy an existing business in the ghetto. Bankers who normally discourage loans for the purchase of a business, or refunding credits, should take a more constructive view of these loans when they are sought by a Black borrower.

Who are the potential lenders in a position to supply commercial business credit in the slum economy? Which institutions, for sound business reasons, do not lend in ghetto areas? The 14,000 commercial banks are the backbone of America's lending system. But since they operate under stiff regulatory restraints, they make direct business loans only to established businesses having "bankable" credit. Long-term mortgage loans come mainly from the savings banks and life insurance companies, who, also, are highly regulated and restricted as to permissible loan risks. Personal-loan companies have found it difficult to lend in slum areas, in which legal limits on interest rates do not cover the unusual risks and expenses in making and servicing these loans. In some cases, these loan companies have shown remarkable mastery of the skills of making high-risk loans, but more often the economic anarchy of the ghetto credit economy has bested them.

Commercial finance companies are a most important group of business lenders. Respected institutions, particularly in New York City and Chicago, specialize in high-risk nonbankable business loans. These lenders measure business credit risk in terms of interest rates of 10 percent and higher. They are considered expert in evaluating the ability of marginal or undercapitalized business to repay a loan. "Nimble" high-risk secondary lenders have played a vital role in the growth of small and untested businesses. Unlike the bank loan officer, who may be tied to more conservative lending practices, the secondary lender or finance-company officer often possesses great competence in appraising the promise of a business which will be operating in a cultural and economic environment completely foreign to his own experience. He often has special experience in loan "work-outs"— salvaging a loan and a business that is in trouble—a common problem with slum-area business credits.

In recent years, many banks have developed new expertise with the high-risk or "controlled-risk" loans. Banks such as First National City Bank in New York City and the First National Bank of Boston have moved into areas of risk financing which formerly belonged to the secondary lenders and commercial finance companies. Special departments in these banks have developed great agility in taking unusual banking risks with appropriate compensation in the form of higher interest rates and valuable training privileges for junior credit officers. These banks are ideally qualified to establish additional programs of commercial lending to businesses in the disadvantaged areas of their cities.

I suggest that an automatic compensating credit incentive, predetermined yet unregulated, is necessary to move vital business credit into the Black markets. No incentive can give the ghetto lender the high degree of income certainty that his directors and his examiners normally expect of prime commercial borrowers. The incentive cannot insure the lender against riot, fire, or a business failure resulting in nonrepayment of the loan. However, a credit incentive is capable of overcoming much of the ghetto risk-aversion. This incentive, operating together with the program I suggested earlier for self-executive federal repayment guarantees of ghetto loans, eliminates all of the legitimate arguments against lending in the slum economy.

I suggest that any federal or state regulated lender, such as a bank, insurance company, or loan company, should be entitled to a special annual addition to its allowable bad-debt reserve (over and above normal bad-debt reserve allowances) of 6 percent of the average balance during the year of loans made to businesses and service establishments doing business in poverty areas designated by the Secretary of Commerce. This credit incentive would allow the corporate lender, who is normally in a 50 percent income tax bracket, an additional 3 percent after tax yield on commercial business loans made in ghetto areas.

This tax credit would be allowed even if the loan was secured by a mortgage, which would be the case for plants and supermarkets located in the ghetto. The bad-debt tax reserve credit would also be allowed any lender who successfully processed an application for a business-loan guarantee with the Small Business Administration. Such perseverance should be rewarded with both the incentive and the repayment guarantee of SBA. However, tax credit would not be available for residential non-business loans.

This program contemplates an "enforced" federally subsidized export of private business credit to the ghetto. In time, the "free market" interest rates of the ghetto credit merchants, who presently lend to ghetto shopkeepers at rates ranging from 50 to 250 percent annually, would be replaced by those "near to prime" rates of 7 to 10 percent that white businessmen pay downtown. Hopefully, the country would finally achieve a reciprocating flow of credit from all parts of our cities so that the distinctions between the ghetto credit market and the mainstream loan markets would become blurred.

NEW LIQUIDITY FOR GHETTO-ORIGIN INSTALLMENT PAPER

During the bleakest period of the great depression, Walter Bimson, one of the nation's most creative bankers, sent a message to his staff at Phoenix's Valley National Bank:

Make loans! This is the way to recovery, and I want this period of automatic loan refusal to end and end now. Make loans! The biggest service we can perform today is to put money into people's hands. Especially, let us go into mass-production on small loans. Plain people at this very moment need to borrow for all kinds of useful buying purposes. So great is their need for credit that some of them are paying heavy interest to loan sharks, and this is the bank's fault. This bank's credit capacity isn't what it will be, but we have some capacity, and I want it used. Use it to get buying under way, to get building under way, to get business and farm production under way.

The relevance of this plea to building installment loan credit in the ghetto economy is clear. But how do we get normal retail credit moving in the slum? In an area in which income certainty does not exist, collateral is weak, and few people can sign a bankable unsecured note for $500, how do we rout the loan sharks and legally marginal lenders who destroy the possibility of building a reasonable system of installment credit?

Since the turn of the century, social workers have urged eliminating profit on consumer credit in the ghetto. They convinced the legislatures that criminal sanctions against usurious loans were the only method of rooting out the merchant credit gouger and loan shark. The nation's experience with legal prohibition of liquor should convince us that criminal penalties for violation of credit laws are almost always futile and naive. These laws put loan sharks in jail, but do not remove the ghetto's need for credit, or add to the meager supply of loanable money. Enforced legal ceilings on interest rates do not reduce the buyer's determination for goods; he merely turns to those who exact an even higher price for credit. Recent laws which restrict the negotiability and liquidity of installment paper taken in unconscionable installment purchase transactions have the same effect of excluding normal credit in the slums. Institutions which lend at low rates, and which are unable to distinguish an unconscionable or fraudulent sale of merchandise which is sold on credit shun the purchase of all installment paper originating in the ghetto. The loan shark accepts the paper and exacts his "toll."

Plainly, the objective is not to destroy the vestiges of low-cost bank credit that remain in the ghetto, but rather to build into the slum normal patterns of retail credit. A sound approach to this problem is to create new incentives or profit opportunities for lenders which will result in the export of low-cost credit from the normal economy into the ghetto. This can be achieved by compensating regulated commercial banks and finance companies for the extra credit risk they take in purchasing (discounting) installment loans which originate in poverty areas. If the legitimate lender's compensating incentive is sufficient, ghetto installment loans will become attractive to lenders, or at least competitive with the safe loans available elsewhere.

I suggest that an institution which purchases an installment loan contract originating in an eligible poverty area should be entitled to an additional income tax deduction (over and above its normal bad-debt reserve deduction) on an annual basis equal to 6 percent of the face amount of the purchased loan. This program would return to the lender a 3 percent additional after-tax yield on installment loans originating in ghetto areas. The auditor of the lending institution would be required to certify that to his best knowledge:

1. The loan was made directly to a resident of an eligible poverty area and was secured by a first lien on new or used appliances, automobiles, or other hard goods; or

2. The loan was purchased from an automobile or hard-goods dealer in an eligible poverty area and was so certified by the dealer.

The tax deduction would be claimed by the lending institution holding the paper at the end of his tax year. Since the special tax benefit would be negotiable and "ride along" as an endorsement on the installment paper, the tax credit would give extra value and buoyancy to retail commercial paper in downtown credit markets.

A criticism of this form of incentive is that the gouging appliance dealer in a ghetto area not only is perfectly free to overcharge the customer, but also is privileged to "lay off" the loan on a downtown bank anxiously bidding for the commercial paper because it carries the tax incentive. I suggest, however, that as a ghetto credit market develops and a supply of bank installment credit becomes available, the new credit will drive out the credit merchant, who will gradually lose his monopoly over ghetto loans. Since the credit gouger is a financial intermediary whose cost of capital is high, it will become impossible for him to compete at free-market bank rates. If it becomes feasible for downtown banks to lend in ghetto markets at, or near, downtown interest rates, new bank branches will open in the ghetto and existing branches will become aggressive lenders.

### STIMULATING DEPOSITS IN SLUM-AREA BANKS

The specific credit incentives I have just proposed are designed to enforce exports of outside banking credit to the ghetto market. Obviously, these incentives do not work toward immediately creating new banking offices or deposits within the slum economy. Rather, they permit the credit-starved slums to tap the world's largest reservoir of private capital: the $300 billion of deposits held in 14,000 commercial banks in America.

Yet, we have also seen that white-controlled banks are not always the most effective vehicle to grapple with the problems of developing business loans in the slums. The ghetto's hostility to downtown banks, its opposition to the export of credit, the often excessive "ghetto credit risk-aversion" of the Main Street banker, and his inability or unwillingness to enforce collection of a loan from a ghetto borrower place limitations on our program for moving credit into the ghetto from the "outside" economy.

The internal banks of the ghetto, the so-called interracial or Black-controlled institutions, have no such problems. The Black banks recognize higher ghetto credit risks; they charge a higher interest rate on loans than prevails in the downtown economy without running afoul of charges of discrimination; they press regularly for collection of their loans. Moreover, the ghetto bank has greater skills, agility, and understanding in dealing with the special business and credit problems of the slum economy.

Although for Blacks the ghetto banks have lending advantages over white-controlled banks, their power to change the credit economy of the slum is insignificant. To strengthen the lending capabilities of the slum-area banks, I propose an annual income tax credit for any corporation or person, including a correspondent bank, which maintains a deposit in any bank whose principal office is located in an eligible poverty area.[3]

The income tax credit would operate as follows.

1. *For demand deposits* (non–interest-bearing[4]). An annual tax credit to the depositor equal to 2 percent of the average daily balance maintained, as certified in writing at the end of the depositor's tax year by the cashier of the ghetto bank.

2. *For time deposits*. An annual income tax credit to the depositing individual, corporation, or correspondent bank equal to 25 percent of the established interest rate on the time deposit. The tax credit would be limited to time deposits maintained for one year or more. The time deposit is more enriching to the ghetto economy than is the demand deposit, since it more closely approximates permanent capital. The relative permanence of this type of deposit gives the ghetto bank greater flexibility in making community loans.

3. *Negotiable certificates of deposit or investments in ghetto bank debentures*. Holders of these instruments would be entitled to a year-end tax credit equal to 25 percent of the established interest rate on the certificate of deposit or debenture.

Since many corporate treasurers would not feel comfortable with large deposit balances in the undercapitalized ghetto banks even if aided by the deposit incentive program, I suggest that the present Federal Deposit Insurance coverage limit of $15,000 be increased to $50,000 for demand deposits and time deposits maintained in banks doing business solely in the poverty areas.

The scope of Federal Deposit Insurance coverage could be expanded to include debentures issued by ghetto-area banks. The "capital debenture" route is becoming an increasingly more attractive method of raising bank capital. Allowing ghetto-bank debenture issues to carry, within limits, a Federal Deposit Insurance Corporation guarantee should be a most effective method of coaxing new funds into slum-area banks. The limited debenture guarantee would also reduce the cost of capital and give these banks the edge they need for lending in the profitless slum economy.

The program of tax incentives for deposits in ghetto banks, combined with increased Federal Deposit Insurance coverage, should persuade large metropolitan banks to establish healthy correspondent relations with ghetto banks. These correspondent bank balances deposits would place new funds in the hands of ghetto bankers who have a special expertise in handling the high-risk ghetto loan. A bank such as the First National in Boston cannot put out installment loan money in the Roxbury ghetto at, say, a 1 percent premium over what it charges downtown. However, First National is in a position to maintain a $1 million balance with the interracial Unity National Bank in Roxbury; Unity Bank, in turn, could then be in a position to spread this money around the Roxbury ghetto in installment loans at a 0.1-percent interest premium over the downtown rate.

The program for strengthening ghetto banks should also lure demand and time deposits from the treasurers of the great national corporations. Portfolio managers of life-insurance companies and other institutions[5] will improve their investment performance by acquiring low-risk tax-sheltered debentures issued by ghetto banks. Because of the new tax incentives available to depositors and investors, it is likely that credit markets will establish a beneficially low interest rate on debentures or certificates of deposit payable by ghetto banks.

GHETTO DEVELOPMENT BANK: PUBLIC AND PRIVATE

Our program has focused first on incentive credits for the direct development of commercial and business loans—a necessary element in building working patterns of Black business and commerce. The next aspect of the credit program, the tax-incentive endorsement which rides on the back of ghetto-origin installment paper, is geared to encourage consumer credit in ghetto markets. It would reduce interest charges and ease repayment terms on the purchase of automobiles, appliances, and other hard goods. The next credit incentive is aimed at encouraging deposits in the interracial banks. This feature is designed to develop new and independent sources of credit within the slum, and at the same time to harness the special lending advantages of Black banks.

The first three incentive programs should quickly aid and directly initiate our strategy of normalizing credit in the ghetto. However, there are vast urban core areas in America, housing hundreds of thousands of Black people, where not one functioning commercial bank is evident. The ghetto is totally underbanked. Credit failure is so massive that an entirely new ghetto banking system is required.

Two basic approaches to this problem are available. One strategy calls for a completely new system of federal-, state-, or community-sponsored development banks. The other suggests an extension and expansion of the existing commercial banking system, with concurrent adoption of adequate lending incentives for the ghetto area.

Influenced by the success of the World Bank abroad, there is bipartisan support in Congress for creating a new bank, or a system of banks, to lend in the ghetto. A leading advocate of this approach is Senator Javits of New York. In October 1967, the senator introduced a comprehensive program for setting up a Domestic Development Bank and a separate Economic Opportunity Corporation to provide technical assistance to Black businesses, and to develop ghetto entrepreneurship.

Under the senator's plan, the Domestic Development Bank would be established, by an act of Congress, as a profit-making corporation for financing business and commercial projects (plants, equipment, and working capital) in or near poverty areas where capital is not available on reasonable terms. Loans would be made to companies of all sizes for job-producing enterprises. For smaller businesses, the Domestic Development Bank would be authorized to guarantee loans made by local banks.

A more recent proposal suggests a new national system of community-development banks, patterned after the National Land Bank Associations set up to provide farm credit during the depression years. These banks would be established as part of the Community Self-Determination Bill,[6] introduced in the Senate in July 1968. The bill contemplates setting up a series of Community Development Corporations owned by the residents of poverty neighborhoods. The CDC's would be essentially ghetto business conglomerates, with broad powers to control the economic development of their neighborhood. They would own the local community-development banks. These banks would be funded by capital contributed by the parent CDC, and by the sale of income bonds backed by a Federal Reserve escrow fund. A National Community Development Bank would also be established to assist the CDC program.

Proposals for a new federal development bank and, as an alternative, for a new system of community-controlled development banks, repeat some errors of antipoverty programs of the past. It seems likely that a new federal development bank, independent of Congress and the executive branch, would yet develop many of the disincentives such as delays, red tape, and rigidity that have infected ambitious ghetto programs entrusted, in the past, directly to the Small Business Administration and the Federal Housing Administration. Greater disadvantages, in my view, are the delays inherent in recruiting and staffing, financing and launching a completely new nationwide system of banks. The community-development banks are not likely to attract the more effective wealth-builders to their loan staffs. Most important, the system of CDC banks does not take any advantage whatsoever of the lending skills of 100,000 or more trained American banking executives.

Supported by at least twenty senators, liberal as well as conservative, this program for establishing a new system of community-development banks stands an excellent chance of enactment during the ninety-first Congress, as part of the Community Self-Determination Bill. The thrust of the new banking legislation—a massive injection into the ghetto community itself—is sound. Despite its disadvantages, the program deserves total support from American business and banking.

The alternative, developing a system of private development banks that would undertake high-risk loans and investments in the ghettos, is philosophically opposed to legislation calling for a new system of federal or community-sponsored banks. Private development banks would be set up as subsidiaries of existing banks, or as joint ventures undertaken by a consortium of banks and insurance companies, all of which would have a common interest in the regeneration of a particular city or area. The private development bank could be established as a business corporation for profit, or as a nonprofit community corporation. It would be largely funded from local banks, insurance companies, and other business corporations. The private development bank would commit for a broad range of equity loans, second mortgages, and front-end capital investments in the ghetto, which are presently illegal investments for life-insurance companies and banks.

The prototype of a bank-originated private development bank is the Citizens and Southern Community Development Corporation, formed by Georgia's one-billion-dollar Citizens and Southern National Bank. Capitalized in May 1968, by its parent bank at $1 million, the new unit makes second-mortgage loans and provides equity capital for new small businesses in the slums of Savannah. It will also lend second-mortgage and equity money to enable slum dwellers to buy their own homes. The bank anticipates that, on most home loans, first- and second-mortgage payments will be no higher than the rents now being paid. This program is a brilliant innovation, uniquely calculated to build ownership and equities in the ghetto.[7]

A different approach has been taken by the nonprofit Interracial Council for Business Opportunity in New York City. An ICBO Fund had been organized which plans to raise about $300,000 in capital funds. Unlike the Citizens and Southern National Bank plan, the ICBO Fund does not lend directly to Black businesses. The fund guarantees repayment of ghetto business loans made by private commercial banks that have agreed to participate in the program.[8] Through the use of the guarantee technique, it is obvious that greater lending leverage is obtained. The fund estimates that $300,000 in capital will support $1 million in loan guarantees to Negroes. The ICBO Loan Guarantee Fund hopes to commit ghetto guarantees with a minimum of red tape—possibly even by telephone request. The program puts private banks and businesses directly in the role of recruiting and funding loans to promising Black businessmen. Since the guarantee makes the loan bankable, the credit can be committed at the lower rates prevailing outside the ghetto. The ICBO program removes two fundamental weaknesses of the direct loan functions and loan-guarantee program of federal agencies: (1) administrative delays in approving loan applications; and (2) the inability of government agencies to recruit and recognize promising Negro borrowers.

The concept of a nationwide system of private ghetto development lending institutions with broad powers to make "free-wheeling" risk loans and equity commitments carries extraordinary potential. New sponsorship of these projects should be encouraged through a specially tailored and controlled system of incentives.

I suggest that sponsors of private ghetto development banks be permitted to deduct from taxable income, spread ratably (amortized) over a three-year period the amount of any investment in the capital stock of any corporation chartered to take equity positions; make business, mortgage, or personal loans; or acquire real estate in the designated poverty areas. For maximum efficiency, I would suggest that the incentive apply only when 40 percent or more of the capital stock, or debenture capital, of a new development bank is held by insurance companies, commercial and savings banks, and other institutional lenders regulated by law.

The subsidiary private banking development corporation would also be entitled to the benefits of the categorical credit incentives I suggested earlier to encourage ghetto installment credit, commercial and business loans, and deposits in slum-area banks.

Under present income tax laws, the type of private ghetto lending subsidiary formed in Georgia by Citizens and Southern National Bank is not encouraged. The initial commitment of funds is a nondeductible business investment, not a deductible charitable contribution. The parent bank obtains no tax deduction except as ghetto loans are written off as worthless, or unless the whole ghetto development subsidiary fails and is written off as worthless stock in the parent bank's income tax return. The tax premium therefore attaches to failure. There is no reward for initiating a successful slum business loan, except satisfaction from full repayment of the loan with interest (taxable at the usual 50 percent rate). The plan I suggest of granting an income tax benefit to banks that organize ghetto development banks applies the tax incentive to a very early and difficult stage of the process we wish to encourage—actually forming and putting hard money into a ghetto development organization.

Unlike proposals for chartering a new federal or a community-sponsored system of ghetto development banks, the plan for private development banks makes immediate and effective use of the lending skills of both the white-controlled and the Black banks. Staffing is not a problem, and the program can go into effect immediately. This program creates an immediate need on the part of the nation's banks and insurance companies to fund new high-risk subsidiaries uniquely qualified to build credit enrichment into the ghetto.

## Front-end Incentives

### COAXING SAVINGS IN THE GHETTO

The banker's ethic to the contrary, few people in the normal economy grow rich or even affluent through the simple process of faithfully and periodically depositing money in a savings account. Personal affluence is more likely to come from converting a stake of money or savings into a business or investment opportunity. A sum of savings enters the process of building wealth only when, by a bold act of the owner, the thrift fund is changed into risk capital or front-end money. The companion wealth-producing factor of leverage—typically a line of credit from a bank—operates only in conjunction with this risk capital. It is rarely possible to start up a new business on borrowed money unless someone supplies some element of margin money, equity, or front-end money. A tradition-bound economy, such as we find in the American ghetto, cannot grow and innovate without developing these discretionary risk funds.

If the formation of risk capital has been such a vital part of the process of growing affluent in the normal economy, then it is necessary to work on the available pockets of potential savings in the ghetto, so that they may find their way into a thrift institution or mutual-fund shares. Emerging opportunities for Blacks in commerce and business tend to remove the argument, popular in the ghetto, that there is "no use in savings." But these entrepreneurial and investment opportunities must be reinforced so that the motivation for the savings will be for "investment" as well as for "security." The Black man's need to have money in the bank for a rainy day is no greater than his need to have it so that he can seize an entrepreneurial opportunity. I develop later a specific set of incentives which are designed to make certain adjustments in ghetto economics so as to encourage Negro entrepreneurship. These incentives should boost motivation to save money in order to enter commerce; yet the importance of the very process of savings in reversing the direction of a declining or undeveloped economy commands a specific savings incentive program.[9]

It would appear that an inducement could be given directly to the ghetto resident and businessman to encourage him to save. The normal approach might be a federally subsidized bonus to the ghetto saver in the form of an increment of 1 percent or more to the normal 5.5 percent interest paid by the savings institution. But there are serious obstacles in administering a savings incentive which is applied directly to the depositor. Savings from the outside economy will too readily find means of acquiring the benefits of the savings credit by channeling funds through a ghetto resident or businessman. Moreover, I suggest that if the ghetto purchaser or businessman is willing to disregard the interest charge on his installment purchases from the ghetto credit merchant (which frequently varies from 20 percent to 100 percent per annum), no reasonable additional credit to the interest column in a savings passbook is likely to produce savings in the ghetto in preference to spending discretionary funds.

For this reason, and for reasons of more efficient administration, the incentive is more effectively applied to the ghetto savings institution than to the saver.

To persuade the resident of the ghetto to open and maintain a conventional savings account requires some marketing skill and maybe a little sorcery. During the years after the 1933 bank holiday, when nobody trusted a savings bank, American banks showed great resourcefulness in coaxing savings from a poor economy. Banks advertised for savings; they merchandised savings by offering casseroles, clocks, and set of dishes. The potential for building personal capital in an underdeveloped economy has been demonstrated in the Soviet Union, where one of world's largest pools of personal savings has been created in 70,000 government-owned savings banks. The Soviet banks aggressively advertise and merchandise savings— virtually the only exception to the communist prohibition against advertising. In the United Kingdom, banks traditionally have merchandised savings by giving the depositor the option of applying one-half of his interest dividend to the purchase of national lottery tickets. Banks cannot sell lottery tickets in the United States, but they do have access to trading stamps, television advertising, and a host of merchandising techniques which have never been used to encourage personal savings in ghetto areas.

At the present time, ghetto banking economics are so distorted that the ghetto institutions actually discourage savings accounts. Black banks have low-profit margins because they are plagued with high bookkeeping and administrative costs incurred in servicing a large number of tiny, active savings accounts. Unlike other banks, those in the ghetto are not favored with a high percentage of the more profitable demand deposits or checking accounts, or with substantial and rewarding time deposits.

Therefore, I suggest that an incentive should be applied which compensates the ghetto savings institution for (1) the extra administrative costs of maintaining savings accounts in slum areas and (2) the extra marketing and promotional costs that are necessary to lure the money of ghetto savers away from the numbers operator and into a passbook account where, ultimately, it may be converted into risk capital or even into the purchase of mutual-fund shares.

The incentive to ghetto-area savings institutions would operate in the following way:

Every ghetto bank (savings bank, savings-and-loan association, or commercial bank with its main office and branch offices located exclusively in the designated poverty areas) would be entitled to a year-end payment from the federal government.[10] The federal credit would be 1.5 percent of the savings accounts held by individuals who, at the time the account was opened, were residents of a designated poverty area. The credit would be smaller, 0.5 percent, for year-end savings balances which admittedly originate from non–poverty-area depositors or from sources which the ghetto bank is unable to identify.

This incentive gives the ghetto institution a fund for promoting ghetto savings. It also compensates the bank so that it will no longer tend to discourage the small, active savings accounts which are so costly for the banks to maintain. The incentive will encourage the formation of new branch banks in the ghetto areas. It will also have the effect of causing the slum-area banks to persuade a few middle-class or affluent residents of the ghetto to transfer their savings accounts from downtown banking offices to slum-area or independent interracial banks. Giving the ghetto bank a bonus for funds deposited from *outside* the ghetto does not build thrift *within* the ghetto, yet it strengthens the capital structure of the interracial ghetto banks. The effect is a desirable infusion of capital into the slum banking community, where it will be available for commercial and mortgage loans.

The direct federal subsidy to ghetto banks for time deposits is in addition to the tax credit proposed earlier, which is applied directly to any person maintaining balances in ghetto institutions.

GHETTO-ORIGIN STOCK PLACEMENTS

During such time as the ghetto economy remains poor and has very limited capability of generating savings and risk capital internally, the need to attract risk funds from outside the ghetto is urgent. Just as uncertain patterns of ghetto income and risks to invested capital block bank and other credit from moving into the slum from downtown institutions, so the nation's underwriting industry does not bring to the market new stock issues for financing new ghetto plants or real estate improvements. Until 1969, when a Wall Street brokerage house underwrote shares for a stock offering of Parks Sausages, Inc., a new "hot issue" in the shares of a Negro firm was unknown on Wall Street—or, for that matter, on 125th Street in Harlem.

The occasional public issue, or private placement of shares, in an untested Negro enterprise is not bought with any real expectation of profit. The underwriting is more often an act of philanthropy. A stock issue in Harlem's Freedom National Bank was marketed with difficulty in 1964, although Jackie Robinson, of Brooklyn Dodgers fame, was chairman of the board.[11] Mutual Real Estate Investment Trust (M-REIT), a publicly owned real estate trust formed to purchase white apartment buildings and open them up to all races, took two years to market its first share offering of $4 million. In his efforts to prove that integrated housing can be profitable, the sponsor, Morris Milgram, offered a second stock issue of $10 million in 1968. *Business Week* reported that only one-tenth of the issue had been sold one month after the offering date, but that the assassination of Martin Luther King created new interest in this offering.[12]

These laborious efforts to market securities for enriching the ghetto stand in sharp contrast to the current frenzy of new issues in the main economy. Hardly a week goes by that Wall Street markets do not make millionaires of men who have new ideas for a restaurant franchise or for an electronic product. Since new security issues are such an important catalyst of wealth in the normal economy, I suggest that incentives should be developed to start building normal patterns of new security issues for projects in the Negro market.

Our income tax laws now permit any investor in a qualified small business corporation to deduct in full against income any loss on the sale of stock in the corporation. This provision allows full tax benefits from the loss, even if the securities are sold "long-term." This incentive was enacted in 1958 in line with congressional policy to encourage risk-capital investment in small business ventures.

I suggest that these special income tax privileges for small business corporations should be expanded for stock or debenture investment in all corporations formed to develop new plants, office buildings, apartment houses, retail outlets, or other new facilities in the certified poverty areas. Losses in these security investments should be allowed in full against the investor's ordinary income, plus an extra deduction against ordinary income of 10 percent of the loss. Profits on resale of ghetto-origin stock investments should be taxed in the usual way but reduced by a special poverty-area tax credit of 7.5 percent of the capital gain.

As a further inducement encouraging ghetto ownership of business and real estate equities, I propose that the poverty-area tax-loss deduction or credit on taxable profits be increased by 30 percent in cases in which, after the financing is completed, 50 percent or more of the equity securities of the issuing corporation are owned by ghetto residents or firms.

These specific incentives for new security issues should lure risk capital out of the normal economy and force it into the subsidiary ghetto economy. Investors in the normal economy will be encouraged to seek out creative new ways of combining their risk capital with SBA- and FHA-guaranteed credits to build examples of entrepreneurship in the urban slums.

## THE CORE-AREA SERVICE CLUSTER

Leverage, or the compounding of value, develops most efficiently in concentrated form. Real estate men and city planners know that a concentrated $5 million real estate investment in a blighted area will produce greater aggregate value or wealth than the equivalent money dispersed over the entire area. A massive concentration of investment in a ghetto neighborhood can basically reverse the direction of a decaying slum. Significant investments focused on a limited area produce new values in surrounding real estate. This added value of leverage is lost when programs for economic enrichment of the ghetto are dispersed in various pockets which gradually become overwhelmed by the decaying character of surrounding neighborhoods.

Several decades ago, Metropolitan Life Insurance Company's massive investment in New York's Stuyvesant Town added hundreds of millions of dollars in tax assessments, and transformed much of this Lower East Side ghetto of New York City. Value was added to properties many miles away from the actual point of investment. In 1959, the $175 million Lincoln Center project, built on Manhattan's decaying West Side, set off a rejuvenation of the area from 42nd Street to 79th Street. Billions of dollars of value was added to dilapidated real estate in an area shunned by institutional lenders. The proposed New York State government office building to be located at 125th Street has stimulated speculative interest in Harlem real estate, dampened only slightly by the riots following the assassination of Martin Luther King in the spring of 1968. The most significant rehabilitation of a ghetto area has been undertaken by the Bedford–Stuyvesant Restoration Corporation. This project, originally sponsored by Robert Kennedy, involves restoration of 640 square blocks of the nation's most depressed poverty area. The project ambitiously contemplates renovation of most of the area's deteriorated three- and four-story row housing. Planned are two "superblocks" linked to central green belts, two rehabilitation centers for skill training, a $4 million athletic and cultural center, and a huge office-and-shopping center with perhaps a branch store of Macy's. The plan contemplates some twenty-five new businesses and plants, a network of health centers, a local TV station, and a four-year work–study college. The Bedford–Stuyvesant Restoration project was introduced in the fall of 1960. Progress has been slow. Aside from the support of foundation and government grants, the ultimate success of the project depends on the continuing drive of the businessmen and bankers who have been associated with it. But the future of a project of such magnitude should not rest only on the goodwill and voluntary desires of the businessmen who are "pledging" their time. Large core-area projects offer such potential of leverage for the complete and efficient transformation of a ghetto economy that special assistance and direct inducements should be applied.

I suggest a specific incentive program for new investments in contiguous facilities in an eligible ghetto area of $100 million or more in a city with a population of five million or more (the amount of required investment to be scaled down for smaller cities).

The incentive would apply to an investment in a cluster of facilities which includes three or more of the following:

1. A department store, shopping center, or cooperative market
2. A plant, or business service facility, such as an automobile diagnostic service center
3. Entertainment facilities (theaters,[13] bowling alleys, roller- and ice-skating rinks)
4. Medical centers, hospitals, and extended-care facilities
5. Day-care facilities for children
6. Low-income housing
7. New ghetto-resident-controlled banks and other regulated credit institutions

This tax incentive should be directed to the supplier of the risk capital, as well as the participating lending institutions:

1. The sponsor and owner (or consortium of owners) should be entitled to normal accelerated-depreciation deductions and new facilities tax credits, plus an automatic annual incremental tax credit of 5 percent of equity investment cost without "strings," restrictions, or regulatory approvals. The effect of this incentive is to add a 5 percent tax-free investment return on equity.

2. Participating construction lenders and holders of long-term mortgages should be entitled to a tax exemption of 2 percent of interest income received or accrued. The exemption on interest received would apply, whether or not the construction or long-term loan was insured under any existing federal or state programs for the guarantee of loans.

Corporations such as Alcoa, Gulf Oil, and ITT have expressed interest in building entire new towns and cities in America. The federal government must use its taxing powers to direct these efforts into the ghetto and poverty areas, where the greatest leverage for slum rehabilitation can be achieved.

The program I suggest for core-area clusters is an exception to the principle which excludes investments in leveraged real estate from the benefits of ghetto tax credits. The exception is made because the program for new ghetto service clusters offers such great opportunities for reversing decay in our cities.

# Notes

1. However, expanding the powers of banks to make commitments in the ghetto provides the necessary legal environment in which ghetto credit incentives can operate.

In October 1968, the author testified before the Senate Financial Institutions Subcommittee on proposals to amend federal banking laws in order to channel more bank credit into the Black economy. At that time I recommended to the committee: (1) expanding the investment powers of national banks to permit them to form credit-development subsidiaries to make high-risk commitments in poverty areas; (2) empowering national banks to directly acquire and develop real estate in designated poverty areas; (3) removing the limitations on maturities and repayment terms of slum-area mortgages held by national banks; (4) permission for a national bank to invest up to 2 percent of its capital in shares of so-called interracial banks; (5) increasing Federal Deposit Insurance coverage of deposits in slum-area banks, and expansion of coverage to include debentures and capital debentures issued by these institutions; (6) modification of laws in certain states which forbid the operation of branch banks; (7) removal of Small Business Administration regulations which limit loans for start-up financing for small groceries, beauty parlors, and carry-out food shops in disadvantaged areas, and for financing change of ownership of a ghetto business.

2. At an American Management Association Seminar in June 1968, Thomas F. Murray, Vice President, Mortgages, of The Equitable Life Assurance Society, of the United States, described the most valuable type of "refunding loans" which the Equitable is making on ghetto real estate: "We soon found that the most expeditious way to get going was to invest in mortgages on one to four family residences. These mortgages usually permitted the owner or purchaser to obtain terms which were more favorable than were heretofore available, and often provided financing where none was obtainable before. We found, in many cases, that our mortgage refinanced a first and second, and possibly even a third mortgage whose combined monthly payments were practically impossible to meet for this Negro family that was seeking to establish itself as an owner in a community often characterized by absentee landlords. Very often our funds permitted the owner to rehabilitate his home, or he could use the decrease in monthly payments to modernize or improve his dwelling. We are delighted, accordingly, that our program has helped foster and support resident ownership in ghetto areas—nearly 85 percent of our funds have gone into this phase of our ghetto lending program."

3. Ghetto branches of metropolitan banks are excluded because their principal offices are not in an eligible poverty area. Deposits in ghetto branches of the large metropolitan banks do not stick in the ghetto; they are more likely to flow back downtown seeking safer credit risks in the normal economy.

Under certain circumstances it might be desirable to expand the benefits of the tax credit to deposits made in *nonghetto* banks where the deposit is earmarked for an unusually enriching program. An example would be bank deposits made under an innovative deposit program sponsored by the Bicentennial Improvement Corporation in St. Louis. This group arranges for undercapitalized Blacks to obtain home ownership under conventional non-FHA mortgages. The Improvement Corporation sponsors individual and corporate deposits with ghetto mortgage lenders. The deposit is pledged as additional security for mortgage.

Of course the incentive would apply to any banks which might be established in the impoverished Indian reservations in the South or Southwest, or in any of the great rural poverty areas of Appalachia and northern California.

4. By almost universal law in the United States, banks may not pay interest on demand deposits (usually checking accounts).

5. One of the most aggressive depositors in ghetto banks is the tax-exempt New

York Synod of the Presbyterian Church. Without the impetus of tax incentives, the church deposited $15,000 in Harlem's Freedom National in 1968, and spread $250,000 around in various slum-area banks and savings institutions.

Also in 1968, the Executive Council of the Episcopal Church deposited $675,000 in forty-five ghetto banks. The council's only requirement is that the deposits be federally insured and that the institution be locally owned and managed for the benefit of those who live in the community.

At last count, General Motors held cash and marketable securities of $2.3 billion. No published figures reveal how much of this resides in ghetto banks (probably more than the combined capital and surplus of any one of them), yet the ghetto banks hardly cause a ripple in our banking system.

6. Senate Bill 3876.

7. The program was approved by the Comptroller of the Currency in April 1968. The plan is therefore legal for any national bank. It is doubtful if any state regulatory authority would fault a parallel project undertaken by a state bank provided the financial commitment was reasonable in relationship to the sponsoring bank's capital funds. Under the Citizens and Southern plan, the capital at risk is less than 0.01 percent of the total assets of the bank.

8. The original participating banks in the ICBO program were all in New York City: Bankers Trust Company, The Chase Manhattan Bank, Chemical Bank New York Trust Company, and Harlem's Freedom National Bank. A similar guarantee fund, Puerto Rican Forum, Inc., has been established in New York City to help finance small businesses operated by minority-group members. The fund is sponsored by Manufacturers Hanover Trust Company and San Juan's Banco Popular de Puerto Rico under a Ford Foundation grant. In July 1968, the first loan of $6,000 at 7.5 percent simple interest was made by Manufacturers Hanover to Tony Bonilla of 69 Irving Place, New York City, for refinancing existing obligations of his printing shop. The fund guarantees half the loan on a prorated basis. The bank thus accepts one-half of the risk.

9. A program encouraging the development of savings in the ghetto will be more effective if it is combined with the more urgent program of bringing ghetto incomes above the poverty level and reducing immigration to the slums. The ghettos of America are unable to control either births or immigration, which now aggregate about half a million people a year. The program for generating savings in the ghetto must recognize that significant gains will not occur until the slum has first provided for minimum consumption needs. A federal program which encourages new plants (and jobs) in the South obviously tends to break the economic grip of the ghetto in the North.

10. The federal payment or subsidy to the ghetto bank would be made *outside* the federal income tax system because most ghetto banks show an operating loss. Therefore an income tax credit holds no advantages.

11. The stock prospectus was hardly designed to excite stock traders downtown. It explained that Freedom National had been "planned as a community enterprise that will in every way belong to the people it is to serve. . . . Moreover, it is intended that these people shall be represented in the formation and administration of the policies of this bank to assure its role in helping to eradicate those financing practices that restrict the economic growth of the community and erode the money power of its members."

12. *Business Week*, April 13, 1968, p. 118.

13. The new New York City zoning code already encourages construction of legitimate theaters in new office buildings by granting the builder more liberal legitimate office-space allowances in new buildings which also contain a legitimate theater.

# 20 ]] Community Development Corporations:

# A New Approach to the Poverty Problem

*Harvard Law Review*

## 1. Introduction

Concern over poverty in America has spurred efforts to develop effective new approaches to the problems of economically depressed areas. One approach which has received widespread bipartisan support[1] is embodied in the Community Self-Determination Bill recently introduced in Congress.[2] The stated purpose of the bill is to help the poor to play "a more meaningful and rewarding role in building a better, stronger, and more confident America." [3] It finds that there exists within the United States a "nation within a nation" consisting of millions of Americans living in poverty.[4] Handouts to these Americans, the bill continues, are demeaning, stripping the poor of dignity and breeding resentment toward the total social system.[5] Efforts must be directed toward assisting the poor to "achieve gainful employment and the ownership and control of the resources of their community. . . ." [6] Such ownership would generate profits which could be used to fund needed social services.[7] In addition, organization of the poor would allow them to make "public policy decisions on issues which affect their everyday lives." [8] The role of government in this endeavor should be directed towards supporting and reinforcing local self-help measures while avoiding all undue interference with local policy decisions.[9]

The bill's response to these findings and to the general statement of purpose is to create a National Community Corporation Certification Board (NCCCB), which will have power to grant federal charters and "seed money" in the form of an initial allocation of federal funds[10] to community development corporations (CDC's),

organized by the people of an urban or rural community . . . for the purpose of expanding their economic and educational opportunities; increasing their ownership of productive capital and property; improving their health, safety, and living conditions; enhancing their personal dignity and independence; expanding their opportunities for meaningful decisionmaking and self-determination; and generally securing the economic development, social well-being and stability of their community.[11]

These enumerated CDC purposes, viewed in light of the bill's findings and general statement of purpose, suggest that the CDC as an institution

From 82 *Harvard Law Review* 644 (1969). © 1969 by the Harvard Law Review Association.

is intended to achieve three primary goals. First, as a political institution, it provides a mechanism through which the poor can achieve meaningful participation in the control of significant aspects of their community life. Second, the CDC as a service organization provides needed services to the community while avoiding the handout syndrome surrounding public welfare. Third, as an economic institution, the CDC promotes the economic development of the community through investment in community businesses.[12]

This note will examine the bill's main provisions for forming and operating a CDC,[13] as they relate to the fulfillment of these three primary goals. First we will focus on the incentives for ownership of CDC stock and for participation in its affairs, then examine the proposed procedure for managing CDC business enterprises. Next we will be concerned with the tax measures proposed in the bill to allow the CDC to retain a high proportion of its profits and to encourage outside assistance in local economic development. The last section will discuss the applicability of state corporation law to the CDC. This note will concentrate on structural modifications which may be necessary within the CDC framework if the experiment is to have a fair chance of success. But the very choice of the corporate model of development rests on empirical assumptions, which will be isolated during the discussion.

## 2. The Role of Residents in the CDC

### A. FORMATION OF THE CDC

The bill's formation procedures are designed to ensure that the CDC finally established in a community is acceptable to its residents and that the power of those who ultimately gain control is recognized as legitimate.[14] This goal is presumably to be achieved by requiring majority approval and by convincing all that they had a fair opportunity to compete for a final charter.

For this purpose the bill prescribes an elaborate procedure for the establishment of a CDC. At the outset those seeking to incorporate a CDC file with the NCCCB a letter of intent specifying the precise geographical boundaries of the proposed CDC community.[15] They then prepare and file an application for a charter which includes the letter of intent, the articles of incorporation, and an organization certificate. Upon request, the NCCCB is authorized to help in the compilation of data necessary for the completion of the certificate.[16] The certificate contains economic statistics[17] showing that the community qualifies for participation in the community development program and pledges for stock by five percent of the community residents who are over sixteen.[18] Upon satisfaction of these requirements a conditional charter issues.[19] If the group then can procure enough additional stock pledges to bring its total up to 10 percent of the residents and collect a total of $5,000 from at least 500 residents,[20] a referendum is held to determine whether residents want a CDC to be formed in the described community.[21] If several groups propose different geographical areas, the area described in the first letter of intent filed plus all other proposed areas having some overlap with it is voted upon first.[22] If a majority of the residents voting approve the area, the CDC group with the largest vote becomes eligible for a final charter and for a grant from the NCCCB equal to the amount invested by the shareholders.[23] If a majority does not vote in favor of a CDC, a new referendum is held in the largest geographical area described by the articles of an eligible group, and the process is continued until a majority selects one group's area as the community. The bill prescribes a maximum of 300,000 residents over sixteen years old and a minimum of 5,000 for the CDC community.[24]

This formation procedure creates a bias for communities with larger populations within the statutory limits.[25] While it is possible that individual areas will withhold support until an acceptable community size is presented, the fact that the largest area is voted upon first reduces the likelihood that smaller areas will ever become the subject of a referendum. This seems especially true in light of the NCCCB's responsibility to encourage consolidation of competing groups prior to the referendum.[26] In addition, since all groups which have satisfied the procedural requirements participate in the intial referendum, groups whose articles describe smaller areas are placed in a paradoxical position. On the one hand they must urge that the voters disapprove the establishment of a CDC serving the larger community in which the first vote is taken. On the other hand, they must prepare to campaign actively for election[27] as the area CDC in the event that the majority approves establishment of a CDC for the geographical area being voted on in the referendum.

This bias toward larger communities may seriously impair the capacity of the CDC formation procedure to legitimate the power of the CDC since it reduces the opportunity for small grass roots movements to mobilize the support necessary to defeat those already possessing influence and power in the community. Yet it would seem that if those segments among the poor who feel themselves unrepresented by presently visible leadership in the community are to accept the CDC and recognize its leaders as legitimate, they must believe that they had a fair opportunity to participate in the process eventually resulting in the selection of a CDC group to represent the community.

One possible solution to the problem would be to reverse the bias so that the first referendum could be held in the smallest community described in the articles of a CDC group. In a smaller community it would be significantly easier for relatively unknown groups to reach all residents with information concerning the advantages of their organization. Moreover, the smaller a particular CDC community, the greater is the likelihood that the activities of the CDC will be conducted in accordance with the desires of that particular community. Further, even though a larger

CDC would require a larger staff, a greater number of small CDC's would probably increase the number of poor people holding responsible positions within the CDC organization. Nevertheless, reduction in the size of the community involves the sacrifice of benefits of scale highly conducive to achievement of community economic development. A larger CDC would be better able than a small CDC to afford the substantial cash outlays involved in industrial projects. Moreover, it could coordinate its business efforts in a consistent scheme for development of the whole economically depressed area.

Perhaps a better solution would be to provide campaign funds and resources to all groups who have qualified to participate in the referendum.[28] Thus, at the outset all would have the means to inform the community of the advantages of their organization. Furthermore, a campaign battle with its continual flow of information may have the additional advantage of generating enthusiasm among the residents and thereby increasing the level of stock ownership in the CDC which eventually is chartered.[29] To outside observers such a battle might seem a luxury which, considering the risk of animosity's potentially impairing the CDC's operation, poor communities can ill afford. But the CDC is to be viewed as an institution representative of the interests of the whole community, previously apathetic or hostile groups should be encouraged to come forward and bid for local support. Proliferation of competing groups may force groups to unite with competitors in order to gain control. Even if coalitions should not result, the emergence of such groups is likely to increase the opportunity for those dissatisfied with the board of directors eventually elected to remove them. Under such circumstances the members of the board may be expected to be responsive to the wishes of as many shareholders as possible.

### B. POSTORGANIZATION PARTICIPATION

### 1. Incentives for Continued Investment

The enthusiasm generated by an intensive campaign promoting establishment of a CDC may secure relatively widespread stock ownership at the time of final incorporation. But if shareholders are to retain their shares in the corporation[30] and are to participate actively in its functions, and if new shareholders are to be encouraged to invest after formation, then concrete benefits must derive from stock ownership. However, unlike investors in business corporations, shareholders in the CDC cannot realize capital gains because of the restriction on transferability and the continuing offer of shares by the CDC at the $5 par value. Moreover, distribution of CDC profits to shareholders ordinarily may be made only in the form of community services.[31] Intangible considerations, such as community pride or pride in being a shareholder–owner of visible and tangible assets, may serve to secure participation at the outset, but these are thin reeds on which to rest a continuing financial commitment by the poor. As presently drawn, the bill limits drastically the concrete value of stock ownership.

All business management functions[32] of the CDC reside in a business management board (BMB) whose members are not elected by the shareholders but are appointed by the board of directors to staggered three-year terms.[33] BMB members are removable only for cause,[34] and a majority always will have two years left to serve. The bill here seems to reflect a fundamental compromise between the goals of participation and economic development; community participation in the economic development function is rendered remote and indirect by insulation of the BMB's majority from shareholder control. Thus, shareholder influence in business management decisions is not a significant incentive for share ownership.

This seems to leave the community service function of the CDC as the remaining source of effective incentives. The bill vests responsibility for this function in the board of directors, who are elected by the shareholders for terms of up to two years.[35] But the bill leaves to the bylaws the determination of the degree to which accesses to "the programs, services, benefits, and opportunities resulting from the activities of the corporation" shall be restricted to shareholders.[36] Presumably these programs, services, and benefits may include child day-care centers, job-training centers, recreational facilities, and anything else the residents themselves desire.[37] If the bylaws make benefits available to shareholders and nonshareholders alike, then accessibility to services can be no incentive to stock ownership.[38] The only remaining advantage appears to be the right to vote for directors and thus to determine indirectly the specific services provided by the CDC. Whether the value of this right alone is sufficient to induce continued stock ownership is questionable, especially in large CDC's where each shareholder has minimal influence in electing directors favorable to the types of services he wants distributed. Thus, distribution of services to nonshareholders seems to eliminate the only concrete incentive to continued financial investment in the CDC.

Furthermore, a distribution of services to nonshareholders seems to conflict with the statutory purpose of destroying the handout syndrome accompanying provision of community services. One of the great advantages of a CDC as a service organization is that the recipient of services has some basis for believing that he is receiving not a handout, but rather a return on his investment in the CDC. When these services are distributed to nonshareholders, however, their character as handouts remains unchanged. While handouts from one's fellows may be less demeaning than handouts from outsiders, their "something-for-nothing" status remains undesirable.

These considerations argue for restricting the distribution of services to shareholders and their immediate families.[39] Limiting the distribution of services has the collateral benefit of increasing the monetary value of services available to each shareholder. It also ensures that the individuals receiving services will be those who have had the opportunity to express their preferences through election of the board of directors, thus making services more responsive to the needs of the recipients.

Nevertheless, limiting distribution might seem to create an exclusive class in the community, those who are shareholders of the CDC and are thereby entitled to special services. However, the fact that anyone can buy a share in the CDC at any time with his labor as well as with his money[40] goes far to obviate this problem. But some probably will remain apathetic to all organizational efforts, and the CDC will have no obligation to care for them. Thus, the CDC never will be able to be a complete substitute for existing welfare organizations. However, the strict limitations on cash distributions,[41] which comprise a significant portion of modern welfare services, indicate that it has never been so intended. Perhaps a more serious problem is that the limitation on distribution seems to entail some loss in the promotion of a sense of community responsibility for the fate of nonshareholders. However, the sacrifice of concrete incentives to invest resulting from a distribution of services to all seems to outweigh this consideration.

### 2. Facilitating Active Participation

Even if restricted distribution of services maintains widespread stock ownership, the statutory goals of participation will not be fulfilled unless shareholders also participate actively in the CDC by voting in shareholder ballotings. Such participation is necessary to secure maximum responsiveness of corporate activities to shareholder desires. Moreover, participation may have a value in itself by promoting a sense of self-worth and responsibility among the poor. As in the case of shareownership, widespread community participation seems attainable only if adequate incentives are provided to motivate shareholders to action. The bias toward large CDC's would seem to have a tendency to reduce participation by reducing the influence of individual votes. To counteract this tendency, the bill modifies traditional corporate voting and control procedures in several important respects.

First, the bill provides that regardless of the number of shares one man holds he is limited to one vote in CDC ballotings.[42] The purpose evidently is to keep relatively small numbers of people from capturing control of the CDC and to motivate the poor man to participate despite his small stockholding.

Of course, such a modification discourages individual investments in more than one share of stock since additional shares would provide neither additional votes nor increased services. Further, strict adherence to the one-man, one-vote principle entails sacrifice of the opportunity to reward active participation with additional votes. Perhaps the principal should be altered to permit issuance of fractional shares of voting stock to all shareholders participating in a balloting or to all shareholders doing other necessary work, even if not directly related to the business or service functions of the CDC, such a circulating information about subsequent elections. To the extent such services would have been necessary expenses of the CDC, the potential loss in capital investment resulting from the lack of incentive to purchase additional shares could be reduced. Making an exception for additional voting shares issued in return for participation in or service to the CDC would not seem inconsistent with the political concept of egalitarianism implicit in the one-man, one-vote concept: participation rather than class status or economic ability would determine who received a greater say in the operation of the CDC. Nevertheless, those who enjoy a greater opportunity to participate through their position in the CDC or to provide services through their possession of special skills might take advantage of such a scheme and obtain large blocks of stock to gain or to perpetuate control. Thus, the size of stock dividends would have to be strictly limited and the situations under which they could be issued clearly defined by the corporate bylaws.

A second change in traditional corporate doctrine relates to shareholder proxy rules. The bill allows shareholders to provide in a bylaw for proxy voting, evidently recognizing the proxies may be necessary in order to make shareholder meetings feasible in large CDC's.[43] Such proxies, however, must be "expressly executed with respect to the particular matter submitted to the shareholders" and they may be effective for a maximum of thirty days.[44] Presumably this restriction on blank check proxies is intended to encourage each shareholder to make an individual judgment on an issue[45] rather than to delegate that judgment to a particular group, especially the management group.

But if the shareholders are to have real decision-making power, they must have an opportunity to choose among alternative proposals and must receive information sufficient for a reasoned judgment. If management alone solicits proxies, the shareholders will have no such choice and may receive only a minimum of information. Thus, the bill encourages other groups to solicit proxies by providing them with the "opportunity to counter the corporation's statement of a balloting's purpose and recommendations of proposed shareholder action, if any, in the same media and to the same extent" and by specifying that "the corporation shall bear the cost thereof."[46] This solution, however, is not entirely adequate. If incumbents do not solicit proxies or solicit proxies with a minimum of accompanying information, the rights of their opposition are drastically reduced. Because of the burden the opposition must overcome, perhaps they should be guaranteed at least some opportunity to express their views and to solicit proxies at CDC expense, regardless of the incumbents' action. If this were done, shareholders would be assured of receiving continuous information about the operation of the CDC and the issues confronting the board. The opportunity for meaningful decision making would increase, and the existence of smaller groups organized around proxy solicitation and maintained by the hope of future control would provide an outlet for those seeking broader participation and a spur for director responsiveness to shareholder wishes.

A third modification of corporate doctrine under the bill is increased shareholder control over the board of directors. A majority of shareholders may elect the board members, and a majority may remove them at any time with or without cause.[47] This procedure seems designed to ensure the responsiveness of board action to shareholder demands. However, by granting a majority such extensive control over the CDC, the bill runs the risk that legitimate minority interests will go unattended.[48] This danger is aggravated by the statutory bias toward large communities which may force many divergent groups to organize within one CDC.

The obvious and traditional corporate procedure for securing minority representation is cumulative voting. In the context of one man, one vote, the procedure would involve giving each shareholder the number of votes equal to the number of directors to be elected, with the option to cast all votes for one director or to distribute them as he wished.[49] However, cumulative voting is of little help in a situation where a group with a secure majority[50] has so alienated the minority that their incentive for shareownership and participation has been vitiated. In such a case the board could continue to act with impunity in the face of protestations by minority representatives on the board. In the more common situation where the controlling group is not completely secure, cumulative voting has the disadvantage of polarizing dissent in such a way as to institutionalize opposing views. In place of a system in which a control group must accommodate itself to a variety of interests, it substitutes a system where the director elected by a specific group need be responsive only to that group's interests. Nevertheless, the added inducement to minority participation provided by cumulative voting seems necessary if minority groups are to remain in the CDC, especially where minorities such as racial minorities already exist in the community. The extreme case where cumulative voting has not prevented the disregard of minority interests might be dealt with under the bill's annexation and secession provisions.[51]

Although shareholder control over the directors is achieved primarily by the continual threat of removal without cause, it would probably be unwise to require resort to such extreme measures as the only means of expressing shareholder views. Alternative procedures should be made available in the form, for example, of advisory shareholder resolutions.[52] Although not binding, such resolutions, by providing a continuing means of monitoring shareholder sentiment, would give the directors significant guidance as to how to direct their efforts. And a continual polling of shareholders would seem to promote shareholder interest by increasing their information about and their role in CDC activities. The disadvantage of advisory resolutions seems to be the expense, especially if shareholder support is solicited through proxy machinery whose cost is borne by the CDC. But this cost seems to be offset by the potential expense and inconvenience involved in the special meetings necessary for removal of directors and in the cost of seating an entirely new board. If, however, the procedure for advisory resolutions proves too expensive, CDC funds could be denied this type of proxy solicitation.

## 3. Corporate Management of Community Development

### A. ALLOCATION OF FUNDS

The procedures outlined above for promoting shareholder participation depend for full effectiveness on the assumption that each vote is valuable because it represents a valuable shareholder interest. Because of the insulation of business management decisions, this interest has been seen to be the right to determine what services will be distributed by the CDC.[53] Presumably, the greater the value of services to be distributed, the greater the incentive for each individual to participate in CDC ballotings. The value of services depends in part on the profitability of the CDC, but it also depends upon the amount of profits allocated to community services.

Responsibility for determining the percentage of profits to be allocated to services[54] resides in the BMB.[55] The BMB is the group in the corporate structure which is least responsive to shareholder desires.[56] Moreover, its function is to manage the business enterprises of the CDC, and faithful performance of this function would seem to lead it to favor reinvestment of profits in business opportunities rather than distribution of profits in the form of shareholder services. Although this allocation of power is conducive to economic development of the community, it may result in a drastic reduction in shareholder participation and finally in stock ownership if the value of CDC services is kept at too low a level.[57]

One alternative is to vest responsibility for allocation of profits in the board of directors. However, because of the responsiveness of directors to shareholders, the former probably would favor a maximum distribution of profits in the form of services satisfying immediate and pressing needs. The long-range benefits to the community from economic growth would seem to be substantially less attractive to a poor man confronting day-to-day problems. Thus, the shifting of responsibility for profit allocation to the board of directors is likely to result in serious handicapping of the economic development function of the CDC.

To maintain a proper balance between the competing functions of shareholder participation and economic development, perhaps a procedural check should be instituted to prevent either the BMB or the shareholders from favoring one function to the exclusion of the other. Responsibility for the initial allocation would remain in the BMB, but the board of directors would be given a veto power if it found the allocation unsatisfactory. The final allocation would then be hammered out in a conference between the BMB and the board, a conference not unlike a joint congressional conference where divergent versions of legislation must be reconciled. Of course, this procedure is subject to the criticism that the board might always veto in order to gain additional funds in conference, and that the BMB consequently would initially take a greater proportion of funds than it actually required. Even if this were the case, however, the final result might be expected to represent a more satisfactory resolution of conflicting purposes than is possible if one group had complete power. And it is not likely that the veto would be exercised excessively since the prospect of long sessions necessary to reconcile widely disparate claims for funds would probably lead the BMB to submit realistic estimates and the board to approve them. In addition, an understanding as to what constitutes an appropriate allocation would probably develop over time as the needs of the CDC became more clearly defined. If this should result, the veto would maintain a satisfactory balance between competing CDC activities.

### B. THE ROLE OF THE BMB AS MANAGERS

As suggested above, the BMB plays a central role in the CDC through its control over allocation of profits. But even within its strictly managerial capacity,[58] the BMB must make decisions affecting the ultimate goals of the CDC.

The statutory language investing the BMB with responsibility for managing the property and assets of the corporation is similar to the language of many state corporation statutes investing such responsibility in a board of directors.[59] In light of the bill's incorporation of relevant state law,[60] the conclusion might be reached that the managerial role played by the BMB is intended to be comparable to the role played by a board of directors in an ordinary business corporation. But there are significant differences between the purposes of an ordinary corporation and those of a CDC. Under traditional corporate law, corporations operate "primarily for the profit of the stockholders," and the role of directors is to implement this purpose.[61] To be sure, long-range development may serve as a justification for programs not producing immediate rewards, but the profit-making function of a corporation lies behind all business decisions. The purpose of the corporation thus provides the directors with a standard by which to guide their actions.

The diverse goals of the CDC subsumed under the general purpose of economic development include, but are not limited to, profit making. Subgoals also include the creation of jobs, the raising of salary levels, and the improvement of the physical condition of the community. Clearly an overemphasis on profit making could result in the neglect of these other aspects of economic development. Nevertheless, a deemphasis of profit making could hamper the fulfillment of other valid CDC purposes, such as the distribution of needed community services. Thus the BMB, unlike the directors of a regular corporation, cannot rely on the profit standard to guide its decisions since the profit standard, while conducive to achievement of some CDC goals, does not adequately encompass all the purposes of the CDC. It would be of little value, for example, in helping the BMB to decide between investments with low-profit but high-employment potential and investments with high-profit but low-employment potential; or investments which will generate a few permanent, high-paying jobs and investments which will create many seasonal, low-paying jobs.

Nevertheless, the BMB should be given some guidance when it approaches such important policy questions.[62] Otherwise, it may flounder between one goal and another without ever reaching a satisfactory resolution of competing objectives. In place of a standard with its necessary emphasis on particular factors to the exclusion of others, a list of priorities seems to be more appropriate because it can provide the BMB with guidance as to which subgoals to prefer without forcing decisions which would be impractical in terms of the generally understood meaning of economic or community development. In making a decision the BMB either could follow the list of priorities or in unusual cases could deviate from the list and take advantage of an exceptional opportunity with the justification that it was especially well-suited to achievement of a subgoal not preferred but nonetheless included in the concept of economic development. The necessity for the BMB to rationalize its decisions in terms of a list of priorities would allow flexibility while at the same time providing a check on BMB action.

The strong feeling among the leaders in economically depressed areas that they must be permitted to make policy decisions without outside interference[63] indicates that if the CDC is to retain its character as an institution representing purely local interests, responsibility for formulating a list of priorities should be vested in the NCCCB;[64] nor should priorities be incorporated into the statute. A rigid set of priorities has the additional disadvantage of freezing the CDC within a particular set of goals which may not be shuffled as circumstances change.

Perhaps the best place to vest responsibility for determining priorities would be in the board of directors.[65] As particular business opportunities presented themselves to the CDC, the board could change priorities as circumstances demanded, thereby maintaining the relevance of priorities to community needs. Moreover, a list of priorities handed down by the board would reflect the desires of the shareholders to whom statutory procedures make the board highly responsive. This method of developing priorities would heighten the shareholders' sense of control over CDC functions and hence have the additional advantage of promoting increased levels of shareholder participation. Continual supervision of the priorities would allow shareholders to express satisfaction or dissatisfaction with the results of CDC action and thus promote the responsiveness of CDC activities to its shareholders' wishes.

## 4. Tax Benefits To Aid the CDC

Profits earned through investment in businesses and in service contracts are necessary for the support of the social-service functions of the CDC, while at the same time they contribute to increased efforts towards economic development. However, the limitations on profit maximization imposed by competing goals, and on business expertise imposed by residency requirements for shareholders and directors[66] make realization of profits an uncertain prospect. To assist the CDC in carrying out its profit-making function, the bill not only grants federal seed money to match private investment at the time of incorporation but also provides extensive tax benefits both to the CDC itself[67] and to private investors outside the community who assist the CDC.

### A. INCOME TAX BENEFITS FOR THE CDC

The bill softens the impact of the federal income tax on CDC earnings. Instead of the limitations on surtax exemptions in the present code,[68] all individual surtax exemptions are retained and the tax rate on the first $25,000, of earnings of CDC subsidiary corporations is kept at 22 percent.[69] Moreover, the tax rate is reduced and the surtax exemption increased in inverse ratio to the development index[70] of the CDC community so that CDC subsidiaries in some areas may pay no tax on the first $50,000 of taxable income and may claim a surtax exemption of up to $200,000.[71] Finally, the profits of subsidiary corporations may be transferred to the CDC with no additional taxation.[72]

But all income tax benefits will, of course, be worthless if the CDC does not turn a profit since their effect is to allow a greater retention of profits once earned. It would seem that especially in the early years provisions should be made for a positive source of income to reduce probable losses.

Perhaps in recognition of the fact that the CDC will be providing community services previously funded by municipal, state, and federal governments, some provision should be made for compensation to the CDC for the expense of the services it assumes. Of course the objection can be raised that if the government is footing the bill anyway, it does not need a CDC to distribute its funds. Moreover, if the CDC becomes too dependent on government contracts, it may lose its independence of outside controls. But reliance on government payments, as well as the payments themselves, could be reduced as the need for them diminishes over time. In any event the advantages of a well-funded CDC during its formative years seem to outweigh these objections.

### B. TAX INCENTIVES FOR OUTSIDE INVESTMENT

The CDC will require outside assistance if it is to establish in the community profitable businesses with valuable plants and facilities and potential for employing large numbers of workers in relatively high-paying jobs.[73] To motivate major businesses to contribute such assistance, the bill provides a variety of tax incentives designed to make it financially profitable for businesses to erect buildings, purchase equipment, train residents, and then, after establishing a money-making operation, to sell out to the CDC and with the profits begin another enterprise while continuing to improve the profitability of the first. Arrangements for the venture sponsored by the outside corporation would be made in a "turnkey contract" negotiated between it and the CDC.[74] This contract would specify the obligations of both parties and include a timetable for sale to the CDC.[75]

To induce private corporations to enter such contracts six types of tax incentives are provided. These are (1) rapid amortization of turnkey facilities,[76] (2) exemption from recapture of investment tax credit for machinery and equipment in turnkey facilities,[77] (3) 10 percent tax credit for wages and salaries of shareholder employees in turnkey facilities,[78] (4) nonrecognition of capital gains on sale of the turnkey facility to the CDC if proceeds are reinvested in a new turnkey facility or in class B stock of a Community Development Bank,[79] (5) exemption from recapture of depreciation if the proceeds are reinvested in a new turnkey facility,[80] and (6) tax credit equal to 15 percent of profits generated by the turnkey facility for five years after sale.[81] Tax benefits, therefore, promote initial creation and operation of a turnkey facility through rapid amortization of equipment and credits for wages and salaries, encourage reinvestment through deferral of capital gains and nonrecapture of rapid amortization, and encourage future transactions with the turnkey facility and its establishment as a profit-making enterprise through a tax credit depending for its existence and amount on the continued profitability of the facility. The eventual result of the turnkey arrangement is the ownership of profitable businesses in economically depressed areas by the residents of those areas. The businesses will alleviate unemployment by providing training and job opportunities, and their profits will fund needed community service programs. With something for everyone, high levels of community participation are hopefully assured.

To achieve this ideal, however, the businesses originally established by the turnkey agreements must be self-perpetuating and successful. Attracted by the chance to avail themselves of all the tax advantages except the tax credit for future profitability, outside businesses may be led to promote turnkey businesses which would be unprofitable absent the significant tax benefits provided by the bill, or they may be led to promote businesses which offer short-range profits but lack long-range growth potential. Tax credits alone provide no assurance that the businesses established will be well suited to the locality either in terms of market accessibility or employment potential. To be sure, the 15 percent tax credit may be lost, but the immediate benefits of significant deductions may far outweigh the loss, especially for a business experiencing unusually high profits.

The key to preventing such distortions of the statutory purpose lies in the turnkey contract itself. Since the contract is a prerequisite for the enjoyment of all tax advantages, the CDC can choose only those businesses which it considers to offer the best investment. Moreover, the contract could contain a multiple of earnings formula for sales price which would provide a strong incentive for the outside contractor to create a profitable business. And it could secure a continued business relationship through long-term supply contracts. Underlying these advantages is the assumption that a sufficient number of reputable businesses will seek turnkey arrangements so that CDC's will not be forced to enter turnkey arrangements with businesses offering less attractive investment prospects. But this assumption seems reasonable in light of the substantial tax incentives and the apparently growing concern of large businesses to help reduce poverty.[82]

The CDC, however, must be able to recognize the better business prospects when they present themselves. And the potential lack of expertise on the BMB may prevent sophisticated analysis. To assist the BMB it may be useful to establish an advisory group for the purpose of preparing a report upon which a final judgment by the BMB could be based. The seeds of such an advisory system may be present in the powers of review granted the treasury, which may deny tax benefits to a turnkey contract it finds to be unwise.[83] In addition, the Small Business Administration is authorized to make grants to the CDC to help defray the cost of projects directed towards increasing the efficiency and profitability of CDC businesses.[84]

## 5. Applicability of State Corporation Law

Significant aspects of the CDC may be affected by the application of state corporation law. State law, for example, may determine the permissibility of advisory resolutions,[85] the standard to guide BMB action,[86] and the applicability of cumulative voting.[87] The bill includes a provision governing the applicability of state corporation law:[88]

A national community development corporation shall be subject to the provisions of this title, to such reasonable rules and regulations as the Board may make to interpret or implement any provision of this title and to the laws of general applicability relating to business corporations of the state wherein such corporation is located, except insofar as such state laws are inconsistent with the provisions and purposes of this title or such reasonables rules and regulations as may be made by the board.

The presence of this provision would seem to preclude the development of a federal common law of national community development corporations. Perhaps this is unfortunate; the CDC as an instrument of social organization combining political and economic goals under statutory guidance is different from business corporations traditionally governed by state law. If it is to succeed, a considerable amount of experimentation will be necessary at the outset. The range of permissible experimentation very probably cannot be anticipated within the bounds of the organizing statute. Hence, it may be desirable to permit a federal common law of national community development corporations to emerge as a guide to the long-term development of this form of social organization.

At the very least,[89] these considerations argue for a liberal construction of the word "purpose" in the present statutory provision to include implicit statutory purposes. If "purpose" were read narrowly to permit application of state law where not conflicting with stated statutory purposes, particular state corporate doctrines might seriously impede development of CDC's. For example, the BMB might be bound to a standard of profitability[90] despite the fact that profitability at some point might interfere with shareholder participation or high employment. Or state cumulative voting might be made applicable to protect minority rights[91] without consideration of the difference[92] between the character of CDC minorities and that of the minorities of ordinary corporations. On the other hand, if consistency with implicit purposes is the test, such problems would be avoided, while state law might still be applied where it is consistent with the bill's broader purposes. For example, the present omission in the bill of a provision covering reimbursement of insurgents beyond the expense incurred by incumbent directors in a proxy contest[93] might be filled by a state law allowing reimbursement of successful insurgents for all reasonable expenses if ratified by the stockholders.[94] While state law in this case and others might not provide as satisfactory a solution as one which could be incorporated in the bill, it nevertheless would provide useful rules to govern situations which the bill cannot anticipate.

## 6. Conclusion

Although the bill on its face acknowledges community organization as a goal of the CDC, it seems clear that the bill subordinates realization of this goal to maximization of economic development. Its procedures seem designed to promote participation only so far as is necessary to legitimate the CDC as a community representative. Presumably, the drafters believed that the increased standard of living resulting from economic development would be more beneficial to residents than community organization, or at least represented a more appropriate goal for the Community Self-Determination Program. It is unclear, however, whether such benefits will reach the most apathetic and poorest elements of the community unless concerted efforts are directed toward involving them in the CDC and thus motivating them to partake of increased economic opportunity. Moreover, organization can raise the self-respect and dignity of the poor by instilling in them a sense of community pride. And, of course, organization can produce better representation of the interests of the poor.[95] One of the purposes of this note has been to suggest methods by which participation within the CDC form can be promoted.

Nevertheless, by taking a new approach to the problems of poverty, the Community Self-Determination Bill seems to avoid many of the problems plaguing existing poverty programs. By eliminating continued financial dependence on the federal government, it creates in the CDC an institution free from the threat of outside interference exercisable through control of appropriations.[96] In addition, by replacing the staff of "outsiders" characteristic of present programs with local residents, it allows the poor people themselves to exercise control over programs intended to minister to their needs. And by drawing upon the community itself, it exploits resources which presently are going untapped. Finally, the incorporation of community organization, welfare-type services, and economic development into one institution is a promising experiment.

However, it is unclear whether a corporate vehicle is the most appropriate form for the achievement of the stated goals. Implicit in the general term "corporation" are concepts that require the observance of certain formalities. For example, the initial investment must be in the form of a share of stock representing partial ownership of the corporation. And such ownership raises the issue of return on and recovery of the initial investment. The procedure for management involves the concepts of "shareholders" and "directors," each of which is encrusted with overlays of judicial and statutory elaboration. This note has discussed these and other problems in the corporate terms in which the bill has cast them. But perhaps the goals of the bill could be better served by an institution with a different character. For example, the model might be a municipal corporation where all would have the right to vote in general elections for officials responsible for everyday operations. Capitalization could be provided by a local tax levied in accordance with a statutory formula. Or perhaps a cooperative form might be appropriate, in which residents could view themselves as joining together to achieve the economic advantages accompanying large-scale operations. Corporate procedures for management could be maintained, but the initial sum paid in would be characterized as membership dues and not as an investment entitling the investor to dividends. Similar to this would be a labor union characterization where residents would join together to gain a better bargaining position, against established outside interests in the community.

While the bill incorporates into the CDC aspects of each of these institutions, the corporate form in which the CDC is cast may reduce its appeal to poor residents. A straightforward appeal to community spirit may represent a more honest and effective approach to organizing the community to achieve the bill's stated goals. Such possibilities at least should be examined and their advantages and disadvantages compared with those of the proposed corporate model.

## Notes

1. See 114 CONG. REC. 9749–9752 (daily ed. July 30, 1968) (statement by Vice President Humphrey, July 20, 1968); *id.* at 7020 (daily ed. July 18, 1968) (statement by former Vice President Nixon, July 12, 1968); PLATFORMS OF THE DEMOCRATIC PARTY AND THE REPUBLICAN PARTY at 31 (U.S. House of Representatives pub.) (Democratic Party); *id.* at 56 (Republican Party).
2. H.R. 18715, 90th Cong., 2d Sess. (1968); S. 3875, 90th Cong., 2d Sess. (1968). Throughout this note the bill will be referred to only by section. The bill was referred

to the House Committee on Ways and Means and the Senate Finance Committee. Since it was not acted on prior to the adjournment of the Ninetieth Congress, a new bill will have to be introduced in the Ninety-first Congress. The bill will be substantially revised in the interim. Telephone interview with a member of Senator Percy's staff, in Washington, D.C., November 21, 1968.

3. § 3.
4. § 2(a).
5. § 2(b).
6. § 2(c).
7. § 2(e).
8. § 2(f).
9. See §§ 2(f), 2(i).
10. §§ 101–103.
11. § 110(a).
12. The draftsmen of the bill consider the economic development function of the CDC to be the most important. Interview with John McClaughry, Special Assistant to President-elect Nixon for Community Affairs and formerly Legislative Assistant to Senator Percy, in Cambridge, Mass., November 16, 1968 [hereinafter cited as McClaughry Interview].
13. The bill is divided into five titles. This note will focus on Title I, National Community Development Corporations, and Title IV, Amendments to Internal Revenue Code. Title II provides for the creation of National Community Development Banks to make loans to local CDC's and other community small business concerns. Title III provides for the creation of a United States Community Development Bank "to serve as a secondary financial institution and as a source of technical, managerial, and financial expertise to community development banks. . . ." § 301.
The bill is intended to aid residents of both urban and rural communities. §1. Most of the discussion in this note will assume a large urban context, although it may also be relevant to problems of rural communities.
14. When he introduced the bill, Senator Percy stated that the purpose of its organizational provisions is "to guarantee to all the residents of any area in which a CDC is proposed, and to all representatives thereof, a full and fair opportunity to participate in the process of organizing the CDC and influencing the direction that it will take once it has been finally chartered." Thus, the bill "insures that all elements within an area will have equal opportunity to define the community and the objectives of the CDC. . . ." 114 CONG. REC. 9280 (daily ed. July 24, 1968) (remarks of Senator Percy).
15. §§ 130(a)–131(a). Apparently, incorporators may be nonresidents as well as residents.
16. § 133(b). Upon receipt of a letter of intent the NCCCB is also required to set up a temporary branch office in the proposed community to "give prominent notice of such initial letter of intent, its contents, and the effect thereof to the residents . . . ." § 135(a).
17. The bill employs a development index composed of either the ratio between community unemployment and the national or relevant metropolitan average, or community income and the national or relevant metropolitan median, whichever ratio is the lesser, to determine whether a community is depressed sufficiently to merit a CDC. § 138. This index is also used to determine the amount of income tax imposed on a CDC, § 402, see p. 661 *infra*, and to determine whether a particular community has been developed sufficiently to allow the CDC to make cash distributions to its shareholders. § 120(b); see p. 650 and note 31 *infra*.
18. §§ 130(a)–(b), 131(a)–133(c).
19. § 135(e).
20. § 136(a).
21. § 137(a).
22. § 137(b). This area is the "potential community." § 135(a).
23. §§ 137(b), 140(b). The bill refers to the grant of funds as intended "for such sundry administrative expenses as it [CDC] may previously have incurred . . . ." After expenses are defrayed, presumably the remainder will constitute initial capitalization.
24. §§ 137(b), 110(b). The term "resident" is defined as "a natural person who resides within the community area." § 4(d).
25. § 110(b). This conclusion is based on the assumption that geographical area and population are related.
26. § 136(b).

27. Of course, there is no assurance that the incorporators of the conditionally chartered CDC selected in the communitywide referendum will be elected as directors at the initial balloting of shareholders. See § 112(c). Nevertheless, their close identification with the CDC receiving final approval makes the prospect of their election as directors highly likely.

28. This is not a novel suggestion. The bill already provides some funds for opposition groups during the solicitation of proxies. § 111(d); see p. 654 *infra*.

29. The bill does not include mechanisms designed specifically to motivate large numbers of residents to pay the requisite $5.00 for a share of stock in the CDC. See § 117(a). But widespread stock ownership seems necessary if the recipients of CDC services are to feel that they are receiving not handouts but dividends earned through investment in the CDC. Moreover, the greater the initial investment in stock the greater the amount of federal funds to be granted for initial capitalization. See § 140(b). Nevertheless, motivating poor men to invest rather than spend their money on immediate needs represents a considerable obstacle, to be overcome only if a high level of enthusiasm is generated among residents. Saul Alinsky has suggested that such motivation is impossible unless the poor already are organized. He believes that only such organization can overcome the distrust engendered by a long series of disillusioning experiences with past poverty programs. He has remarked that if the poor were given shares of stock, probably most would lose the certificates. Interview with Saul Alinsky, Executive Director, Industrial Areas Foundation, Chicago, in Cambridge, Mass., October 25, 1968.

30. The bill in § 118 requires individuals who cease to be residents in the CDC area to redeem their shares for the $5.00 par value. No provision, however, guarantees residents the right to redeem their shares. Such a right could be highly detrimental to the smooth operation of the CDC since it would allow a run on the treasury by dissident groups. Moreover, shareholders might continually redeem and then repurchase their shares. Nevertheless, if investment in the CDC is to retain the character of a voluntary act of self-help, resident shareholders should have some opportunity to terminate ownership and recover at least part of their investment. Even though the initial decision to purchase is voluntary, it may well be made under the influence of optimism generated by the referendum campaign. Further, the option to withdraw adds a final check on nonresponsiveness by the CDC in the event that dissident groups are unable to organize within the community. Relaxation of transferability restrictions, at least between residents, may be one solution. However, additional shares of stock have little value for residents already holding a share, see p. 653 *infra*, and therefore the sales price would be well below the $5.00 at which a share could be purchased from the CDC unless an anxious buyer presently owning no CDC stock is found. Perhaps shares should be made redeemable from the CDC, but the total volume redeemable during any one period should be limited.

31. An exception to this rule, however, allows distribution of a limited percentage of profits if after five years of operation special tax advantages, see pp. 660–661 *infra*, are waived and requirements relating to the level of community development are met. § 120(b). Because of the high level of uncertainty as to whether such distributions ever will be made, their influence on shareholder participation may be disregarded.

32. See note 58 *infra*.

33. § 113(a).

34. § 113(e).

35. § 112.

36. § 116(c).

37. The bill is ambiguous as to the character of the services which may be provided. At one point it seems to restrict these services narrowly to those which expand "economic and educational opportunities available in the community." § 119(a). These words, however, may be construed broadly to include whatever the board considers to be necessary to the welfare of the community. See generally pp. 664–665 *infra*. Moreover, the bill at other points suggests that the services provided by the CDC may include those which improve "health, safety, and living conditions" and enhance "personal dignity and independence." § 110(a). Senator Percy has listed as types of services: "basic education, child welfare, day care, preschool training, health, consumer education, home ownership counseling, college placement assistance, job finding, recreation, [and] legal aid." 114 Cong. Rec., *supra* note 14, at 9279.

38. Nevertheless, some individuals may be moved to own shares of stock so that they can feel that they are receiving dividends earned through investment and not merely handouts.

39. The bill provides for this alternative by permitting the bylaws to specify that shareholders and their immediate families shall receive "preferential or exclusive treatment." § 116(c).

40. § 117(b)–(c).

41. § 120(a).

42. § 111(e).

43. § 111(b). Three forms of shareholder balloting are permitted: shareholders may cast secret ballots at various specified locations, or they may vote at one shareholder meeting, or at one of a variety of meetings held in the community. It is unclear whether proxies are allowed if shareholder balloting is in the form of a secret ballot cast at specified voting locations. A requirement that each shareholder must produce his certificate in order to vote seems to indicate that proxies in this situation are prohibited.

44 § 111(b)(3).

45. Except for the election of directors, it is unclear what issues are to be submitted to shareholders. Presumably, these will be defined in the articles of incorporation. It is equally unclear whether shareholders may execute proxies delegating the authority to select particular directors, or whether they must specify the director for whom the proxy vote is to be cast. Specification of particular directors seems desirable since delegation of the choice of directors appears to cut too deeply into the bill's emphasis on individual decision making.

46. § 111(d).

47. §§ 111(f)–112(d), 112(g).

48. This risk may be mitigated somewhat by the enactment of a bylaw specifying that individual directorships may be elected from geographic subdivisions of the community. § 112(d). The success of this procedure in protecting minority rights depends, however, on the existence of identifiable geographic subdivisions in which residents share common views. If such subdivisions are in fact recognized for the purpose of electing directors, they may have the unfortunate effect of fragmenting the community by institutionalizing divergent views.

49. It is possible that state laws requiring cumulative voting may be applied to CDC's. See pp. 664–665 infra.

50. Such a majority may be present in a community composed of several ethnic groups, each of which tends to vote as a bloc. Where over half the residents are members of one ethnic bloc, the likelihood of that group's losing control through defections may be small.

51. §§143–144. A situation where, for example, the interests of a minority racial group included in the CDC community are being disregarded may be remedied under the bill either by its seceding from the CDC to form its own CDC or by its joining another CDC already in existence. However, strict requirements must be met before such drastic action may be taken. Nevertheless, it would seem that the threat of such action may increase board responsiveness to minority interests. See 114 CONG. REC., supra note 14, at 9281.

52. Other possibilities are the shareholder referendum or initiative. These, however, would be binding on directors and might go too far in hampering the directors' sense of individual responsibility.

53. See pp. 650–651 supra.

54. The statutory limits are no more than 80 percent and no less than 20 percent. § 119(a).

55. Id.

56. See p. 650 supra.

57. It must be remembered that unlike an ordinary corporation where reinvested profits may produce capital gains to the shareholders, the primary benefit to CDC shareholders is services, since the price of shares even if redeemable or transferable can never exceed the par value offering price of new shares continually made available by the CDC.

58. Although the bill does not define what "management" specifically entails, it apparently includes the purchase of stock in community businesses and the exercise of general shareholder prerogatives in those businesses, including the election of directors. Thus, the BMB has the responsibility for deciding what corporations should be purchased and, through appointment of directors, what policies they should pursue. See 114 CONG. REC., supra note 14. Presumably management of noncorporate business involves similar obligations. Cf. §§ 113(a), 119(a).

59. Compare § 113(a) ("The property and assets of the corporation shall be

managed by the business management board") with, e.g., DEL. CODE ANN. tit. 8, § 141(a) ("the business of every corporation . . . shall be managed by a board of directors . . .").

60. § 110(c); see pp. 665–666 *infra.*

61. Dodge v. Ford Motor Co., 204 Mich. 459, 507, 170 N.W. 668, 684 (1919).

62. The development index created by the bill to measure economic development for purposes of participation in the community development program, see note 17 *supra*, does not seem suitable as a guide for BMB action because it fails to delineate the point at which efforts to achieve high employment and to raise salaries interfere so seriously with the achievement of other valid CDC goals that they must be abandoned.

63. E.g., Panel discussion including Thomas I. Atkins, City Councilman of Boston, Harvard Law School Forum, in Cambridge, Mass., October 25, 1968.

64. The bill may allow the NCCCB such power under its authority to promulgate rules and regulations implementing statutory provisions. § 103(m). A liberal construction of this provision, however, seems inconsistent with the concept of self-determination.

65. It may seem that the power of the board of directors to manage "the affairs" of the CDC, see § 112(a), includes the power to determine priorities. This interpretation was not intended, however, by the drafters of the bill. McClaughry Interview, *supra* note 12.

66. §§ 117(a), 112(a).

67. The tax benefits enjoyed by CDC businesses give them a substantial advantage over their competitors within and outside the community. This form of subsidy shifts part of the cost of the bill's program from society at large to competitors of CDC's.

68. INT. REV. CODE OF 1954, §§ 1561–1563.

69. §§ 401–402.

70. See note 17 *supra.*

71. § 402.

72. § 403. Income tax benefits are limited solely to corporate earnings by CDC subsidiaries. Profits earned in divisions operated directly by the CDC or on contracts with government agencies presumably are taxed at the regular rate. Hence, the apparent effect of these tax provisions will be to force CDC's to incorporate all divisions as subsidiaries and to create a subsidiary service corporation. Otherwise, in its early years of operation, when it must rely heavily on service contracts, see 114 CONG. REC., *supra* note 14, the CDC would have no income tax benefits.

73. *Gf. id.* at 9283; 114 CONG. REC. 7017 (daily ed. July 18, 1968) (remarks of Congressman Curtis).

74. § 4(e).

75. See 114 CONG. REC., *supra* note 14, at 9283.

76. § 404.

77. § 405.

78. § 406.

79. §§ 407–408. Class B stock is defined in § 201.

80. § 408.

81. § 409.

82. *Cf.* Statement by Vice President Humphrey, in Washington, D.C., July 20, 1968, reprinted in 114 CONG. REC. 9749–9752 (daily ed. July 30, 1968).

83. § 406.

84. § 503.

85. See pp. 655–656 *supra.*

86. See p. 658 *supra.*

87. See p. 655 *supra.*

88. § 110(c).

89. By promulgating rules and regulations, the NCCCB may prohibit the application of undesirable state law. In fact, NCCCB promulgation might serve much the same function as a federal common law. Nevertheless, such expansive activities by the NCCCB seem undesirable because of the extent of their interference with the soverignty of individual CDC's.

90. See, e.g., Dodge v. Ford Motor Co., 204 Mich. 459, 507, 170 N.W. 668, 684 (1919).

91. E.g., N.C. GEN. STAT. § 55–67 (1965); CAL. CORP. CODE § 2235 (West 1955).

92. See p. 655 & note 50 *supra.*

93. § 111(d); see pp. 654–655 *supra.*

94. See Rosenfeld v. Fairchild Engine & Airplane Corp., 309 N.Y. 168, 128 N.E.2d 291 (1955).

95. Senator Percy has recognized "[r]epresentation of community interests in other areas of public policy and concern" to be a valid function of the CDC. 114 CONG. REC., *supra* note 14, at 9279. See generally Kotler, *Two Essays on the Neighborhood Corporation*, in SUBCOMM. ON URBAN AFFAIRS OF THE JOINT ECONOMIC COMM., 90TH CONG., 1ST SESS., URBAN AMERICA: GOALS AND PROBLEMS 170 (Comm. Print 1967).

96. See generally Cahn & Cahn, *The New Sovereign Immunity*, 81 HARV. L. REV. 929 (1968).

# PART IV

*Black Economic and Business Development: The Future*

# Introduction

There is a great diversity of opinion on various aspects of Black economic development. The readings in this part were selected because they are much more evaluative than the previous selections. Together they provide a significant commentary on the strategies and philosophical issues that will essentially determine the outcome of Black developmental activity.

Green aud Faux have written an excellent piece that returns to a topic treated much earlier in the volume. Their discussion of the separatist–integrationist debate takes the form of the pros and cons of ghetto dispersal versus ghetto investment and development. Perhaps their most important contribution is the effort to establish a framework for the evaluation of Black economic development.

The Kain and Persky article is included because it is important to sensitize ourselves to the pitfalls of an argument rooted in shallow economic analysis. The authors spare no pain (and would not spare Blacks any) to "eradicate" the ghetto. They would accept segregated (but dispersed) suburban Black communities and would deny an improvement in the quality of urban life in pursuit of their goal. Alan Haber operates on the assumption that the ghetto is a colonial appendage of American society that shows little sign of disappearing. He views the major solution to the problem as the removal of institutions that victimize the ghetto, if *any* solution to the plight of Blacks is possible in this country.

Reflecting the widespread sentiment (at least among Black folk) that it is they who must ultimately define the nature of their problems and find the way to their economic, political and social freedom, the writings of three Black commentators close the volume. James Forman asserts that racism is so pervasive that its end will have to await a Black-controlled government. Robert Browne discusses the necessity of formulating an economic plan for Black America. Viewing the limitations to Black development in American society, the author suggests that in the short run Black people should strive to support those programs with widely acceptable ends. Talmadge Anderson critically assesses the potential and pre-conditions for the economic liberation of Black people in the American economic system. These three selections should be a sharp reminder to those who might tend to think otherwise that, in America, many things are not as they should be. And that some people will not rest until they are!

# 21 ]] The Social Utility of Black Enterprise

*Gerson Green and Geoffrey Faux*

"Green power" movements have been developing among minority groups at a very rapid pace over the past two years causing government, foundations, and the business leadership to grope for policy and program guidelines.

Although there is general agreement that the development of Black enterprise efforts is necessary and desirable, there is little actual program experience upon which to base judgments as to scale and type of programs. Most urban Black enterprise projects are still in the development stage; few have been operational for more than two years.

Roughly, the debates, both within the ghetto and without, fall into two schools. One school emphasizes the cost side of the cost–benefit question, holding that the ghettos present the least fruitful areas for enterprise development, in that land, facility, and maintenance costs are exceedingly high, circulation is congested, housing amenities and transportation are inadequate, crime and hostility in the ghettos prevent the employment of competent management and clerical staffs, and insurance costs are excessive. This argument represents the majority view in government and business, and has resulted in the almost sole dependence on employment programs supported by social services to achieve economic well-being in the ghetto.

The second school emphasizes the benefits, or social utility, side of the equation. It holds that the economic structure which puts the ghetto at a competitive disadvantage is not due to natural market forces but to specific resource allocation policies (highways, housing, tax policies) which have built up the infrastructure of the suburbs and small cities at the expense of the urban core. Those in this school will argue that our investment policies could and should be changed to aid ghetto areas and that, in effect, the "cost-effectiveness" position is another variant of "socialism for the rich, free enterprise for the poor." The need is to concentrate upon the social utility of the program, just as we emphasize the benefits of the defense, space, and highway programs, and rarely their costs.

These two views are complicated by the current clash of integrationist and separatist philosophies. In general the "cost effectives" hold the integrationist view that Blacks can best assimilate into American life through opening up housing and jobs in suburban growth areas, and that the tools, legal and programmatic, are now at hand. The National Alliance of Busi-

From Gerson Green and Geoffrey Faux, "The Social Utility of Black Enterprise" from William F. Haddad and G. Douglas Pugh, eds., *Black Economic Development.* © 1969 by The American Assembly, Columbia University. Reprinted by permission of Prentice-Hall, Inc., Englewood Cliffs, N. J.

nessmen proceeded on this view. The "social utilitarians" argue that recent data indicates a slight opening-up of the suburbs to Blacks and that the trend will increase, but that such movement has affected only the Black upper-middle class and has thus further reduced the leadership in the ghettos, leaving the great mass of Blacks doomed to decades of existence in deteriorating neighborhoods. Black planners and architects are providing an additional view holding that if American cities are to survive as viable social systems, the ghettos must be made to flower into desirable total living environments. On this issue, the cost effectives argue that the function of the ghetto is a transition to assimilation into suburban life. This is a maintenance view leading to minimal investment in physical and economic development of the ghettos and stressing ameliorative social service and employment programs to help more residents up and out of the ghetto. The social utilitarians hold that the Blacks now occupy prime land in our inner cities which will ultimately be reclaimed and rebuilt, and that large numbers of Blacks should remain and benefit from the rebuilding. The current mood of the ghetto would appear to require a policy of rebuilding for current residents.

This represents, in crude form, the policy context from which our argument follows.

## The Benefits

The War on Poverty (appropriations to the Economic Opportunity Act) currently costs some $2 billion per year. Over eight hundred millions are invested in OEO's Community Action Program, for both rural and urban areas, in the heart of the self-help organizational effort in the ghettos. With the advent of the Model Cities Program, the urban areas may receive a significant increase in resources. Little, if any, of the current and projected resources are earmarked for the economic development of Black ghettos, principally because government planners continue to place their main reliance on manpower training and social service programs.

The question of whether the economic development of poor ghetto areas should be an appropriate goal of federal anti-poverty policy usually dissolves into a simplistic comparison between "employment" programs and "investment" programs. The question is then posed, should we bring people to the jobs or the jobs to the people? From the outset, the focus is upon jobs and it is an easy step from there that jobs are the ultimate measure of program effectiveness.

Despite the fact that an investment program, the Area Redevelopment Act, was the first major new program established by the Kennedy administration, for most of the sixties the argument has been carried on by those supporting the "employment" or "manpower training" alternative. The debate, of course, has a history of its own. It has involved specific personalities and political relationships which themselves have had no small impact upon policy decisions. But the basic thrust of program analysis has consistently, almost exclusively, favored employment programs, implicitly concluding that either the costs of economic development were too high, the benefits too low, or both.

Even on its own terms (i.e., the primacy of the employment goal), the analysis upon which the conventional conclusion is based has not been very thorough. Comparative costs of employment and investment programs have not been established, and the variables of the employment goal (who is hired, what kinds of jobs, etc.) rarely isolated and tested separately. In addition, the variety of possibilities on the economic development side are almost never postulated. However, even if the techniques and data were available for making valid comparisons between training programs and economic development, the conceptual basis for making such comparisons would still be in error. Job training cannot be compared with economic development on an either/or basis, because job training programs have one single objective—employment—while economic development is a program with multiple objectives, one of which is employment. Thus the real issue is whether or not there should be an *exclusive* reliance upon manpower and other similar employment programs, or whether some mix of economic development and job training would be more cost effective in the long run.

Before addressing the basic issue, there should be an understanding of what is meant by economic development in the context of domestic urban problems. Terminology is a problem here. Clearly, we are not talking about economic development as the term is usually applied to underdeveloped nations; that is, the problem of increasing the output and productivity of the population of a large, more or less self-contained geographical unit, the solution to which involves the techniques and strategies of capital accumulation. While there are certain analogies between a ghetto community and an underdeveloped country, the analogy as an operating principle breaks down quickly, mostly because of the difficulties in defining the ghetto in economic terms and in identifying and controlling such economic indicators as imports and exports. The problem in our inner cities is somewhat different. It deals ultimately with the redistribution of income, employment, and ownership among income classes, and to a degree, among racial groups through the development of a business infrastructure in the ghetto itself.

Thus far there is no significant national program for this kind of economic development. Title IV of the Economic Opportunity Act, which provides loans and technical assistance to poverty area entrepreneurs, was an attempt to add a modest economic development dimension to the poverty program. It proved inadequate to the task for administrative reasons, and because of the concentration of effort on small high risk "mom-and-pop" stores. Recently, SBA has tried to move away from reliance on small marginal enterprises and may be having some effect upon improved access to capital and technical assistance by Black and other minority businessmen. The Economic Development Administration operates what is essentially a rural area and small town program. It does have an urban technical assistance program which has engaged in some creative projects but that program has been limited both in money and program authority. OEO has funded several demonstration projects in this area, but thus far has not looked upon economic development as an area of major program interest.

The history of the Kennedy–Javits Amendment to the Economic Opportunity Act, . . . which calls for massive investment in poverty areas but has been assigned a minuscule role in the poverty program, is evidence that economic development has not been taken seriously as part of a total antipoverty strategy.

Thus those who argue for exclusive reliance upon employment programs have been in the ascendancy during the short history of the War on Poverty. The basic argument for this position centers around two propositions: (1) that employment programs at all times are more efficient in the development of jobs than investment programs; (2) that economic development programs will increase segregation and encourage separatism.

These points, as well as the identification of some additional social benefits of economic development are discussed below.

## EMPLOYMENT

It should first be understood that the authors of this chapter do not believe that there is any realistic substitute for job training and related employment programs. The majority of the hard-core unemployed in our ghetto areas will find jobs located outside the ghetto. However, over the past few years a huge assortment of these programs have been funded. Some have succeeded; many have failed. While the failure of individual programs as a result of inadequate techniques or poor management does not necessarily mean that the strategy of training ghetto dwellers is wrong, it has brought the strategy of *exclusive* reliance upon such programs into serious question. Part of the problem lies in the basic assumption that any job paying something above subsistence is a sufficient inducement to the Black ghetto dweller for him to travel long distances and subject himself to the psychological pressures attendant upon breaking into employment areas traditionally held by lower-middle-class whites. It is, of course, hard to say just how much of current chronic unemployment is a result of this problem. Estimates have been made but reliable information on the reasons for high failure rates of employment programs are simply not available. The reports of people running through training program after training program without ending up in a permanent job indicate that it is enough to be concerned about.

Certainly, part of the failure of conventional employment progress can be traced to technical and administrative problems rather than to the concept itself. Lack of experience in training the inner-city unemployed and sluggishness of institutions responsible for the programs have taken their toll. As experience accumulates, these problems should diminish.

Another part of the problem comes from a lack of sufficient demand for unskilled and semiskilled labor at the upper limits of acceptable price increase in the economy, which thus creates a pool of unemployed workers at any given period of time.

However, a third reason for the continued existence of so many hard-core unemployed certainly is an insufficient understanding and appreciation of the race problem in America. Consider the case of the "hard-core" young Black male adult who successfully completes a training course and for whom a job is available (a situation which often does *not* result from training programs). So far his life has been one humiliating failure after another. As a result, he has little confidence in his ability to cope with the difficulties emanating from his being Black and poor in a white middle-class society. He gets his job as a result of a highly publicized employment program in his city, through which firms in the suburbs agree to make jobs available to Black inner-city residents. He is thus greeted by a *white* personnel manager, a *white* foreman, and *white* co-workers. They resent the "special" treatment he is getting and they let him know it. The pressures on him to succeed become enormous, and in a few weeks he drops out. He adds another failure to his personal history and returns to the economically less satisfying but psychologically tolerable life on the streets. At the same time, the experience, repeated over and over, convinces the plant manager, the personnel manager, the foreman, and the white workers that "these people" just do not want to work. The next time an employment program is launched with new and better publicity and "out reach" our friend in the ghetto just does not respond.

The response of the program planners to this phenomenon is illustrated by the Kerner Commission's recommendation that "Special emphasis must be given to motivating the hard-core unemployed." The problem is perplexing. The poor have low self-esteem, lack of drive. We must therefore deal with the "motivational problems" of the poor. In other words, the problem is *them*, not *us*. We do not ask the objective question, "What is wrong?" We ask, "What is wrong *with them*?" The predictable response of a society which, if not racist, responds along remarkably racist lines.

The commission was certainly not blind to the failing of white society; it recommended special training for supervisory personnel on how to deal with the hard-core. Well and good, but white racism is not simply an individual characteristic. It is a characteristic of the social structure supported by a huge portion of the population. Most Americans do not see themselves as racists. Thus the personnel manager "impartially" administers an aptitude test which by its nature is biased to the disadvantage of Black ghetto dwellers. Or their foreman "impartially" decides that promoting a Black to a supervisory position will make white workers hostile and therefore impair plant efficiency, which he is being paid to maximize.

Racism appears to be a very complex phenomenon. Few of us have the confidence to state for certain how deep its roots go or what is required to root it out. It is clear, however, that an important element in the picture is economic competition. It is no accident that the white group most vehemently opposed to having Black Americans enjoy equal opportunity in justice are those with the most to lose—the white lower middle class. It is curious, therefore, that until quite recently little attention has been paid to this group, and little analysis made of the impact of poverty programs upon their overt racism.

It is an economic truism that job training and other employment programs do not create jobs. In order for training programs to raise the absolute level of employment (in the short run) there must be, or about to be, vacancies for which qualified personnel are not available and for which training is being given. Under other conditions training merely provides the trainees with the opportunity to become more competitive. The same is true with so-called job development programs. Unless jobs are not being filled because of some gross malfunctioning of the employment market, these programs merely give Black applicants a *competitive edge* over others. While this may be difficult for some to understand, it is readily perceived by the steel workers and cab drivers of the nation that George Wallace quotes so often.

Whether we operate JOBS (Concentrated Employment Program), or any other purely employment program, the result is to increase the competition among Blacks and whites for the same number of jobs in an environment which operates to the disadvantage of the Blacks.

All this is occurring in an economic context of shrinking job opportunities for the unskilled and expanding opportunities for the skilled and educated. The greater ease with which Black professionals are integrated is commonly attributed to the enlightened attitudes of their white, educated colleagues. One wonders, however, how quickly Black engineers and economists would be integrated if the job opportunities in these areas were declining.

The point is not that employment programs should not continue, but that we must recognize the great effort and determination it requires on the part of the Blacks, and that there is a substantial number of people who do not naturally possess the qualities it takes and therefore cannot succeed in the present system.

To some extent this is recognized in the general conclusion of the Kerner Commission that what is needed are short-run programs to "enrich" the ghetto and long-run programs to integrate the people of the ghetto. (Distinction should be made between enrichment as a goal and enrichment as a stage toward the goal of integration. . . . It is the latter concept with which we are most concerned.) Thus we need programs aimed at restructuring the economic environment of the ghetto to provide a chance for programs emphasizing individual "treatment" to work. In addition to creating the skills necessary to work at a particular occupation, programs will have to create the occupations themselves in an environment free of the pressures of prowhite bias so that the hard-core ghetto adult can develop into a confident competitive worker. This means creating an economic foundation within the ghetto itself to provide jobs and opportunities where the people are.

It may mean a great deal more in cost and subsidy (including the provision of protected markets), than that which is being invested in the successful unemployed ghetto resident who finds a permanent job in the suburbs through an employment program, but it must be remembered that we are talking here about those who are not able to compete in that environment and for whom that trip to the suburbs is truly going to another country. For those people it may be that "gilding the ghetto" in the long run is the most effective policy we can have.

## SEPARATISM

The charge that economic development of ghetto areas will encourage racial segregation and undo the progress toward integration of the past eight years is a serious one. It must be seriously addressed because, despite some rhetoric to the contrary, a dual society or dual economy is not a realistic solution for anyone, Black or white. If ghetto economic development has the effect of encouraging racial segregation, it is not a justifiable program.

We should begin, however, by acknowledging that integration is not merely an interaction between Black and white individuals, but a relationship based upon a recognition and respect for the opposite party's equal status. An economic institution such as slavery is clearly not integration (although in the limited sense of personal interaction, the plantation may have been a great deal more integrated than today's typical American metropolitan area). A negotiation between a free buyer and free seller of a product or service clearly is integration. At first glance the employee–employer relationship would seem to qualify. But because the Black man's image, both in his own eyes and the eyes of the white, has been one of inferiority, the employee–employer relationship often reinforces this sense of inferiority and makes little headway against a segregated society. If the jobs currently being developed were career jobs which carried with them a sense of worth, one might have some hope that jobs alone could break down the racial barriers dividing our society. But this has not been the case.

## ECONOMIC INTEGRATION

What is currently lacking in the Black ghetto is the development of institutions which interact with the white community on the basis of equality. The point has been made in many places that such institutions have played an important part in the successful integration of European immigrant groups. Jewish retail stores, Irish police forces, Italian construction companies are the easily recognized examples of this. They all provided a group support for individual contacts with the surrounding dominant ethnic groups. Through this mutual support these institutions developed a power base that forced a respect for their members and at that point real integration became possible.

The function of these institutions is not only to gain respect for the ethnic group involved, but to provide shelter and assistance for the weaker, less competitive individuals. A successful strong business or political machine can afford to carry a few people for the sake of ethnic solidarity. In turn, these institutions can expect the support of their constituencies when they are in competition with institutions controlled by the dominant ethnic groups.

It is clear that this kind of institution-building has been lacking in the Black ghetto. The reasons are not difficult to discern, given a knowledge of the unique history of the Black man in America. The task now, however, is to help accelerate the building of these institutions by allowing for the development of Black economic and political power within the ghetto.

The creation of a Black-owned business goes far beyond the incremental income that may accrue from ownership of a business. The real significance is its control over resources. The Black manager or entrepreneur buys. He hires. He deals with suppliers. He establishes credit. He is engaged in a continual relationship with the white community and by so doing acts as a bridge to the long-run goal of a socially and economically integrated society.

It is unlikely that the benefits from this sort of operation can be precisely measured. It involves a process which has implications far beyond the balance sheet of a Black-owned business. An investment in opening up a menial job for a Black man in a white firm, at the most, mildly increases the total level of Black–white interaction and hardly has any impact at all on integration. The establishment of a Black business, however, increases the amount of real integration in the nation by creating situations in which both parties bargain as equals. Rather than being an obstacle to integration, the growth of Black economic power has as a major goal the building of meaningful links between the races, a goal which will not be achieved by exclusive reliance upon employment programs.*

COMMUNITY DEVELOPMENT

The events of the past few years have demonstrated how difficult it is to accelerate the pace of residential integration for poor Blacks. Even the most optimistic projection of expenditures for public programs aimed at solving this problem implies that a large portion of those currently trapped in urban ghettos will continue to live there for years to come.

That life must be improved. As part of efforts to improve it, the provision of adequate shopping facilities and consumer services would play an important role. Compared to the typical suburban area, the typical ghetto is woefully underserviced in terms of food and clothing stores, laundry services, banks, etc. Clearly, some of this is attributable to low income, but much of it is a result of the generally deteriorating conditions of life in the ghetto. Threat of riot, refusal of landlords to improve com-

---

* For greater elaboration on this point see Stewart E. Perry, "Black Institutions, Black Separatism, and Ghetto Economic Development" (Paper read at Society for Applied Anthropology meeting, Mexico City, April 9–15, 1969).

mercial property, impossibly high insurance rates, refusal of suppliers to supply credit and often even to deliver goods to the ghetto merchant, all have drastically reduced the number of businesses serving the inner city. The result in turn is a further drift into hopelessness and an aggravation of the tensions between the ghetto population and the community at large.

Economic development programs aimed at the development of the commercial sector of the ghetto economy will not only increase access to services and quality goods but can help in reducing the higher prices that the poor have to pay to obtain goods. Economic development can provide such things as access to reasonable credit for ghetto businesses, cooperative arrangements to improve merchants' bargaining power with suppliers and financing for decent facilities to attract a greater flow of customers. It can also provide for sufficient competition among ghetto businesses to help assure that reductions in the cost structure are, in turn, passed on to the consumers.

The ultimate goal of community-based ghetto economic development should be the total renewal of the ghetto and not only the creation of minor and modest scale ghetto-controlled enterprises. This leads us to the issue of ghetto urban renewal programs which, once begun, have either foundered upon the resistance of the ghetto to be renewed, or, *were* never begun due to the obvious hostility of the ghetto to the traditional method utilized in the urban renewal of low-income residential enclaves. Urban renewal of primarily residential ghettos, unlike the development of specific businesses, provides the opportunity for adequate scale investment to radically alter the living environment and, at the same time, create large-scale entrepreneurial opportunities for ghetto-controlled community corporations in construction of housing, office buildings, and retail centers, and also in the financing and management of such structures and businesses.

Ghetto-controlled urban renewal will also provide the opportunity to exploit new production–construction systems now proven in Europe and Israel and soon to be imported into the United States. This will represent a major opportunity for ghetto entrepreneurs to share in a new technology at the earliest stage of its development.

This may be seen as "separatism" with a vengeance, but it appears to be the only approach available to the government that would be acceptable to current ghetto leadership. It is the only alternative to governmental paralysis in urban renewal. Such an approach may well achieve the stated goals of both urban renewal and Black economic development.

### LEADERSHIP MODELS

Another social benefit is the establishment of a Black entrepreneurial and managerial class within the ghetto itself to provide the leadership and models for male behavior which the ghettos so sorely lack. One of the great failures of poverty programs is the failure to attract the uneducated young adult males upon whose shoulders the destiny of the Black ghetto ulti-

mately rests. Aside from paid professional staff, the activists in most of
these programs have been the "preachers and the women." Manpower
training programs which at the beginning did attract the young males
have in too many cases resulted in dead ends. The result is that the models
are still not there and we still search in vain for motivation. A principal
hypothesis of ghetto enterprise development programs is that they can
attract and engage the interest of young males. Business in American
society is man's work. It carries with it the independence and power and
the promise of reward which no other program can match.

THE BENEFITS OF NEIGHBORHOOD CONTROL

The renewed interest in Black enterprise has moved beyond the traditional organizational modes of doing business. Some of these new organizational arrangements, such as those which involve joint ventures between
Black businessmen and established white firms, protected subcontract
markets, and franchises are variations on old themes. In one way or
another they continue the basic models of individual entrepreneurship or
corporate capitalism. Thus aid is given to existing or potential individual
businessmen in an effort to overcome and compensate for the patterns of
discrimination they face. In this regard the Black businessman is treated
like a separate problem group—like the aged, or prekindergarten children,
or high school dropouts between the ages of seventeen and twenty-one.

It is undeniable that minority businessmen are discriminated against.
The great exertions a Black businessman must go through in order to
obtain the considerations other businessmen take for granted have
severely restricted the growth of a Black middle class. Programs to expand
credit availability, to provide technical assistance, to liberalize bonding and
insurance standards and to provide easier access to markets for minority
entrepreneurs should be immediately intensified. It may be, however, that
by limiting our energies to solving the problems of the Black businessman
we are missing another, somewhat different, opportunity for helping to
resolve the urban crisis.

This opportunity reflects the evolution of ghetto poverty programs and
ghetto organizations over the past four or five years. While any generaliza-
tions about so complex a system as the urban ghetto should be made with
great care, many, if not most, of the active leadership groups seem to have
gone through roughly parallel experiences. At the beginning, the poverty
organizations had a decidedly welfare and social service orientation. The
people running programs by and large were those who began from some
organizational base—churches and civil rights groups, settlement houses,
social service organizations, etc. After a while, however, the increase in
resources and power represented by the local community action program
and its affiliates began to draw in younger people and, in staff jobs, Black
male leaders. At the same time, the program orientation changed. Manpower training became the major thrust, which reinforced the development of Black male leadership. For the reasons cited in the previous sec-

tion, manpower programs have been disappointing and the belief in (and thus the importance of) short-term integration on the part of this new leadership has diminished.

We are now, therefore, at a point where a new generation of Black male leadership is emerging in the neighborhoods and ghetto organizations. This is a leadership anxious to test its strength and eager to build on the growing Black consciousness of its constituency. For many, the next most logical program step is in the area of economic development. Economic development programs not only have the promise of creating employment and income and entrepreneurial experience, but in the eyes of many Black leaders, they offer freedom from the white man's charity which they feel is essential for the growth of self-confidence and self-respect among the Black population. Since federal programs and federal bureaucrats are the most immediate manifestation of the white man's charity, they are often the first target.

From the local level, federal grant programs appear extremely haphazard, and often sinister. They are uncoordinated (an approach which has certain virtues) and are subject to delays, red tape, and political whimsy. Attempting to increase "administrative efficiency" is not the answer. The trouble is not with the people who run the bureaucratic system but with the system itself. As long as programs are subject to fiscal year funding and as long as the critical decisions are made by individual bureaucrats (no matter how bright or well-intentioned) and thereby subject to political pressures, rational planning and mutual confidence will be hard to come by.

Inasmuch as "independence" is so often equated with "financial independence" in our society, it is quite natural that the recent experience should generate an interest in controlling resources through ownership of business. At times this results in the naive assumption that meaningful social programs could be financed from the immediate profits of Black-owned businesses. But short of this, there is much sense in the notion that (aside from whatever income benefits may occur) ownership and control of businesses and other economic institutions provide an independent base for the extension of influence that federal programs cannot provide. It may well be that in the long run an expansion of business ownership by the Black community organizations will do more to change the schools, attitudes of policy, etc., than categorical federal grants could ever do. A fundamental change in the milieu of the ghetto may produce such a serendipitous effect.

The fact that community organizations perceive that economic development meets their needs does not by itself justify a public investment in economic development programs. There are, however, at least two important programmatic reasons for establishing economic development programs with broad-based community support. First of all, it is becoming increasingly more difficult for any federal program to operate in a ghetto without reference to the social and political forces within the ghetto. The civil rights movement and several years of operating community action programs have made a change in the ghetto environment. Poor Black people are generally more sophisticated about their plight than used to be the case, and they have become skilled in the techniques of organization and communication with the relevant elements in the white community. As a result, it has become virtually impossible to implement any meaningful program without active community participation. The drive for community control is not a figment of some social scientists' imagination. Regardless of the ultimate fate of the concept, it is an honest alternative generated by the failure of traditional institutions to respond to the legitimate human needs of the ghetto population. The recent history of every new program dealing with inner-city problems testifies to this. Model Cities, in which the demands of inner-city residents all over the country have led to more "citizen participation" than Congress had ever dreamed of, is a case in point. Ghetto economic development must be predicated on these new institutional structures controlled by the ghettos themselves.

The second program reason for community control is directly related to the fact that the social utility of ghetto economic development involves multiple benefits. As long as programs involve single, separate, quantifiable outputs such as total employment, total number of houses built, etc., a strong case can be made for having the ultimate control of the program in the hands of the technicians who are better equipped to achieve these goals and to optimize the various combinations of benefit–cost relationships. As previously described, however, ghetto economic development involves multiple goals and thus requires that tradeoff decisions be made involving nonquantifiable comparisons. Given the fact that the state of the art of cost–benefit analysis is, and for the near-term future will continue to be, much too crude to permit any semblance of objective cross comparisons of social benefits, the question becomes, Who should decide between social benefits? If both cost the same, does a program that brings a supermarket to a ghetto area result in more social benefit than an electronics subcontracting plant which hires more men but does not add to the living environment? Is it better to invest a given amount in such a way as to create ten entrepreneurs or thirty unskilled workers? These are questions that will involve subjective and arbitrary judgments. If someone has to make these judgments, it is a reasonable assumption that the perception of the community which has to suffer any mistakes is a better guide than the perception of outside professionals who lack both the conceptual framework and the data for rational analysis. The population of target areas know what it is to live without adequate shopping facilities. They know what it is to live amid an army of unemployed, unskilled males.

This does not mean that ghetto residents can develop their community without outside help. It is as wrong-headed to think that poor unskilled people can operate successful programs alone as it is to assume that professionals can operate programs alone. This is particularly true in programs of business development which by nature involve complex interrelationships between people, considerable technical competence, and presume a certain common frame of reference among participants. The trick, therefore, is to find the combination of community control and technical capability which will produce responsive policies and competent programs. In effect, the authors support the partnership concept between Black ghetto institutions and the reigning white establishment, with government playing a "marriage broker" role by equipping the ghetto institutions with the fiscal base to negotiate as equals. Without this governmental role it is unlikely that such "marriages" will be consummated in our time.

From the point of view of public policy, there is a final advantage in community-controlled programs. Conventional programs in this area, such as those run by the Small Business Administration and the Economic Development Administration, are built upon an assumption of arbitrary power by the administering bureaucracy. The power to finance one man and deny another lies in most instances with individual bureaucrats whose interests and goals may or may not be in sympathy with the stated goals of a program. More important, perhaps, is that the existence of arbitrary power makes every decision subject to political pressure.

In the private sector, the existence of this kind of power on the part of individuals in financial institutions can be rationalized since, in theory at least, all action can be judged on the basis of maximizing profitability. In the public sector, however, there is no profit guide and political decisions (constrained only by the possibility of large losses) are made much more easily.

The question, therefore, arises as to why individual bureaucrats should have the power to grant public resources to individuals. It would seem that allowing representative community organizations to make the judgments with the aid of competent technical assistance is basically a more legitimate means of disbursing the public treasury.

EVALUATION

Identification of social benefits is just a first step. The probability of a continued shortage of public expenditures on ghetto problems suggests that each and every investment in economic development as well as other programs must be scrutinized closely in order to gain the maximum effectiveness for such expenditures.

If the foregoing description of the multiple benefits of ghetto economic development and the nature of those benefits is valid, it is clear that much broader and more sophisticated evaluation techniques must be developed. The problem is not unique to economic development programs. In fact, the absence of evaluation procedures adequate to deal with multigoal programs and nonquantifiable benefits may be a critical bottleneck to the development of innovative programs. As long as numbers are the only possible justification for program judgments (other than politics) our ability to resolve our domestic problems will be inhibited, even if available resources expand. The spectacle of federal officials solemnly describing to the Congress the numerical benefits of programs which all objective observers agree have failed, but which continue because they generate quantifiable outputs, is a commentary on the *real* failure of social science.

In developing new evaluation techniques for ghetto business programs, the following principles must be considered:

1. Since the participation in decision making by the target community is essential in order to arrive at tradeoffs, the evaluation of the program must also include the community's own perception of the net effectiveness of a given program or set of programs.

Random samples of the ghetto population should be made periodically. Questions can be designed to provide information on postulated benefits of specific programs, e.g., the effect of local Black entrepreneurship on the aspirations of young males, the extent to which ownership and control of resources has increased the degree of respect being shown ghetto people by representatives of the community at large.

Questions can also be designed to gather information on degree of total satisfaction with programs, thus implicitly dealing with the effectiveness of tradeoffs between goals. All programs involving substantial expenditures should be subject to an ongoing evaluation by the ghetto residents and no major program decisions should be made without an analysis of this kind of data.

2. Both economic development programs and the problems to which they are addressed exist in a relatively long-term framework. The building up of an economic power base in the ghetto as a means of attaining the full integration of society cannot be judged a success or failure in the space of a fiscal year. It is not unusual for successful new businesses to take three years to come into the black, and it will certainly take as long for complex community-based programs to begin to show significant measurable final outputs. This does not mean that programs cannot be evaluated at all before several years have elapsed. Incidents in the process of program implementation can be identified and used to measure individual performance. It does mean, however, that short-term payoffs are likely to be rare and if the expectation of such benefits is aroused economic development programs are sure to fail. It would be the height of irresponsibility to establish evaluation requirements which do not allow for a sufficient length of time for economic development programs to work out their impact.

3. Finally, the evaluation of social utility must proceed beyond the analysis of available quantifiable data. If the program goals involve more than employment and income, then they must be evaluated in terms which also include more than employment and income. This requires courage. The attractiveness of conventional statistical data is its ability to serve as a substitute for individual judgment and therefore absorb the blame for program mistakes. In this capacity, it serves congressmen and bureaucrats (in both public and private sectors) and provides a sound long-term market for highly specialized statistical services. The attempt to go beyond the easily quantifiable must be made, however, for without some understanding of the social benefits of economic development the program will not survive long enough to be effective.

4. Due to the absence of adequate evaluation methods, and recognizing that everything related to programming in the ghetto appears to be charged

with an exaggerated rhetoric generating either excessively hopeful expectations or a feeling of being "conned" again, it is the authors' conviction that it is most important that Black economic development not be oversold as a panacea. Community-based Black economic development should be presented as the latest weapon in the fight against poverty and racism, but not meant to supplant or supersede the manpower and social service programs currently extant. In the age of promotion this is an essential caution.

To sum up, the development of Black-owned enterprises with a strong community base can achieve a number of social benefits that other programs cannot. It may well be that the cost "per achievement" will be higher than the cost "per job" of the conventional approaches of the anti-poverty program. If so, the nation will have to decide whether the social benefits described above, which include those aimed at helping provide a permanent resolution of our social crisis through the creation of strong economic institutions, are worth the cost.

# 22 ]] Alternatives to the Gilded Ghetto

*John F. Kain and Joseph J. Persky*

Nothing less than a complete change in the structure of the metropolis will solve the problem of the ghetto. It is therefore ironic that current programs which ostensibly are concerned with the welfare of urban Negroes are willing to accept, and are even based on, the permanence of central ghettos. Thus, under every heading of social welfare legislation—education, income transfer, employment, and housing—we find programs that can only serve to strengthen the ghetto and the serious problems that it generates. In particular, these programs concentrate on beautifying the fundamentally ugly structure of the current metropolis and not on providing individuals with the tools necessary to break out of that structure. The shame of the situation is that viable alternatives *do* exist.

Thus, in approaching the problems of Negro employment, first steps could be an improved information system at the disposal of Negro job seekers, strong training programs linked to job placement in industry, and improved transit access between central ghettos and outlying employment areas. Besides the direct effects of such programs on unemployment and incomes, they have the added advantage of encouraging the dispersion of the ghetto and not its further concentration. For example, Negroes employed in suburban areas distant from the ghetto have strong incentives to reduce the time and cost of commuting by seeking out residences near their work places. Frequent informal contact with white coworkers will both increase their information about housing in predominantly white residential areas and help to break down the mutual distrust that is usually associated with the process of integration.

Prospects of housing desegregation would be much enhanced by major changes in urban renewal and housing programs. Current schemes accept and reinforce some of the worst aspects of the housing market. Thus, even the best urban renewal projects involve the government in drastically reducing the supply (and thereby increasing the cost) of low income housing—all this at great expense to the taxpayer. At best there is an implicit acceptance of the alleged desire of the poor to remain in central city slums. At worst, current programs could be viewed as a concerted effort to maintain the ghetto. The same observation can be made about public housing programs. The Commission on Civil Rights in its report on school segregation concluded that government policies for low cost housing were "further reinforcing the trend toward racial and economic separation in metropolitan areas."

From John F. Kain and Joseph J. Persky in *Race and Poverty: The Economics of Discrimination*, John F. Kain, ed. (Englewood Cliffs, N.J.: Prentice-Hall, 1969). Reprinted by permission.

An alternative approach would aim at drastically expanding the supply of low income housing *outside* the ghetto. Given the high costs of re-claiming land in central areas, subsidies equivalent to existing urban renewal expenditures for use anywhere in the metropolitan area would lead to the construction of many more units. The new mix by type and location would be likely to favor small, single-family homes and garden apartments on the urban periphery. Some overbuilding would be desirable, the object being the creation of a glut in the low income suburban housing market. It is hard to imagine a situation that would make developers and renters less sensitive to skin color.

These measures would be greatly reinforced by programs that increase the effective demand of Negroes for housing. Rent subsidies to individuals are highly desirable, because they represent the transfer of purchasing power that can be used anywhere in the metropolitan area. Other in-come transfer programs not specifically tied to housing would have similar advantages in improving the prospects of ghetto dispersal. Vigorous en-forcement of open housing statutes would aid the performance of the "impersonal" market, perhaps most importantly by providing developers, lenders, and realtors with an excuse to act in their own self-interest.

## Suburbanization of the Negro

Even in the face of continuing practices of residential segregation, the suburbanization of the Negro can still continue apace. It is important to realize that the presence of Negroes in the suburbs does not necessarily imply Negro integration into white residential neighborhoods. Suburbaniza-tion of the Negro and housing integration are not synonymous. Many of the disadvantages of massive, central ghettos would be overcome if they were replaced or even augmented by smaller, dispersed Negro *commu-nities*. Such a pattern would remove the limitations on Negro employ-ment opportunities attributable to the geography of the ghetto. Similarly, the reduced pressure on central city housing markets would improve the prospects for the renewal of middle-income neighborhoods through the operations of the private market. Once the peripheral growth of central city ghettos is checked, the demands for costly investment in specialized, long-distance transport facilities serving central employment areas would be reduced. In addition programs designed to reduce de facto school segregation by means of redistributing, bussing, and similar measures would be much more feasible.

Although such a segregated pattern does not represent the authors' idea of a more open society, it could still prove a valuable first step toward the goal. Most groups attempting to integrate suburban neigh-borhoods have placed great stress on achieving and maintaining some preconceived interracial balance. Because integration is the goal, they feel the need to proceed slowly and make elaborate precautions to avoid "tipping" the neighborhood. The result has been a small, Black

trickle into all-white suburbs. But if the immediate goal is seen as destroying the ghetto, different strategies should be employed. "Tipping,"
rather than something to be carefully avoided, might be viewed as a
tactic for opening large amounts of suburban housing. If enough suburban
neighborhoods are "tipped," the danger of any one of them becoming a
massive ghetto would be small.

Education is still another tool that can be used to weaken the ties of
the ghetto. Formal schooling plays a particularly important role in preparing individuals to participate in the complex urban society of today.
It greatly enhances their ability to compete in the job market with the
promise of higher incomes. As a result, large-scale programs of compensatory education can make important contributions to a strategy of weakening and eventually abolishing the Negro ghetto. Nevertheless, the important gains of such compensatory programs must be continually weighed
against the more general advantages of school desegregation. Where real
alternatives exist in the short run, programs consistent with this latter
objective should always be chosen. It is important to note that truly
effective programs of compensatory education are likely to be extremely
expensive and that strategies involving significant amounts of desegregation may achieve the same educational objectives at much lower costs.

Bussing of Negro students may be such a program. Like better access
to suburban employment for ghetto job seekers, bussing would weaken the
geographic dominance of the ghetto. Just as the informal experience of
integration on the job is an important element in changing racial attitudes,
integration in the classroom is a powerful learning experience. Insofar as
the resistance of suburban communities to accepting low-income residents
and students is the result of a narrow cost-minimization calculus that
attempts to avoid providing public services and in particular education,
substantial state and federal subsidies for the education of low-income
students can prove an effective carrot. Title I programs of the Elementary
and Secondary Education Act of 1965 and grants to areas containing large
federal installations are precedents. Subsidies should be large enough
to cover more than the marginal cost of educating students from low-
income families, and should make it *profitable* for communities and school
districts to accept such students. The experience of the METCO program in Boston strongly suggests that suburban communities can be
induced to accept ghetto school children if external sources of financing
are available.

Because the above proposals would still leave unanswered some immediate needs of ghetto residents, a strong argument can be made
for direct income transfers. Although certain constraints on the use
of funds, for example rent supplements, might be maintained, the emphasis should be on providing resources to individuals and not on freezing
them into geographic areas. The extent to which welfare schemes are
currently tied to particular neighborhoods or communities should be determined, and these programs should be altered so as to remove such
limitations on mobility. Keeping in mind the crucial links between the

ghetto and the rural South, it is essential that southern Negro share in these income transfers.

## The Ghetto and the Nation

Although there are major benefits to be gained by both the Negro community and the metropolis at large through a dispersal of the central ghetto, these benefits cannot be realized and are likely to be hindered by programs aimed at making the ghetto a more livable place. In addition to the important objections discussed so far, there is the very real possibility that such programs will run afoul of major migration links with the Negro population of the South. A striking example of this problem can be seen in the issue of ghetto job creation, one of the most popular proposals to improve the ghetto.

Although ghetto job creation, like other "gilding" programs, might initially reduce Negro unemployment, it must eventually affect the system that binds the Northern ghetto to the rural and urban areas of the South. This system will react to any sudden changes in employment and income opportunities in northern ghettos. If there are no offsetting improvements in the South, the result will be increased rates of migration into still restricted ghetto areas. While we need to know much more than we now do about the elasticity of migration to various economic improvements, the direction of the effect is clear. Indeed it is possible that more than one migrant would appear in the ghetto for every job created. Even at lower levels of sensitivity, a strong wave of in-migration could prove extremely harmful to many other programs. The South in 1960 still accounted for about 60 percent of the country's Negro population, more than half of which lived in nonmetropolitan areas. In particular, the number of *potential* migrants from the rural South has not declined greatly in recent years.

\*       \*       \*

Although the differential in white and Negro migration is clearly related to differential economic opportunity, the overall level of southern out-migration must be ascribed to the underdeveloped nature of the region. A more rapid pace of southern economic development could change these historic patterns of Negro migration. Tentative research findings indicate that both manufacturing growth and urbanization in the South reduce Negro out-migration. Although the holding effect of these changes is not so strong for Negroes as for whites, the difference between the two responses can be substantially narrowed. If development took place at a higher rate, the job market would tighten and thus encourage Negroes to stay. Moreover, the *quid pro quo* for large scale subsidies for southern development might be strong commitments to hire Negro applicants. A serious program of southern development is worthwhile in its own right as a cure to a century of imbalance in the distribution of economic activity in the nation. From the narrow viewpoint of the North, however, the economic development of the South can play a crucial role in providing leverage in the handling of metropolitan problems.

Belated recognition of the problems created for northern metropolitan areas by these large-scale streams of rural migration have led in recent months to a large number of proposals to encourage development in rural areas. Not surprisingly the Department of Agriculture has been quick to seize the opportunities provided. A "rural renaissance" has been its response. Full-page advertisements headed, "To save our cities, We must have rural–urban balance," have appeared in a large number of magazines under the aegis of the National Rural Electric Cooperative Association. These proposals invariably fail to recognize that Negro migration from the rural South differs in important respects from rural–urban migration and has different consequences. Failing as they do to distinguish between beneficial and potentially disruptive migration, these proposals for large-scale programs to keep people on the farms, everywhere, are likely to lead to great waste and inefficiency, while failing to come to grips with the problem that motivated the original concern.

## Improving Skills

A second important approach to easing the pressure on the ghetto is to improve the educational and skill level of incoming migrants. An investment in the under-utilized human resource represented by the southern white and Negro will pay off in either an expanded southern economy or a northern metropolitan job market. Indeed, it is just this flexibility that makes programs oriented to individuals so attractive in comparison to programs oriented to geography. To the extent that a potential migrant can gain skills in demand, his integration into the metropolis, North or South, is that much eased. In light of these benefits, progress in southern schools has been pitifully slow. Southern Negro achievement levels are the lowest for any group in the country. Southern states with small tax bases and high fertility rates have found it expedient in the past to spend as little as possible on Negro education. Much of the rationalization for this policy is based on the fact that a large proportion of southern Negroes will migrate and thus deprive the area of whatever educational investment is made in them. This fact undoubtedly has led to some under-investment in the education of southern whites as well, but the brunt has been borne by the Negro community.

Clearly it is to the advantage of those areas that are likely to receive these migrants to guarantee their ability to cope with an urban environment. This would be in sharp contrast to migrants who move to the ghetto dependent on the social services of the community and unable to venture into the larger world of the metropolis. Nor are the impacts of inadequate southern education limited to the first generation of Negro migrants. Parents ill-equipped to adjust to complex urban patterns are unlikely to provide the support necessary for preparing children to cope with a hostile environment. The pattern can be clearly seen in the second generation's reaction to life in the ghetto. It is the children of migrants and not the migrants themselves who seem most prone to riot in the city.

Thus, education of potential migrants is of great importance to both the North and South. The value of the investment is compounded by the extent to which the overall level of Negro opportunity is expanded. In the North, this is dependent on a weakening of the constricting ties of the ghetto. In the South it depends on economic development per se.

## Concluding Thoughts

This article has considered alternative strategies for the urban ghetto in light of the strong economic and social link of that community to the metropolis in which it is imbedded and to the nation as a whole. In particular the analysis has centered on the likely repercussions of "gilding programs."

Included prominently among these programs are a variety of proposals designed to attract industry to metropolitan ghettos. There have also been numerous proposals for massive expenditures on compensatory education, housing, welfare, and the like. Model cities programs must be included under this rubric. All such proposals aim at raising the employment, incomes, and well-being of ghetto residents, *within* the existing framework of racial discrimination.

Much of the political appeal of these programs lies in their ability to attract support from a wide spectrum ranging from white separatists, to liberals, to advocates of Black power. However, there is an overriding objection to this approach. "Gilding" programs must accept as given a continued growth of Negro ghettos, ghettos which are directly or indirectly responsible for the failure of urban renewal, the crisis in central city finance, urban transportation problems, Negro unemployment, and the inadequacy of metropolitan school systems. Ghetto gilding programs, apart from being objectionable on moral grounds, accept a very large cost in terms of economic inefficiency, while making the solution of many social problems inordinately difficult.

A final objection is that such programs may not work at all, if pursued in isolation. The ultimate result of efforts to increase Negro incomes or reduce Negro unemployment in central city ghettos may be simply to induce a much higher rate of migration of Negroes from southern rural areas. This will accelerate the already rapid growth of Black ghettos, complicating the already impressive list of urban problems.

Recognition of the migration link between northern ghettos and southern rural areas has led in recent months to proposals to subsidize economic development, educational opportunities, and living standards in rural areas. It is important to clarify the valuable, but limited, contributions well-designed programs of this kind can make to the problems of the metropolitan ghetto. Antimigration and migrant improvement programs cannot in themselves improve conditions in northern ghettos. They cannot overcome the prejudice, discrimination, low incomes, and lack of education that are the underlying "causes" of ghetto unrest. At best they are complementary to programs intended to deal directly with ghetto problems. Their greatest value would be in permitting an aggressive assault on the problems of the ghetto—their role is that of a counterweight which permits meaningful and large-scale programs within *metropolitan* areas.

What form should this larger effort take? It would seem that ghetto dispersal is the only strategy that promises a long-run solution. In support of this contention we have identified three important arguments:

1. None of the other programs will reduce the distortions of metropolitan growth and loss of efficiency that result from the continued rapid expansion of "massive" Negro ghettos in metropolitan areas.

2. Ghetto dispersal programs would generally lower the costs of achieving many objectives that are posited by ghetto improvement or gilding schemes.

3. As between ghetto gilding and ghetto dispersal strategies, only the latter is consistent with stated goals of American society.

The conclusion is straightforword. Where alternatives exist, and it has been a major effort of this article to show that they do exist, considerable weight must be placed on their differential impact on the ghetto. Programs that tend to strengthen this segregated pattern should generally be rejected in favor of programs that achieve the same objectives while weakening the ghetto. Such a strategy is not only consistent with the nation's long-run goals, but will often be substantially cheaper in the short run.

# 23 ]] Economic Development:
# Liberation or Liberalism

*Alan Haber*

Economic development, the latest battle cry of social reformers, has replaced, or at least equaled, community action and social services as the chief hope for progress in the ghetto. Such hope reflects continued optimism that constructive and substantial programs can be found to rescue the country from the crossfire of riot and repression that is destroying our cities.

The avalanche of proposals, organizations, coalitions, task forces, demonstrations, proclamations, embryonic development corporations and pledges of money bespeaks the urgency with which the leaders of White America now view the ghetto situation. And the convergence of response suggests that even if all else has failed, business and the tried-and-true methods of entrepreneurship can and will save us from the consequences of our history.

I am concerned here not with describing the varied plans or evaluating their specific features. Nor is it necessary to judge the sincerity of the motivation behind them or the keenness with which the eye is kept on profits as well as public interest. There is no point in arguing that massive investments in the ghetto should not be made. The investments will be made, and they are needed. Whatever form they take, they will probably yield some benefit for ghetto residents. What is important at this point, while these programs are still in their infancy and perhaps subject to influence, is to suggest what needs to be done.

It is axiomatic that unless economic development deals with the real problems and forces of the urban situation, it will simply be another false hope, leaving in its wake greater frustration, confusion and human destruction. Since it is not possible to separate the economic issues of jobs and income from the whole complex of oppression, unfreedom and colonization in the ghetto, a development program must address the totality of the problem. If priorities have to be drawn, the pattern of victimization and racism is probably more critical a problem to be attacked by such a program than is the persistence of economic poverty.

The first fact of the ghetto is that it is an economic and administrative colony. The land, housing, businesses and jobs are owned by outsiders

The article "Economic Development: Liberation or Liberalism" by Alan Haber appeared in the Spring 1968 issue of *New Generation*, a quarterly journal of the National Committee on Employment of Youth pp. 18–21.

and, along with governmental "public services," are run in the interests of and according to the rules of outsiders.

The second fact of the ghetto is that it is a racial compound and concentration camp. Except for a tiny minority, there is no way out. The segregation is complete. The arbitrary, largely hostile authority of outside guardians penetrates every aspect of personal and community life.

The third fact of the ghetto is that it exists in a society that is both racist and capitalist. The overwhelming thrust of the dominant culture conveys the inferiority of blackness; the measure of man is his material acquisitions and his status in productive enterprise. The power of money is such that those with much can control those with little.

It is this complex and inseparable reality that produces, and makes legitimate and necessary, the urban rebellions, the rhetoric of black power and the consciousness of black as a mark of "nationality" trapped in the bosom of an alien society. This reality is not made or chosen by the ghetto dweller. If it is to be changed, the work lies not in the "development" of the ghetto but in the reconstruction of the business-as-usual institutions of White America.

For the black, the job is to find, as best he can, liberation within the given situation. It is in terms of this job that the requirements of economic development must be defined.

A development program must get rid of the economic institutions that directly victimize the ghetto. It cannot rely simply on expanding the ghetto economy to produce more opportunities. The economy must be transformed at its core. The nonresident businessmen and absentee property owners must be forced out. Many means are legitimate in reaching this fundamental objective: buying them out; or forcing them out through competition, or boycott, or fear; or burning them out. But so long as property ownership is the essential basis of authority, then the ghetto must *own* the property on which it lives and works.

Self-determination, though, is not the only reason the transfer of ownership is imperative. The development process itself rests on it. Such capital as is now accumulated in the ghetto is quickly taken out, because it is either reflected in the profits of absentee owners or expended in purchases of consumer goods outside the ghetto. The whole potential of internal financing of community development programs is dependent on blocking the leaks by which money leaves the ghetto in profits, rents, interests and consumption. Gaining internal ownership of productive resources is critical to this process. Without the potential for internal financing, development must rely on the availability of outside funds and thereby on the terms set down by outside interests.

Economic development must also be linked to political organization. It must facilitate the creation of a political instrument through which the ghetto can deal with the wider range of institutions that dominate its life—the welfare administration, the school board, the police, the city government and governments beyond the city. Unless the Black community has the political means to affect these governmental and administrative forces, there will be little substantive change in the quality of daily life, even if good jobs are created.

There are many types of links between economic and political development. For instance, internally controlled development corporations should be the agencies—and the only agencies—to accumulate capital and make investment decisions. The form of ownership of new enterprises should draw people together and contribute to collective responsibility. There is a clear preference for cooperative (over private) ownership since co-ops function as community organizing instruments and as democratic decisional structures, as well as economic units. The surplus produced by enterprises should be allocated, in part, to support political organization and action programs, rather than being wholly plowed back into the business or distributed as personal income.

Development efforts must also seek to create a cohesive, self-conscious community structure that increases people's interdependence on one another and their independence from white-dominated institutions. This means the primary emphasis should be on enterprises serving high-demand consumer needs—housing, food, clothing, furniture, repairs and maintenance, entertainment, etc.—even if these are areas of lower profit margin than, say, manufacture for an "export market." It also means the support of noneconomic activities such as social services, cultural institutions and communication media.

Initial focus on distribution of products should be linked to wholesaling and even production. Markets should be expanded by interlock among several or more Black communities, rather than the autonomous development of each ghetto economy or the dependence of ghetto retailing on white manufacturing.

The need for these enterprises to have an organic relation to the ghetto community suggests that a large measure of internal financing must be paired with external capital. The requirement of internal financing makes it likely that development will proceed at a slower rate of growth than that hoped for through massive infusions of outside money.

Finally, development must build economic instruments capable of penetrating the walls of the ghetto. The process of integration must take place, if it is to take place, not by Blacks being absorbed, one by one, into the suburbs, or downtown offices or other frames of reference controlled by the white majority. Instead, blacks must find a way to penetrate white society on a basis that allows them to maintain ties to the power and identity generated in the ghetto.

Thus housing corporations might be concerned not only with rebuilding the ghetto, but also with acquiring land and building beyond the ghetto. Businesses which are to contract to provide services or products outside the ghetto might be focused in markets where they have the potential to become intergral participants in nonghetto economic processes. Ghetto-financed financial institutions might buy into white economic structures—not to produce an ownership stake in the white economy but to have a political voice in the operation of those structures.

Given these requirements of ghetto development, the major proposals emanating from corporation and government circles appear much less promising. For however inventive they are in new financing schemes, new modes of job development, and new types of entreneurship, they do not satisfy the needs of the Black community. They certainly do not contemplate displacing the white-owned core of the ghetto economy, or surrendering the critical investment decisions to the ghetto, or subsidizing political organization, or sacrificing a market return on investment, or excluding themselves from the markets they generate. And they certainly do not envision building an independent economic power that can penetrate the workings of the white economy.

On the other hand, of course, the elements of local ownership I have outlined do not insure that economic development will achieve liberation within the context of the existing American reality. Nor do they insure that particular development decisions will always be "correct" or in the "best interest" of the Black community, though it is obvious that there is no insurance of this under any plan.

It may be that there is no solution to the ghetto problem within the context of American society as its central features are now defined. But at least this approach focuses the critical decisions within the community and makes their handling accessible to the people affected by those decisions. This would create the potential for an internal political and economic democracy, a democracy in which the issues dividing the Black community can be crystallized and fought out concretely rather than rhetorically or by proxy at the behest of white patrons.

It is not for white society to decide for Blacks the questions of separation or integration, nationalism or Americanism, communalism or individualistic capitalism. White society should deal with racism and the perversions of the profit system that have produced the ghetto. Beyond that, it should seek to insure that programs in aid of the ghetto contribute to an internal democracy that allows Black people an opportunity to define for themselves how to come to terms with the reality of the separate and unequal world in which they now live.

# 24 ]] The Black Manifesto: Total Control as the Only Solution to the Economic Problems of Black People

*James Forman*

Brothers and Sisters: we have come from all over the country, burning with anger and despair not only with the miserable economic plight of our people, but fully aware that the racism on which the Western world was built dominates our lives. There can be no separation of the problems of racism from the problems of our economic, political, and cultural degradation. To any Black man, this is clear.

But there are still some of our people who are clinging to the rhetoric of the Negro and we must separate ourselves from those Negroes who go around the country promoting all types of schemes for Black capitalism.

Ironically, some of the most militant Black nationalists, as they call themselves, have been the first to jump on the bandwagon of Black capitalism. They are pimps: Black power pimps and fraudulent leaders and the people must be educated to understand that any Black man or Negro who is advocating a perpetuation of capitalism inside the United States is in fact seeking not only his ultimate destruction and death, but is contributing to the continuous exploitation of Black people all around the world. For it is the power of the United States government, this racist, imperialist government that is choking the life of all people around the world.

We are an African people. We sit back and watch the Jews in this country make Israel a powerful conservative state in the Middle East, but we are not concerned actively about the plight of our brothers in Africa. We are the most advanced technological group of Black people in the world, and there are many skills that could be offered to Africa. At the same time, it must be publicly stated that many African leaders are in disarray themselves, having been duped into following the lines as laid out by the Western imperialist governments.

Africans themselves succumbed to and are victims of the power of the United States. For instance, during the summer of 1967, as the representatives of SNCC, Howard Moore and I traveled extensively in Tanzania and Zambia. We talked to high, very high, government officials. We told

Presented by James Forman to the National Black Economic Development Conference in Detroit, Michigan, April 26, 1969. Reprinted in *The Review of Black Political Economy*, Spring–Summer 1970, pp. 36–44. Reprinted by permission.

them there were many Black people in the United States who were willing to come and work in Africa. All these government officials who were part of the leadership in their respective governments, said they wanted us to send as many skilled people as we could contact. But this program never came into fruition and we do not know the exact reason, for I assure you that we talked and were committed to making this a successful program. It is our guess that the United States put the squeeze on these countries, for such a program directed by SNCC would have been too dangerous to the international prestige of the United States. It is also possible that some of the wild statements by some Black leaders frightened the Africans.

In Africa today, there is a great suspicion of Black people in this country. This is a correct suspicion since most of the Negroes who have left the states for work in Africa usually work for the Central Intelligence Agency (CIA) or the State Department. But the respect for us as a people continues to mount and the day will come when we can return to our homeland as brothers and sisters. But we should not think of going back to Africa today, for we are located in a strategic position. We live inside the United States which is the most barbaric country in the world and we have a chance to help bring this government down.

Time is short and we do not have much time and it is time we stop mincing words. Caution is fine, but no oppressed people ever gained their liberation until they were ready to fight, to use whatever means necessary, including the use of force and power of the gun to bring down the colonizer.

We have heard the rhetoric, but we have not heard the rhetoric which says that Black people in this country must understand that we are the vanguard force. We shall liberate all the people in the United States and we will be instrumental in the liberation of colored people the world around. We must understand this point very clearly so that we are not trapped into diversionary and reactionary movements. Any class analysis of the United States shows very clearly that Black people are the most oppressed group of people inside the United States. We have suffered the most from racism and exploitation, cultural degradation and lack of political power. It follows from the laws of revolution that the most oppressed will make the revolution, but we are not talking about just making the revolution. All the parties on the left who consider themselves revolutionary will say that Blacks are the vanguard, but we are saying that not only are we the vanguard, but we must assume leadership, total control and we must exercise the humanity which is inherent in us. We are the most humane people within the United States. We have suffered and we understand suffering. Our hearts go out to the Vietnamese for we know what it is to suffer under the domination of racist Amercia. Our hearts, our souls and all the compassion we can mount goes out to our brothers in Africa, Santo Domingo, Latin America and Asia who are being tricked by the power structure of the United States which is dominating the world today. These ruthless, barbaric men have systematically tried to kill all people and organizations opposed to its imperialism. We no longer can just get by with the use of the word capitalism to describe the United States, for it is an imperial power, sending money, missionaries and the army throughout the world to protect this government and the few rich whites who control it. General Motors and all the major auto industries are operating in South Africa, yet the white dominated leadership of the United Auto Workers sees no relationship to the exploitation of Black people in South Africa and the exploitation of Black people in the United States. If they understand it, they certainly do not put it into practice which is the actual test. We as Black people must be concerned with the total conditions of all Black people in the world.

But while we talk of revolution, which will be an armed confrontation and long years of sustained guerrilla warfare inside this country, we must also talk of the type of world we want to live in. We must commit ourselves to a society where the total means of production are taken from the rich people and placed into the hands of the state for the welfare of all the people. This is what we mean when we say total control. And we mean that Black people who have suffered the most from exploitation and racism must move to protect their Black interest by assuming leadership inside of the United States of everything that exists. The time has passed when we are second in command and the white boy stands on top. This is especially true of the welfare agencies in this country, but it is not enough to say that a Black man is on top. He must be committed to building the new society, to taking the wealth away from the rich people such as General Motors, Ford, Chrysler, the DuPonts, the Rockefellers, the Mellons, and all the other rich white exploiters and racists who run this world.

Where do we begin? We have already started. We started the moment we were brought to this country. In fact, we started on the shores of Africa, for we have always resisted attempts to make us slaves and now we must resist the attempts to make us capitalists. It is in the financial interest of the United States to make us capitalists, for this will be the same line as that of integration into the mainstream of American life. Therefore, brothers and sisters, there is no need to fall into the trap that we have to get an ideology. We *have* an ideology. Our fight is against racism, capitalism and imperialism and we are dedicated to building a socialist society inside the United States where the total means of production and distribution are in the hands of the state and that must be led by Black people, by revolutionary Blacks who are concerned about the total humanity of this world. And, therefore, we obviously are different from some of those who seek a Black nation in the United States, for there is no way for that nation to be viable, if in fact the United States remains in the hands of white racists. Then too, let us deal with some arguments that we should share power with whites. We say that there must be a revolutionary Black vanguard and that white people in this country must be willing to accept Black leadership, for that is the only protection that Black people have to protect ourselves from racism rising again in this country.

Racism in the United States is so pervasive in the mentality of whites that only an armed, well-disciplined, Black-controlled government can insure the stamping out of racism in this country. And that is why we plead with Black people not to be talking about a few crumbs, a few thousand dollars for this cooperative, or a thousand dollars which splits Black people into fighting over the dollar. That is the intention of the government. We say . . . think in terms of total control of the United States. Prepare ourselves to seize state power. Do not hedge, for time is short and all around the world, the forces of liberation are directing their attacks against the United States. It is a powerful country, but that power is not greater than that of Black people. We work the chief industries in this country and we could cripple the economy while the brothers fought guerrilla warfare in the streets. This will take some long-range planning, but whether it happens in a thousand years is of no consequence. It cannot happen unless we start. How then is all of this related to this conference?

First of all, this conference is called by a set of religious people, Christians who have been involved in the exploitation and rape of Black people since the country was founded. The missionary goes hand in hand with the power of the states. We must begin seizing power wherever we are and we must say to the planners of this conference that you are no longer in charge. We the people who have assembled here thank you for getting us here, but we are going to assume power over the conference and determine from this moment on the direction in which we want it to go. We are not saying that the conference was planned badly. The staff of the conference has worked hard and has done a magnificent job in bringing all of us together and we must include them in the new leadership which must surface from this point on. The conference is now the property of the people who are assembled here. This we proclaim as fact and not rhetoric and there are demands that we are going to make and we insist that the planners of this conference help up implement them.

We maintain we have the revolutionary right to do this. We have the same rights, if you will, as the Christian had in going to Africa and raping our motherland and bringing us away from our continent of peace and into this hostile and alien environment where we have been living in perpetual warfare since 1619.

Our seizure of power at this conference is based on a program and our program is contained in the following manifesto:

## The Manifesto

We the Black people assembled in Detroit, Michigan for the National Black Economic Development Conference are fully aware that we have been forced to come together because racist white America has exploited our resources, our minds, our bodies, our labor. For centuries we have been forced to live as colonized people inside the United States, victimized by the most vicious, racist system in the world. We have helped to build the most industrial country in the world.

We are therefore demanding of the white Christian churches and Jewish synagogues which are part and parcel of the system of capitalism, that they begin to pay reparations to Black people in this country. We are demanding $500 million from the Christian white churches and the Jewish synagogues. This total comes to $15 per nigger. This is a low estimate for we maintain there are probably more than 30 million Black people in this country. Fifteen dollars a nigger is not a large sum of money and we know that the churches and synagogues have a tremendous wealth and [their] membership, White America, has profited and still exploits Black people. We are also not unaware that the exploitation of colored peoples around the world is aided and abetted by the white Christian churches and synagogues. This demand for $500 million is not an idle resolution or empty words. Fifteen dollars for every Black brother and sister in the United States is only a beginning of the reparations due us as people who have been exploited and degraded, brutalized, killed, and persecuted. Underneath all of this exploitation, the racism of this country has produced a psychological effect upon us that we're beginning to shake off. We are no longer afraid to demand our full rights as a people in this decadent society.

We are demanding $50 million to be spent in the following way:

1. We call for the establishment of a southern land bank to help our brothers and sisters who have to leave their land because of racist pressure; for people who want to establish cooperative farms but who have no funds. We have seen too many farmers evicted from their homes because they have dared to defy the white racism of this country. We need money for land. We must fight for massive sums of money for this southern land bank. We call for $200 million to implement this program.

2. We call for the establishment of four major publishing and printing industries in the United States to be funded with $10 million each. These publishing houses are to be located in Detroit, Atlanta, Los Angeles, and New York. They will help to generate capital for further cooperative investments in the Black community, provide jobs, and an alternative to the white-dominated and -controlled printing field.

3. We call for the establishment of four of the most advanced scientific and futuristic audiovisual networks to be located in Detroit, Chicago, Cleveland and Washington, D.C. These TV networks will provide an alternative to the racist propaganda that fill the current television networks. Each of these TV networks will be funded by $10 million each.

4. We call for a research skills center which will provide research on the problems of Black people. This center must be funded with no less than $30 million.

5. We call for the establishment of a training center for the teaching of

skills in community organization, photography, movie making, television making and repair, radio building and repair, and all other skills needed in communication. This training center shall be funded with no less than $10 million.

6. We recognize the role of the National Welfare Rights Organization and we intend to work with it. We call for $10 million to assist in the organiztion of welfare recipients. We want to organize the welfare workers in this country so that they may demand more money from the government and better administration of the welfare system of this country.

7. We call for $20 million to establish a National Black Labor Strike and Defense Fund. This is necessary for the protection of Black workers and their families who are fighting racist working conditions in this country.

* 8. We call for the establishment of the United Black Appeal (UBA). This United Black Appeal will be funded with no less than $20 million. The UBA is charged with producing more capital for the establishment of cooperative businesses in the United States and in Africa, our motherland. The United Black Appeal is one of the most important demands that we are making for we know that it can generate and raise funds throughout the United States and help our African brothers. The UBA is charged with three functions and shall be headed by James Forman:

a. Raising money for the program of the National Black Economic Development Conference.

b. The development of cooperatives in African countries and support of African liberation movements.

c. Establishment of a Black Antidefamation League which will protect our African image.

9. We call for the establishment of a Black University to be funded with $130 million to be located in the South. Negotiations are presently under way with a southern university.

10. We demand that IFCO allocate all unused funds in the planning budget to implement the demands of this conference.

*In order to win our demands we are aware that we will have to have massive support, therefore:*

1. We call upon all Black people throughout the United States to consider themselves as members of the National Black Economic Development Conference and to act in unity to help force the racist white Christian churches and Jewish synagogues to implement these demands.

2. We call upon all the concerned Black people across the country to contact Black workers, Black women, Black students and the Black unemployed, community groups, welfare organizations, teachers' organizations, church leaders and organizations explaining how these demands are vital to the Black community of the United States. Pressure by whatever

* (Revised and approved by Steering Committee).

means necessary should be applied to the white power structure of the racist white Christian churches and Jewish synagogues. All Black people should act boldly in confronting our white oppressors and demanding this modest reparation of $15 per Black man.

3. Delegates and members of the National Black Economic Development Conference are urged to call press conferences in the cities and to attempt to get as many Black organizations as possible to support the demands of the conference. The quick use of the press in the local areas will heighten the tension and these demands must be attempted to be won in a short period of time, although we are prepared for protracted and long-range struggle.

4. We call for the total disruption of selected church-sponsored agencies operating anywhere in the United States and the world. Black workers, Black women, Black students and the Black unemployed are encouraged to seize the offices, telephones, and printing apparatus of all church sponsored agencies and to hold these in trusteeship until our demands are met.

5. We call upon all delegates and members of the National Black Economic Development Conference to stage sit-in demonstrations at selected Black and white churches. This is not to be interpreted as a continuation of the sit-in movement of the early sixties but we know that active confrontation inside white churches is possible and will strengthen the possibility of meeting our demands. Such confrontation can take the form of reading the Black manifesto instead of a sermon or passing it out to church members. The principles of self-defense should be applied if attacked.

6. On May 4, 1969 or a date thereafter, depending upon local conditions, we call upon Black people to commence the disruption of the racist churches and synagogues throughout the United States.

7. We call upon IFCO to serve as a central staff to coordinate the mandate of the conference and to reproduce and distribute en masse literature, leaflets, news items, press releases, and other material.

8. We call upon all delegates to find within the white community those forces which will work under the leadership of Blacks to implement these demands by whatever means necessary. By taking such action, White Americans will demonstrate concretely that they are willing to fight the white-skin privilege and the white supremacy and racism which has forced us as Black people to make these demands.

9. We call upon all white Christians and Jews to practice patience, tolerance, and understanding and nonviolence as they have encouraged, advised and demanded that we as Black people should do throughout our entire enforced slavery in the United States. The true test of their faith and belief in the Cross and the words of the prophets will certainly be put to a test as we seek legitimate and extremely modest reparations for our role in developing the industrial base of the Western world through our slave labor. But we are no longer slaves, we are men and women, proud of our African heritage, demanding to have our dignity.

10. We are so proud of our African heritage and realize concretely

that our struggle is not only to make revolution in the United States, but to protect our brothers and sisters in Africa and to help them rid themselves of racism, capitalism, and imperialism by whatever means necessary, including armed struggle. We are and must be willing to fight the defamation of our African image wherever it rears its ugly head. We are therefore charging the steering committee to create a Black Anti-Defamation League to be funded by money raised from the United Black Appeal.

11. We fully recognize that revolution in the United States and Africa, our motherland, is more than a one-dimensional operation. It will require the total integration of the political, economic, and military components and therefore, we call upon all our brothers and sisters who have acquired training and expertise in the fields of engineering, electronics, research, community organization, physics, biology, chemistry, mathematics, medicine, military science and warfare to assist the National Black Economic Development Conference in the implementation of its program.

12. To implement these demands we must have a fearless leadership. We must have a leadership which is willing to battle the church establishment to implement these demands. To win our demands we will have to declare war on the white Christian churches and synagogues and this means we may have to fight the total government structure of this country. Let no one here think that these demands will be met by our mere stating them. For the sake of the churches and synagogues, we hope that they have the wisdom to understand that these demands are modest and reasonable. But if the white Christians and Jews are not willing to meet our demands through peace and good will, then we delcare war and we are prepared to fight by whatever means necessary. We are, therefore, proposing the election of the following steering committee:

| | | |
|---|---|---|
| Lucius Walker | Ken Cockrel | Mike Hamlin |
| Renny Freeman | Chuck Wooten | Len Holt |
| Luke Tripp | Fannie Lou Hamer | Peter Bernard |
| Howard Fuller | Julian Bond | Michael Wright |
| James Forman | Mark Comfort | Muhammed Kenyatta |
| John Watson | Earl Allen | Mel Jackson |
| Dan Aldridge | Robert Browne | Howard Monroe |
| John Williams | Vincent Harding | Harold Holmes |

*Brothers and sisters, we no longer are shuffling our feet and scratching our heads. We are tall, black and proud.*

And we say to the white Christian churches and Jewish synagogues, to the government of this country and to all the white racist imperialists who compose it, there is only one thing left that you can do to further degrade Black people and that is to kill us. But we have been dying too long for this country. We have died in every war. We are dying in Vietnam today fighting the wrong enemy.

The new Black man wants to live and to live means that we must not become static or merely believe in self-defense. We must boldly go out and attack the white Western world at is power centers. The white Christian churches are another form of government in this country and they are used by the government of this country to exploit the people of Latin America, Asia and Africa, but the day is soon coming to an end. Therefore, brothers and sisters, the demands we make upon the white Christian churches and the Jewish synagogues are small demands. They represent $15 per Black person in these United States. We can legitimately demand this from the church power structure. We must demand more from the United States government.

*But to win our demands from the church which is linked up with the United States government, we must not forget that it will ultimately be by force and power that we will win.*

We are not threatening the churches. We are saying that we know the churches came with the military might of the colonizers and have been sustained by the military might of the colonizers. Hence, if the churches in colonial territories were established by military might, we know deep within our hearts that we must be prepared to use force to get our demands. We are not saying that this is the road we want to take. It is not, but let us be very clear that we are not opposed to force and we are not opposed to violence. We were captured in Africa by violence. We were kept in bondage and political servitude and forced to work as slaves by the military machinery and the Christian church working hand in hand.

We recognize that in issuing this manifesto we must prepare for a long-range educational campaign in all communities of this country, but we know that the Christian churches have contributed to our oppression in white America. We do not intend to abuse our Black brothers and sisters in Black churches who have uncritically accepted Christianity. We want them to understand how the racist white Christian church with its hypocritical declarations and doctrines of brotherhood has abused our trust and faith. An attack on the religious beliefs of Black people is not our major objective, even though we know that we were not Christian when we were brought to this country, but that Christianity was used to help enslave us. Our objective in issuing this manifesto is to force the racist white Christian church to begin the payment of reparations which are due to all Black people, not only by the church but also by private business and the U.S. government. We see this focus on the Christian church as an effort around which all Black people can unite.

*Our demands are negotiable, but they cannot be minimized, they can only be increased and the church is asked to come up with larger sums of money than we are asking. Our slogans are:*

ALL ROADS MUST LEAD TO REVOLUTION
UNITE WITH WHOMEVER YOU CAN UNITE
NEUTRALIZE WHEREVER POSSIBLE

**FIGHT OUR ENEMIES RELENTLESSLY**
**VICTORY TO THE PEOPLE**
**LIFE AND GOOD HEALTH TO MANKIND**
**RESISTANCE TO DOMINATION BY THE WHITE CHRISTIAN**
**CHURCHES AND THE JEWISH SYNAGOGUES**
**REVOLUTION BLACK-POWER**
**WE SHALL WIN WITHOUT A DOUBT**

# 25 ]] Toward an Overall Assessment of Our Alternatives

*Robert S. Browne*

Aware and Concerned Brothers and Sisters, It is with great humility that I have accepted this invitation to deliver the keynote address for this important conference on Black economic development. We are all aware in what a critical period we Black people in America now find ourselves. In the richest nation which the world has ever known, we find ourselves in a position of relative impoverishment. In a nation which boasts of its democratic processes, we find ourselves relatively powerless. In a nation which worships education as the magic key to success, our children are going unlettered. In an era of global nationalism, we are a people without a nation.

Obviously I have only begun to enumerate a few of the ways in which we are a disadvantaged people in this society. And indeed, there is nothing which I have stated which Frederick Douglass, or Booker T. Washington, or Dr. DuBois could not have declared with equal validity sixty-nine or more years ago, as we entered upon this cataclysmic twentieth century. Indeed, they did make many of these very observations to groups not unlike this one. But I feel there is a difference today—not merely the obvious difference that for us today is real whereas they are history—but a qualitative difference which derives from the differing mood of Black people generally. I sense that today's Blacks, and especially the younger ones, are a new breed of Black person. I sense that the old passivity and dependency psychology has been replaced by a psychology of independent action and I sense that the old gradualism has been replaced by a new urgency. And I also suspect that the several hundred people in this auditorium enjoy a capacity for implementation which far surpasses that of any audience which Douglass or Washington or DuBois ever addressed.

It might of course be argued that the obstacles to Black achievement have increased at least as much as has our potential for achievement. I would not agree however. Our oppressors are probably no more vicious than they ever were; naturally their desperation can be expected to increase as they feel more threatened by our successes in fighting free from their grasp, but this is inevitable. Meanwhile, the general world situation has evolved in a manner more favorable to our cause. We have sympathetic allies in every corner of the globe, and modern communications insures

Keynote speech delivered at National Black Economic Development Conference, Detroit, Michigan, April 25, 1969. Reprinted in *The Review of Black Political Economy* Spring–Summer 1970, pp. 18–26. Reprinted by permission.

that world opinion remains constantly apprised of the major happenings in our noble struggle.

However, lest I mislead you into thinking that my address will be cast in an optimistic vein, allow me to move on to some more sobering considerations. The subject of my talk is "the need for formulating an economic plan for Black people." What is an economic plan? The term initially gained its popularity from its usage by the Soviet Union.

In 1928, about a decade after the 1917 revolution, the Soviet Union announced that it was launching a five-year plan for economic development. Since that time it has undertaken several more such plans, and the practice has been widely copied by other Socialist countries as well as by many nonsocialist countries such as India and many of the smaller nations. Indeed, such plans have become a regular part of the economic development process for a growing number of nations. Although differing in some details, the heart of these economic plans is the setting forth of specific goals to be achieved by a certain date, and some plan for attaining these goals. Goals are likely to be such things as: achieving a certain level of industrial productivity in designated categories, a certain level of agricultural production, a certain volume of exports, a certain rise in per capita income, lowering illiteracy by "x" percent, training "x" number of teachers, graduating so many doctors, etc. Obviously, such a plan must be internally consistent if it is to succeed, i.e., a large increase in agricultural production cannot be achieved unless plans are also made for producing (or importing) the necessary fertilizer, farm equipment, etc. Considerable research and data collection must precede the making of any economic development plan so that the goals will in fact be within the realm of possibility.

Does such an economic plan have meaning for Black people in America? It seems to me that the answer is both yes and no. The answer is no because this type of a plan assumes the existence of a nation which has title to a cluster of contiguous resources and which exercises *sovereignty over both itself as a community* and over its members, who must feel themselves to be a part of this community. This sovereignty may be exercised either by consent or by coercion, but it must be effective if there is to be a nation. In effect, there must be a government with the power to govern. Short of this there can be no sovereignty, no nation, no economic development plan in the customary sense of the word.

Black America clearly fails all of these tests. The concepts of gross national product, imports and exports, agricultural or industrial output, etc., are not only measurable for the Black community; they have no meaning. In a rather crude fashion we can measure Black purchasing power, the capitalization of Black-owned business establishments. And with extreme difficulty we might succeed in measuring Black savings and Black land ownership. Next year the census bureau will presumably attempt to measure the magnitude of the Black population and will view with alarm its rate of increase, but I suggest that these magnitudes at present have little meaning in a national sense. It may be quite useful to get these measurements—indeed, urgent to do so—but the mere gathering of such data will not create the necessary conditions for nationhood or for an economic development plan. We are not yet a consciously cohesive community; we do not have sovereignty over ourselves as individuals; we do not have sovereignty over ourselves as a community. That is to say, we cannot draw up final rules for governing ourselves, for taxing ourselves, for conducting foreign relations and trading, for law enforcement, for property rights, for immigration and emigration, nor can we establish our own monetary unit. No, we are far from enjoying the basic prerogatives of nationhood, and despite the presence at this conference of some distinguished brothers who are doing groundbreaking work along these lines, I sense that this conference is not primarily to be concerned with the question of whether national sovereignty is desirable for Blacks or how it can be achieved.

Rather, it seems to me, we have been brought here to discuss the more modest question of what is achievable by Black people within the existing limitations of our *not* enjoying national sovereignty. That is, given the reality that we are, for the moment, inseparably attached to the larger, white, capitalistic American society, what are the most promising techniques which we can utilize to maximize Black well-being.

Admittedly, this is a much more modest objective than the building of a Black nation. It is clearly not an objective which will bring Black people a major degree of control over their destinies. But it may put some additional bread on their tables and ease some chronic illnesses and therefore it is probably worth doing. For the achievement of this more limited objective I think that the concept of an economic plan can have considerable significance—obviously not the classical type of economic planning appropriate to an independent nation, but it is of the utmost importance that Black people sit down and take inventory of where we are, where we hope to get to, and what series of steps seems most likely to get us there. Clearly, this conference did not convene in order to discuss simple band-aids which might be applied to some of the more painful sores on the Black community. As a matter of fact, the white establishment has not been ungenerous with its bandaids—but any child knows that a bandaid is of little help when the limb is broken and bleeding profusely. Surgery may be necessary but short of that, major treatment is certainly called for. The task then of this conference, it seems to me, is to begin to prescribe that treatment. I am even hesitant to suggest that the conference should spend very much time diagnosing our malady, for we have been diagnosed thousands of times and I suspect that there is little new to be said on that count.

Essentially, the illness is that Black people have no handle on the basic levers or sources of power in this country which I conceive to be six in number: (1) accumulations of private wealth—if you want to know who these families are I refer you to the May 1968 issue of Fortune magazine, where most of them are listed together with an estimate of their assets. (2) some 200 major corporations, most of whose annual incomes far exceed the budgets of most of the nations of Africa. The annual revenues of

General Motors Corporation are larger than the gross national product of all but the top fifteen of the nations of the world. (3) The military–industrial complex, centered in the Pentagon and obviously overlapping with the 200 largest corporations which I have just cited. (4) The federal and state governmental apparatus. (5) The federal legislative apparatus. (6) The crime syndicate. In deference to our host city I might add a close seventh—organized labor.

We lack access to these levers of control because of a combination of reasons, the main one being of course the history which we have experienced in this country. When the country was being divided up and raped, we were slaves. Indeed, we were part of the very property which was being divided and raped—literally. So we didn't get in when the melon was being cut and now almost the only way to get a really significant hunk of it is to wrest it away from someone else. We also lack access because we are numerically too small a group, and too dispersed, to have been able to seize control of any one of these levers. This lack of access to the instruments of power, supplemented by white America's vicious racial prejudice toward Black people, has led to our perpetual impoverishment, our self-hatred and psychological insecurity, our poor educational attainment, and our social disorganization.

If this diagnosis is correct, and I suspect that it is a diagnosis to which most Blacks would subscribe, the question then arises: Should our attack be focused on the causes of the malady or on the symptoms? Do we focus on raising Black peoples' wages, enlarging their education and skills, overcoming their psychological insecurities, and building up their social organization? Or do we focus on the causes of our poverty and degradation, namely, our powerlessness, our lack of access to the levers of power in the society?

There will be a natural tendency to respond by saying "Attack the causes, not the symptoms." This is obviously what we usually do in medicine and I am quite sympathetic with this view. If only surface manifestations are changed while the underlying causes are left intact there is always the likelihood of a reeruption of the malignancy. Realistically speaking, however, I see very limited possibility for our grasping the levers of control in this society. True, we have an excellent potential for exercising a sort of negative power, a limited veto so to speak, over how the white establishment uses its power. And we should work toward building this sort of negative power, essentially I suppose via the electoral process but not forgetting that our brothers in the streets have been rather creative about devising other techniques as well.

If we were to decide to go after the causes of our oppression, the sole avenue which might offer some hope for our grabbing a tenuous hold onto one lever of control, and an avenue which could serve a dual purpose of also helping us toward achievement of Black nationhood, would be for Blacks to capture control of one or more state governments. Unlike control of a municipality, control of a state government not only offers tremendous opportunities for developing an extensive corps of Black

technicians but also provides Black people with a somewhat viable economic unit from which to build a tangible sense of community and of
cultural autonomy. Where today are the Black men who can design, build,
and operate giant bridges, hydroelectric installations, water works and
sewage disposal plants, massive port facilities, and other basic elements of
the physical infrastructure of a modern society? If there are such people,
and they can't be many, they are lost in a vast white ocean. There is no
identifiable corps of Blacks with these capabilities. Perhaps as a result, we
have few Blacks studying these skills. I have never forgotten how, in 1961,
at the height of the Lumumba era, I was asked by an official of the
Congolese government if I could recommend about sixty Black mining
engineers to come to the Congo to take over the direction of the Katanga
mines from the Belgians. I hardly need to tell you that I was unable to
produce even one such person. Indeed, as far as I could determine, there
was no record of any Blacks having finshed from the Colorado School of
Mines, which is perhaps the major institution for such study in this
country. Mining engineering is of course only symbolic for an entire range
of very basic technical activities which it would rarely occur to a Black
youngster to pursue, but which Black possession of a state government
might offer some access to. Hopefully, the Cleveland and Gary experiences,
though they may be mere tokens of Black control, and other Black-run
municipalities soon to come, will provide vitally needed opportunities for
our Black youth to gain some new skills and experiences. But a city is a
relatively limited economic unit; it is usually not a viable financial unit
these days; and physically a city is an extremely vulnerable unit in that
it raises no food and is totally dependent on outsiders for its external
communications. Thus it could not serve even as a symbolic homeland for
Black people—nor could a series of such enclaves. For me, the currently
popular "parallel economy" concept takes on meaning not with Black control of a series of geographically separated communities or cities but only
with Black control of a unit at least as large as a state. One avenue of
effort by this conference then might be to explore the feasibility of a legal
Black takeover of one of the fifty states. Such a program would require
extensive research and planning; it would require channeling millions of
dollars into a concentrated voter registration drive in the designated state;
the quiet buying up of large properties and the provision of an economic
base for attracting Black immigrants, etc. The new towns provision of the
Housing Act of 1968 might be of some use here, but needless to say, once
the whites realized what was happening the resistance would be substantial. And let me reiterate that such an effort, although I put it forth
as a form of direct thrust for real power in America, would—even if highly
successful—represent the accretion of only a modest amount of additional
power for Blacks. But it would enormously enhance our capability for
further advance.

Let us, however, return to our consideration of whether we are better
off to focus our attack on the causes of our disadvantage or on the symptoms. Can we launch an effective, direct attack on Black poverty, Black

illiteracy, Black insecurity despite our exclusion from the national power structure? I feel that we can. Our achievements will be of limited scope and will certainly not bring into being The Black nation. But in putting some more bread on the table, in bringing us a greater degree of self-reliance, it will justify itself. It is in this sense that the numerous local development projects, small business programs, job training, consumer education, vocational guidance, school improvement and other community programs are all helpful. I believe such limited goals to be achievable because they do not threaten the superestablishment, the six power centers which I earlier specified. Achieving these limited goals may require expropriating some local landlords and businessmen, it may undermine some petty white racketeers and party hacks, it may deny some government-salaried jobs to some white middle-class professionals, and it may weaken some racist union locals. But none of these groups are part of the national power structure anyway. The superestablishment, recognizing that Blacks must be placated in some way, will be prepared to sacrifice the small fry local white exploiters so that it may continue uninterrupted with its global strategies. Thus we are presented an opportunity and a danger. The opportunity is to utilize our wits to exploit this willingness of the national power structure to meet some of our demands at the expense of the local exploiters. The danger is that we may find ourselves unwitting collaborators in a system which does long-run damage to our self-interest. It is a tricky bag in which we niggers find ourselves.

Certainly we must assume control of our communities. Certainly we must acquire ownership and control of income-producing properties, and most especially those located within our communities. The real estate, the businesses, the public facilities must belong to the community in some form or another. Racketeering, prostitution, the numbers—if they are to continue—must be put into the hands of the community. Education must be made more effective for Black children. We must develop some industry. A larger portion of tax revenues must flow through our hands. I will not dwell on this because I suspect most everyone here agrees. But the implications of some of these demands cut many ways. Fifty percent of federal tax revenues currently go into military expenditures. We are already getting a healthy share of the portion of these expenditures which go for enlisted men's salaries. Do we want to increase this share? Do we want to lobby Washington to award a few defense contracts to the Black community so that we can make tanks and napalm to be used on Black Africans—and on us? Do we want more of our Black brothers in the State Department and the CIA if in fact it means that they will be flying about the world carrying out the Pentagon's repressive policies toward nonwhite nations?

What I am suggesting is that any significant economic development which we achieve will come about largely through political maneuvering, and we must therefore be very together and know exactly what we are doing. There is considerable resistance among Black intellectuals to the concept of Black capitalism and strong support for some sort of communal or cooperative ownership. This is desirable I think, but there is a risk of exagerating the importance of such institutional differences.

In a capitalist, imperialist society, is a cooperatively owned Standard Oil Company likely to be any less exploitative than a privately owned one? If so, is it likely to succeed for very long? To repeat what I suggested earlier; the amount of self-determination which we can achieve while remaining a part of white, capitalistic American society is extremely limited and we should clearly understand this. Otherwise, there is likely to be great disappointment. It is probably true that Black control of our communities may provide us a much broader power base than we now have from which to attempt to make a leap to the power table. But it is far from being a guarantee that we can successfully make such a leap.

I do not bring you answers; if so, the Conference could be just about winding up now. Rather, I bring you questions . . . questions which you must wrestle with today and tomorrow, and perhaps for some time to come. I have purposely avoid detailing specific actions which we might take, such as forming Black construction unions, demanding a guaranteed income, channeling Black savings into the community, and many other tasks which you will certainly be taking up in your workshops.

In developing plans for dealing with these specifics, however, may I point out that an economic plan is not a plan unless it comes to grips with the question of priorities. A shopping list of desirable things to be done is not a plan. To be a useful guide, the plan must have, first of all, clearly defined goals. Fanon, incidentally, in his revolutionary writings, placed great stress on the importance of being clear about your goals and being certain that the populace clearly understands the goals. Secondly, a development plan must have an overall logic, it must recognize the interdependence of each part with every other, it must state what is to be done first, what next, etc. Developing such a plan is an enormous task. It can't be completed in a week or a month, and in a sense such plans are never really completed because they must be flexible enough to change as the dynamics of the situation change. For Blacks in America the question of an economic plan is further complicated by the fact that no group is likely to be given a mandate to draw up such a plan. Personal and institutional jealousies as well as valid ideological factionalism within the Black community insures that no development plan will be accepted as satisfactory by all segments of the Black population. It is a source of some distress to me that the head of one major national Black organization intimately involved in economic development work complained to me that he had not been invited to attend this conference. I do not know if he was telling me the truth, but I do feel strongly that at this stage we should be inclusive. Nevertheless, this conference will have made an unprecedented contribution to Black economic development if it seriously explores some of the grand issues which must necessarily be raised by such a planning effort.

For instance, it is believed that Black people in the South have been selling their land holdings—sometimes rather substantial ones—and moving to cities; an action which is perhaps justified from the point of view of the individual but which may be contrary to the best interests of Blacks as a group. Such questions demand exploration and research. If it appears that such actions are in fact harmful to us then we might need to develop a fund to purchase such land and to decide its disposition on the basis of some rational Black program. In exploring such an undertaking one should consider what resources Blacks already have which might be useful. For example, there are a half dozen or more land grant Negro colleges in the South: Prairie View, Alcorn, A&T, Tennessee A&I, etc. What are these schools doing with regard to rural Black populations? What should they be doing? What can we get them to do, and how? All such questions can be meaningfully explored as part of a Black economic development plan.

On yesterday afternoon another national conference on Black economic development opened in New York—organized by white academic and money interests. I attended yesterday's deliberations, which were participated in by about thirty white and thirty Black persons from around the country. Obviously, a biracial conference of that nature has certain built in inhibitions, a principal one being that Black economic development cannot be discussed separately from Black political development, and Blacks don't easily discuss this with whites.

But within its limitations, the conference was instructive. One of the brothers who was there but who was also invited to be here summed up his dilemma by saying that he couldn't decide whether it was more instructive to listen to the folks who had the dough or to those who were trying to get it away from them. (Actually, we need people to do both.) The spectrum of Black opinion at that conference is probably less broad than this audience here. But I did meet two or three beautiful cats whom I had never heard of before, and there are probably more whom I didn't meet. The same thing has already begun to happen to me here. I am really struck by the endless numbers of sharp, dedicated, together Black guys who are appearing as if from nowhere. This suggests to me an additional benefit of an economic plan.

It is possible that the arduous task of forging an economic plan for Black people, which would necessarily involve the intense interaction of most of these brothers with one another, could begin to produce the degree of unity which we so desperately need for the next stages of our liberation process.

In conclusion then, I suppose that the meat of my address has been that the first step in Black economic development is not economic at all, but political. There is no question of "pulling ourselves up by our bootstraps." We have no bootstraps. We are starting with so few economic resources of our own that our tactic must be to utilize cleverly what strength we do have, namely, the political force of 25 million potentially united Black minds, for extracting some economic resources from those who do have them. In many cases, of course, the resources morally belong to us anyway. But obtaining control of them will not be easy. A commitment even prior to the political one is implied in my statement, however, for I referred to our political force being based on 25 million potentially united

Black minds. Achieving a substantial degree of unity is an obvious pre-requisite for rendering the political force effective as a lever for extracting resources. As Harold Cruse well said: our revolution must take place on three levels: cultural, political, and economic. As this conference proceeds with its discussions focused on economic issues I feel certain that the cultural and political—which is to say ideological—factors will inescapably impose themselves into your framework. It is inevitable and essential that they do so. But ideology is divisive as we all know, and can paralyze us totally. Therefore, as we begin this important work here this weekend I feel it to be of foremost importance that we recognize the tremendous implications of what we are about and that we approach our task soberly, humbly, and with a spirit of tolerance and Black love.

I would urge that each of us concentrate our efforts on discovering what are the short-run tasks that we can find common agreement on—irrespective of the fact that the brother who is pushing any particular program may indeed be our bitter personal rival or ideological opponent. Although we have had rather tragic experiences with Black spokesmen and Black cabinets in the past—whether Booker T. Washington, Mary McLeod Bethune, or the Civil Rights Leadership Conference, I can't help but feel that a great deal could be gained were we able to develop a united position on at least some aspects of how we would like to see government and private money used in the Black community. This would be at least the beginnings of an economic plan.

Brothers and Sisters, what you do here this weekend may significantly influence where Black people go from here. Shoulder your responsibilities well! Uhuru!

# 26 ]] Black Economic Liberation

## under Capitalism

*Talmadge Anderson*

The economic system of America is not exalt and immune from criticism by Black people. Moreover, the exploitive nature and intent of American capitalism by its racial subjugation of Black people, naturally, should provoke the most vociferous attack on the system by Black economists and academicians.

This is not to say that white society or the dominant culture, in the absence of humanistic values, should not laud and defend American economic practices. Putting aside moral considerations, it is senseless to expect white beneficiaries to condemn a pseudo-democratic system that has provided them the apex of privilege and affluence. Likewise, it is equally illogical and perhaps even unnatural for Black people to cherish a socio-economic system or institution which demeans and exploits, so blatantly, on the basis of Black color.

Paradoxically, Black business educators and most of the relatively few Black economists have made the tragic mistake of embracing, unequivocally, the principles and practices of American capitalism; the same system that white people manipulate and scheme to deny Black people significant participation. Black involvement and participation in the economic system is simply peripheral and subservient by the design and tactics of the white capitalist. This does not imply that Blacks are not essential or maybe even indispensable to the system; for Black people are the "bargain" of the labor factor of production. And on the end of the product-flow, the Black consumer (approximately 30 million) is generally swindled and over-charged for goods and services. Because of white domination and the lack of Black alternative, the white capitalist is automatically assured of Black patronage at very little, if any, extra advertising and promotional effort.

Ghetto residents pay more for all kinds of goods and services than do people living in white neighborhoods. According to testimony by Paul Rand Dixon, Chairman of the FTC, an item selling wholesale at $103 would retail on the average for $165 in a general merchandise store and for $250 in a low-income specialty store.[1]

Then it is very obvious that it would not be in the best interests of the white capitalist to allow Black people to move up from their status of subservience to controlling and policy-making positions within the system.

Reprinted with permission from *The Black Scholar*, October 1970, pp. 11–14.

To assure further the perpetuation of this successful strategy, Black men are suppressed at the pyramidal base of the business and governmental power structure. Restriction to the base guarantees minimal income in order to diminish and thwart ambitions for ascension.

Walter Heller, Milton Friedman and Paul Samuelson, noted white "liberal" economists, have presented papers and drawn economic models showing in essence the unfavorable economic costs of racial discrimination. These and other economists claim that no positive economic advantage is gained by the exclusion of Black people from full and equal participation in the system. In fact, the Council of Economic Advisers in 1965 reported that:

If Negroes received the same average pay as whites having the same education, the personal income of Negroes and of the Nation would be $12.8 billion higher. If Negroes also had the same educational attainments as white workers, and earned the same pay and experienced the same unemployment as whites, their personal income—and that of the Nation—would be $20.6 billion higher. The entire economy would benefit from better education of Negro workers and an end to job discrimination. Industry would earn additional profits. The total Gross National Product would rise by an estimated $23 billion, or an extra 3.7 percent.[2]

Obviously, this admission by this elite group of white economists would cause Black people to wonder then, why is economic and educational opportunity denied? If full enfranchisement of all Blacks would boost the general prosperity of the country, the enfranchisement of the Indians, Mexicans and Eskimos would increase Gross National Product an even greater 10 or 15 billion. And since the white man is such an ardent worshipper of profits, prosperity and power, why doesn't he hasten to admit these potential money-makers into the economic mainstream of American society? Fully and shrewdly comprehending the risk and fallacy of this theory, white people explain that it is simply a matter of tradition, culture and custom the reasons for Black exclusion from within the system. This is a much too easy "cop out," based on Thorsten Veblen's, *The Theory of the Leisure Class*.

To dismiss human subjugation and exploitation as due to tradition, culture or mores inclusively, is an over-simplification. It will behoove Blacks to conceive white American inhumanism as tactics rather than tradition; conspiracy as against culture; and perhaps mania over mores.

Nevertheless, the theory proffered by the Council of Economic Advisers must be debated in the context of its practicality relative to white opportunism. An ordinary student of Euro-American economics will discern that to admit and elevate Black people to a significant level of economic participation after centuries of deprivation would require a massive financial investment in people. An investment in human resources, like any other form of investment, will not automatically *guarantee* a sufficient personal income expansion and consumption function to create optimum growth in Gross National Product. In fact, this type of investment initiative at a time of near or full employment could result in an adverse economic condition.

Consequently, there is a high element of risk associated with the theory that remedial Black participation might result in long-term gain for the economy as a whole. High risk quells the incentives of the profit-maniacs. The surety of short-term exploitive gain from Black exclusion outweighs the high risk of aggregate long-term economic benefits possible from Black inclusion.

The avowed support of Black capitalism by the Nixon Administration; special Small Business Administration projects; and joint industry-government programs designed to give Blacks a semblance of capitalistic participation have met with the intended limited success. These programs are mere compromising, gratuitous, piece-meal and political appeasers to the white power structure. To prove sincerity of intent in the economic reconstruction of Black people, white industry and government would be required to spend hundreds of billions more than the few millions presently allocated. After twenty years it is still easier for the son of a Mississippi sharecropper to attend West Point than for a Black businessman to obtain a Small Business Administration Agency loan or acquire a major corporation franchise.

Andrew F. Brimmer, Black economist and Governor of the Federal Reserve Board, degraded the awakening efforts of Blacks to exercise franchise and control over the economic potentials and resources within the Black community. In a 1969 speech, Brimmer is quoted in a Paul A. Samuelson textbook as stating that:

Economic separatism has been tried in the past, and it has failed to provide genuine opportunity for Negro businessmen—and it certainly has failed to provide economic well-being for our Negro population.[3]

In another paper prepared for the American Economic Association, Andrew F. Brimmer was joined by Henry S. Terrell, a Black Federal Reserve official, in saying:

Self-employment offers a poor economic future for colored people, . . . in the long run, the pursuit of black capitalism may retard economic advancement by discouraging many from the full participation in the national economy with its much broader range of challenges and opportunities.[4]

These statements by Brimmer and Terrell are most unfortunate from a Black point of view. Admittedly, Black capitalism has not proved successful as a means for achieving economic equality for Black people, but the point is that its failure has assured the continued affluence and well-being of white people. This fact implies that white businessmen benefit and profit from the failure of Black capitalism.

It is striking and peculiar that the proud attainment of self-employment and racial-ethnic capitalistic practices by the Irish, Jew, and Italian are lauded, while at the same time some deem it impractical for Black people. The reason being that the Black man is easily conscripted for capitalistic "service" because of a conspicuous color identity which prevents him from assimilating with the white majority without detection. Therefore, he is exploited by white people of all national origins in America.

However, the color factor that establishes a racial boundary between

Black and white does not reciprocally impose on each the same restrictions. White people have always been free to apply and reap the benefit of capitalistic practices in the Black community, but the encroachment by Blacks in the economic resources of the white community is either discouraged or tacitly forbidden. Thus, the disadvantageously unequal role of the Black is that of profit-giver, and that of white profit-taker. It would be naive to assume that the white power system would permit the Black and white economic positions altered voluntarily.

It is not surprising that many people adopt the wishful concept of integration, "the Negro dream," as a solution towards the economic liberation of Black people. Economic integration would appear logical. E. Franklin Frazier seemed to express skepticism relative to Black economic separation in his book, *Black Bourgeoisie*. Had he lived through the turbulent sixties and witnessed the blatant contrivances and violent protest on the part of white people in preventing the full economic franchisement of Black people, and also witnessed the growing polarization of the races today, his opinion may have been affected. For the old excuses such as not ready, unprepared, uneducated and unqualified with reference to integration are substantially not valid today. Although token social or physical association has been advanced, Black integration into the economic power base of America is yet distant.

Gunnar Myrdal's observation a few decades ago deserves careful analysis today:

On the one hand, they (Black people) find that the caste wall blocks their economic and social opportunities. On the other hand, they have, at the same time, a vested interest in racial segregation since it gives them what opportunity they have.[5]

In other words, the Black capitalist is given little choice by the white power system. For all practical indications integration as a social means of ameliorating economic inequities between the races, Black and white, is proving to be a myth. What popularly has been termed integration has economically meant the mere hiring of a limited number of Black people by white firms in relatively unimportant positions at base levels. The exception being a few high paying showcase jobs that serve as government moral appeasers or as a token of goodwill to satisfy Black pressure groups. Basically, the implementation of integration has given Black people the privilege of being in closer physical proximity with white people in some commercial establishments and public institutions. As Malcolm X put it, "Integration means that now Black people can sit next to white people and eat a hamburger or sit side by side and use the toilet." Integration of the lunch counters will not ever likely be followed with an integration by Blacks on the board of directors tables.

Realistically, it is evident that white society, by bent and design is dedicated to limiting the economic power of Black people. Assuming this to be true, the inequitable integration of a Black minority with a dominant white majority will lead to a disastrous dilution and diffusion of the potential power of Black solidarity. Integration is real and workable only if all people share equitably in the economic decisions shaping the power structure of a society. Without violence, the threat of revolution, or massive Black economic boycotts, it is unlikely that true integration will ever prevail in America.

If Black people are to be liberated under capitalism, it must be under Black determination of educational, social and economic values in terms of Black relevancy. Black people must control the land and the institutions affecting the Black community. In order to achieve this objective, it might mean the temporary, but strategic separation on an economic basis. This would enable Black people to develop into a formidable economic power unit. Power respects power. Power is never relinquished voluntarily, it is usually pressured, tricked or forced from the holder. Any cohesive independent power poses a threat to another power, and is therefore regarded and feared. This has always been the basis of conciliation, treaty and eventual acceptance.

If Black people are to achieve economic liberation under capitalism it is imperative that the potential power inherent in Black unity not be diffused and dissolved prematurely into a hostile white power system that is dominant. Strategic economic withdrawal in feasible and selective areas must be achieved rapidly. Further attempts at being absorbed in the white system will not result in Black and white integration, but Black disintegration.

## Notes

1. *Report of the National Advisory Commission on Civil Disorders* (New York: Bantam Books, 1968), p. 276.

2. From a staff memorandum of the CEA (March 26, 1965).

3. P. A. Samuelson, *Economics* (New York: McGraw-Hill, 1970), 8th ed. p. 787.

4. "Black Capitalism Under Fire By Federal Reserve Official," *The Afro-American*, January 10, 1970, p. 18.

5. Gunnar Myrdal, *An American Dilemma* (New York: Harper and Brothers, 1944), p. 305.

# Bibliographical Notes

The rapid pace which has characterized the unfolding of activities that make up the field of Black economic development makes any compilation of readings on the topic a somewhat risky undertaking. And related to this is the lag in the gathering of available literature. These brief notes are intended to alert the reader to sources that will provide elaboration on various aspects of Black economic and business development, in addition to those previously cited in various places throughout this volume.

There are several bibliographies which provide fairly comprehensive coverage of general sources and sources specifically covering Black business development. Elizabeth Miller's *The Negro in America: A Bibliography* (Cambridge: Harvard University Press, 1970), an extensive and recently up-dated listing of references organized by topic areas, gives background sources on the economic, political, and social plight of Blacks. The Business and Defense Services Administration of the U.S. Department of Commerce has published an annotated "Bibliography on Marketing to Low-income Consumers" (Washington, D.C.: Government Printing Office, 1969), which includes sources treating the characteristics and problems of low-income consumers and various programs to solve these problems. An excellent bibliography is one compiled by Howard University's Small Business Guidance and Development Center, "The Negro in Business" (1969). This annotated listing is the most comprehensive available on the subject.

The writings of several Black people give a good overview of many important historical factors: Booker T. Washington's *The Negro in Business* (Chicago: Hertel, Jenkins and Company, 1907) and a report on a conference in Atlanta edited by W. E. B. DuBois under the title, *The Negro in Business* (Atlanta: Atlanta University Press, 1899) are two volumes that should be used in developing a perspective on the period. The works of Marcus Garvey are very important also. See, for example, Amy Jacques-Garvey, ed., *Philosophy and Opinions of Marcus Garvey* (New York: Arno, 1969). A widely cited study of banking and business among Blacks is Abram L. Harris's *The Negro As Capitalist* (Philadelphia: American Academy of Political and Social Science, 1936). Other sources include Gunnar Myrdal's *An American Dilemma* (New York: McGraw–Hill, 1964) and E. Franklin Frazier's *The Negro in the United States* (New York: Macmillan, 1957).

Very few contemporary writers have recognized the importance of presenting and synthesizing the historical aspects of Black business and economic development. Such an effort is undertaken by Harold Cruse in his admirable study of Black intellectual traditions, *The Crisis of the Negro Intellectual* (New York: Morrow, 1967). An even more explicit treatment of this problem is contained in his "The Economics of Black Nationalism" in *Rebellion or Revolution?* (New York: Morrow, 1968). A more recent effort is Charles Tate's "A Survey of the Conceptual Origins of Black Economic Development and a Review of Residual and Contemporary Forms," a working paper of The Urban Institute, Washington, D.C.

There are several topics closely related to the issues in Black economic development. For discussion of the social and political context in which this developmental thrust is taking place, Kenneth Clark's *Dark Ghetto: Dilemmas of Social Power* (New York: Harper, 1965) and Stokely Carmichael and Charles Hamilton's *Black Power: The Politics of Liberation in America* (New York: Random House, 1967) are good sources. *The Report of the National Advisory Commission on Civil Disorders* (Washington, D.C.: Government Printing Office, 1967) is a recent effort to sort through the intricacies of the plight of Black folk in this country. Wilbur R. Thompson's *A Preface to Urban Economics* (Baltimore: Johns Hopkins, 1965) focuses on related economic topics. William Tabb's *The Political Economy of the Black Ghetto* (New York: W. W. Norton, 1970) is perhaps the best effort to develop the idea of "domestic colonialism."

The recent thrust in Black business development is chronicled in sources that are surprisingly scattered. *Black Economic Development* (Englewood Cliffs, N.J.: Prentice–Hall, 1969) edited by William Haddad and G. Douglas Pugh, a compilation of papers presented to the American Assembly, treats the broader economic development aspects. Theodore L. Cross's *Black Capitalism* (Boston: Atheneum, 1969) is the most substantive work on the subject. Cross endeavors to describe the "wealth-abolishing" characteristics of the ghetto economy and then outlines a series of corrective measures required to strengthen financial and commercial operations in ghetto communities. Frederick Sturdivant in *The Ghetto Marketplace* (New York: Free Press, 1969) carries the analysis of ghetto economics a few steps further. A critique of Black capitalism—termed "corporate imperialism"—is found in Robert L. Allen's *Black Awakening in Capitalist America* (Garden City, N.Y.: Doubleday, 1969). Another discussion from the perspective of Black folk in America is found in *Ebony* magazine, August 1970. The issue, entitled "Which Way Black America—Separation? Integration? Liberation?," contains articles by economists Andrew Brimmer, Dunbar McLaurin, and Robert S. Browne on themes related to Black economic development.

Much has been said about the role of business in solving America's urban problems. *Business Leadership and the Negro Crisis* (New York: McGraw–Hill, 1968) by Eli Ginzberg is an edited volume of comments by selected businessmen, Blacks and others. *Business and Society*, edited by Milton Moskowitz, is a biweekly report on business and social responsibility. *White Power, Black Freedom* (Boston: Beacon Press, 1969) by Arnold Schucter provides a framework for the involvement of business enterprise in rehabilitating the urban area.

The community-based economic development thrust is one of the most promising contemporary movements. A very current and highly informative source is Nels S. Ackerson and Lawrence H. Sharf, "Community Development Corporations: Operations and Financing," *Harvard Law Review* (May 1970) 83:1558–1671. The Center for Community Economic Development (56 Boylston Street, Cambridge, Mass.) has been created to conduct research on the problems of community development corporations and other community-based economic organizations. The center has published, in conjunction with the Cambridge Institute, an occasional paper which reports the *Proceedings of the Information Exchange* (October 1969). A bibliography on the subject is available, in addition to a number of excellent papers on various aspects of community-based economic development. The partial listing of cooperatives and community development corporations provides an opportunity to view first hand the process of implementing the concept. Recently organized and hopefully a source of future information and action is the National Congress for Community Economic Development, Washington, D.C.

A considerable portion of the literature discussing Black economic development is found in periodical and other forms. Some information is available from the various federal agencies involved in minority business enterprise, especially the Small Business Administration, the Office of Minority Business Enterprise, and the Office of Economic Opportunity. A biweekly newsletter on minority economic development is *Urban Enterprise* (Chicago: Urban Research Corporation). Another recent publication, *Black Enterprise* (New York: Earl G. Graves Publishing Company), is tailored to the informational needs of Black interests in business. *The Review of Black Political Economy*, published by the Black Economic Research Center, New York, will certainly develop into a prime source of critical comments on Black economic development among Black folk in this country.

# Index

accommodation philosophy, 55, 57
Accord (Detroit), 109
Ackerson, Nels S., 347
ACT, 129–130
adult education, 249
advisory services, 227
affluence: and poverty, *viii*; and savings, 261; *see also* wealth
Africa, 327; attitude of Black Americans toward, 321–322, 327; business in, 27; socialism in, 92; U.S. influence in, 320–321; *see also* underdeveloped nations
African heritage, 326–327; and Black bourgeoisie, 90
Agency for Corporate Transfer, *see* ACT
Alabama, land developing corporation in, 245
Alabama Penny Saving Bank, 33
aluminum industry, relations between U.S. government and, 127
America, Richard F., 99, 147, 175
American culture, influence on Black business, 63
*American Dilemma, An*, 4, 33, 345
American Economic Association, 173, 341
American economy, *see* U.S. economy
American Indians, 102, 161; reservation system for, 119, 209
American Jews, *see* anti-Semitism *and entries under Jewish*
antebellum period, Black business during, *see* Black business, in antebellum period
antipoverty programs: attitudes toward, 233–234; and capital ownership, 241–242; failures of, 234–240; theme of, 234; *see also* War on Poverty
anti-Semitism, 66, 80
Appalachia, 102, 153, 161
Aptheker, Herbert, 92, 163
Architects Renewal Committee in Harlem, 198–199, 202, 204n
Area Redevelopment Act, 295
Arkansas, "operation green thumb" in, 249
Asia, 328; *see also* underdeveloped nations
Association for the Study of Negro Life and History, 173
Atlanta Savings Bank, 33
Atlanta University, 79; Fourth Conference at, 73–75
AT&T, and COMSAT, 206
automation, 237–239

"Back to Africa" expeditions, 6
bad-debt reserve, 254
balance of payments, in Harlem, 193–194

banking laws, 267n; liberalization of, 251
banks, 6; and credit to Black business, 108–109; deposit incentive program for, 256–258; and Ghediplan, 192; ghetto branches of, 267n; and rush financing, 251–253; *see also* Black banks; Domestic Development Bank
Bedford-Stuyvesant, 122, 208, 251
Bedford-Stuyvesant Development and Services Corporation, 208
Bedford-Stuyvesant Renewal and Rehabilitation Corporation, 208
Bedford-Stuyvesant Restoration Corporation, 265
benevolent societies, 29, 32
Bicentennial Improvement Corporation, 267n
"big business": and Negro business, 34; and Negro-white caste system, 39; *see also* Capitalism
Black Anti-Defamation League, 325, 327
Black audiovisual networks, demand for, 324
Black banks, 169; causes of failures of, 79–80; in Chicago, 70–71; development of, 32–33; lending capabilities of, 256–258; in 1910, 76; origins of, 29–30
Black barbers and beauticians, 6, 63, 69–70, 169, 170
Black bourgeoisie: attitude toward Black business, 23; and Black masses, 80–81; and capitalism, 93; and gradualism, 89–91; and myth of Black business, *see* myth of Black business
Black business development, 7, 55; after 1865, 31–34; after 1890, 6–7; during antebellum period, 47–53; and availability of capital, 31; before 1865, 27, 31; bibliographies on, 345–347; as Black capitalism, 173–175; and capitalism, *see* capitalism; in Chicago, 71n; community control of, 303–306; and community development, 301–303; and corporate power transfer proposal, *see* corporate power transfer proposal; corporate sponsoring of, 110; current status of, 102–103; developing new evaluation techniques for, 306–308; and economic environment, 166–168; and economic integration, 300–301; effect of failures of, *see* Black business failures; effect of isolation on, 35–38; effect of Negro population growth on, 57–58; as extension of segregation, 300; Federal interest in, 10–11, 105–106; ghetto dispersal as

Black business development (*cont'd*)
alternative to, 309–315; and growth of
Negro market, 63–65; impact of segregation and desegregation on, 164–166;
and increased employment opportunities, 37–38, 82–83; and inevitability of
separation, 56–59; influence of historic
background on, 25–26; and isolation of
Negro population, 35–37; *vs.* job training, 294–295; and lack of support from
Black market, 67–69; as leadership
model, 302–303; location of, 34; methods of assisting, 109–110; motivations
of advocates of, 7; and Negro consumer
income, 40; and Negro-white caste system, 38; new opportunities for, 108;
numbers and types of, 8–10; organizational assistance for, 104, 110–113;
pre–Civil War, 5–6; prestige: value of,
41–42; problems of, 65–66, 186–187;
producer industries, 185; and racial
equality, *see* racial equality; reasons
for lack of, 103; after Reconstruction,
6; role of church in, 31–32; and role of
white business, 106–107; in rural south,
34–35; as small business, 27; social
myth of, *see* myth of Black business;
as solution for ghetto problems, 56,
101–102; studies of, 79–80; and structure of Black business, 168–171; and
trade outside the ghetto, 147–148; trends
and philosophies on, 41–45; types of,
168–171; in urban areas, 35–37; and
war and race, *vii*; in Watts, 122; *see
also* Black economic development; Black
capitalism; *and under individual types
of, i.e., Black banks; Black newspapers*
Black business failures, 91–92; and capitalist system, 174–175; causes of, 146–
147, 185; and investors in ghetto areas,
142; and lack of business training, 42;
and myth of Black business, 78, 79;
and refunding loans, 252; white aid to,
112–113; *see also* Black business failures; Black businessmen; Black capitalism; Black economic development
Black businessmen: and advantages of
segregation, 39, 42; attitudes toward
Black customers, 67–68; and CDC plan,
117–118; credit difficulties of, 40; identification of potential, 199; in 1906, 75;
and policymaking, 126
Black capitalism, x, 11; alternatives to,
175; analysis of Brimmer's critique of,
173–179; attitudes toward, 11, 99–100,
159; and Black economic development,
13–14; and Black nationalists, 320–321;
and CDC proposal, 114–115, 120–121;
compared with cooperatives, 335–336;
and continuation of exploitation, 154;
and corporate power transfer, *see* corporate power transfer; definitions of, 6,
159, 173–175; and El Mercado de Los
Angeles, 119–120; and failures of capitalist system, 174–175; Federal attitude

toward, 114; and Garvey, 93–94; intended limited success of, 341–342; as
myth of white capitalists, 152; origins
of phrase, 18*n*; and poverty of Black
people, 175–177; and powerlessness of
ghettos, 177–179; and Progress Plaza,
120; proposal for advancement of,
121–122; and white power structure,
342–343; *see also* Black business development; myth of Black business
"Black Capitalism: An Assessment," 173
Black church: and doctrine of the "double-
duty dollar," 61–63; role of, 31–32
Black communications system, 160
Black community, *see* ghetto; Negro community
Black construction unions, 336
Black corporations, absence of, 127
Black customers, *see* market for Black
business
Black economic development: along Afro-
centric lines, 19*n*; alternatives for, 183;
analysis of goals and obstacles of, 12–
17; and attitudes of big business, 229–
232; Black nationalism as requirement
for, 159–160, 162–163; and Black self-
determination, 175; and capital ownership, 241–242; and capitalism, 332–335,
339–343; categories of activity for, 11;
and causes of underdevelopment, 152–
153; compared with economic development of whites, 5; and concept of
separate Black nation, 160–161; concepts necessary for, 160; and Economic
Opportunity Program, 211*n*; economic
organization program for, 225–228; and
expulsion of exploiters, 154; and failures of Black capitalism, 341–342; financing plans for, 224–226; five-year
comprehensive programs for, 158; and
Ghediplan, *see* Ghediplan; goals of, 19,
336–337; government-private industry
plan for, 216–232; and Harlem project,
*see* Harlem project; and investments,
*see* investments in ghetto; and job training programs, 155–156; and land reform and acquisition, 156–157; liberal
and liberation points of view on, 316–
319; methods of planning for, 337–338;
and migration to North, 5; and migration to urban areas, 18*n*; objectives of,
218; and OEO Harlem plan, *see* OEO
plan; participation of youth in, 157–
158; and partnership with corporations,
211–232; political basis for, 162–163;
and present Black economic needs, 160–
161; and rejection of Black capitalism,
159; required pace for, 154–155; Ribicoff Committee hearings on, 205–208;
role of private sector in, 205–211; and
separation-integration controversy, 3;
and slavery, 5; social ownership *vs.*
private enterprise, 156–158; and struggle, 154; validity of plans for, 331–332;
and view of ghetto, 184–187; views on,

185–187; and war economy, 81; and war and race, *vii*; and World War II, 81; *see also* Black business development; Black Economic Development Conference; Black Manifesto; CDC

Black Economic Development Conference, 6, 99, 159;

Black economy: challenge to white economy, 87; creation of, 126; DuBois on, 94–95; *vs.* economic reform, 88–89; and Garvey movement, 91–94, and gradualistic economic philosophers, 89–91; and lack of economic theory, 92–93; and Marxism, 95; necessary ingredients for, 87–88; semiseparate, 43; separation and integration of, 42–43; and white exploitation of Harlem, 88–89; *see also* separatism

Black employment, *see* employment of Blacks

Black family income, *see* family income

Black farmers, 75, 245

Black fraternal orders, and life insurance, 25

Black grocery stores, CMA, 77–78

Black insurance companies, 70, 165, 166

Black journalism, role of, 30

Black leaders: Black businessmen as, 302–303; and democratic control of planning, 89, 231; and economic development, 304; inadequacies of, 88; and political power, 90; of revolution, 322–323; types of, 36

Black liberation, *see* liberation

Black management, 134–135, 178; and Black control, 128–129;

"Black Manifesto," 159, 162; prologue to, 320–323

Black manufacturing companies, 169, 175, 218–224; and CDC plan, 116

Black market, *see* market, for Black business

Black militants: aims of, 175; attitudes toward Black business, 11; attitudes toward white aid, 112–113; and ghetto development plans, 231–232

Black millionaires, myths on, 77

Black Muslims, 175

Black nationalism, 159; attitudes of "infantile leftists" toward, 159; and Black bourgeoisie, 90; and Black capitalism, 320–321; and Black economy, 86–87; and capitalism, 93–94; economic thinking of, 92; and Garvey, 91–94; and NNC, 91; as requirement for Black economic development, 159–160, 162–163

Black newspapers: during antebellum period, 52; after emancipation, 31; and myth of Black business, 84;

Black-owned businesses, *see* Black business development

Black people: in abolitionist movement, 51; attitudes toward capitalism of, 99; causes of disunity among, 161; compared with European immigrants, 195;

and countervailing force concept, 126; economic and business development of, *see* Black business development, Black economic development; effects of capitalism on, 339–343; financial status of, 167–168; and group responsibilities, 88; and inadequacies of Federal programs, 124–125; income of, *see* income; living conditions of, *viii*; migration to North of, 35–36; needs of, 124–125; occupations of, 9–10; and other oppressed people, 161; percent of "nonwhite" category, 8*n*, 9*n*; and policy decisions, 125–126; progress of, *x*; and reform *vs.* revolution, 137; regional shifts of, 4–5; savings incentives for, 261–264; as vanguard force, 321–323; and Vietnam war, *ix*; and violence, *viii*; in white community, 342.

Black Panthers, 160; and cultural nationalism, 162

Black political power, *see* political power of Black Americans

Black population: census of, 331; free-slave comparisons of, 48–49; growth of, 57–58, 64; and pace of economic development, 154–155; in proportion to total U.S. population, 47–48; in U.S. cities, 178

"Black Power," 231; historical background of, 3

Black pride, and business ownership, 101

Black publishing and printing industries, 324

Black radicalism, 90, 160; and socialism, 92

Black real estate companies, 169

Black resources, 337

Black retail establishments, 168

Black revolution, *see* Black Manifesto

Black savings, *see* savings

Black service businesses, 168

"Black socialism," 163

Black solidarity, and integration, 342–343

Black Star Line, 91–92

Black underdevelopment: causes and nature of, 14, 152–153; role of capitalism in, 13, 150–151; underdeveloped nation approach to, 187–188

Black undertakers, in Chicago, 69

Black unit approach, 43

Black university, demand for, 325

Black-white ownership of businesses, 40

Black-white relations, *see* race relations

Black women, employment opportunities for, 37–38

Black youth, 37; businessmen as leadership models for, 302–303; and job training programs, 155–156; participation in planning and development of Black community, 157–158

BMB, 282; and CDC fund allocation, 277–278; and CDC management, 278–279, 287*n*; and state corporation law, 282–283

Boggs, James, 99

Bond, Julian, 327
bonding, for black business, 199, 303
Boston: Black business during antebellum
  period in, 50–51; corporate combinations with Black business in, 106; segregated schools in, 51; small-industry
  development in, 219
boycott movement, 43–44, 64
Brimmer, Andrew F., 12, 14, 99, 341, 346;
  critique of Black capitalism by, 173–179
Brokerage service, for Black businessmen,
  199
Bronzeville, see Chicago
Brooklyn, N.Y., development corporation
  in, 208
Browne, Robert S., 176, 293, 327, 346
Browne, W. W., 32, 33
building and loan societies, 33
business: definition of, 25; role in American life of, 26–27; see also Black business development; white business
business associations, 70
business education: and Black economic
  development, 18n, 42; Negro colleges
  giving, 78
business failures, see Black business
  failures
Businessmen's Development Corporation
  (Phila.), 109
busing of Negro students, 311
buying pools, 87

California Golden Oaks Products Company, 175
Cambridge Institute, 347
Camp Kilmer Job Corps Center, 234
Canada, Black business during antebellum
  period in, 50–51
capital, 55; accumulation of, 238; and
  affluence, 240–242; and Black business
  development, 18n, 42, 239–242; methods
  of infusing, 108–109, 121; and pre-Civil
  War Black business, 29; during Reconstruction period, 31; as solution for
  ghetto underdevelopment, 180; Third
  World need for, 160; see also equity
  capital; risk capital
capitalism, 95–96; and Black business
  failures, 174–175; and Black economic
  development, 12, 92, 339–343; and
  Black economic objectives, 332–335;
  and Black ideology, 322; Black liberation under, 343; and Black underdevelopment, 150–153; defined, 26; and
  development of Black community, 154;
  and economic exploitation, 89; of Garvey, 93; and ghetto economic development, 138–139, 317; and gradualism,
  90; vs. survival economics, 159–160;
  see also capitalism in ghetto areas
capitalism in ghetto areas: and concept
  of corporate power transfer, 139–140;
  and education, 148–149; lessons and
  guidelines, 144–149; requirements for
  success of, 140–142; role of investors
  in, 139–140, 142–144

Carmichael, Stokely, 19n, 163, 346
catering business, 6, 30, 51
CDC, see Community Development
  Corporation
Census of Negro business, 72n
Center for Community Economic Develop-
  ment, 347
Central Intelligence Agency, see CIA
charity, 233–234; see also giveaway
  programs
Chase Manhattan Capital Corporation,
  141, 143–144
Chayra, Arturo, 119
Chicago: Black businesses in, 23, 63–71;
  Black population growth in, 57–58;
  boycott approach in, 43; corporate as-
  sistance plans in, 107; Operation
  Breadbasket movement in, 104–105;
  purchasing power of Blacks in, 65, 66;
  Sears, Roebuck and Company of, 221;
  small-industry development in, 219
China, nationalism in, 93
churches, 328; Black disruption of, 326;
  and reparations to Blacks, 324–325
CIA, 321; control of, 176
Citizens and Southern National Bank,
  260, 261
city contracts, and long-term unemployed,
  217
Civil Rights Act of 1875, 57
civil rights demonstrations, results of, 178
Clark, Kenneth, 346
clearing house, for ghetto loans, 251–252
colonial system, x; compared with ghetto
  system, 15, 125; and Black communities, 152–153; struggle against, 161
Colored Men's Professional and Business
  Directory of Chicago, 63
Colored Merchants Association, 77
Columbia University: Development Planning Workshop, 198, 204n; School of
  Social Work, 210
Communication Satellite Corporation, see
  COMSAT
Communists: and Garvey, 91; and Harlem, 95; and Republic of New Africa,
  162–163; and W. E. B. DuBois, 95
community control: of Black business development, 11, 87, 303–306; and Black
  capitalist orientation, 13–14; economic
  implications of, 178–179; evaluation
  techniques for, 307–308; of ghetto institutions, 134; and government supported
  private investors, 212–213; limitations
  of, 335–336; and racism, 14; see also
  social ownership
community development, related to business development, 301–303; see also
  Community Development Corporation
community development banks, 281; public and private, 258–261
Community Development Corporation, 133,
  175, 183, 208–209, 216, 223, 224, 231,
  258–261, 347; allocation of funds by,
  277–278; altered role for, 120–121; applicability of state corporation law to,

282–283; BMB control of, 276–279; criticism of, 118–119; dangers of, 115–118; and economic development index, 288n; facilitation of active participation in, 274–276; formation procedure, 270–272; and ghetto segregation, 143; incentives for continued investment in, 272–274; and loss of freedom, 117–118; and maximization of economic development, 283–284; proposal for, 114–115; purposes of, 269–270, 285n; tax benefits for, 279–282

community ownership, 175; of worn-out white businesses, 175

community participation, and role of private sector in ghetto, 208

community self-determination, 99

Community Self-Determination Act, 175, 183, 259; evaluation of, 283–284; see also community development corporations

community service functions of CDC, 273–274

"community socialism," x

company stores, 34–35

competition: between Black- and white-owned businesses, 41, 43, 64–65, 68–69, 173–174; and Black business, 164; between CDC's, 271–272; vs. cooperation, 19n; and corporate power transfer, 130–131; for jobs, 299; as viable tool for Black liberation, 13

COMSAT, 205–207, 212; and ghetto problems, 195–196

conduits, local, see Ghediplan

Congress of Racial Equality, see CORE

conservatism: and gradualism, 90; and isolation of Black community, 36

Consumer Attitude Survey, 198

"cooperative commonwealth," 92–93

cooperatives, 183; in African countries, 325; compared with Black capitalism, 159, 335–336; compared with CDCs, 284; see also poor people's cooperatives

CORE, 11, 12, 175, 179, 183

core-area service cluster, 265–267

Cornish, Samuel E., 30

corporate assistance programs, 106–107

"corporate colonialism," 210–211

corporate combinations, 106

corporate managers, social initiative by, 229

corporate power transfer proposal, 124–125, 175; alternative approaches, 128–129; bidding procedures, 131–132; candidates for, 130–131; effect on company's operation, 134–135; feasibility of, 136–137; mechanism of, 129–130; precedents for, 127–128; reactions of market to, 140; restrictions on buyers, 133–134; safeguards, 132–134; sources of opposition to, 135–136

corporation law, and CDCs, 282–283

corporations: compared with CDC, 274–276; and employment of Blacks, 82; and service cluster approach, 266–267;

see also white business; white businessmen

corrective incentives: development banks, 258–261; and new liquidity for ghetto-origin installment paper, 254–256; risk reduction, 251–254; for stimulation of deposits in slum-area banks, 256–258

cost-benefit question, and business development vs. job training, 294–295, 296

counseling, by white businessmen, 106–107, 109–110

credit for Black business development, 40, 108–109, 224–225, 303; and development of Black banks, 32; in pre-Civil War period, 29; special needs for, 252–253; see also credit incentives; financing; loans

credit incentives, laws on, 267n; see also corrective incentives

credit unions, 33, 243

crop diversification, 245

Cruse, Harold, 3, 23–24, 163, 338, 345–346

"cultural nationalism," 162

cultural revolution, 162

culture, of Blacks and whites compared, 36

Cybernetics Revolution, changing nature of, 236–239

Datamation, 238

day-care facilities, 266

death rate, among Negroes, 48

decision-making, 175–176; in poor people's cooperatives, 246–247; see also policy-making

Delany, Martin R., 3, 41, 90

delinquencies and defaults, on loans to Black businessmen, 105, 108–109

democratic capitalism, myth of, 87–88

Depression of 1929: and Black business, 58–59, 64; boycott movements during, 80

discrimination, see racial discrimination

disposable income, 241; in Harlem, 194; and income-producing capital, 241–242; of nonwhite persons, 10; see also income

Domestic Development Bank, 224, 258–259; at national level, 216; role of, 199

Domestic Marshall Plan, 125

double-duty dollar, doctrine of, 61–63; and idea of a separate Negro economy, 80; origin of term, 71n

Douglass, Frederick, xi, 3, 51, 54, 55

Drake, St. Clair, 23, 176

dressmaking, 37

DuBois, W. E. B., 3, 57, 86, 87, 90, 92–93, 94–95, 163

Dusk of Dawn, 92, 94, 163

Eckstein, Otto, 178

economic base for Black business, 10–11

Economic Development Administration, 296–297, 306

economic opportunity: changing nature of, 236–239; meaning of, 234–240

Economic Opportunity Act, 184, 205, 224–225, 234, 236, 296; and CDC plan, 117; critique of, 236, 239–240; *see also* War on Poverty

Economic Opportunity Corporation, 206–207, 258–259

Economic Opportunity Loans, 105–106, 108, 224–225

education: and Black Americans, *ix*; and Black business development, 50–53, 148–149; for ghetto development, 228; and ghetto dispersal, 311; for management, 247; of rural Southern Blacks, 246, 314; *see also* school segregation

efficiency gaps: and Harlem Project, 202, 204; and self-determination, 119–120

elections, in CDC, 286*n*, 287*n*

Elijah Muhammad, 163

Emancipation Proclamation, 47; effects of, 4

employees: available to ghetto residents, 196; by Black businesses, 170, 171; in Black- and white-owned businesses, 9; of Blacks and whites compared, 13; and boycott movement, 43–44; and corporate power transfer, 135–136; and development of small industry, 220; and economic opportunity, 238–239; evaluation of programs for, 297–300; future outlook in, 177–178; and income parity, 14; *vs.* self-employment, 174; as solution for Black economic underdevelopment, 177–178; and trend of infiltration and integration, 44; by white merchants, 28; *see also* job training; unemployment

entertainment facilities, 266

EOL program, *see* Economic Opportunity Loans

equity capital, 109; *see also* capital

European immigrants: and Black employment, 29; compared with Black Americans, 195; integration of, 300–301

exploitation: and Black capitalism, 99, 152, 159; of Black community, 153–154, 321; and capitalism, 151; causes of, 340–341; and cooperatives, 249–250; vulnerability of Blacks to, 177

family income: of Blacks and whites compared, 10, 40, 166, 194; in Harlem, 193; and wage-dependence and capital ownership, 239

Fanon, 163, 336

farm cooperatives, *see* poor people's cooperatives

farm subsidies, *vii, viii, ix*

feasibility studies, of potential Harlem businesses, 201–202

Federal government: antipoverty program of, *see* antipoverty program; and Bedford-Stuyvesant restoration project, 265; and Black business, 9, 10–11, 18*n*, 105–106, 124–125; Black business development *vs.* job training controversy in,

294–297; and Black capitalism, 114; Black participation in, 54; and community controlled economic development, 306; and Community Development Corporations, 269; and cooperatives, 249–250; and corporate power transfers, 130, 134; political and economic attitudes toward Blacks, 175–176; and private development corporations, 127–128, 209–210; and private investors in ghettos, 212–232; subsidies to ghetto banks for time deposits, 263

Federal Manpower Development and Retraining Act, 240

Federal Reserve Board, 12, 173, 341

Federation of Southern Cooperatives, 244

finance companies, 253

financial assets, of Blacks and whites compared, 166–167

financial liabilities, of Blacks and whites compared, 167–168

financing: of CDCs, 270–271; for cooperatives, 244, 247; guaranteed, 189–190; through tax incentives, 223; through reparations, 324–325

First National Bank, Boston, 253, 257–258

First National City Bank, New York City, 253

First Pennsylvania Banking & Trust Company, 120, 251

Food Price Survey, 198

Food-Stamp and commodities distribution programs, *ix*

Ford Foundation, 120, 244

foreign policy, and racism, 321–322; *see also* policy-making

Forman, James, 14, 163, 293

*Fortune*, 127, 130

Frazier, E. Franklin, 23, 90, 91, 342, 345

free Negroes: as businessmen, 28, 29, 41; as percent of antebellum period Negro population, 48–49; *see also* Black business, during antebellum period

freedom, *see* liberation

Freedom Budget, 125

Freedom National Bank, 109, 264, 268, 268*n*

*Freedomways*, 88, 89, 92, 93

Freeman, Renny, 327

Friedman, Milton, 340

front-end incentives: core-area service clusters, 265–267; ghetto origin stock placements, 263–265; for savings in ghetto, 261–263

Fuller, Howard, 327

Galbraith, John Kenneth, 126

Garvey, Marcus, 90, 91–94, 163

General Education Board, 79

General Electric Company, 213

General Motors Corporation, 268*n*, 322, 333

genocide, *vii*

Georgia, ghetto lending subsidiary in, 261

Getty, J. Paul, 233

"Ghediplan," 14–15, 175, 183; basic requirements for, 188; cost and financing of, 191–192; goals of, 189; and guaranteed financing, 189–190; and guaranteed markets, 189; operative machinery of, 190; supportive machinery of, 190–191; "underdeveloped nation" philosophy of, 187–188

ghetto: alternatives in dealing with the problem of, 118–119; colonial character of, 15, 316–317; effects of Black business on, 101–102; effects of CDC on, 115–118; elimination of, 11, 187; eradication of, 293; housing, 177; job creation in, 312–313; need for jobs in, 299–300; rebellions, and Black economic development, 8; renewal, business role in, 205–211; responsibility for the existence of, 177; role of capitalism in, see capitalism in ghetto areas; tax credit plans for investment in, 209–210; see also ghetto dispersal; Harlem; Negro community

ghetto dispersal, 19, 118; vs. Black business development, 309–315

Ghetto Economic Development and Industrialization, see Ghediplan

"Ghetto National Product," methods of increasing, 185

"gilding" programs, 309–315

Ginzburg, Eli, 346

giveaway programs, 141–142, 149, 233–234, 269; and Ghediplan, 184

Goodman, Roy, 192

gradualism, 55, 89–91, 154–155

Grand Marie Vegetable Growers Association, 243

Grand United Order of True Reformers, 32

Great Migration, and creation of Negro market, 63–64

Grenala Citizens Federal Credit Union, 243

Gross National Product, and Black America, 331, 340

gross receipts, of Black- and white-owned businesses compared, 9

guarantee technique, for ghetto business loans, 260

guaranteed annual income, 249–250

guerrilla warfare, in U.S., 322

Guevara, Che, 163

Hamer, Fannie Lou, 327

Hamilton, Charles, 19, 346

handouts, see giveaway programs

hard-core structural affluence, 240–241

hardcore unemployed programs, 101, 106, 297–300; and pacification of ghettos, 155–156

Harding, Vincent, 327

Harlem, viii; Black business in, 102; community control of schools in, 179; description of, 193–194; "Ghediplan" for, 14–15; health facilities in, 193; OEO plan for, see OEO plan; opening of the

CMA stores in, 78; white economic exploitation in, 87, 88–89; see also ghetto; Harlem project

Harlem Commonwealth Council, 110, 199, 204n

Harlem Corporation, role of, 199–200

Harlem project: description of problem, 195–196; implementation of, 204; industrial planning, 200–204; institutional planning, 199–200; instruments of, 197; objectives of, 196; use of existing economic structure by, 198–199

Harmon, J. H., 32, 41

Harrington, Michael, 230, 231

Harris, Abram L., 7, 41, 43, 73, 79, 345

Harvard Business Review, 99, 121, 139–140

health care, see medical care

hiring practices, 13; of Sears Roebuck, 221; see also employment

Hoffman, Frederick L., 32

Holiness sects, 62

Holmes, Harold, 327

Holt, Len, 327

home ownership, of Blacks and whites compared, 168

Hoover, J. Edgar, ix

Hope, John, 73–74

hospitals, see public institutions

housing: desegregation, 301, 309–310; in Harlem, 193; integrated, 264; low-cost, 154–155; outside ghetto, 310; segregated, viii; and suburbanization, 310; in urban ghettos, 195, 318

Howard University: 1946 conference at, 81–82; Small Business Guidance and Development Center, 345

HUD, 208, 211

"human resources," 220, 235

Humphrey, Hubert H., 234, 284n

ICBO Fund, 260, 268

illiteracy, and Black business during antebellum period, 50–53

immigrants, see European immigrants

imperialism, viii; and Black ideology, 322

incentives, for continued investment in CDCs, 272–274; see also corrective incentives; front-end incentives

income: of Black businesses, 170, 171; of Black farmers, 245; of Blacks and whites compared, viii, 5, 13; and meaning of economic opportunity, 235; and political power, 177–178; of self-employed whites and Blacks compared, 166

income tax, see taxes

income transfers, 311–312

independent political power, 90; see also political power

India, economic development plans for, 331

Indians, see American Indians

individualism, as tool for Black liberation, 13, 124

industrial development, in ghetto, 200–204, 216, 218–224, 225–226, 249–250
industrial loan associations, 33
Industrial Revolution, 236
infant deaths, in Harlem, 193
"infantile leftists," 159
infiltration, into white business, 44–45
Innis, Roy, 11, 12, 179
installment debt, of Blacks and whites compared, 167–168
installment paper, liquidity for, 254–256
institutions, control of, 178–179, 300–301, 317
insurance companies, 6; and credit to Black business, 108–109, 303; see also life insurance companies
integration, x; and Black business activity, 7; and Black solidarity, 342–343; economic, 95–96, 300–301, 342; as a goal, 19; and nationalism, 91; into overall American economy, 44–45; vs. separation, see integration-separation controversy; and suburbanization, 310
integration-separation controversy, 3, 23–24, 86–88, 342–343; and attitudes toward Black capitalism, 99–100; and Black economic development, 173–174; and business development vs. job training, 294–297; and economic development goals, 16, 17n, 18n
interest charges, and savings, 262
Interracial Council for Business Opportunity, 106, 260
investments in ghetto, 141–144; for Black banks and insurance companies, 33–34; in CDCs, 209–210, 270–274, 278–279; and core-area service cluster approach, 265–267; and development banks, 258–261; front-end incentives for, 261–267; and Harlem project, 197; and installment paper liquidity, 254–256; and risk reduction, 251–254

Jackson, Jesse, 105
Jackson, Mel, 327
Javits, Jacob, 114, 184–185, 205, 224, 258
J. C. Penney Company, in CDC area, 116
Jews: attitudes of Black people toward, 91; as businessmen in Black neighborhoods, 68, 69, 80; self-employment among, 341; see also anti-Semitism; synagogues
job competition, 235
Job Corps camps, 249
job training center, demand for, 324–325
job training programs: and Harlem project, 199; for small-industry planning, 227–228
Johns, Vere S., 44
Johnson, James Weldon, 30
Johnson, Lyndon Baines, 108, 221

Karenga, Ron, 163
Kennedy, Robert, 205, 207–209, 213–215, 217, 222, 224, 265, 297

Kerner Commission, 8, 11, 14, 19, 19n, 101, 188, 298–299
King, Martin Luther, Jr., 104, 118, 264, 265
Ku Klux Klan, 56
Kuomintang, 93

labor unions, see unions
labor-management force, available in Harlem, 198
land: as economic opportunity, 237; for farm co-ops, 248; in ghetto, 222; owned by non-whites, 245; sale by Blacks of, 336–337; see also land reform
land reform, ix, 160, 245–246, 250; and Black economic development, 156–157
Latin America, 328; and American Blacks, 321–322; see also underdeveloped nations
law-enforcement agencies, see police, public institutions
lawlessness, and police organizations, 156
leasing arrangements, 223
leverage, see incentives
liberals: Black attitudes toward, 91; and Black economic development, 16–17; under capitalism, 343; and "ghetto dispersal" goal, 19n; and "gilding" programs, 314
life insurance companies, attitudes toward Blacks of, 32, 165
Lincoln Center project, 265
link deposit plan, 190, 192
Litton Industries, 249
loans: to Black and white businessmen compared, 18n; to El Mercado, 119; for ghetto development, 224; and Harlem Project, 199; and installment paper liquidity, 254–256; and risk reduction, 251–254; for transfer of ghetto businesses, 252–253; see also credit
Local Development Corporation, 190
looters, attitudes toward, 102
Los Angeles' Black-operated Bank of Finance, 108
low-income housing, 266
"lumpen-bourgeoisie," 83, 85n

McCarthy, Eugene, 125
McKersie, Robert, 12, 99
McKinsey & Company, 252
McKissick, Floyd, 125
McKnight, Albert, 243
McLaurin, Dunbar, 14–15, 175, 346
Mafia, and group solidarity, 87–88
Malcolm X, 163
management, of co-ops, 247
management training, 109–110; as solution for ghetto underdevelopment, 180, 199
managerial skills, lack of, 12, 103
Manifesto for a Black Revolutionary Party, 151
manufacturing space, available in Harlem, 198–199
markets for Black business, 165–166, 303,

318; and Black business development, 37–38; changing status of, 80–84; competition for, 64–65, 68–69; effects of slavery on, 49, 52; estimate of, 34; growth of, 63–65; guaranteed, 189; low purchasing power of, 36; limitations of, 108; and loyalty, 61–63, 67–69, 174; and odds against Black business, 65–66; outside of ghetto, 147–148; percent of expenditures in Black-owned groceries, 72n; in rural South, 34–35; and selection of small-industry enterprises, 227
Marxism: and Black economic thought, 93, 95–96, 159; and Black nationalism, 162
mass media, control of, 176
Medicaid, 252
medical centers, 266
medical care, 155
Meier, August, 163
Mercado de Los Angeles, El, 119–120, 122
Metropolitan Council of Governments, 217
Metropolitan Life Insurance Company, 265
Metroregional Development Corporation, 216, 231
Mexican-Americans, 102, 161; and El Mercado, 119–120; and Sears, 221
Michigan Survey, 167
Mid-South Consumers Oil Co-op, 243
migration to Northern ghettos, 57–58, 312; economic effects of, 18n
military power, and Negro-white caste system, 38
military-industrial complex, 176, 333
Miller, Elizabeth, 345
Mills, C. Wright, 85n, 176
Mississippi, Negro banks in, 76
Mississippi Freedom Democratic Party, 245–246
Model Cities Program, 208
money crisis, signs of, 251–252
Monroe, Howard, 327
Moore, Howard, 320
Morris, Jesse, 243
mortality rate, in Harlem, 193
mortgage debt: of Blacks and whites compared, 168; on ghetto residences, 267n; of industries and retailers in the ghettos, 224
Moskowitz, Milton, 346
moving and storage men, 64
Muslims, business activities of, 175
mutual aid societies, role of, 30, 104
Mutual Real Estate Investment, 264
Myrdal, Gunnar, 4, 30, 33
myth of Black business: and changing status of Negro, 80–84; institutionalization of, 74–75; origin of, 73–74; propagation of, 75

National Advisory Committee on Civil Disorders, see Kerner Commission
National Black Economic Development Conference, 176; speech by Robert S.

Browne at, 330–338; Steering Committee of, 327; see also Black Manifesto
National Black Labor Strike and Defense Fund, 324
National Business League, 75–77
National Civil Rights Law, 54
National Community Corporation Certification Board, 269, 270–271, 285n
National Congress for Community Economic Development, 347
National League on Urban Conditions of Negroes, 77
National Negro Business League, 7, 39, 41–42, 74, 82, 93
National Negro Business League, The, 83
National Rural Electric Cooperative Association, 313
National Urban Resources Development, 224
National Welfare Rights Organization, 325
nationalism, see Black nationalism
Nation's Business, 173, 174
"Needed: A New Homestead Act," 249
Negro Alliance of Washington, 43
Negro as Capitalist, The, 73, 79, 345
Negro colleges, 337; schools of business in, 40, 78
Negro community, 35–38; and doctrine of "double-duty dollar," 61–63; as protected market, 165
Negro Potato King, The, 75
Negroes, see Black people and entries under Black
New Deal, 83, 90; and Black business development, 58–59
New School for Social Research, Center for Economic Planning of, 200 204n
New York City: bid specifications in, 217; trade pact agreement approach in, 43
New York State Job Development Authority, 223
New York Times, The, 124
Nickel Savings Bank, 33
Nixon, Richard, 136, 159; Black capitalism, program of, x, 10, 12, 173; see also Nixon administration
Nixon administration: and Black capitalism, 173; and welfare reform, ix
nonviolence, 326
"nonwhites," Negroes as per cent of, 102
North: Black business during antebellum period in, see Black business development, during antebellum period; land reform in, 157, 160; post-Emancipation migration to, 5
nursing profession, 37

occupations, of minority citizens, 9–10, 30–31
OEO Plan, see Harlem project; Office of Economic Opportunity
Office of Economic Opportunity, 104, 224–225, 347; and cooperatives, 244
Office of Minority Business Enterprise, 347

open housing statutes, and ghetto dispersal, 310
Operation Breadbasket, 104–105, 110, 111, 113
"Operation Green Thumb," 249
*Opportunity Magazine*, 43
oppression, and Christian churches, 328; *see also* exploitation; racism; segregation
output increases, 238–239; and Black Americans, 331

pacification, and government development programs, 158
Parks Sausages, Inc., 264
Panic of 1873, 55
Payne, Evans, 33
Percy, Senator, 285n, 289n
personal services businesses, Black- and white-owned compared, 8
PERT, 138
Philadelphia: bid specifications in, 217; Black business in, 50–51, 102; housing in, 195; Progress Plaza of, 120
Philadelphia Plan, 15
philanthropists, and Black business, 79
Phillips, Gerald L., 215
Pierce, Joseph, 23
Piven, Frances Fox, 210–211
Point de Saible, 71
police: and Negro-white caste system, 38; in political organizations, 156
policymaking, role of Blacks in, 125–126
political power of Black Americans, 322–326; and Black liberation, 343; and economic development, 210–211, 231, 317–318; and income, 177–178; lack of, 332–335
poor people, vii; objectives of, 233; unity among, 161; *see also* poor people's cooperatives; poverty
poor people's cooperatives: criteria for assessing, 244; external problems of, 247; internal problems of, 247–248; organization of, 243–244; potential of, 248–250
Poor People's Corporation, 243
population, of CDC areas, 116, 285n, 271–272
poverty: and American political and economic system, 175–176; in Chicago, 105; and community development corporations, *see* community development corporations; elimination of, 125; after Emancipation, 32; and Ghediplan, 188; and public and private programs, 101; and reactions of investors in ghetto, 145–146; *see also* antipoverty programs; poor people
Prejean, Charles, 244
President's Message on Poverty, 234
pressure groups, and separation of Negro economy, 43–45
price differentials, in ghetto, 198, 204n, 339; and support for Black businesses, 67–68

private enterprise: as CDC investors, 280–282; changing nature of, 237–238; incentives for, *see* corrective incentives; social responsibilities of, 212–213; *see also* capitalism; corporate power transfer; corporations
professionals, and support of Black business, 66
profit-sharing, 219, 222
profits: of Black businesses, 170, 171; and Black enfranchisement, 340–341; from CDCs, 269, 272–273, 277–278, 286n; from commercial enterprises in Harlem, 87; on consumer credit in ghetto, 255–256; in ghetto areas, 142–143; on ghetto investments of private equity capital, 205, 207, 230–231; as goal of American business, 26–27; from slavery, 4; and stocks in ghetto businesses, 264
Progressive Labor Party, 159, 162
Progress Plaza, 120, 122
"Project Own," 18
"protected businesses," 71
public institutions, community control of, 154, 156
public opinion, control of, 176
public-private corporations, federally chartered, 206n, 207
Puerto Ricans, 161
Pugh, G. Douglas, 346
purchasing power of Blacks, 84n–85n; in Chicago, 65; and production, 239

Quakers, 51

race pride, and lack of support for Black business, 67
race relations: and colonial problem, 125; and concept of countervailing force, 126; and ideological conflict, 3; and white aid to Black business, 112–113; *see also* racial discrimination; racism
*Race Traits and Tendencies of the American Negro*, 32
racial discrimination: and Black business, 34–38, 50–51; institutionalized, 15; of insurance companies and banks, 32; and migration to North, 58; and Negro-white caste system, 38
racial equality, Black business development as means to, 7–11; *see also* liberation
racial segregation, *see* segregation
racial solidarity, and support for Black business, 39
racism: and Black control, 293; and Black economic underdevelopment, 14; in construction trades, 15; economic advantages of, 340–341; effects of, 321–322; and ghetto economic development, 317; and hardcore unemployed, 298–299; and migration to North, 58; in North and South, x; as product of capitalism, 150–151; struggle against, 161–162, 323; and white support for Black business, 6

Randolph, A. Philip, 91
Reconstruction period, 31; Black poverty during, 176; and development of separatism, 54–56
recruitment of Black personnel, 135; and Black business development, 165–166
"refunding loans," 252, 267$n$
religious practices, and Negro-white caste system, 38
rent subsidies, and ghetto dispersal, 310–312
reparations to Black people, 162, 324
repayment terms of loans, 225–226
Report of the National Advisory Commission on Civil Disorders, 184, 346; see also Kerner Commission
Republic of New Africa, 160, 162
Republican party: Black newspapers of, 31; during Reconstruction period, 54
research institutes, Black-controlled network of, 160
research skills, demand for, 324–325
restaurants, Black-owned, 63
retail commercial space availability, 198–199
retail trade businesses, 6; Black- and white-owned compared, 9, 166
Ribicoff Committee, 205–207, 208, 213–215
risk capital, formation of, 261–263
risk financing, 251–253; see also credit, loans
Robeson, Paul, 90
Robinson, Jackie, 264
Rochester, New York, corporate combinations with Black business in, 106
Rochester Business Opportunities Corporation, 111–112
Rockefeller, David, 206
Roosevelt, Franklin D., 83, 137
Rose, Arnold, 56
Rosenwald, Julius, 79
Rouse, James, 211, 211$n$
rural communities: and CDCs, 285; and Negro colleges, 337
Rural Electric Cooperatives, 249
Russworm, John B., 30

Samuelson, Paul, 340
Santo Domingo, and American Blacks, 321–322
savings, 336; of Blacks and whites compared, 166–167; incentives for, 261–263, 267$n$–268$n$; by pre-Civil War Blacks, 30
SBA, see Small Business Administration
school segregation: during antebellum period, 51; and business separatism, 56; and housing segregation, 309–310; see also education
schoolteaching, 37
Schuyler, George S., 44, 90
Sears, Roebuck and Company, Chicago, 221
"second-income plan," 183
secret societies, 32
"seed money," for CDCs, 269

segregation: and accommodation philosophy, 55–56; and Black business, 7, 33–43, 61–63, 174, 309–310; and Black business failures, 173–174; and Black economic development, 18$n$, 164–166, 216; see also integration-separation controversy; separation
Select Committee on Small Business, 164
self-determination, 317; and capitalism, 122; and CDC, see CDC; and efficiency, 119–120; and equity capital infusion, 109; and federal programs, 125
self-employment, 53; vs. salaried employment, 174
self-made man, 237–238
seniority, 13
separatism: and Black underdevelopment, 160–161; and CDC, see CDC; and control of Negro market, 66; and economic development of ghetto areas, 300; impossibility of attaining, 82; inevitability of, 56–59; and migration and urbanization, 57–59; and myth of Black business, 80; origins of, 54–56; see also integration-separation controversy; segregation
sharecropping system, 5
Sharf, Lawrence H., 347
Shriver, Sargent, 233, 234
skills: during antebellum period, 52; development of, $x$, 174; and ghetto dispersal, 313–314; see also job training
slave insurrections, and Black employment, 28
slavemasters, as employers of emancipated Blacks, 55
slaves, small businesses of, 28
slavery: and Black business development, 28, 47, 49–51; and Black journalism, 24; economic and social consequences of, 4, 103
slums, see ghettos
small business: in ghetto, see Black business development; relationship to big business, 27
Small Business Administration, 18, 105, 108, 191, 224, 226, 296, 306, 341, 347; and El Mercado, 119; loan policies of, 253; survey of U.S. business, 8–10
Small Business Development Centers, 190, 191–192, 225
Small Business Investment Companies, 190
Smith, Stephen, 29
social ownership, vs. private ownership, 156–158
social services, of CDCs, 286$n$
social work, 37
socialism, and Black economy, 94–95
Socialist countries, economic development plans in, 331
South: Black business in, 28–29, 34–35; Black migration from, 312–313, 336–337; boycott technique in, 43–44; integration in, 44–45; land reform in, 157, 160; and myth of Black business, 78–79;

South: Black business in (*cont'd*)
  poor people's cooperatives in, *see* poor
  people's cooperatives
Southern California Edison Company, 109
Southern Consumers Cooperative, 243,
  246
Southern Consumers Education Foundation, 244
Southern land bank, proposal for, 324
Southern Leadership Christian Conference,
  104–105
Soviet Union: and economic development
  plans, 331; savings in, 262
Spelman Fund, 79
Standard Industrial Classification industries, 200
Standard Life Insurance Company, 33
status: of Black business, 61–63; and employment opportunities, 37–38; and
  myth of Black business, 80–84; and
  Negro-white caste system, 38
Stevens, Hope, 89, 92, 93, 94, 95–96
stock investments: of Blacks and whites
  compared, 166–167; in CDCs, 270–271,
  272–273, 286*n*; of ghetto origin, 263–
  265
storefront centers, 228
Sturdivant, Frederick, 99, 346
Stuyvesant Town, 265
subsidies: for cooperatives, 249; rent,
  310–312
suburbanization of Black people, 310–312
success stories, pre-Civil War, 6, 52–53
Sullivan, Leon, 120, 175
Sun Yat-Sen, 93
"Survey of the Conceptual Origins of
  Black Economic Development, A," 346
survival economics, 159
SWAFCAs, 247
synagogues, 328; Black disruption of, 326;
  and reparations to Blacks, 324–326

Tanzania, 320–321
Tate, Charles, 99–100, 346
tax credit programs, 217–218, 217*n*, 224;
  for banks making high-risk loans, 254;
  and CDC proposal, 116–117, 280, 288*n*;
  for community corporations, 209–210;
  and corporate power transfers, 134; for
  depositors in slum area banks, 256–258;
  267*n*; for ghetto investment, 209–210;
  *see also* tax incentives
tax incentives, 121, 213, 222; for CDCs,
  279–282; and stocks in small business
  corporations, 264–265; *see also* tax
  credit programs
technical assistance, for Black business,
  303
technology: and Black economic development, 155; effects of, 237–238; and increased production, 239; and job
  changes, 239–240; for small-industry
  planning, 227
Terrell, Henry, 173, 341
*Theory of the Leisure Class, The*, 340

"Third World," 160
Thompson, Wilbur R., 346
Tillma, Johnnie, 233
Tower, John, 114
trade unions, *see* unions
Tripp, Luke, 327
True Reformer Bank, 33
Tubman, Harriet, 51

"Ujamaa," 19*n*
underdeveloped nations, 218; compared
  with Black communities, 152–153, 185–
  188, 296, 331; compared with Harlem,
  193–194
undertakers, 6
unemployment: of Black and white families compared, 5; and CDC tax advantages, 116–117; in Chicago, 105; in Harlem,. 193
unions, 176, 322, 333; discriminatory policies of, 15; membership rules of, 13
United Auto Workers, 322
United Black Appeal, 325, 327
United Kingdom, saving incentives in, 262
United States: and Africa, 320–321; Department of Agriculture, 313; Department of Commerce, 10, 209, 345; Department of Housing and Urban Development, 209; Department of Labor,
  209; functions and nature of business
  in, 26–27; State Department, 321; and
  underdeveloped nations, 187; violence
  in, *viii–ix*
United States Commission on Civil Rights,
  *viii*
United States Congress: and Black ownership, 10–11; and Community Self-Determination Bill, 114; and War on Poverty,
  105–106
United States Constitution, Thirteenth
  Amendment to, 47
United States economy: and prospects for
  Black business, 82; and separate Black
  economy, 87; *see also* capitalism
United States government, *see* federal government
United States House of Representatives:
  Committee on Ways and Means of,
  284*n*; Education and Labor subcommittee of, 233
United States Senate: Finance Committee,
  285*n*; Subcommittee on Executive Reor-
  ganization, *see* Ribicoff committee
United States Supreme Court, *ix*; and re-
  peal of Civil Rights Act of 1875, 57
University of Michigan, Institute for Social Research at, 137
Urban Coalition, 111
Urban Employment Opportunities Development Act of 1967, 208–209, 222
Urban-Grant University, 223, 226–227,
  231; and management-training, 228
Urban League, 111
urban renewal: ghetto-controlled, 302; as

precedent for power transfer proposal, 127–128
urban unrest: and elimination of poverty, 125; need for new approaches to, 184; *see also* ghetto
urbanization of Black people, 6, 35–36

Valley National Bank, Phoenix, 254–255
Van Buren, Martin, 234
Vandyke, Peter, 29
Veblen, Thorsten, 340
Venable, Abraham S., 103
Vesey, Denmark, 51
Vietnam, 327
Vietnam War, *vii, viii*; and American Blacks, 321–322
violence, *viii–ix*, 163, 322
vocational training, 55–56; critique of, 239–240; and pacification of ghettos, 155–156; *see also* Job training programs
voting rights, *x*; in CDC, 274–276

Walker, Lucius, 327
Wallace, George, 299
war industries, 81; and status of Black workers, 37–38
War on Poverty, 105–106; job training *vs.* business development approach to, 294–297; *see also* antipoverty program
warfare state, *viii*
Washington, Booker T., 7, 18*n*, 30, 38, 57, 79, 82, 87, 90, 92, 94, 345; and Garvey, 91; influence on today's Black leaders, 163; and myth of Black business, 74, 75–77
Washington, D.C., Black-owned businesses in, 168–171
Watson, John, 327
Watts: business community in, 121–122; in late 1960s, 251
Watts Manufacturing Company, 122
wealth, 240–241; appropriation of, 322; among Chicago Blacks, 71; distribution of, *vii*; production of, 71, 238, 240–241
welfare organizations: Black control of, 322; CDC as substitute for, 274
welfare recipients, 148; organization of, 325
welfare state, *viii*
West Batesville Farmers Association, 243
"What Do the Negroes Want?" 124
white business: aid to Black business, 112–113; and Black business development, 106–107, 205–207; in Black community, 36–37, 43–44; and CDC plan, 116; competition with Black business, 64–65, 68–69; and doctrine of double-duty dollar, 61–63; effects of recruitment of Black personnel on, 165–166; in ghettos, and looting, 102; as sponsors for Black business, 110
"white" churches, and reparations for Blacks, 162
White Front, 122
white people: attitudes toward Black businesses, 31; attitudes toward hardcore unemployed, 298; in Black community, 43–44, 342; and Black takeover of white corporations, 129, 140; effects of enfranchisement of minorities on, 340; effects of isolation of Black population on, 35–36; "emancipation" of, 4–5; and myth of Negro business, 83; in Operation Breadbasket movement, 104; as potential customers for Black businesses, 56; support for Black manifesto from, 326; unity with Black people, 161–162; *see also* white business
white power structure: and Black capitalism, 152, 342; and Black decisions, 319; and Black economic development, 332–335; and Black poverty, 175–177; and community corporations, 210–213
white-collar jobs, 102, 177–178
*Who Rules America*, 176
Wiles, P. J. D., 96
Wilkins, Roy, 92
Williams, John, 327
Woodson, Carter G., 90
Wooten, Chuck, 327
work force, Black percentage of, 178
World War I: and Black business, 57
World War II: and Black economic development, 81; and status of Black workers, 37–38
Wright, Michael, 327
Wright, Robert, 99

Young, Elmer, Jr., 120

Zambia, 320–321
Zion Investment Program, 175
Zuber, Paul B., 86, 87, 89